OH JOE!

I HOPPE THIS BOOKE
HELPES YOU TO FIND
INSPIRASION FOR
A LOTTA OF THOSE
FUNNEE JOKES
YOU WRITA!
AW AW AW AW

(ALL VERY LOUD) CARLO
AND WITH

# ALAN PARTRIDGE: EVERY RUDDY WORD

## ALL THE SCRIPTS. FROM RADIO TO TV. AND BACK

**STEVE COOGAN, PETER BAYNHAM, ARMANDO IANNUCCI AND PATRICK MARBER**

MICHAEL JOSEPH

an imprint of PENGUIN BOOKS

MICHAEL JOSEPH

Published by the Penguin Group
Penguin Books Ltd, 80 Strand, London WC2R ORL, England
Penguin Putnam Inc., 375 Hudson Street, New York, New York 10014, USA
Penguin Books Australia Ltd, 250 Camberwell Road, Camberwell, Victoria 3124, Australia
Penguin Books Canada Ltd, 10 Alcorn Avenue, Toronto, Ontario, Canada M4V 3B2
Penguin Books India (P) Ltd, 11 Community Centre,
Panchsheel Park, New Delhi – 110 017, India
Penguin Books (NZ) Ltd, Cnr Rosedale and Airborne Roads,
Albany, Auckland, New Zealand
Penguin Books (South Africa) (Pty) Ltd, 24 Sturdee Avenue,
Rosebank 2196, South Africa

Penguin Books Ltd, Registered Offices: 80 Strand, London WC2R ORL, England

www.penguin.com

First published in Great Britain by Michael Joseph 2003
1

*Knowing Me, Knowing You* Radio Show, scripts copyright © Armando Iannucci,
   Steve Coogan and Patrick Marber 1992
*Knowing Me, Knowing You* TV Show, scripts copyright © Armando Iannucci,
   Steve Coogan and Patrick Marber 1994
*Knowing Me, Knowing Yule* TV Show, scripts copyright © Armando Iannucci,
   Steve Coogan and Patrick Marber 1995
*I'm Alan Partridge* TV Show, scripts copyright © Armando Iannucci,
   Steve Coogan and Peter Baynham, series 1, 1997, series 2, 2002
Photographs copyright © BBC photo library 2003
Illustrations copyright © Phosphor Art 2003
The moral right of the authors has been asserted

Set in 9/12pt Plantin
Designed and typeset by Smith & Gilmour, London
Printed in Great Britain by Clays Ltd, St Ives plc

A CIP catalogue record for this book is available from the British Library

ISBN 0–718–14678–6

# CONTENTS

**Knowing Me, Knowing You, Radio Show**

Programme 1  1

Programme 2  18

Programme 3  34

Programme 4  50

Programme 5  67

Programme 6  86

**Knowing Me, Knowing You, TV Show**

Programme 1  99

Programme 2  117

Programme 3  135

Programme 4  150

Programme 5  166

Programme 6  183

**Knowing Me, Knowing Yule, TV Show Christmas Special**  200

**I'm Alan Partridge, TV Show, Series 1**

A Room with an Alan  225

Alan Attraction  242

Watership Alan  260

Basic Alan  278

To Kill a Mocking Alan  295

Towering Alan  314

**I'm Alan Partridge, TV Show, Series 2**

The Talented Mr Alan  336

The Colour of Alan  353

Brave Alan  371

Never Say Alan Again  390

I Know What Alan Did Last Summer  408

Alan Wide Shut  425

# KNOWING ME KNOWING YOU

## RADIO SHOW 1

*Music: 'Knowing Me, Knowing You'*

**Alan**

Ah-haa! *(Applause)* Ah-haa. No, please, please, shh. Welcome to *Knowing Me, Knowing You*. Knowing me, Alan Partridge, knowing you, the you, the audience, here in the studio, or you, the you, the listener at home, in the car, or somewhere else, but with a radio. Those of you who know me from the world of sport will know that I like having a bit of a chat with brawny men on the rugby field and, er, having a bit of a chat with the soft fair waif-like moist creatures who you find in ladies' sports. Please, don't write in saying that's, saying that's sexist – it's not. So what better place to continue that chat than here on a chat show, my show, my own show? My first guest: he's one of the world's great heavyweights, not in the boxing sense, he's sixty-seven, huh, but intellectually speaking. He's a novelist, his new novel, *The Soul of Time*, weighs in at nearly eight pounds, 950,000 words of thick dense type, all telling the story about, well – let's get the potted version from the man of letters himself. Dip thy quill and clappeth loud for Britain's greatest living novelist, Lawrence Camley.

*Music: 'Knowing Me, Knowing You'*
*Applause*

1

**Alan**
Knowing me, Alan Partridge, knowing you, Lawrence Camley, ah-haa. Welcome.

**Lawrence**
Ah-haa.

**Alan**
Glad to have you on the show. Now, I've got to say, first reaction to your book – don't drop it on me foot!

**Lawrence**
Yes, it is a heavy book, but if I may be so bold there are, of course, certain literary precedents. One thinks of Proust's *A La Recherche De Temp Perdu*, Dante's *Divina Commedia*, Chaucer's *Canterbury Tales*, which I'm reliably informed could cripple one. Maybe that's what happened to Lord Byron?

**Alan**
Why, what … what happened to him?

**Lawrence**
He, he had a clubbed foot.

**Alan**
Right. Ha ha! Um, *The Soul of Time*, that's the name of your book. Sounds a bit deep, is it?

**Lawrence**
Well, it's a serious novel. I deal with the great, er, contemporary themes. But I like to think there are one or two jokes in it.

**Alan**
Oh great. Go on, tell us a joke. Ha ha ha! We like to start the show with a joke. It's always great to get it off on –

**Lawrence**
I see I've got myself in sticky, sticky mud already. They're not, they're not jokes in the traditional Knock-Knock sense, they're

more, er, comic vignettes woven into the general fabric and architecture of the novel.

**Alan**
It's more funny-peculiar than funny-ha-ha then, is it? What I want to ask you is, and this is a question I've been dying to ask you, if you were stuck in a lift, what, what one book would you have with you?

**Lawrence**
Well, I would actually choose for sheer bloody-minded entertainment value, I would be stuck in a lift with *The Hound of the Baskervilles*.

**Alan**
I don't believe it, Sherlock Holmes. Now you're making sense. I am his number one fan. I've read all his books.

**Lawrence**
Ye-es, I've read them.

**Alan**
I've read all of them. Have you read all of them?

**Lawrence**
Probably not all of them.

**Alan**
I've read all of them. Read all of them. I love Sherlock Holmes. I've got all his books, leather-bound. What I thought was great about Sherlock Holmes was that not only was he a supersleuth, he was also a hard worker. Because, not only did he go out and solve the crimes, he came home and wrote it all down. Fantastic. That, that's why I admire him.

**Lawrence**
Yes. I've always thought it was a shame that Conan Doyle had to kill him off.

**Alan**
No, I think you'll find it was Moriarty that killed him.

**Lawrence**
Yes, I know, but ultimately of course it was Conan Doyle.

**Alan**
No, it was Moriarty, it was definitely –

**Lawrence**
Yes, I know, in the books it was Moriarty, but of course the ultimate responsibility was Conan Doyle's.

**Alan**
Yep, hang on. As far as I know, Moriarty acted alone. Or did he? This is interesting. You, you think that there was some sort of conspiracy involving this shadowy Doyle figure? All right, OK, fair enough. Who solved all the cases?

**Lawrence**
Sherlock Holmes.

**Alan**
Exactly.

**Lawrence**
Yes, but the cases were fictional too, it's all make-believe.

**Alan**
All right. Who lived on Baker Street?

**Lawrence**
I don't know.

**Alan**
Moriarty?

**Lawrence**
No!

**Alan**
Did the, did the Doyle live there?

**Lawrence**
The Dail, the Dail is the Irish Parliament.

**Alan**
The Irish Parliament! This conspiracy's getting bigger. You can't trust anyone these days. You've got the Doyle, Moriarty, the Irish Parliament, it's – On that bombshell, I think we'll move on.

**Lawrence**
No, no, no. I'm sorry, Alan, I, I, I'd like to let this go, but, ha, I really can't. Sherlock Holmes did not exist.

**Alan**
He did.

**Lawrence**
Look. If he had existed, how would he have been able to describe in intimate detail the circumstances of his own death?

**Alan**
*(Long pause)* Um. The Nobel Prize for Literature. You never won it. What went wrong?

**Lawrence**
Ha, you are an extraordinary man, Mr Partridge. I am an artist and I don't write for prizes or acknowledgement. I write to satisfy my muse.

**Alan**
It's a big fish. Your net's full of holes.

**Lawrence**
All nets are full of holes.

**Alan**
Granted, granted. But your, your holes are too big to catch the Nobel Peace Prize fish of Literature. This, this cleverness thing. It real—, I want to get to the bottom of this. Being clever. Do you know what? I reckon that we could ask you any question and you'd know the answer.

**Lawrence**
I am, I am not a puppet.

**Alan**
Anything. Let's just try that. I reckon that if we went to the audience, got them to ask you a question, you'd know the answer.

**Lawrence**
I will not take part in this ridiculous charade.

**Alan**
He's a bit modest. I'm just going into the audience here. Sir, what question do you want to ask?

**Female Audience Member**
What is the capital of Kenya?

**Alan**
Good question. What's the capital of Kenya, do you know the answer?

**Lawrence**
I have already told you, I refuse to participate in this ridiculous charade.

**Alan**
Fair enough, but it's not the answer. What's the capital? Come on, do you know?

**Lawrence**
I know the answer.

**Alan**
You don't – He doesn't know.

**Lawrence**
I do know the answer.

**Alan**
He doesn't know.

**Lawrence**
I do know the answer.

**Alan**
What's the answer?

**Lawrence**
It's bloody Nairobi.

**Alan**
Well done. That's really fantastic. Once more, there he is. Do you know he could get a lot of work on the conference circuit doing clever stuff like that? Listen. That's all we've got time for.

**Lawrence**
Yes.

**Alan**
Got another question about your dog here, but there's no time for that.

**Lawrence**
No, no time.

**Alan**
So, another big round of applause for Lawrence Camley, a clever man.

*Applause*

**Alan**
Now, my next guest is a woman who first stamped her feet with the women's movement eighteen years ago. Her book, *Livid Doll*, was read by angry, angry and irritable women alike. Since then, she's written for journals as varied as *Woman's Own* and the *Radio Times*. And now she hosts the hugely popular therapy show, *Problem People*, on cable TV. Please welcome the intelligent, and not unattractive, Ali Tennant.

*Music: 'Dancing Queen'*
*Applause*

**Alan**
Hello, Ali, I've just come out to meet you here. Um, for the listeners. Now listen. You've got something very special for us today, haven't you?

**Ali**
I've actually got two very special people with me. They are Linda and Peter.

**Alan**
Hi, Linda and Peter.

**Ali**
And they're two people who are currently working with me on my therapy show, *Problem People*, on cable TV.

**Alan**
Right. So these are two of the disturbed people that you –

**Ali**
No, no, no. They are not, it's very important, they're not disturbed people. They're normal people with normal problems.

**Alan**
Right, um, so if anyone's concerned, these two – just, bit harmless. Right. OK. Right. So what are you going to do with them?

**Ali**
Well, I'm going to do just a brief demonstration of the kind of therapy that we work on.

**Alan**
Good. You got your plug in there. I'll leave it in your capable hands. Ali Tennant and the two disturbed people.

**Ali**
OK. Hello, Linda.

**Linda**
Hello.

**Ali**
Hello, Peter.

**Peter**
Hi.

**Ali**
Now we've been working together on my three-point therapy plan, and I'll just run through that very quickly. The three points are: the birthing of the emotions, the dialoguing about those emotions, and, finally, pledging towards a better future. So, let's begin with birthing. Linda, would you like to birth your emotions, please?

**Linda**
Yeah. Um. Anger, frustration, jealousy, loathing, bitterness, um, deep resentment and, um, hate.

**Ali**
Bit, bit of inner turmoil.

**Linda**
Yeah, inner turmoil, yeah. Inner turmoil, yeah.

**Ali**
Thank you very much, and well done. Peter, would you birth your emotions, please?

**Peter**
Yes. The same really, um, but no loathing.

**Ali**
Thank you, Peter, and well done. Phase three, Linda. Sex with Peter.

**Linda**
Well, I mean, it's obvious isn't it? I mean, it's just not happening. I mean it hasn't been happening for a very *long* time.

**Ali**
Well done. Peter. Sex with Linda.

**Peter**
Well, it's not happening for me either, is it?

**Linda**
Well, I mean, that's because you're never there.

**Peter**
What do you mean – I'm never there? I sleep in the bed with you.

**Linda**
Can I just say something? That he comes – that he often comes back smelling of dog.

**Peter**
Oh come on. Don't start with the dog again. Every time –

**Ali**
OK. End of dialogue. Very good. Well done. We've reached pledging time.

**Alan**
*(Offstage)* You've got about a minute.

**Ali**
OK. Thank you. All right. Peter, we're going to start with your pledge. I'd like you to say in front of all these people here and all the people who are listening at home – that's about thirteen million people rooting for you. OK. I want you to say: I pledge to spend more time with Linda, and more time with baby Sam.

**Peter**
Samuel.

**Ali**
Whatever, OK, and that is my pledge. Will you say that now, please?

**Peter**
Yep, um, I pledge to spend more time with Linda and with Samuel.

**Ali**
And that is my pledge.

**Peter**
That is my pledge.

**Ali**
Well done, Peter, well done. Marvellous. Well done. OK, we're nearly at a resolve. Linda, it's your turn to pledge. I want you to pledge now: I pledge to spend more time with myself, and to take a lover to ease my frustrations.

**Peter**
Hold on – hold on a moment.

**Linda**
No, we're not dialoguing.

**Peter**
No, I don't think –

**Ali**
Peter.

*Peter continually attempts to interrupt while Linda is speaking.*

**Linda**

I pledge to spend more time with myself and to take a lover to ease my frustration.

**Ali**

And this is my pledge.

**Linda**

This is my pledge.

**Ali**

Well done, Linda. That's marvellous. Well done. Well done, Linda, that's brilliant.

**Alan**

Great stuff. Hang on. I'm just coming over to meet them now. That was absolutely fabulous. Thanks you two for doing your pledging and stuff. I hope you're not so disturbed any more. Let's, er, say goodbye to you and hello to Ali Tennant. Please, come and take a seat. Come and sit down. Just, sit there. Right, sit down. Now, now. Ali. Was that good therapy or barmy old cack?

**Ali**

I'll leave it for you to decide really. I mean, your audience saw it work. So, um –

**Alan**

Right, and you've got a pretty successful success rate.

**Ali**

Very successful. There are people queuing up for the cable TV show, which I think is incredibly brave.

**Alan**

Absolutely fantastic. Well, I've got a – Let me give you a little problem.

**Ali**

Um-hum.

**Alan**

Let's, let's say, take a hypothetical situation, that a bloke in his mid-thirties, got a good job, maybe in the papers, maybe in the media, who knows, and he's got a problem at home with his wife. He's doing quite well. He's got a nice house, nice furniture, World of Leather sofa. Nice car, electric windows, power steering.

**Ali**

OK, yeah.

**Alan**

Central locking. Now he thinks, he's not quite sure, but he thinks his wife's having an affair. Where's the problem?

**Ali**

With him, with him.

**Alan**

Right.

**Ali**

Frankly, he's clearly paying too much attention to his material possessions. I mean, God help us, his World of Leather sofa, even.

**Alan**

They're, they're actually quite comfortable sofas.

**Ali**

Well, whatever, but you see the point? The point you were obviously trying to make.

**Alan**

Yes. It's just an example.

**Ali**

And I don't blame her. I really don't blame her.

**Alan**

You say it's all his fault, but let's try and paint the picture more clearly. Um, let's say she never talks to him. She's always going out to fitness twice a day, every day. Why, why does she do it?

**Ali**

Well. In the dialoguing phase, what we do is we'd explore why she's going out quite that frequently, and, as you saw there, we give equal weight to each partner, so, so what would happen is that she would say: 'I resent you spending all your time waxing your car, whatever.'

**Alan**

Yeah, yeah.

**Ali**

He'd say: 'I resent you going out to fitness three times a day.'

**Alan**

Fair enough. But if this man's in the media his car's got to look good. If he's got a –

**Ali**

Well, I mean, the car is obviously just an example.

**Alan**

But if the car was maroon, say, that looks terrible when it's dirty.

**Ali**

Well, yeah, but I mean we're sort of –

**Alan**

As an example.

**Ali**

We're sort of, we're getting off the point, Alan.

**Alan**

It's just an example.

**Ali**

I mean that really is the basic point. We need to just air those problems as we did there.

**Alan**

Right. Now, tell me about sex. I mean –

**Ali**

Well, of course, ninety-nine per cent of the problems that I deal with are sexually related. Clearly that's the case even if they don't appear to be on the surface.

**Alan**

So, sort it out downstairs then sort it out upstairs. To crystallize it.

**Ali**

That's a way of putting it, yeah.

**Alan**

Right, fine.

**Ali**

Right. Um, if the woman in question is frequently denying sex, then clearly there's an emotion behind that and that emotion is anger. And clearly there's an emotion coming from the man, and that emotion is fear of castration.

**Alan**

No. No it's not. It's not that, no.

**Ali**

No, that's, I mean that's a very, again it's an extreme way of putting it, but it's basically impotence. Fear of impotence, fear of castration.

**Alan**

No it's not. Now, let's, let's move on. Er, you've said your stuff, you've got a leaflet, got the helpline, pens, all that. Now, I say, I'm normal, me, Alan Partridge, normal.

**Ali**

Good, good.

**Alan**

You, you Ali Tennant. Bit strange. I read, I read in, I read a bit in your book that was highlighted in yellow by a researcher for me that, er, that you're quite, you're quite into female orgasms. You like them, don't you?

**Ali**

*(Laughs)* Well, don't you?

**Alan**

Yes. But, but, but, I mean, I, I'm quite curious as a man. What –

**Ali**

Good.

**Alan**

What – the female orgasm. What is it? I mean, I don't mean what, I don't, I don't mean what is it, I don't mean what – what I mean – how, how does it manifest itself . . . ? When you hear, when, when it's how, what is it, what is it, what is it, what is it, what is it, what is it?

**Ali**

What's a female orgasm?

**Alan**

Yes.

**Ali**

Um. It's a very good question actually, and the answer that I would give you is: what's a male orgasm? Describe what happens when you achieve an orgasm.

**Alan**

Uh – no.

**Ali**

No, I'm serious, honestly, really.

**Alan**

No, I don't think so. No, no.

**Ali**

Because it's really important. Just describe the process.

**Alan**

No. Uh, no. OK.

**Ali**

No, there's no comparison.

**Alan**

OK, let's leave it there. It's over. Leave it. A great lady or a mad old trout, you decide – Ali Harris.

**Ali**

Ali Tennant.

**Alan**

Ali Tennant. Ali Tennant. Sorry, er, sorry, Ali, for getting your name wrong at the end. Ali Tennant not Ali Harris, getting names confused there, but hadn't heard of you before tonight. Now, um, let's move on. What I want you to do, by the way, is just go and move over to the other comfy chair.

**Ali**

Fine, OK.

**Alan**

Um, I'm going to bring on my next guest. What I want you to do is obviously keep quiet for a bit, and then when I've got going, chatting to my next guest, please feel free to chip in. Now, my next guest is a man who first made his name back in the 60s. He was voted Carnaby Street's 'Mister Boutique' of 1969. He knew all the pop stars. He was at all the parties. Whenever David Bailey was seen with a beautiful woman, you can bet that my next guest had been there first. These days, his retail empire is enormous. No high street is complete without its branch of Wishing Wells, and I wish *him* well. Super green, super sexy, eco-friendly and bloomin' rich, here he is, Adam Wells.

*Music: 'Money, Money, Money' (instrumental)*
*Applause*

**Alan**

*(Laughing)* The end of his mike's come off there. Adam Wells, welcome to the show.

**Adam**

Cheers, cheers. It's a plesh.

**Alan**

Money – money, money, money, must be funny in a rich man's world. Now, you're here to launch your new drink, your new vegetable drink.

**Adam**

Vegina.

**Alan**

Vegina. It's, er, made from vegetables, it's a fizzy vegetable drink.

**Adam**

A fizzy vegetable drink in an edible can.

**Alan**

That's fantastic. Now –

**Adam**

It's gonna be in the shops from next week, go out, kids, and buy millions.

**Alan**

All right.

**Adam**

Buy them in buckets.

**Alan**

Shh. Er, right. Now, back in the 60s.

**Adam**

Yeah.

**Alan**

That's when it all happened. Everyone was partying. All night long, all day long. Wasn't it, wasn't it a great time? What was it all about, the 60s?

**Adam**

It, it was great –

**Alan**

Those parties –

**Adam**

Ali and I knew each other then, of course.

**Alan**

Did you?

**Ali**

Oh, very well, yes.

**Adam**

We didn't notice you at any of the parties, Alan.

**Alan**

Now, well, I was, my 60s were in Norwich, really, it was – We kind of called it Naughty Norwich. And it was. We had a great time, just partying all day long, all night long. I remember during one summer we just, hot summer, for about three weeks, we just had barbecues non-stop, all day long. Amazing.

**Ali**
Sounds, sounds incredible.

**Alan**
Crazy.

**Adam**
It sounds fabulous.

**Alan**
Yeah. Suppose you were having orgies, were you?

**Adam**
*(Laughing)* I was actually. Well, I mean, we all were.

**Ali**
It was the thing to do.

**Alan**
Did you go? You went to an orgy?

**Ali**
I went to many, yes, yes.

**Alan**
How, how?

**Adam**
They were mixed.

**Alan**
How, how do you start, how did you, how did you have an orgy then? What did you do?

**Ali**
Ha! It's fairly self-explanatory.

**Adam**
Come on. It was twenty-five years ago. I can't remember the actual mechanics –

**Alan**
You must be able to. Try and remember.

**Adam**
– blow-by-blow.

**Alan**
Try and remember.

**Adam**
I can't remember.

**Alan**
Try and remember! Did you, did you, did you, did you ever, ever see, er, what, did you ever see two girls kissing?

**Adam**
Yeah, yeah, yeah. All the time. It was very free and easy.

**Alan**
Did you ever, did you ever kiss a bloke?

**Adam**
No!

**Alan**
Well, anyway, before you made your name with your vegi-shoes, you had a hit with your first wife, Eve.

**Adam**
Yeah.

**Alan**
Adam and Eve, with that novelty hit.

**Adam**
Yeah, I don't, I don't –

**Alan**
Remember what it was called?

**Adam**
Oh yeah: 'The Smiling Bicycle of Amsterdam'.

**Alan**
'The Smiling Bicycle of Amsterdam'. Well, we've got a bit of a surprise for you because we are going to play that –

**Adam**
Oh, no –

**Alan**
– record that reached number –

**Adam**
– don't embarrass me –

**Alan**
twenty-three in the charts –

**Adam**
– oh, no.

**Alan**
– twenty-four years ago. Let's hear it.

**Adam**
I haven't heard it for years.

**Alan**
Listen to this.

**Music**
'Oh, don't take a bus.
Don't take a tram.
You're my girl and happy I am.
You're my babe, it's a real wham-bam.
On the smiling bicycle of Amsterdam.
All aboard.
Tickets, please.
Room for one more pixie.'

**Alan**
Fantastic. Well, give a round of applause.

*Applause*

**Adam**
Oh God.

**Ali**
Certainly, er –

**Adam**
That was just so –

**Ali**
Certainly brings back memories.

**Adam**
You are, you are, you are a naughty man. That is just so embarrassing.

**Alan**
Yeah –

**Adam**
So embarrassing.

**Alan**
I know, but please, let me just say thanks once again for bringing that copy in. We couldn't find it anywhere. Thanks a lot for that. Now, um, now, that was, that was then, this is now.

**Adam**
Is it?

**Alan**
Now, yes, shh. Now, Wishing Wells, there's a Wishing Well on every street. Adam Wells' shop Wishing Wells – nice link with your name there – on every street. What's the concept behind it, because it's very different from normal shops, isn't it?

**Adam**
That's right.

**Alan**
It's very sort of different.

**Adam**
It is very different. I invented the slogan for Wishing Wells back in '71. At the time I had a boutique on the Kings Road called Flair and in '71 I thought, now I'm going to branch out, and I came out with the slogan which was, 'No tree has died. No child has cried. To make the product that you have buyed.'

**Alan**
Fantastic.

**Adam**

And that slogan, that ethos, still holds true today. The, the whole thing about the shop was that we, we wanted to, like, sell cheap ethnic clobber to the masses, but made in Britain.

**Alan**

Right. So they can buy it and not feel guilty.

**Adam**

That's right.

**Alan**

I don't go in there so often. I'm more a kind of Argos, World of Leather man myself. Now –

**Adam**

You like, you like sitting on a dead cow at home, do you?

**Alan**

As long as they've, er, cut the head off *(laughs)*. That'd get in the way, be flopping about, yeah. Now, I'll tell you what else I bought, I bought, I bought one of those African masks.

**Adam**

Oh, they're terrific.

**Alan**

Tremendous. I, I, it was quite a, it was last Halloween. I had a bit of a joke with it. You'll like this, er, Ali. Um, the, my two, my son and daughter had come home late. They'd been out clubbing with their friends and Denise and Fernando came in, and they, they walked into the living room with their friends. I think they wanted to watch a video or something and I hid behind the curtains, with the African mask on –

**Adam**

Ha! Oh no –

**Alan**

And when they came in and turned the lights on, I jumped out and said: 'Buga, Buga, Luga, I'm a big cannibal. I'm going to boil you in a pot and eat you.'

**Adam**

*(Laughing)* I bet they loved that.

**Alan**

No, they found it very offensive. They said it was racist. Said it was racist.

**Adam**

Yeah, well that's the loony-tuney left, you know.

**Alan**

That's –

**Adam**

You've hit on my Achilles bugbear there.

**Alan**

Yes, er. You're very different, aren't you?

**Adam**

I, I am different.

**Alan**

Did, did, did you go to sch—, did you study at university or – ?

**Adam**

*(Laughing)* You know, or you should know, that I was educated at the Uni –

**Adam and Alan**

– versity of Life.

**Alan**

So was I.

**Adam**

And that's the best place. And I graduated with flying honours.

**Alan**

So did I.

**Adam**
I'm the warden of that university. I'm the rector. I'm the dean.

**Alan**
Well, I'm, I'm there as well.

**Adam**
Ali, Ali, were you there?

**Ali**
I feel terribly left out, actually. No, I was at Keele, but, er, I think I'm probably doing a postgraduate course.

**Adam**
What are O Levels? They're just bits of toilet paper. What are A Levels?

**Alan**
Well, you know.

**Adam**
They're just bits of luxury toilet paper.

**Alan**
Yeah, that's a point, yeah, well, I mean, I agree with you in a way there. I mean I've got O Levels and a couple of A Levels, but, er, you know, maybe they're just bits of paper that you have framed in your office on either side of the – You know, I mean, you know I've got six, um, O Levels. Um, got four, four Bs and two Cs and got, er, I actually got seven because I got a D in French but I retook that and got a B, so that's seven, and got, er, two A Levels. I, I took French and Art and General Studies, but I dropped French because it was too much, but I, I ended up with a C in Art and B, B in General Studies, which, of course, I'm quite pleased about.

**Adam**
Right.

**Alan**
Yeah.

**Adam**
Thanks for letting us know that, Alan. Let's give him a round of applause there.

*Applause*

**Alan**
OK, all right, OK, no, we'll cut –

**Adam**
No, I'm sorry, I was out of order. I know, it's your show, you're the boss.

**Alan**
No, that's all right. You can say that, just – shh. Your new drink, Vegina. The advert's been banned.

**Adam**
The new vegetable drink, Vegina. Yes, there has been problems with the Advertising Standards Authority. Again, loony-tuney left, students, feminists, women, whatever, whoever they are, God knows.

**Alan**
Right.

**Adam**
But these people really just get on my breasts. I mean, they are just –

**Alan**
Let's, let's see what –

**Adam**
Yeah, let's –

**Alan**
– this is about.

**Adam**
– let's hear the advert –

**Alan**
– hear the advert –

**Adam**
– and then, and then – this is the banned advert.

**Alan**
That you won't be hearing.

**Adam**
For the vegetable –

**Alan**
My show. Shh.

**Advert**
*(Alternating female and male voices)*
'Vegina.'
'Carlos Dawson, 42.'
'Vegina.'
'Heart attack.'
'Vegina.'
'Mary Armstrong, 33.'
'Vegina.'
'Knocked down by a car.'
'Vegina.'
'Jerry Davies, 62.'
'Vegina.'
'Kidney disease.'
'Vegina.'
'Paula Wills, 5.'
'Vegina.'
'Never found.'
'Vegina.'
'Maureen Hadley, 87.'
'Vegina.'
'Battered.'
'Vegina. For life.'
'Not death.'

*Applause*

**Adam**
Now, now, what, what is the problem?

**Alan**
That's terrible!

**Ali**
It-It's a disgrace.

**Alan**
The DTI are investigating you at the moment, er. Might as well mention that.

**Adam**
Why not? Why not chuck that in?

**Alan**
Your sweat shops in Thailand –

**Adam**
They are not sweat shops. They are not sweat shops.

**Alan**
Well –

**Adam**
They are factories.

**Alan**
Factories with eleven-year-old boys working eighteen-hour days.

**Adam**
Hold on, hold on, hold on. Let's, let's just get something very, very, very clear here.

**Alan**
All right.

**Adam**
In Thailand, an eleven-year-old boy is considered, in their culture, to be a man.

**Alan**
Ahh –

**Adam**
So when I employ an eleven-year-old boy, he is, in fact, a man. I am employing eleven-year-old men –

**Alan**
Right –

**Ali**
Well, that's not how Amnesty sees it, clearly. I mean, the Amnesty Report was absolutely –

**Adam**
Well, who are Amnesty?

**Alan**
No, he, that's, there is a good point here, actually. Who, who is Amnesty?

**Adam**
I'll tell you, I'll tell you who Amnesty is. Amnesty is five bearded, bitter hippies.

**Ali**
Well, that's great coming from you, isn't it, because when I first met you, you were a bearded hippy. You may not've – You know –

**Adam**
Yeah, but, I, I was never bitter.

**Ali**
Yes, you were.

**Adam**
I was not bitter.

**Ali**
You're bitter, you're bitter now.

**Adam**
Maybe after I met you I was bitter.

**Ali**
OK, let's not get personal.

**Alan**
Hang on. Hey, hey, hey.

**Ali**
I mean, this is not hostility here.

**Alan**
No, wait, wait, wait –

**Adam**
We didn't call you Miss Lemon for nothing.

**Alan**
Listen. Let's just, woah. Let's cool it down. Now then, er *(clears throat)* we'll, er, have Amnesty on next week, with, er, Ken Dodd, hopefully. Thailand. A bit more relaxed the culture there, isn't it?

**Adam**
That's right.

**Alan**
They don't mind eleven-year-old boys. That kind of thing.

**Adam**
Hold on. What, what are you saying?

**Alan**
Just that, you know –

**Adam**
No, no, no, you're always flannelling about.

**Alan**
All right.

**Adam**
What are you saying?

**Alan**
All right. I'll tell you what I'm saying.

**Adam**
Yes, what are you saying?

**Alan**
I, Alan Partridge –

**Adam**
Yes, I know who you are –

**Alan**
– am saying to you, Adam Wells. You, in the 60s, you were a big shot. You, you, you went to loads of orgies with men and women at them –

**Adam**
Yes, and you're jealous –

**Alan**
I'm not jealous.

**Adam**
– because you weren't there.

**Alan**

I was at loads of barbecues. You were all over the place, seeing women here, women there, and, and, dabbling all over the world. Four wives.

**Adam**

How many women have you had, Alan?

**Alan**

That's irrelevant. You –

**Adam**

You've had one. You've had one.

**Alan**

So what. The point is, and I've got two strapping children to show for it and you haven't borne any children, have you?

**Adam**

So what are – what's that?

**Alan**

Right, what am I saying? You have been spreading your seed, but reaping no harvest.

**Ali**

Careful, Alan –

**Adam**

What's that supposed to mean?

**Alan**

You're firing blanks. You are, you are infertile.

**Ali**

Oh, now look. You can't go saying that –

**Adam**

For God's sakes – you can't just sit here on a chat show –

**Ali**

Alan –

**Alan**

*(Talking over Adam and Ali)* And on that bombshell –

**Adam**

You can't just –

**Ali**

Alan!

**Alan**

And on that bombshell, it's time to say, that's all from the show –

**Adam**

Who is Alan Partridge? Who is this guy? What is he? Look at him.

**Alan**

– this week. Me, Alan Partridge. Thanks to my guests, Lawrence Camley, Ali Tennant, Adam Wells. The writers and researchers. Steve Coogan, Doon MacKichan, Rebecca Front, Patrick Marber, David Schneider and, of course, produced by Armando Iannucci. Thanks very much and goodnight.

*Applause*

**Alan**

Thanks very much and goodnight. Well done. Great. All right. Just, er –

*Music: 'Knowing Me, Knowing You'*

# KNOWING ME KNOWING YOU

## RADIO SHOW 2

*Alan Partridge*

*Music: 'Knowing Me, Knowing You'*

**Alan**

Ah-haaaa! *(Applause)* Thank you, thank you! Welcome! Welcome to *Knowing Me, Knowing You*. Now, I have a letter here from a listener, Mr Tim Stringer. It says, 'Dear Alan, I love the show, but please could you tell me, is your theme tune, "Knowing Me, Knowing You", available on record? If so, who's it by? Yours sincerely, Tim Stringer.' Well, Tim, 'Knowing Me, Knowing You' was originally recorded by the Swedish power-pop combo Abba, sadly no longer with us, but the version we use, we use instead, use a version of the song recorded by the Jeff Love Orchestra, which I have to say, in my opinion, is superior in essence to the actual original. So I hope that answers your question, Tim! My first guest tonight

is, I have to say, the PITS! That's a joke – because – it's a joke with a point – because I met him in the pit at the Monaco Grand Prix, because he is France's second best racing driver! He's sophisticated, he's suave, please give a loud cheer and *cri de coeur* for second best, French racing driver, *le très bon* Michel Lambert!

*Music: 'Voulez-vous'*
*Applause*

**Alan**

Knowing me, knowing you, Ah-haa!

**Michel**

Ah-haa.

**Alan**

Ah-haa! Or should I say, 'Je sais moi, Alan Partreedge, Je sais toi, Michel Lambert, Oh-ho!'

**Michel**
*(Laughs weakly)*

**Alan**
Now, you are a celebrity, you're France's second-best racing driver, you get interviewed all the time. Do you get bored of the same old questions –?

**Michel**
Yes, that's very true, there's nothing worse than an interviewer who cannot be bothered to find an interesting angle –

**Alan**
Yeah, I can imagine. When did you first want to be a racing driver?

**Michel**
Yes! Exactly!

**Alan**
Yes – yes, exactly WHEN?

**Michel**
*(Quietly) Mon Dieu. (Replies)* Well, ironically, Alan, I never wanted to be a racing driver, I actually wanted to be a chat show host, like you. But I turned up to the wrong job interview and I ended up as a racing driver –

**Alan**
That can't be true!

**Michel**
No it's not, it's a joke.

**Alan**
Of course, the famous French sense of humour there – Now, you're nearly at the top of your profession, and what I want to know is, how do you cope with the pressure?

**Michel**
I take a lot of drugs.

**Alan**
*(Whisper)* Yeah – Michel, in this country drugs are frowned upon, so – better not to mention them –

**Michel**
*(Whisper)* I was joking, Alan.

**Alan**
*(Whisper)* Right. Right. If you joke in future, could you wink at me or something? Just to let me know – they won't notice, it's radio.

**Michel**
Fine, OK.

**Alan**
Right! Now, what do you think about when you're racing your car? What do you think about?

**Michel**
Surprisingly, I think about the race.

**Alan**
Right. Um –

**Michel**
What do you think about when you're interviewing someone?

**Alan**
Well, nothing – But do you, when you're driving along, do you ever think, 'Oooh, sacre bleu! I've forgotten to set the video to record, I don't know, *Top Gear* –'?

**Michel**
What is – what is *Top Gear*?

**Alan**
Oh, it's – Oh, all right then, you've forgotten to tape Cyrano de Bergerac with Gerard Depardue.

**Michel**
Depardieu.

**Alan**
Depardur.

**Michel**
Depardieu.

**Alan**
Depardiur.

**Michel**
Depardieu.

**Alan**
Depardiure.

**Michel**
De!

**Alan**
De.

**Michel**
Par!

**Alan**
Par.

**Michel**
Dieu!

**Alan**
Dieu.

**Michel**
Dieu!

**Alan**
Dieu.

**Michel**
Dieu!

**Alan**
Dieu –

**Michel**
It's so important, Alan.

**Alan**
Right.

**Michel**
I think, I think what you're trying to ask me is, 'Do I ever get distracted when I'm driving?' No I don't.

**Alan**
No, no, no, no, I'm quite specifically asking you, do you forget to tape Cyrano de Bergerac with, er, Gerard –

**Michel**
Depardieu –

**Alan**
Him, yeah!

**Michel**
No, I don't ever forget to tape it because I saw it at the cinema when it came out.

**Alan**
Right.

**Michel**
Have you ever seen this film?

**Alan**
Yes. Yes, I did see it –

**Michel**
You like it?

**Alan**
I'm – not – so keen on it, I mean, I don't like what they did with the idea, they set it in the seventeenth century, gave him a long nose, maybe it made it a bit funnier – but, but for the British, Bergerac *is* John Nettles – I – I thought you ruined it really – I'm just glad you haven't got your hands on *Lovejoy* – Probably set it in the future! When, of course, antiques will be even more expensive – Not a bad idea really!

**Michel**
And – the question is –?

**Alan**
The, the question is, yes, um, right. Are you – are you winking at me?

**Michel**
No, I was sniffing.

**Alan**
Oh right.

**Michel**
Because I take drugs.

**Alan**
Do you really?!

**Michel**
No, I was winking – See, I managed to sniff and wink at the same time, it's a French trick.

**Alan**
*(Quietly)* Very clever – Erm, now, well –

**Michel**
Alan, I don't mean to be rude, but I think we're wasting our time here –

**Alan**
Er, well – I'll be the judge of that! If we're wasting anyone's time – which, I concede, we may be – then it's the listeners' –

**Michel**
Yes, but at least the listeners have the opportunity to turn their radios off –

**Alan**
Ah, wrong again! You see, a recent survey reveals most of my listeners are infirm, or –

**Michel**
But, Alan, they could at least bash the radio with their walking sticks, you know, and escape!

**Alan**
No! No! A lot of hospitals have it piped in, they have no control. I've got a list of questions as long as the channel tunnel here and I'll –

**Michel**
Well, just get through them –

**Alan**
Right, OK. Now, right. What's your favourite colour car?

**Michel**
*(Pause)* Have another go, Alan.

**Alan**
OK – fair enough – What's your favourite haute cuisine – hot food?

**Michel**
*Alors! Encore*, Alan, *encore*!

**Alan**
There are some bad questions – er – Right, I'll just read through them all, you stop me if you like one.

**Michel**
Fine.

**Alan**
Right, what's the biggest road you've driven on? What's the furthest you've driven without stopping? No? Er – what's the fastest car you've driven? What's the slowest car you've driven? Thought that'd be quite – bit of a twist on that –

**Michel**
Alan, just read the questions, I'll stop you when it's appropriate.

**Alan**
OK, all right – do you own a bicycle? Do Formula One cars use unleaded petrol?

**Michel**
No, they use leaded petrol.

**Alan**
Right, is –

**Michel**
No, there's no conversation there. That's it.

**Alan**
Right, OK. Have you ever driven a lorry? Have you ever driven a tractor? A minibus? A tank? A taxi? A rocket? What's your

favourite mode of transport, land, sea, air?
When you crashed three years ago, did you
ever consider gi—

**Michel**
Giving up motor racing for good? No,
I didn't, next question.

**Alan**
No! I wasn't going to say that!

**Michel**
No, you weren't?

**Alan**
No, I was going to say –

**Michel**
A more original question!

**Alan**
Yes, I was going to say – Did you ever
consider – the scenery? No, no, I –

**Michel**
Yes! I did! I looked out of the window and I
thought, 'Oh! Look at the scenery!'

**Alan**
No, I wasn't, no, I –

**Michel**
No, you weren't.

**Alan**
No, I wasn't. Right.

**Michel**
How long more have you got to kill, Alan?

**Alan**
*(Whispers)* I've got two minutes.

**Michel**
You got any more questions?

**Alan**
*(Whispers)* No, I've run out.

**Michel**
Now, there is a, a traditional French
custom, we always give our guests, er,

special French smelling salts – so I have
some here –

**Alan**
Yes –?

**Michel**
If you want to take this, put them in your
nose and open up this little package here –

**Alan**
Well, this is –! Right, this is a – this is a
French smelling salt?

**Michel**
Yeess – it's a traditional French ritual – OK.

**Alan**
What do I do now?

**Michel**
Just roll up this ten pound note –

**Alan**
It's like the *Generation Game* this, isn't it!

**Michel**
Just roll that up so it's kinda like a straw –
You see this line here, just sniff that line –

**Alan**
I – put this, what – what do I do with this?

**Michel**
Put it up your nose –

**Alan**
Right – you sure?

**Michel**
Yes, that's fine –

**Alan**
You're absolutely –

**Michel**
It's good for you, you'll feel really good –

**Alan**
Right, what do I do now?

**Michel**
Just sniff it up –

**Alan**
Through there? OK – *(Alan sniffs)*

**Michel**
That's good, and the other nostril –

**Alan**
Yeah, OK, right – *(Alan sniffs again)*

**Michel**
That's good – yeah, nice!

**Alan**
Well, thank you for that nice ritual!

**Michel**
You'll find in about twenty minutes' time
you'll feel really good and kind of – up –

**Alan**
Thanks for the smelling salts! Feeling
better already! And, er, now time for me
to say to you, *Merci beaucoup! Au revoir!*
Michel Lambert!
*(Applause)*
Great – what a nice, what a nice man – Now
– my next guest is a woman who is always
popping up, and, popping out if you've seen
her chest – She's a friend of the stars, and
has a story for everyone. If British industry
had half her energy, we wouldn't be in a
recession! I'm exaggerating, of course – But
please give a round of applause as hopefully
I get a kiss and a cuddle from Shirley Dee!

*Music: 'Super Trouper'*
*Applause*

**Shirley**
Thank you, ladies and gentlemen! Oh,
aren't they lovely? What a lovely audience
you've got here! Aren't they lovely? Oh, I'm
so proud to be here, Alan, you are so lovely!
Isn't he gorgeous, girls? Don't you think?
Put on a bit of weight though since I last
saw you, haven't you!

**Alan**
Just a bit! Ha ha!

**Shirley**
Sorry, darlin', what d'ya wanna ask me?

**Alan**
Shh! Now – woooah! Now. Right. Knowing
me, A–

**Shirley**
You'll have to shut me up because I will just
carry on!

**Alan**
Yeah – shh – all right. Knowing me, Alan,
knowing you, Shirley Dee, Ah-ha!

**Shirley**
Ah-haaaaaaaa! Ooooh! I just love it! It's
such a brilliant catchphrase!

**Alan**
Right. Yeah. Now.

**Shirley**
This is a wonderful programme, darlin' –

**Alan**
Yeah – right –

**Shirley**
– because it is just wonderful, really.

**Alan**
Yeah, right, c'mon, c'mon woooah –

**Shirley**
Sorry, darlin', I'm goin' on again, aren't I?

**Alan**
Yeah, yeah – getting a bit tiresome –

**Shirley**
Yeah!

**Alan**
Now! Now –

**Shirley**
I'll shut up –

**Alan**
It's all right, now let me ask you a question –

**Shirley**
I'm terrible, I wear myself out!

**Alan**
Yeah – you can't half talk –

**Shirley**
I know! I'm terrible! I mean you should-a known that, you should-a been forewarned, because you've seen me in hospitality with that French geezer who's also a bit of a looker, ain't he, girls? Oh! Wouldn't mind a bit o' that one! But, you saw me, I was nattering away nineteen to the dozen –

**Alan**
He understood your Cockney accent then?

**Shirley**
No, we was talkin' in French, darlin'!

**Alan**
Really?

**Shirley**
Yeah, we were havin' a right ol' natter! Marvellous he is!

**Alan**
*Tu parles français?*

**Shirley**
Ooooh! Yeah! I do a bit! So do you by the sound of it!

**Alan**
*Oui, oui, un peu!*

**Shirley**
Oh, *oui, oui, bien sûr évidémment je parle français, je passe souvent mes vacances en France* –

**Alan**
Ooh – *(struggling) Très bien!*

**Shirley**
*Mais, bien sûr un homme sophistique comme toi, Alan, tu connais très la France super bien* –

**Alan**
*Oui, oui, très bien!*

**Shirley**
Oh yeah, you gotta watch me though seriously, Alan, because I will take over! I mean, I really will – in a coupla weeks' time this will be *Knowing You, Knowing Me, with Shirley Dee*, y'know –

**Alan**
Ha, ha, ha, ha! No no no no no, that's not going to happen. Erm – now, you, let's not beat about the bush – You are fifty-two.

**Shirley**
I'm nearly fifty-three, darlin'.

**Alan**
Yeah. But you've still got an eye for the fellas!

**Shirley**
I certainly have! Not just an eye an' all! Ha ha!

**Alan**
Right. And, er, presumably now, of course, the added bonus of not having to worry about getting pregnant?

**Shirley**
Yeah – That is, that is so – yeah, it's true –

**Alan**
Right.

**Shirley**
He comes out with 'em, don't he, eh?

**Alan**
Yeah, right, now – *(sniffs)*

**Shirley**
You're coming down with a bit of a cold, darlin', ain't cha?

**Alan**
Yeah, it's all right. I took some smelling salts before – Now, the thing about you is, you're very difficult to categorize, because, one minute you'll be on *Celebrity Squares*, and the next day you're on *Give Us a Clue*.

**Shirley**
That's right, yeah.

**Alan**
You see what I mean?

**Shirley**
That is my favourite, actually.

**Alan**
And then suddenly, you'll turn up on *Blankety Blank*, so – Now! The great thing at the moment is that they're, they, they are making a film –

**Shirley**
Yeah! About me, darlin', I know!

**Alan**
About you, set in the 60s.

**Shirley**
Yeah!

**Alan**
It's called, *Our Shirley*.

**Shirley**
I know – I'm ever so proud.

**Alan**
And it's about all the people you knew –

**Shirley**
Yeah, that's right, it's about the East End –

**Alan**
All those – in the 60s –

**Shirley**
In the 60s, yeah –

**Alan**
Right.

**Shirley**
And I'm in the film, but I'm not playing myself in it, which is even more interestin'.

**Alan**
No – Helena Bonham Carter is playing you?

**Shirley**
Yes – the young me, yeah!

**Alan**
That's right –

**Shirley**
Which I thought was ever so weird when
I heard about it.

**Alan**
Yeah – she wanted to get away from playing
the sort of flowery types –

**Shirley**
Yeah –

**Alan**
And play someone a bit, a bit rougher –

**Shirley**
She's ever so good, darlin', she's
marvellous!

**Alan**
And, and of course, Tom Bell is in
the film –

**Shirley**
Plays me Uncle Dennis, yeah.

**Alan**
Yes. Very good at playing those shady –
types.

**Shirley**
Well, what Tom Bell has got is the warmth,
the magic of my Uncle Dennis. This
wonderful, kind, lovely, nice, nice man –

**Alan**
Well, you see –

**Shirley**
It's so exciting for me, darlin', really.

**Alan**
Yeah, I know – you, now you say 'nice', but
your Uncle Dennis did commit murder –
Served his sentence.

**Shirley**
Yes, he did, I mean he was in with a dodgy
crowd, it was the East End, y'know, to me
he was lovely –

**Alan**
Right, OK, now, well, well with that
in mind, I have here a pathologist's
report on –

**Shirley**
Oh, come on, darlin', he has been tried,
he's served his time –

**Alan**
I know, I know – it's a forty-page report
condensed into, er, this, this paragraph
here, and it's by Home Office Pathologist
and it says 'Re Mickey Rowlands', the
victim – 'The victim was subject to what I
can only describe as a barbaric and frenzied
attack. He incurred multiple fractures to
the ribs and skull and sustained massive
internal injuries due to multiple stab
wounds. It was a combination of organ
malfunctions and loss of blood which led
to death from heart failure. The victim's
disfigurement was such that identification
was only possible with reference to dental
records –' Now, there's nice, and there's
nice, and there's Uncle Dennis.

**Shirley**
You know – he did a bad thing, a very bad
thing, and he –

**Alan**
'Identification only possible –'

**Shirley**
Yes, I know, Alan!

**Alan**
'– with reference to dental records.'

**Shirley**
He went to prison, he served his time and
he regrets it. That is all I can say.

**Alan**
'Massive internal injuries –'

**Shirley**
And now he's – don't go on, Alan – he's
a reformed man.

**Alan**
'Organ malfunctions –?'

**Shirley**
Yeah, I know! It was a terrible thing,
it was a terrible case!

**Alan**
'Barbaric –'

**Shirley**
Everybody knows the details, it was famous
at the time.

**Alan**
' – frenzied attack –'

**Shirley**
You know, it's over, darlin'. *(Beginning to
sound upset)* You can't live in the past, really
I'm not defending him, but you know –

**Alan**
OK – all right.

**Shirley**
You gotta carry on livin'.

**Alan**
*(Quietly)* 'Organ malfunctions –' Now! But
you, you're not in contact with him any
more, which is –

**Shirley**
Yes, I am, darlin'.

**Alan**
Really?

**Shirley**
'Course I am, I mean he was like a father
to me. I go and see him every Christmas –
he lives on the Costa – we go, we spend
Christmas with him – it's marvellous!

**Alan**
Right, and he follows everything you do?
He watches –

**Shirley**
Yeah! He watches everything I'm on, on
telly, all the programmes, he listens to
everything – he'll be listening, hello, Uncle
Dennis! He'll be listening now, you're
probably out on the World Service, ain't
you?

**Alan**
He'll be listening to this?!?

**Shirley**
Yeah! 'Course he will – he never misses a
trick! He doesn't –

**Alan**
He – he doesn't run that boxers' club any
more though?

**Shirley**
Yeah! You know about that, do you?

**Alan**
Really? Oh –

**Shirley**
Yes, he does – boys' club on the Costa.
Those boys – he drags them up from
nothing, and they would do anything for
him – they'd go to the ends of the earth –
it's marvellous really.

**Alan**
Really?

**Shirley**
It's really sort of warming to see.

**Alan**
Umm – he will realize – if, if he's listening –
he will realize that that was – just a joke,
reading that pathologist's report. If he's
listening, I'll address him directly –

**Shirley**
Alan, there's no need, it was just a little joke!

**Alan**
No! Wait – no! Dennis! If you're listening –

**Shirley**
Alan!

**Alan**
Shhhh! I have to say this – Dennis, it was, it was just a joke, I'll probably edit it out, don't – it's no reflection on you – I realize it was a long time ago, and – things in the past should be dead and buried – I, I – unfortunate phrase there – but I –

**Shirley**
Alan, just leave it!

**Alan**
Wait, no! I've got to say this – y'know, it was a long time ago, you, it was, you lost your temper, you murdered a man, it, it, it, it – by all accounts, he was a rather unsavoury character – and, y'know, the world's probably a better place without him – and, and in a, in a way, thank you – for, er, for bringing him to the final court of justice. So – once more – Uncle Dennis, thank you for stabbing him to death, and thank you Shirley Dee for being my guest! Shirley Dee!

*Applause*

We're gonna change the tone a bit now. *(Clears throat)* 'It's cold – it's damp, it's dark, I want to go home, I want to be in a warm bed, but I can't because I'm chained to a radiator in a cell.' Of course, I'm not – my next guest was because he was a hostage for two years in Liberia in the civil war. Don't expect him to be too perky, he was only released six months ago, and – he's still suffering from post-traumatic stress disorder! Please welcome, Chris Lester!

*Music: 'SOS'*

**Alan**
Knowing me Alan Partridge, knowing you, Chris Lester, Ah-haa!

**Chris**
Ah-haa!

**Alan**
Right. Erm, thank you for being my hostage today – I assure you, I, I won't be keeping you for longer than ten minutes. Right, now, you were confined, you were confined for two years –

**Chris**
Two years, that's right.

**Alan**
Now, how long is that, exactly?

**Chris**
Well – it – yeah it's a, it's a long time when you, when you don't know when it's going to end, I mean it's a long time out of anyone's life.

**Alan**
Right – yeah – I mean, let's sort of break it down – it's a hundred weeks – it's – it's eighteen thousand – hours. Eighteen thousand episodes of *The Darling Buds of May*, if you like – erm – or, or in another way, thirty-six thousand episodes of *Knowing Me, Knowing You* – it sounds like torture. Was it? Was it torture?

**Chris**
Well, obviously psychologically, I mean we weren't – we were just, we were just political pawns, you see.

**Alan**
Pawns in a game of – cruel chess!

**Chris**
Yeah –

**Alan**
Who were the bishops?

**Chris**
Yeah. I don't think the metaphor stretches really.

**Alan**
OK. All right. Now, how, how – a question I'm sure everyone wants to know is, how did you relieve the boredom?

**Chris**
Yeah, um – well you have to keep yourself mentally active all the time, because you can't be active physically, so you invent games, you play games, for example, 'Shopping' – I don't know if you know the shopping game, where you say –

**Alan**
No –

**Chris**
'I went shopping and I bought an apple.' And then, 'I went shopping and I bought an apple and a banana.' You see – A – B – 'I went shopping and I bought an apple and a banana and,' something beginning with C, a cucumber or a carrot –

**Alan**
Cake!

**Chris**
Cake –

**Alan**
Or coat! Or –

**Chris**
Coat, yeah, it could be anything beginning with C – and you have to –

**Alan**
Or, or cheese!

**Chris**
Yeah –

**Alan**
It's not got a 'ker' sound but it, it counts!

**Chris**
Cheese is fine – apple, banana, cheese –

**Alan**
So – D – D –, er –

**Chris**
Are we going up to Z on this, are we?

**Alan**
No, no, no – it's not a good idea to – go to – to Z – Zebra! Whilst you were there, what I want to know is, there must have been some – funny incidents. There must have been – something funny must have happened.

**Chris**
Well – no, no not re— I mean you've got to imagine the situation – you're in the cell basically for twenty-four hours a day.

**Alan**
I know –

**Chris**
There's no exercise –

**Alan**
I know it was depressing, I just don't want to dwell on that. I really don't want to – it, it's –

**Chris**
I – I really can't – you know, it wasn't that sort –

**Alan**

I'm not asking for that, look, I'm just saying will you do something amusing? Can you tell us an amusing story? C'mon!

**Chris**

Erm. Well. After about six months in prison, I found, scuttering across the floor, a little beetle, and I called it Hope. And after about six months, I fell asleep and the matchbox was open and Hope escaped, but – in a way I wasn't sad because Hope had escaped and I felt that pre-figured in a way my own escape, which indeed it did, because I escaped twelve months later –

**Alan**

Hmm. You're absolutely sure that's the funniest thing –? Li-listen, if you can remember anything, please, this is very important –

**Chris**

Well, I can't guarantee –

**Alan**

If you can remember anything funny in the rest of the interview just cut straight in with it.

**Chris**

OK. Right. Fine –

**Alan**

*(Whispers)* D'you know – and if you want – you can make something up, it doesn't matter, doesn't really matter –
in fact – if you want to get one of the researchers to get *Frank Muir's Book of Anecdotes*, just dress it up, change the location but it doesn't matter, and, I just want you to get the audience on your side – because, er, I have to say, at the moment, you're coming across as a bit of a sour-puss – I don't want the punters to think you're a bad egg, I know you're not.

**Chris**

I don't think you're quite understanding the situation, you have to make do with what you have in those, in those sort of situations – You don't have much of a choice.

**Alan**

Well! I mean you did have a choice, this is what you've not told the audience! That for two years, you were chained to another human being!

**Chris**

Phil?

**Alan**

Phil! You had a choice between talking to a human being, on one hand, and a dung-beetle on the other!

**Chris**

Yeah, not a dung-beetle, an elm-beetle.

**Alan**

Yeah, whatever, they're all stupid! I mean – Now, I think it's about time we had a surprise – a surprise for you! Yes! He was chained to you for two years! You've not seen him for six months! He impressed us all with his good humour and positive attitude when he was released – please applaud loudly and freely for Chris' comrade in chains, Phil Collins!

*Music: 'In the Air Tonight'*
*Applause*

**Alan**

Knowing me, knowing you, ah-haa!

**Phil**

Ahrr-haaaa!

**Alan**

Now, before we go any further, get it cleared up straight away, you're not the real Phil Collins –

**Phil**
That's right, no, no, I'm not the bald guy in Genesis –

**Alan**
Nah, it's just, just got the same name –

**Phil**
Ha ha! That's right.

**Alan**
Now, you were incarcerated for two years – just to recap on the maths of that, it's, it's as I say, er, thirty-six thousand episodes of *Knowing Me, Knowing You* –

**Phil**
Yup –

**Alan**
Eighteen thousand episodes of *The Darling Buds of May*, and, actually, another way of looking at it, it's nine thousand episodes of *Inspector Morse*! It's not – not so bad when you look at it like that, is it?

**Phil**
Ha! Yeah, I wish we'd had a video! He he he!

**Alan**
Now, the first time I decided to have you on the show –

**Phil**
I don't like the sound of that, Alan! Ha ha ha ha ha!

**Alan**
Great! It's great! Great! Like that! Funny! Now, the first time I decided was at the press conference when you were released –

**Phil**
Yeah –

**Alan**
Because – it was a very momentous occasion, it was televised all round the world – Chris, you came on and gave a very harrowing account of your experience, and

then! You came on, Phil, and you were hilarious! You really were!

**Phil**
I have a very positive view of everything, I always try to keep positive, like yourself, Alan –

**Alan**
Absolutely.

**Phil**
So, on the day, when it was time for me to speak, I stood at the desk, and I picked up this big ball and chain, plonked it on top of the desk, and I said, 'Phew! Glad to see the last of that!'

**Alan**
Ha ha ha ha ha!

**Phil**
And ripped off the chain from the ball, because it was made of polystyrene! And –

**Alan**
Ha ha ha! That –

**Phil**
And everyone fell about!

**Alan**
That – they were big laughs, when you did that!

**Phil**
Yeah, then, if you remember, I stood on the desk –

**Alan**
Hmm.

**Phil**
– and I sort of shook all this sand out of my pockets, like I'd just escaped from Colditz! Like in the film –

**Alan**
Yeah, that didn't go down so well – Now, but the great thing about you is, you've got your book out –

**Phil**

That's right!

**Alan**

I've read it, it's brilliant, it's dynamite!
It really is! It's called, *Hostage* –

**Phil**

Exclamation mark! Don't forget that!

**Alan**

That's right –

**Phil**

And then it's got my name, 'Phil Collins' in
big gold-embossed letters, and then in
brackets underneath it, 'not in Genesis –'
Just so people know, it's clear.

**Alan**

So people know. Right, OK. Now, read an
extract out! Come on –

**Phil**

Yeah, I've got an extract here, prepared –

**Alan**

Really cookin'!

**Phil**

Just so people understand what the plot is,
basically it's, it's as I said, based on me and,
er, Chris, in the cell, but I've kinda changed
it a bit – 'It was morning – early – six. Paul
Carter snapped awake instinctively. Alert,
ready. Les Christopher lay on his side, his
thumb in his mouth, sucking like a baby.'

**Alan**

Yeah!

**Phil**

'Carter rose from his bunk. His feet felt the
hard cold stone grey floor. Feet that had
trod every trouble spot in the world. Feet
that had tasted a touch of danger. Feet
that had seen too much.'

**Alan**

Brilliant!

**Phil**

'A black beetle scuttled across the floor.
Instinctively, Carter crushed it with his
heel. It shattered with a satisfying crunch.
Carter smiled –'

**Chris**

Can you – er, excuse me, Phil, one moment
– was that my beetle?

**Phil**

It's fiction!

**Chris**

Did that happen? Did you crush my beetle?
Is that what happened to my beetle?

**Alan**

Oh! Oh! Uh-oh! Oh! Oh!

**Phil**

Chris! It was six months ago! It was
an accident!

**Alan**

Hang on –

**Chris**

You – it was another accident?!

**Phil**

I didn't crush it on purpose!

**Alan**

Hang on!

**Phil**

I woke up one morning, your beetle
was scurrying –

**Chris**

It cannot be – another thing you
have done –

**Alan**

Look!

**Phil**

I mean if you weren't so busy walking
around – just because your book's not
selling, Chris!

**Alan**

Please! Oi! Hey! Stop, everyone! Are you staring at me?

**Phil**

No –

**Alan**

Err – the thing is – I want to point out that Hope was crushed but it was Hope the cockroach, not hope the, the ideal. Hope, ho – ho – hope the – the – the – what are they laughing at? No –

**Phil**

Alan, are you all right?

**Alan**

*(Stuttering)* Yeah, I'm fine! Erm, you didn't crush a beetle? You didn't crush John Lennon – he's a beetle, didn't crush him. He's – that would have been bad he's already – dead. Paul McCartney's still alive he's doing – with Linda –

**Phil**

Are you sure you're all right?

**Alan**

– McCartney, she's doing the vegetarian dishes – microwave dishes, erm, vitamin deficiency, erm, and *(sniffs)* I'm – I'm – I'm – I'm really hungry, actually! I'm really hungry! Have you got any corn flakes? No? With sugar –

**Phil**

No –

**Alan**

I'm just – I just like frozen food. I like going home, and get the frozen food and cook it up – and it's really nice – put it in a bowl and eat it, right and I put the video on and I've got – TV! And, er, it's the biggest TV you can get –

**Phil**

Alan, have you taken something?

**Alan**

Six feet across! TV – and it's like a big eye, in the room and it sort of stares at me! It scares me! I don't like it!

**Phil**

Alan!

**Alan**

I don't like it! I'm not going home tonight!

**Phil**

Alan!

**Alan**

What? What?

**Phil**

I – I think you've taken some drugs.

**Alan**

I've taken drugs!

**Phil**

Yes.

**Alan**

I, I, I have taken – on *that* bombshell! I, Alan Partridge have taken drugs – Chris Lester! Chris Lester, Phil Collins, Phil Collins, the famous one, er, Shirley Big-tits, er, the Frog! Er, the writers and researchers – Steve Coogan, Patrick Marber, Rebecca Front, David Schneider, Doon MacKichan, produced by Armando Iannucci, see, see, er, next week! Er, right yeah! Right.

*Music: 'Knowing Me, Knowing You'*

# KNOWING ME KNOWING YOU

## RADIO SHOW 3

*Alan Partridge*

*Music: 'Knowing Me, Knowing You'*

**Alan**

Ah-haaaa! *(Applause)* Welcome. Ah-haa, or should I say, Yee-haa! – because I, Alan Partridge, am broadcasting live from Las Vegas, US of A, stateside. I promise you tonight we'll have a real half-pound cheeseburger of a – of a show for you. And it's a cheesburger that contains lots of meaty chat, a salad of wit and a – a flap of amusing cheese, all held together by my sauce of to-mah-to ketchup, or you here in the States, to-may-to catsup *(under his breath)* that's what you say. Now, for those of you listening beneath the Star-Spangled Banner who haven't heard of me, I'm a sort of an English Johnny Carson and, for those of you listening beneath the Union Jack, I'm Alan Partridge.

Now tonight for various reasons my producer and American co-producers here in Vegas thought it would be a good idea if I had an American co-host, and that's great, it's a good idea, I agree with it. So to that end, please welcome my co-host, or should I say hostess – perhaps I shouldn't say hostess, because that in England is a whore, and she's, she's not a whore, she's not a whore, nevertheless, she's the sort of woman you wouldn't mind paying cash to be with, because she's so beautiful and lovely. Please welcome supermodel Kendall Ball. *(Music) (Applause and cheering)* All right, all right, all right, all right, all right, right, right, right, OK, right, shh, shh. Knowing me, Alan Partridge, knowing you, Kendall Ball, ah-haa.

**Kendall**
Ah-haa. Hi everybody, how ya doin'?
*(Applause, whistling)* It's great to be in
Vegas, OK.

**Alan**
Yeah, right, right, fantastic, Kendall, it's
swell or, in English, great to have you on –
great to have you on my show.

**Kendall**
Well, it's great to be on the show, Alan.

**Alan**
My show. Now, now, in case anyone
listening doesn't know who you are or what
you look like, I'll describe you to the
listeners. Now, she's very beautiful, she's
very tall –

**Kendall**
No, please, Alan, I, I have these sticking-out
ears that look like Prince Charles, I –

**Alan**
Oh, come on, you don't look like Prince
Charles.

**Kendall**
Well, I hate them.

**Alan**
His Royal Highness isn't someone who I – I
– share – and I, ah, agree with a lot of what
he says, but he's a deeply ugly man. You've
got a lovely, you've got a lovely little beauty
spot there –

**Kendall**
Well, this is a mole, Alan.

**Alan**
I – I don't like you using that word, it's
not a mole –

**Kendall**
It is, I had it removed –

**Alan**
It's – no, come on, it's not a big fat mole
with a tuft of wiry hair growing in it, it's –
you know, to describe you basically, wh-
what you're wearing, you look like a million
dollars, your legs go right up to your
armpits, uh, not literally that would be
hideous, um, but, er, so remember,
remember, please, to listen to me and
look at her. Don't get it the other way
around, please, that will be, that will be
awful, OK. Our first guests are a married
couple. In fact, they're one of Hollywood's
star couples.

**Kendall**
She is the daughter of legendary star
Mimi Langland and sister of the equally
legendary star Laura Langland, and of
course as a superlative singing star in
her own right.

**Alan**
And he is a British actor, gentleman star,
who first twinkled his bright talent in the
Hollywood galaxy forty years ago when he
starred in the film *Little Lord Fauntleroy*.

**Kendall**
So please give a glittering reception to
Sally –

**Alan**
I say that. Sally Hoff and Conrad Knight!

*Music: 'Thank You for the Music'*
*Applause*

**Alan**
*(In the background)* Oh dear. *(Loudly)*
Knowing me, Alan Partridge–

**Kendall**
Knowing me, Kendall Ball–

**Alan**
Knowing us, Alan Partridge and Kendall
Ball, knowing you Sally Hoff and husband
Conrad Knight, ah-haa.

**Sally**
Ah-haa.

**Conrad**
Ah-haa.

**Alan**
Now, if I can start with you, Sally.

**Sally**
Hi.

**Alan**
Lovely, Sally –

**Sally**
Hello, Alan. Hello, Kendall –

**Kendall**
Oh, it's lovely to meet you, Sally –

**Sally**
Thank you so much –

**Kendall**
I've admired your work for many years –

**Sally**
Oh, Kendall, that is such a lovely thing
to say –

**Alan**
Right, lovely, lovely, shh, shh.

**Conrad**
Isn't Sally terrific?

**Alan**
Yes, she's lovely, yes. Sally, you are the
daughter of the legendary Mimi Langland.

**Sally**
That's right.

**Alan**
Er, sister of the legendary Laura Langland.

**Sally**
Uh-huh.

**Alan**
Now, she is so busy, isn't she? She's –

**Sally**
She's wonderfully busy. I'm very proud
of Laura –

**Alan**
Hectic schedule. She's certainly – I know
for a fact she's working tonight. Um, as is
Collie Simon, Liza Minnelli, Barbra
Streisand, all working tonight, um, but you
are available, that's important. You're here.
What was it like growing up in a famous
family? Must have been marvellous.

**Sally**
Alan, it was magical. I had a fairytale
childhood.

**Alan**
With your mother Mimi Langland. I love
those films she made.

**Sally**
Oh, I'm so happy –

**Kendall**
Sally, tell us about your mother's
alcoholism.

**Alan**
Oh, come on, we want a sole living memory
of – her mother was a fine, wonderful,
musical actress. I don't want to think about
her mother as some drunken woman
wandering around Sunset Boulevard in her
bare feet with mascara running down her
face, directing traffic, holding a bottle of
gin in her hand. I want to think of her
sitting on a haystack and singing
'Hopscotch Girl' in a pink dress.

**Sally**
Well, yes, it was a very private problem.
I've written a book about it, that's all there
is to say.

**Alan**
Conrad, you published your
autobiography, *Agent in LA*.

**Conrad**
*A Gent in LA (laughs).*

**Alan**
Published in – published in 1979, which had very bad reviews. There was a particular babble in *Spy Magazine*. It simply changed one of the words in the title of your book, they changed the first two letters of the word 'gent' –

**Conrad**
Yes.

**Alan**
– and left the last two –

**Conrad**
Yes.

**Alan**
– so it was 'A Something in LA'.

**Conrad**
Yes.

**Alan**
Right.

**Conrad**
And I – I immediately sued *Spy Magazine*.

**Alan**
Hmm.

**Sally**
Sadly he lost the case.

**Alan**
Hmm. In fact you set a legal precedent, because you're one of the few people who can now be referred to in print as that thing, without fear of litigation.

**Conrad**
Yes, that's absolutely right, Alan. Um, but no other medium. Just print.

**Alan**
Just print. So, I couldn't call you that?

**Conrad**
No, but you could fax me.

**Alan**
Right. Or indeed scribble it down on a piece of paper and hold it up to your face.

**Conrad**
That would be perfectly legal, yes. And people do do that.

**Kendall**
Conrad, can I ask you about the McCarthy era? Um, this was a very sticky patch in your career. I wonder if you could eliminate it for us.

**Conrad**
Oh, I wouldn't say it was a sticky patch – it was a time when one had to stick to one's principles and I did.

**Alan**
It was, because at the time you were under a lot of pressure, as were many people, and you were called before the House Commitee of un-American Activities –

**Conrad**
Yes I was.

**Alan**
– before Senator Joseph McCarthy. Very intimidating man –

**Conrad**
He certainly was.

**Alan**
– and I remember hearing the tape. He asked you, he said, 'Will you name any people who you knew to be members of the Communist party?', and you said –

**Conrad**
Humphrey Bogart. Charles Chaplin. Arthur Miller, Elia Kazan, John Huston –

**Alan**
Fantastic. Fantastic. Well done. Well done. Charlie Chaplin especially. I've always, I've heard about him being a Communist, and, whenever I watch those films like *Goldrush*, you know, and see him walking along, that walk seems sinister, somehow.

**Conrad**
Yes.

**Alan**
The walk seems to be saying, 'Be a Communist'. You did the series of dinosaur films, didn't you?

**Conrad**
Yes.

**Alan**
Now, they were rubbish.

**Conrad**
Well, Alan, one of them won an Oscar.

**Alan**
Yeah. Best use of an animated dinosaur.

**Conrad**
Well, I, I've done better work of course.

**Alan**
But have you?

**Conrad**
Well, I have my business interests.

**Alan**
Would you want to tell us about those? What are your business interests?

**Conrad**
Conrad Knight socks.

**Alan**
Wh-wh-wh-what's that?

**Sally**
They're very distinctive socks –

**Conrad**
Conrad Knight socks.

**Sally**
They have a special kind of crest, it's – it's Conrad's historical family crest, which I designed myself –

**Conrad**
Conrad Knight socks.

**Alan**
Hang on a second. You're advertising.

**Conrad**
Conrad Knight socks.

**Alan**
All right. Put a Conrad Knight sock in it.

**Conrad**
Conrad –

**Alan**
Shut up! Now, 1991 was an *annus horribilis* for you two, wasn't it? Conrad, you had a *massive* heart attack.

**Kendall**
Sally, that was a terrible year for you as well.

**Sally**
It was awful.

**Alan**
You had a total nervous breakdown.

**Sally**
Er – hmm. Yep.

**Alan**
Your nerves collapsed completely, didn't they?

**Kendall**
How did you cope?

**Sally**
Kendall, it was very tough. The important thing is that what we experienced then was a tremendous outpouring of love and emotion, from friends and fans.

**Kendall**
Yeah. Beautiful.

**Sally**
I have a letter here. May I read this letter?

**Alan**
Please do read the letter. Is it long?

**Sally**
It's very, very brief –

**Alan**
Good.

**Sally**
– and very beautiful. It's a letter that was from a little old lady from Massachusetts, specifically about Conrad's illness and it simply says this. It says, 'Dear Conrad and Sally, I have heard that Conrad is very ill. I do not know either of you, but I know your work *(starts sobbing)* and I value you. I feel as though I love you both. I have' – I'm sorry – 'have very little left to live for and if you die, I will have nothing – Please, Conrad, don't die!' and it's just, I'm sorry, it's just, it's a very beautiful letter, and it's the kind of thing that –

**Conrad**
And I wrote back to her and I wrote, 'Dear old lady, Thank you for your terrific and moving letter and we love you. Please, don't die.' And I enclosed with the letter a pair of Conrad Knight socks to cheer her up.

**Sally**
It was a lovely gesture.

**Alan**
*(Emotionally)* Did – did she write back?

**Conrad**
No. She died.

**Alan**
*(Sobbing)* Wh-why-y-y? Why do people have to die?

**Kendall**
*(Alan sobbing throughout)* The important thing is, it's a wonderful thing, um, I think we should wind it up here –

**Alan**
*(Still sobbing)* No, no, no. This is – you're listening to Alan Partridge. This is a beautiful moment of emotional outpouring. This is a transatlantic sea of tears that you're hearing now on Radio Four – um – right *(regains composure)* uh, over to you, Kendall.

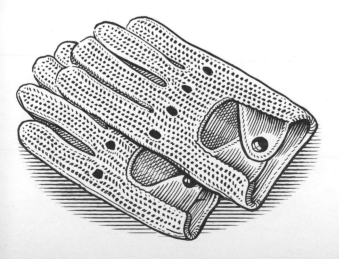

**Kendall**
I believe you two have a little surprise for Alan.

**Sally**
We do, Kendall, we'd like to sing a little song for you.

**Kendall**
Aww.

**Alan**
Ooh, well, thank you.

**Conrad**
Um, more of a surprise, Alan, you're going to sing with us.

**Kendall**
Ooh, yeah.

**Alan**
Oh, I can't sing.

*Audience applaud loudly. The others encourage him.*

**Alan**
Oh, OK

*Music starts.*

**Sally**
*I know you better than I know myself –* Thank you, very kind *– oh, so much better than I know myself.*

**Conrad**
She does, you know.

**Sally**
*I know the tricks you play*

**Conrad**
What tricks?

**Sally**
*I've seen them every day. No wonder I'm bored*

**Conrad**
Bored?

**Sally**
*No wonder I'm mad*

**Conrad**
Conrad Knight socks.

**Sally**
*No wonder I'm crazy over you*

**Alan**
Fantastic!

**Kendall**
Woo-hoo-hoo! Welcome to Vegas!

**Audience**
Woo-hoo-hoo!

**Alan**
*I'm at home in Vegas, 'cos that's where –* you're putting me off *– I belong*

**Kendall**
What a guy.

**Alan**
*You can bet –* oh yeah, you bet *– on Vegas, the only town to move me to say –*

**Kendall**
He's terrific.

**Alan**
*I have seen the best. North, south, east to west. From Shanghai to Timbuktu. O – o – o –* That's quite far way –

**Alan and Sally**
*Oh, we're at home in Vegas*

**Alan**
YES! *And I'm at home in Vegas too. Thanks for being on* Knowing Me, Knowing You.

*Huge applause.*

**Alan and Kendall**
Thank you.

**Kendall**
Thank you. Now, would you all –

**Alan**
Woah-whoah-whoah-whoah-whoah.
I start. Knock-knock!

**Audience**
Who's there?

**Alan**
Alan.

**Audience**
Alan who?

**Alan**
Alan Partridge. Now, you probably
guessed, I'm not a comedian.

**Kendall**
But our second guest most definitely is.
Now, he learnt his comedy skills in the
Catskills. He's got belly laughs in the
borscht belt, and every time he comes to
Las Vegas, he's a surefire comedy winner.
He is my –

**Alan**
Twice – twice this week, I've shouted 'Book
him!' Once, when I was commentating on a
football, or soccer match as you say and
Stuart Pearce committed a particularly
nasty foul, and I shouted 'Book him!' The
second time was when I was having a meal
last night in the hotel carvery and I saw a
very talented New York Jewish comedian,
and I shouted 'Book him!' His name
is Bernie Rosen, so please welcome
Bernie Rosen!

*Applause and music*

**Alan**
Knowing me, Alan Partridge.

**Kendall**
Knowing me, Kendall Ball.

**Alan**
Knowing us Alan Partridge and Kendall
Ball, knowing you Bernie Rosen. Ah-haa.

**Bernie**
Ah-haa. Ya, knowing me, but obviously not
in the biblical sense, ha ha! Though we live
in hope, eh, Kendall?

**Kendall**
Huh, yeah, sure, huh.

**Bernie**
Who are these people here? You know, they
all look so depressed, you know, that's the
thing about Vegas, you know, we Jews, we
got so much money here in Vegas, we call it
Oi-Vegas, yeah. I mean, look. Look at that
woman over there, you know, look at that
lady there, she looks like she just got here
from a funeral, you know, her own –
*(silence in the studio)*.

**Kendall**
Bernie, Bernie, I've noticed the way you
came in was, like, full of confidence –

**Bernie**
Full marks there, Kendall.

**Kendall**
Is your comedy a sort of defence
mechanism?

**Alan**
No, no, can we just, I don't want to get
too heavy, look. Bernie, Bernie.

**Bernie**
Yeah, Alan.

**Alan**
Who's your favourite comedian?

**Bernie**
Well, I s'pose I gotta say Milton Berle,
you know, I –

**Alan**
Who's he?

41

**Bernie**
He's my favourite comedian, y'know.

**Alan**
Right, um, who's your favourite British comedian, that people in Britain might have heard of?

**Bernie**
I-I'm sorry, Alan –

**Alan**
Tommy Cooper?

**Bernie**
No. No, Alan.

**Alan**
Tommy Cooper? Oh come on, he did tricks badly, you know, he died at the Palladium.

**Bernie**
Alan, I tell you something, we've all died at the Palladium, you know.

**Alan**
*(Sigh)* Wh-what's your favourite situation comedy?

**Bernie**
Ah, yeah, oh, my marriage is my favourite sitcom, you know, we're on to our twenty-second series and the ratings are terrible, you know, and the good news is, they're writing my wife out of the next series.

**Alan**
Really, I-I'm sure you're a very funny man, but you never answer the question. I don't know what you're talking about.

**Bernie**
If you don't know what I'm talking about, you should hear my cousin Morris, the Latvian accountant *(gabbles incomprehensibly)*.

**Alan**
Would you just answer the question?!

**Kendall**
Alan, Alan –

**Alan**
What's your favourite sitcom!?

**Bernie**
*The Golden Girls.*

**Alan**
Right. Right. Mine is *Robin's Nest.*

**Bernie**
Right.

**Alan**
It was, it was brilliant, actually. Richard O'Sullivan ran this restaurant and it really was chaos. Yeah, and the man who did the washing up only had one arm. When you think about it, it's ridiculous. Need-need-needless to say that plenty of plates got broken and Robin got annoyed. It was very funny. Now, let's move on, let's not beat about the bush. You are a Jew.

**Bernie**
Alan, hey, you said you wouldn't tell anybody. The secret's out!

**Alan**
What d'you mean? Everyone knows.

**Bernie**
It's a joke, Alan, you know, I was joking.

**Alan**
Oh. You were very funny last night.

**Bernie**
Yeah, well, you know.

**Alan**
Look, in, you see, in Britain there's a rich stream of Jewish comedy, there's, ah, all the famous ones, Shylock, Fagin, Topol, Maureen Lipman in the British Telecom ads, which depict modern Jews accurately and hilariously, but, of course, there are different kinds of Jews, aren't there?

**Bernie**

Oh, sure, yeah, sure, Alan, you know, we got, we got conservative Jews, we got reformed Jews, liberal Jews, orange Jews, apple Jews –

**Alan**

A-apple Jews. Wh-what are they?

**Bernie**

No, Alan, that, you know, it's, it's a joke, Alan, it was juice, Jews, you know it sounds the same.

**Alan**

Did you, did you do that joke in your act?

**Bernie**

No, I wrote it for tonight, yeah.

**Alan**

Well, you shouldn't have bothered.

**Bernie**

Yeah.

**Kendall**

Bernie, could I ask you a question?

**Alan**

Keep it light.

**Kendall**

How do you deal with anti-Semitism in your profession?

**Alan**

Oh, Lord!

**Bernie**

Could I answer that?

**Alan**

Don't! No, look, I don't want to get into this whole dangerous area of anti-Semitism, I, look, please, Bernie, for God's sake, please, tell us a joke about Jews.

**Bernie**

OK, OK, on ya, I'll tell you a Jewish joke. I, I said to my wife, Ida, 'Ida, how come you never tell me when you orgasm?', and she said to me, 'Bernie, it's 'cos you're never there!' You know, when I orgasm, you're never there, you know – it's – you know –

**Alan**

Hang on, hang on – oh yes, yes! *(Laughs hysterically)*

**Bernie**

Yeah, yeah, oh yeah, OK, we have contact! OK.

**Alan**

I've got a great joke about Jews. Right, did you hear about the Jewish hotel keeper? He, he kept a fork in the sugar bowl for goodness sake.

**Bernie**

No, uh, Alan, that's not a Jewish joke, that's an anti-Jewish joke.

**Kendall**

Alan, that stereotypes Jewish people as being mean.

**Alan**

Well, I wouldn't want to say that you were mean, in fact I noticed when I met you tonight the first thing you did when I met you in the bar, you went and bought me a drink, and I – I remembered you did that and I thought, 'Yes. Good.'

**Bernie**

Yeah. I mean, that's very nice of you, Alan, but the important thing is not to generalize, you know, I – I just met you. You're the only person I know from, where're you from, er, Nor-wich?

**Alan**

Norwich.

**Bernie**
Yeah, and, ah, just knowing you I'm not going to think that everyone in Norwich is, is –

**Kendall**
Stupid.

**Alan**
People aren't stupid in Norwich.

**Kendall**
I wasn't – I wasn't saying they were stupid.

**Alan**
No, let me nail this ghost to the coffin, once and for all. Norwich people are not stupid, let me tell you something, let me tell this American audience something. In Britain, we have centres of excellence: Oxford, Cambridge and Norwich. And so people in Norwich are different. Living in Norwich is not just a way of life, Norwich is an attitude. I will not have that kind of prejudice thrown upon me from someone like that. Dis-disgrace. Thank you very much – you were so funny last night.

**Bernie**
Do I, like, go now?

**Alan**
Yeah, give him a round of applause *(sighs)*.

*Applause*

**Kendall**
Bernie Rosen, ladies and gentlemen, Bernie! Woo-hoo!

**Alan**
Our final guest tonight is not so much famous as infamous.

**Kendall**
He's known throughout Las Vegas as one of the biggest high-rolling gamblers of them all.

**Alan**
*Rien ne va plus.*

**Kendall**
Place your bets.

**Alan**
The dice are loaded.

**Kendall**
Stick or twist.

**Alan**
Two fat ladies, eighty-eight. Legs eleven, eleven. All these words are music to his ears.

**Kendall**
Please welcome Mister Ri—

**Alan**
I'll say this. Please welcome Mister Risky Business himself, professional gambler, Jack 'the black cat' Colson.

*Applause and music*

**Alan**
Knowing me, Alan Partridge.

**Kendall**
Knowing me, Kendall Ball.

**Alan**
Knowing us, Alan Partridge and Kendall Ball, knowing you Jack 'the black cat' Colson, ah-haa.

**Jack**
He-he, that is just about the longest introduction I ever had. Ah-haa! – thought you never gonna finish it.

**Alan**
He-he.

**Kendall**
Jack, Jack, I believe that you have played poker w-i-i-i-ith – Telly Savalas.

**Jack**
That's right.

**Alan**
Who loves ya, baby.

**Jack**
Telly Savalas, he's a really keen poker player. He heard I was to be in Vegas, he was shooting some film here. He said, 'Jack Black-cat, how d'you wanna play a bit of poker?' High stakes.

**Kendall**
Yeah?

**Alan**
Book 'em, Dano, murder one.

**Jack**
Nope, man, that's *Hawaii Five-O*.

**Alan**
Right.

**Jack**
Sorry, I had to say that.

**Alan**
OK.

**Jack**
Anyhow, Telly comes up to my hotel room, we s—, I say, 'Telly, you wanna play a little bit of Texas Holding?' You know Texas Holding, Kendall?

**Kendall**
Yeah.

**Jack**
Deal comes, Telly's got a pair of kings, I got bullets in the hole, Aces.

**Alan**
Ooh.

**Jack**
Now I don't know, I figure I'm gonna get Telly all in here.

**Alan**
Ooh.

**Jack**
Flip comes. Deuce, tres, five. Ain't no use to neither of us.

**Kendall**
Right.

**Alan**
Wow.

**Jack**
Telly raises the max. I call. Guess what happens? Four of Clubs comes down here. I just made me an inside straight and hit the middle pin – woo-wee!

**Alan**
Woo-wee!

**Jack**
Telly says to me, 'Well, what you got, Jack "the black cat" Colson?' So I flip over my Aces and I say, 'Telly, I got bullets!' *(Mimics two gunshots)*

**Alan**
You shot Telly Savalas?

**Kendall**
No, Alan. Bullets – it's slang for Aces.

**Alan**
It – it's funny though, isn't it, that his name's Telly Savalas and he's on the telly.

**Jack**
That's real funny.

**Alan**
It's a bit like me being called, uh, Radio Partridge. Of course, it's not that funny when you think about it, because there was, uh, Radio Caroline, isn't there? That's her name.

**Kendall**
Jack, tell us about your famous roulette system, you've been practising it since the age of six.

**Jack**
The thing about roulette, anyone out there listening, is you don't wanna play roulette. Sucker's game, see. You got all these people, they fly over to Vegas to say, 'Hey, I got some big, big-shot roulette system.' Only a sucker's got a roulette system.

**Alan**
I've got a roulette system.

**Jack**
You wanna tell me –

**Alan**
I've got, I've got a foolproof system.

**Jack**
Uh-huh.

**Alan**
I developed it while I was coming over on the plane, club class, and I tried it out several times, now, in my imagination, and it works every time.

**Jack**
I can believe that –

**Alan**
It's – and this is how it works, right. It's like a toss of a coin, look, if I toss a coin, and it's heads, the next time I toss it, it's bound to be tails.

**Jack**
Nope, it's fifty/fifty every single time, Alan. The coin ain't got a brain, ain't got consciousness. No matter what's going on round the coin, the coin just does what the hell it wants to. Bit like yourself, Alan.

**Alan**
Well, I – I bet you any money that if I put my system into practice, it would work. I'll bet you.

**Jack**
Well, I may just have to take you up on that little bet, Alan.

**Alan**
*(Mimicking Jack)* Well, you could just take me up on that little bet.

**Jack**
Well, I may just have to do that.

**Alan**
Well, you can do it if you want.

*Applause*

**Jack**
Well, I may just do that.

**Alan**
Well, do it!

**Kendall**
Woo-hoo! Watch yourself, Alan.

**Alan**
Hang on, hang on. If you –

**Jack**
He knows what he's doing. You wanna make a bet?

**Alan**
I – I think that your Texan belly is going a little bit yellow.

*Audience cheers.*

**Jack**
You do, do you? Well, let's do it, Alan. Thousand bucks –

**Alan**
Thousand bucks.

**Jack**
Let's do it, Alan.

**Alan**
Yep. Thousand bucks.

**Jack**
Call.

**Alan**
Tails.

**Jack**
What's that?

**Alan**
Tails! Yes!

*Applause and cheering*

**Alan**
One thousand dollars to me.

**Jack**
Cheque. Who do you want to make the cheque payable to?

**Alan**
Make it payable to Great Ormond Street Hospital.

**Jack**
You, you wanna raise the stakes a little bit, Alan? Put it up to five thousand bucks?

**Alan**
No, no.

**Jack**
No? *(Mimics a clucking chicken)*

**Alan**
No. Ten thousand. Ten thousand bucks.

**Jack**
Ten thousand bucks? I like the way you speak.

**Alan**
Ten thousand bucks.

**Jack**
Ten thousand bucks.

**Alan**
Yeah.

**Jack**
Call.

**Alan**
Heads.

**Jack**
What's that?

**Alan**

Heads! Yes! *(Applause)* Yes! Ten thousand bucks. Live, from Las Vegas it's Alan Partridge who's just won ten thousand bucks off, supposedly, the greatest gambler who's ever lived.

**Jack**

Shall I make that little cheque here payable to Great Ormond Street Hospital –

**Alan**

No, just – leave that one blank. I'll fill that one in later. It's, er, thanks for being on the show, and thanks for being so gracious in –

**Jack**

My pleasure, Alan.

**Alan**

– your, er, humiliating defeat.

**Jack**

Well, you know me, Alan, it don't matter to me, losing eleven thousand bucks, have a little bit of fun. I still drive home in my brand-new hundred and forty thousand dollar red Mercedes sports car.

**Alan**

Really?

**Jack**

Just drive on home in my –

**Alan**

You got a –

**Jack**

– Mercedes sports car.

**Alan**

Well, here's the big question, buddy boy.

**Kendall**

Alan, don't even think about it.

**Alan**

How do you fancy betting your hundred and forty thousand dollars' worth of German hardware against twenty thousand pounds worth of pure maroon Ford Granda?

**Jack**

You got it, Alan. Call.

**Alan**

Tails.

**Jack**

What's that?

**Alan**

Heads.

**Jack**

Give me the keys, Alan.

**Alan**

Hang on, no you can't. It's my car.

**Jack**

Give me the keys, Alan.

**Alan**

You can't. It's my car. That's my car you can't just –

**Jack**

*(Speaking over Alan)* Just give me the keys.

**Alan**

Best out of three. Please –

**Jack**

Ain't no best of three, Alan. You took a bet. Just give me the keys.

**Alan**

Can I have a chance to win it back?

**Jack**

Whatcha got, Alan?

**Alan**

Do you know what a Nissan Micra is?

**Jack**
Shitty little Japanese car.

**Alan**
It's a Japanese hatchback.

**Jack**
I don't want that.

**Alan**
I have access to one.

**Jack**
Whose car is it?

**Alan**
It – it's my wife's car.

**Kendall**
Alan, don't do that! Alan – no, seriously.

**Alan**
Go powder your nose, babe!

**Jack**
Ooh, big boy!

**Alan**
Come on, yes!

**Jack**
Alan Partridge – Nissan Micra. Go. Call.

**Alan**
Tails.

**Jack**
What's that?

**Alan**
*(Long pause)* On that bombshell, on that, on that double vehicular loss for Alan Partridge in Vegas, it's time to say – I can't say it, you do it, Kendall.

*'Knowing Me, Knowing You' music plays in the background.*

**Kendall**
Well, you have been Knowing Us, Kendall Ball and Alan Partridge, Knowing You, Jack 'the black cat' Colson, Bernie Rosen, Conrad Knight and Sally Hoff. Thanks to our team of researchers David Schneider, Rebecca Front, Doon MacKichan, Patrick Marber and Steve Coogan. Producer, Armando Iannucci.

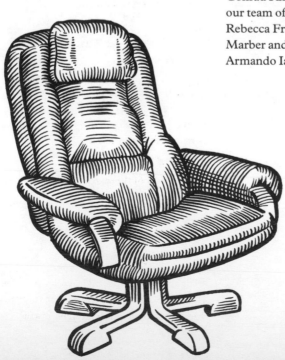

# KNOWING ME KNOWING YOU

## RADIO SHOW 4

*Alan Partridge*

*Music: 'Knowing Me, Knowing You'*

**Alan**

Ah-haaa! *(Applause)* Thank you. Welcome. Welcome. Welcome to *Knowing Me, Knowing You*, and the hot news is, I've got a hit on my hands. This show is a hit according to the *New Statesman* and *Society*. I don't read it myself, but a researcher ran into my office this week brandishing a review. The headline reads, 'Post-Modern Partridge', and it says, it says, 'Alan Partridge is the apotheosis of the three-minute culture. In his hands the essentially complex becomes inordinately simplistic.' So, how about that?

On the way here, my driver, Colin, dropped me off and he said, 'Alan, I hope you've got some good guests on tonight.'

And I have – this is the introduction to them – *(clears throat)* – Two times two is four, two times four are eight, two times eight are sixteen, two times sixteen are thirty-two – that was about my limit when I was nine years old, but it's mere piffle to my next guest, who is a nine-year-old child prodigy and Fellow of Oxford University. *(Audience: Wooooooooo!)* Please give an academic welcome to – with his father – Simon Fisher.

*Applause and music*

**Alan**

Welcome, welcome to Knowing me, Alan Partridge, knowing you, John Fisher, ah-haa.

**John**

Ah-haa.

**Alan**

And, and you, Simon Fisher, ah –

**Simon**

Ah-haa!

**Alan**

Not, not so loud, it's the microphone. Now, Simon, you are a Fellow of Oxford University, and you're a child prodigy. As a child genius what do you do, what do you actually do in the day?

**Simon**

Well I don't exactly do, I – I – I am, I – I see each day as a, as a sort of gift that is to be unwrapped, which I do in my own unique way.

**Alan**

Well of course you, you are very unique.

**Simon**

One cannot have gradations of uniqueness, one either is or is not unique.

**Alan**

Right. You, you know, you're right, you're right. I mean – I mean, you couldn't be more right.

**Simon**

Well, one is either right or not right.

**Alan**

Well, you are – you're right, um and so am I. Now, John Fisher –

**John**

Yes.

**Alan**

– or Simon's dad, as you are more commonly known. Simon is obviously a lot of fun, I can see that, I see that with his little quips, but, erm, when did you first realize that Simon was abnormal?

**John**

Uh, gifted, you mean.

**Alan**

Ab – abnormally gifted.

**John**

Hmm. Well, it's when Simon was about fourteen months old. I remember looking at him there in his cot, and I said to him, 'Who does Daddy love, Simon? Who? Who?', and guess what Simon said?

**Alan**

What?

**Simon**

'*Whom* does Daddy love? *Whom? Whom?*'

**John**

He picked up on my grammatical error with his very first words, and that's when I knew that he was going to be something special.

**Alan**

Yeah, my, my son Fernando wasn't quite as original as that. He said, he said, 'Daddy,' which somehow I prefer.

**John**

'Course he, he was calling me 'Father' soon afterwards.

**Alan**

Not 'Daddy'.

**Simon**

'Daddy' is a vulgarization.

**Alan**

Oh, yeah.

**Simon**

Also is 'yeah'.

**Alan**

Yeah. John, John, do you ever sit alone at night by the fire, with your head in your hands and think to yourself, 'God have mercy on my soul, I have spawned a monster! I've created Frankenstein!'

**John**

No, no, no, I mean Simon's a wonderful child, no, never, never.

**Alan**

Well, that's nice, I'm sure that Frankenstein's parents found it within their hearts to love him.

**Simon**

Interjection, there is no such monster as Frankenstein.

**Alan**

There is, actually, there is, it's in a film and, it's a Certificate X, you wouldn't have seen it.

**Simon**

Well, I've read the book by Mary Shelley, and Frankenstein is the name of a Genevan student who creates Frankenstein's monster.

**Alan**

*(Long pause)* You any good at sport, Simon?

**Simon**

Sport induces violence in the common man.

**Alan**

Yeah, cobblers, I like sport and I'm *not* violent. You're just scared of breaking your glasses.

**Simon**

I don't wear glasses.

**Alan**

Well, you should.

**John**

I, I like sport, in fact I represented my school at the London School Swimming Championships when I was fifteen.

**Alan**

Your bronze medal would probably come in a bit handy, 'cause, you know, if Simon fell

into a canal, you could dive in and save him.

**John**

Yes, I certainly could.

**Simon**

I wouldn't be so stupid as to fall in.

**Alan**

No, but you might get pushed in.

**Simon**

Why don't you just say what you mean, Mr Partridge, as do you think that I deserve to be pushed in a canal, so if you think that I do, then who do you think should push me in, who, who?

**Alan**

Whom? Whom?

**Simon**

No, in this context, 'whom', which is the accusative-dative, is not applicable.

**Alan**

Is he right?

**John**

Yes, he's right, I'm afraid.

**Simon**

Why don't you just say what you mean, which is that you would like to push me into a canal, Mr Partridge?

**Alan**

All right then, I, Alan Partridge, would like to push you, Simon Fisher, into a very deep, disused canal.

**Simon**

There, it's not so difficult, is it?

**Alan**

No. In fact I feel a lot better. Thank you. Thank you very much. You're very honest.

**Simon**

Ay, sir, to be honest as this world goes, is to be one man picked out of ten thousand.

**Alan**
That's very worthy of Shakespeare, very good.

**Simon**
It is Shakespeare.

**Alan**
Well it's, well it's, well it's, it's better than that, it's worthy of the Great Bard.

**Simon**
Have you ever seen *Hamlet*?

**John**
Simon, Simon, please –

**Alan**
Yes, yes.

**Simon**
I saw it with Alan Rickman. Who did you see it with?

**Alan**
My wife Carol.

**Simon**
No, no, no. Who was playing the lead?

**Alan**
Hamlet.

**Simon**
Oh, yes, the great actor Hamlet. No, which actor was playing the lead?

**John**
Simon, Simon, that's enough now –

**Alan**
Ummmm –

**Simon**
Yes?

**Alan**
Bernard Cribbins. I don't know, it was a long time ago, it was before you were born, you wouldn't remember it.

**Simon**
Have you seen *Citizen Kane*?

**Alan**
Yes, I watched every episode. Power to the people, yeah.

**Simon**
Have you seen *Beauty and the Beast*?

**Alan**
Yes.

**Simon**
Jean Cocteau's?

**Alan**
No.

**Simon**
Have you read *Metamorphosis*?

**Alan**
Yes.

**Simon**
Who's it by?

**Alan**
No, I haven't read it.

**Simon**
Have you read any Dickens?

**Alan**
No.

**Simon**
Do you go to the ballet?

**Alan**
No!

**Simon**
Can you play chess?

**Alan**
No! No!

**Simon**
Do you know any Russian –

**Alan**

No! No, what about you? You! Right, right, you, right, you, have you got any pubic hair?

**Simon**

No, I haven't because I'm nine!

**Alan**

No, I'm thirty-seven and I've got plenty, all right. Can you do this *(in a deep voice)* Aaaaahh!

**Simon**

No, because my voice hasn't broken –

**Alan**

Exactly! Don't forget it! And, uh, one more. Are you a boy or a girl?

**Simon**

I'm a boy.

**Alan**

Really?

**Simon**

My name's Simon.

**Alan**

Really? It could be Simone, it could be Simone, because you sound like a girl.

**John**

Alan, stop.

**Simon**

I'm a boy and my name is Simon.

**Alan**

Yeah, you've got something on your shoulder there *(Alan hits Simon)*.

**Simon**

*(Crying loudly in pain)* AAAAARGH!

**John**

Now you've gone too far!

**Simon**

Daddy, he raised his hand to me – in anger! Ahhhhhh!

**John**

Apologize right now!

**Alan**

*(Over Simon's sobbing)* Sorry, I shouldn't have done it, I shouldn't have done it, I'm sorry, it's my mistake, I'm not very good with kids, Carol's – I've got a very bad temper. But you are a little shit. That said, that said, thank you for coming on the show. Ladies and gentleman, the Fishers!

*Applause*

**Alan**

OK, now, if you just want to move chairs, right. Ahem. My next guest. *Look into my eyes! You are feeling very sleepy.* If my soothing voice is soothing enough, it should be sending you listeners at home to sleep. Are you asleep? Well, wake up! Because I, Alan Partridge, am not a hypnotist but my next guest is. I'm told she's going to hypnotize *me*. I might end up like one of those zombies from The Living Dead. Of course, my arms won't be dropping off. She hails from across the Great Lake, good ol' Uncle US of Stateside. She's as American as chocolate chip biscuits and mum's apple tart, but er, that's where comparisons with a tart must end, lest I come to a sticky end. Ladies and gentlemen, she's not a tart, she's a lady hypnotist, with a set of pins that will hypnotize any bloke. The big question is, what's the name of her game? Please welcome Janey Katz.

*Applause and music: 'The Name of the Game'*

**Janey**

Thank you!

**Alan**

Janey Katz. Knowing me, Alan Partridge, knowing you, Janey Katz, ah-haa.

**Janey**
Uh-huh.

**Alan**
No, ah-h*aaa*, you say, ah-h*aaa*.

**Janey**
Ah-haaaaa.

**Alan**
That's right.

**Janey**
OK, right.

**Alan**
What's the name of your game? Is it a game? Has it got a name, other than hypnotism?

**Janey**
Really, what I practise is hypnotherapy, not hypnosis, so I try to distance myself from a kind of showbiz, um, you know, the razzamatazz side of it, I'm not out to make fools of people. I'm there to use hypnotherapy as a form of helping people to open up their minds.

**Alan**
Right, because I saw a brilliant hypnotist, uh, Tony Le – Tony Mesmer he was called, he was brilliant, he, he was fantastic. He had, he had blokes crying like babies, he had women on all fours barking like dogs. It was really first-class entertainment, it really was fantastic.

**Janey**
Yeah, I don't do that.

**Alan**
He's, uh, but he's very popular. He's booked right through to next summer, unavailable, hence your good self. Now, but you – you were in London promoting your new book.

**Janey**
That's right, yes.

**Alan**
I, I, actually know New York quite well.

**Janey**
You do?

**Alan**
Mmm, I popped over there, and I really did get into, as Billy Joel put it, I really did get into a New York state of mind.

**Janey**
I bet you did.

**Alan**
Um, I jumped in a cab and I said, 'Cabbie, take me to the core of the Big Apple. I want to check out the bits, dude.' I really, you know, did say that.

**Janey**
Ha-ha-ha! Oh my God! Just next time, say Manhattan and you'll get there.

**Alan**
Well, no, I want to get to the centre of New York.

**Janey**
Yeah, that is Manhattan.

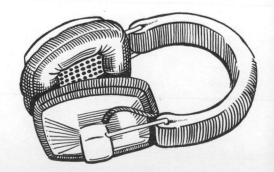

# Knowing Me, Knowing You

**Alan**
Right, that's not where I want to go.

**Janey**
Where do you want to go?

**Alan**
Bloomingdales.

**Janey**
Yeah. You're in Manhattan.

**Alan**
Right OK, I'm in Manhattan. What do I do now?

**Janey**
You just, you get in a cab, and you say to the driver, 'Take me to Manhattan to Bloomingdales.'

**Alan**
OK, I'm outside Bloomingdales, what, what next? What do I do now?

**Janey**
What do you mean?

**Alan**
You've hypnotized me.

**Janey**
No I haven't, no.

**Alan**
Oh, I see! I'm sorry, sorry –

**Janey**
You'll know, Alan.

**Alan**
I thought, I thought you just slid into it. It's just that you are staring at me.

**Janey**
I'm sorry. No, I just find you fascinating.

**Alan**
In wh-wh-wh-what way?

**Janey**
Clinically.

**Alan**
Really? Thank you.

**Janey**
My pleasure.

**Alan**
You, Janey Katz, hypnotist, I, Alan Partridge, clinically fascinating. Thank you. Now, you er, now I believe right now, I'm very fortunate, because you're going to hypnotize me.

**Janey**
I certainly am, yes.

**Alan**
Great.

**Janey**
Um, obviously, we don't have much time, so it's going to be a kind of vague gesture towards it. Uh, but the idea is that what we'll try to do is project on to, let's say, the curtain of your mind, a series of images from your past.

**Alan**
OK, well, I'll draw back my curtains –

**Janey**
Good.

**Alan**
– behind which you will find a net curtain. You may lift that up, should you wish –

**Janey**
Thank you.

**Alan**
– and we'll see if there are any skeletons lurking in – the – cupboard, the curtain, the curtain cupboard.

**Janey**
In your mind.

**Alan**
My mind's curtain cupboard, yeah.

**Janey**
All right. Well the first thing to do is to get you relaxed, so if you can just lie on – What are you –

**Alan**
Just put this peg on my nose.

**Janey**
Why are you putting a peg on your nose?

**Alan**
(Sounding blocked up) Well, because I was told that your blood-pressure increases during hypnotism. It could lead to a nose bleed.

**Janey**
No, no, no. That's nonsense. Who told you that?

**Alan**
The researchers.

**Janey**
I think it was probably a joke.

**Alan**
OK, no, that's all right, that's OK.

**Janey**
Well, I mean, take it off.

**Alan**
I'll take it off if I wish to take it off.

**Janey**
Yeah, you can't relax with a peg on your nose, Alan.

**Alan**
If I, I should be the judge of that whether I should take the peg off my nose, and, as it happens, I have decided to take the peg off. I'll do that now.

**Janey**
OK, just lie back on the couch if you could be so kind.

**Alan**
(Sounding normal again) Right, I'm lying back on the couch, listeners.

**Janey**
OK, just try to concentrate. Now, I'm going to count you down from three and then in that time I want you to relax every muscle in your body, OK, and then you will be hypnotized. Three – two – one. Now, Alan, without opening your eyes, I want you to tell me what you can see.

**Alan**
(In a high, childish voice) A pair of plimsolls.

**Janey**
All right. Now, who do they belong to?

**Alan**
Little boy.

**Janey**
Do you recognize the little boy?

**Alan**
Yes, it's Alan Partridge.

**Jane**
Uh, huh. Now, I want you to just step inside Alan Partridge.

**Alan**
OK.

**Janey**
Now, Alan, would you tell me how old you are?

**Little Alan**
(Sounding frightened) I'm eight years old.

**Janey**
And where are you at the moment?

**Little Alan**
I'm on the bottom of Tandle Hill.

**Janey**
Where's Tandle Hill?

# Knowing Me, Knowing You

**Little Alan**
Near the school.

**Janey**
OK. Now, um, describe what you can
see in front of you.

**Little Alan**
There, there's about eighty boys.

**Janey**
So you're not alone?

**Little Alan**
No, they're at the top of the hill.

**Janey**
And where are you?

**Little Alan**
I'm on the bottom. Can't keep up with
them, it's a cross-country run.

**Janey**
OK.

**Little Alan**
It's cold. It's very cold.

**Janey**
Why are you so cold if you are running,
Alan?

**Little Alan**
I haven't got any shorts on.

**Janey**
Why not?

**Little Alan**
Steven McCoombe's taken them off me.

**Janey**
Can, can you see Steven McCoombe?

**Little Alan**
Yes, he's waving them about with his hands.
He's saying, 'Smelly Alan Fartridge! Smelly
Alan Fartridge!' I'm not smelly!

**Janey**
No, I know that.

**Little Alan**
Smelly Alan Fartridge!

**Janey**
OK, Alan, all right, now look, you're not
happy, are you, no?

**Little Alan**
No.

**Janey**
No. Should we take you away from here?

**Little Alan**
Yes.

**Janey**
Let's take you to some place where you are
happy, OK?

**Little Alan**
Oh good.

**Janey**
We're going there right now.

**Little Alan**
Mmm –

**Janey**
Are you there?

**Little Alan**
Yes.

**Janey**
Now tell me what you can see.

**Little Alan**
I'm in class.

**Janey**
Yeah.

**Little Alan**
The Headmaster's come in.

**Janey**
Right. And what's happening?

**Little Alan**
Oh, he's looking very pleased. He said, he said, 'Someone's won an essay writing competition, someone's written an essay on sport and it's won a prize.'

**Janey**
Mm-hmm. What else is he saying?

**Little Alan**
He said, 'Is there an Alan Partridge in the class? Would Alan Partridge identify himself?'

**Janey**
And what's happening now?

**Little Alan**
I'm standing up. They're all applauding me!

**Janey**
Terrific. And what are you saying, Alan?

**Little Alan**
I'm saying *(reverts back to his grown-up voice)* 'I'm Alan Partridge! I am Alan Partridge! I've won the essay writing competition of that there's no doubt!'

**Janey**
OK.

**Alan**
Yes, I have won it. Things will now be very different. No longer will I be called infantile names – 'cos I won the competition!

**Janey**
Great, now, Alan, we have to, we're running a little short of time, we have to now bring you back, OK?

**Alan**
No, I don't want to come back.

**Janey**
No, you, you'll be fine, you have to come back because you're in the middle of a talk show.

**Alan**
I like it here.

**Janey**
Well, you like it here too.

**Alan**
No, I don't want to go back. I don't want to be on the radio.

# Knowing Me, Knowing You

**Janey**
Come on, Alan. You're very popular –

**Alan**
Nobody listens to Radio 4.

**Janey**
Alan, OK –

**Alan**
Nobody listens to Radio 4!

**Janey**
Now, Alan, just concentrate because
I can't bring you back otherwise.

**Alan**
I want to be on the telly!

**Janey**
Now, I'm going to count to three and you
have to come back.

**Alan**
Let me on the telly! Let me on the telly!

**Janey**
One – two – three.

**Alan**
So what I want to know is when are you
going to hypnotize me?

**Janey**
I've done it.

**Alan**
Really?

**Janey**
Yes, it's been done. Just think about what
is foremost in your mind at the moment.

**Alan**
Oh, the essay writing competition.

**Janey**
That's right, back at school. Anything else
from school, d'you remember?

**Alan**
Yes, cross-country run.

**Janey**
Tandle Hill, do you remember that?

**Alan**
Yeah, great stuff.

**Janey**
That's right, yep, did you enjoy that?

**Simon**
Smelly Alan Fartridge!

**Alan**
What? No one calls me that! No one
calls me that!

**Janey**
Hang on, Simon –

**Simon**
I was just referring him back to his past.

**Janey**
No, Simon, this is a very important point,
you must not abuse this privilege, because
we have been privileged to see inside
Alan's memory.

**Alan**
No, I, I, I did not smell.

**Janey**
Now this is irrelevant, Alan, you don't have
to defend yourself.

**Alan**
*(Agitated)* No, I want to clear this up once
and for all.

**Janey**
There's no need –

**Alan**
This has been hanging in the air for about
thirty years, right, but I want to clear it up,
OK? Steven McCoombe called me Smelly
Alan Fartridge, because he thought it was
funny, Fartridge, Partridge, he said smelly.
I wasn't. My personal hygiene was never in
question. I showered regularly, I was never,
I didn't smell. The question is, what's

Steven McCoombe doing now? That's the question, because I host a chat show, what's he do?

I tell you, he's a forklift truck driver with British Leyland. I'll tell you, he lives in Edgbaston, he's got a pathetic life, I've seen, I've parked my car outside his house, I've watched him come and go, and he's got a sad, pathetic life and McCoombe, if you are listening, what are you now? You're nothing. And I am Alan Partridge! *(Applause)* Yeah, thank you, thank you. Now, that sort of wraps it up. Now – Your book's available in the shops this Christmas?

**Janey**
Ha ha! It's not a very good advert for my book! I assure you it does not make you this aggressive!

**Alan**
OK, well.

**Janey**
Yeah, it's called *'The Future is Behind You'* and it is in fact a therapeutic study.

**Alan**
OK, one for the Christmas stocking, hypnotize your friends.

**Janey**
No, no, it's not a show, it's not a party trick.

**Alan**
Well, OK, in that case, a very serious book. Slap it on top of, er, Stephen Hawking's book on your coffee table and impress your friends. Ladies and gentlemen, Janey Katz!

*Applause*

**Alan**
Now. Order! Order! Silence in court! Order! Order! Silence in court! Of course, I don't say things like that, but my next guest does, because he is a lawyer. But not just any old lawyer, he's a young lawyer who's

known as the 'Bad Boy of the Old Bailey', famous for his natty dress sense and his unconventional behaviour in court. Let us court the *enfants terribles* of the inner temple. Do you want to get to know him? *(Audience: Yes!) Voulez-vous?* OK, *voulez-vous* Nick Ford!

*Music: 'I Fought the Law'*
*Applause*

**Alan**
Sit there, sit there. I don't, I don't know what –

**Nick**
Knowing me, knowing you, ah-haa?

**Alan**
No, there can be no 'ah-haa's'. There's been a dreadful error here. You were supposed to come on to *'Voulez-vous'* by Abba. I don't know *what* that was.

**Nick**
Well, I always come on in court to 'I Fought the Law' by the Clash, 'cause I'm a lawyer, you know, it's kinda cool.

**Alan**
Yeah, but how, how did it get on here?

**Nick**
Well, I just asked the sound guy to play it, you know, thought it'd be cool,

**Alan**
And he just said he'd do it, he didn't say he had to go to anyone else to ask permission?

**Nick**
No, I just said, 'Slap this on, mate', and he said, 'Yeah, cool.'

**Alan**
Right, well, it's not, it's not your fault.

**Nick**
I'm not saying it is.

# Knowing Me, Knowing You

**Alan**
No, it's not, it's not, it's not your job that's on the line. Let's just start again, right, with the music *(clears his throat) Voulez-vous, ah-haa, take it now or leave it, ah-haa, now is all we get, ah-haa, nothing promised, no regrets (fanfare), voulez-vous,* ah-haa! Nick Ford!

*Applause*

**Alan**
Welcome to *Knowing Me, Knowing You*, knowing you, ah-haa!

**Nick**
Ah-haa! I understand the way you work now. Now we've got a rapport.

**Alan**
Right. Indeed. Now, you are –

**Nick**
Great.

**Alan**
– you are a very different kind of lawyer.

**Nick**
That's right. What I say is, like, the law is an ass and I kick it.

**Alan**
Very good, very clever. Yeah. Now, you've done all sorts of things in court, you once abseiled into court –

**Nick**
Uh-huh.

**Alan**
– you once did a partial strip –

**Nick**
That's right.

**Alan**
– and you once simulated a heart attack.

**Nick**
Yeah.

**Alan**
The one that was in the press recently is, um, the robber, the man who robbed the –

**Nick**
Mickey Hall. Basically what happened was he, he robbed a building society, and I felt that there were mitigating circumstances, and so when it came to the summing up, I kind of went in there with all the jewellery on, all the gear and had a baseball cap on with 'Justice' written on it, and I just got them to dim all the lights, one centre spot on me and I went
*(Raps) Ladies and gents, jury. Everybody in the court, hear me one and all, I'm here to plead the case of a guy called Mickey Hall. When he went into the Woolwich on that fateful day, he was an innocent man, he didn't blow no one away. Yeah, he pulled a gun, but the gun was fake, on that piece of evidence I stake – my claim. Society's to blame. Look at its face. I rest my case –*

**Alan**
Very good.

**Nick**
*I rest my case. I rest my case.*
*(Applause)* Said it, said it three times and I just very, very slowly, very dramatically walked backwards into my seat, sat down. The atmosphere was electric. Could've heard a pin drop.

**Alan**
Amazing. What happened?

**Nick**
He got five years.

**Alan**
Well, good for you! Great, well, he won't be doing that again in a hurry, now would he?

**Nick**
I was defending him, Alan. I lost the case.

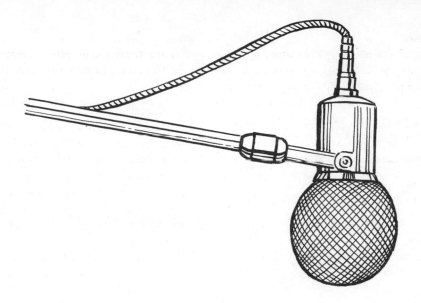

**Alan**
Yeah, it puzzles me, that law. How can you defend a man who, let's say, has been arrested for murder?

**Nick**
Well, 'cos he may be innocent.

**Alan**
Well, with the greatest respect, the police are hardly likely to arrest him if he's innocent, are they?

**Nick**
With slightly less respect, uh, haven't you heard of wrongful arrest?

**Alan**
No.

**Nick**
Guildford four, Birmingham six –

**Alan**
Well, yes, but, no that, that's different. Now, now, they are innocent –

**Nick**
Be, be very careful, Alan. You're on air.

**Alan**
No, I think we should, we should go into it –

**Nick**
No, if I was your lawyer, I would advise you very strongly now to shut your mouth.

**Alan**
Why?

**Nick**
These people will sue and put an injunction on your show and you'll never broadcast again.

**Alan**
*(Long pause)* Where did you get your shirt from?

**Nick**
It's – er, my friend Domo made it.

**Alan**
Not so much a shirt, more a – sort of –

**Nick**
It's a blouse. I think that's the word – you're blushing and groping for –

# Knowing Me, Knowing You

**Alan**
I'm not blushing, I'm not blushing.

**Nick**
It's a big girl's blouse. Kind of Errol Flynn.
Look, if you don't like it, you can be honest,
it's my whole philosophy, this is what I'm
saying, it's like, you know, if there was
more honesty and less repression in our
society there'd be less crimes. That's
the whole point.

**Alan**
All right, all right, I'll be honest.

**Nick**
Well, be honest.

**Alan**
I'll be honest. You are a homosexual.

**Nick**
Bisexual.

**Alan**
Don't pussyfoot.

**Nick**
I'm not pussyfooting.

**Alan**
The point is, there are blokes involved,
that's the important thing.

**Nick**
I mean, you seem very threatened by it,
Alan.

**Alan**
I'm not threatened by you lot, no way. Any
of you lot had a go, I'd deck the lot of you.

**Nick**
Ooh, a tough guy! I meant psychologically
threatened.

**Alan**
Well, whatever.

**Nick**
It's OK to explore your sexuality, you know,
it's OK to be open, I mean, you know, as
the kid here, Simon, let's bring him into it,
I mean, you're just discovering sexuality,
you know. He's got a right to choose –

**Alan**
Oh, leave the kid out of it! Leave him out
of it!

**Nick**
Well, maybe you should have left him out
of it before –

**Alan**
Just cover his ears!

**Nick**
Yeah, well, his ear is still bright red from
where you hit it, Alan.

**Alan**
That was, that was –

**Nick**
Oh, by the way, Mister Fisher, if you're
seeking legal advice on this –

**John**
I don't need any advice from your sort,
thank you very much.

**Nick**
Wo, wo, wo! Welcome to, welcome to
Homophobics Anonymous!

**Alan**
Good one, I like that, Mister Fisher, 'Don't
want any advice from your sort.' Nice.
Right, we should go for a drink sometime.

**John**
No, thanks.

**Nick**
You're hitting kids, you know, you could
end up in jail.

**Simon**

Can I just say something here? No, because, no, please, because technically it wasn't assault because he didn't actually cause any, any bodily harm.

**Nick**

It was assault. He hit you.

**Simon**

Yes, but I was provoking him, I was being precocious.

**Nick**

*(Pause)* The point is, if this was a normal child –

**Simon**

I am normal!

**Nick**

You are not normal. You're a freak!

**Alan**

Come on!

**Nick**

If this was a normal child with a normal father they would sue you immediately. You should be careful, I don't think you'd like it in prison, all those men –

**Alan**

Listen. What are you insinuating? What are you saying? Are you saying that I, Alan Partridge, would end up in prison and maybe, what, get friendly with some bloke –

**Nick**

Who knows, Alan?

**Alan**

– and, maybe, I'd be in the shower with him and, um, and maybe, we'd just start wrestling and mucking about, and then he'd probably start soaping my back down, and, um, and then, you know, we'd kiss each other tenderly. Is that what you're saying? Because that is untrue!

**Nick**

It's all in your imagination, Alan.

**Alan**

Well, if you're insinuating that's what I secretly want –

**Nick**

No further questions, Your Honour! No further questions.

**Alan**

*(Long pause)* Well, um, my researcher said, um, you can get him on *this* question.

**Nick**

I very much doubt it.

**Alan**

It says here – well, I'll read it out, 'Why does he affect a Cockney accent, when he went to Harrow, brackets, which is a public school? So, my question to you is: Why do you affect a Cockney accent, when you went to Harrow, which is a public school?

**Nick**

*(Hesitating)* I – I think that – I don't – I wouldn't say it's affected, I think that – um, you know –

**Alan**

No further questions, Your Honour! Ha, ha, yes!

**Simon**

Can I just say something here? It's because I think we're all here as, as, as fine-minded people, and, and we're, we're sort of wallowing about in a mire, when all the beautiful things we could be talking about, and, and music and art, and we're on this tawdry show –

**Alan**

It's not a tawdry show!

**Nick/Janey/John**

It is a tawdry show.

# Knowing Me, Knowing You

**Alan**
Is it?

**Simon**
– and Mister Ford, and Mister Ford is debasing our beautiful language –

**Nick**
Oh, shut up!

**Janey**
Come on!

**Simon**
– and there's this two-bit, hot-flushing psychotherapist –

**Janey**
What?! OK, Simon, I'm going to say something to you, I'm going to say something to you – I suggest you get a life!

**Alan**
*(Speaking over Janey)* Look, can we –hang on – Order! Order! Order!

**Nick**
Yeah, get a life!

**Janey**
Grow up!

**Simon**
Janey thinks that we need to go and have our heads examined.

**Janey**
Yes, I do.

**Simon**
– well, well, if you think we need therapy, then to who should we go? To who? To who? To who?

**Alan**
Hang on a second. *(Pause)* Sh – surely that should be 'To whom'?

**Nick**
Yeah, he's right, in this context, it is 'To whom.'

**Alan**
To whom?

**Simon**
No, I don't think it's –

**Alan**
You're wrong! *To whom! To whom!*

**Simon**
Please!

**Alan and Nick**
*(Over Simon, struggling to speak)* Whom! Whom! Whom! Whom! Whom! Whom!

**Simon**
I've wet myself, Daddy!

**John**
Oh dear.

*'Knowing Me, Knowing You' music playing in the background.*
*Applause*

**Alan**
And on that bombshell we say goodnight as Simon Fisher, nine-year-old Fellow of Oxford University has wet himself, and I, now, Alan Partridge, dry as a bone saying, 'Knowing me, knowing you', would like to thank my guests Janey Katz, mad hippie, Nick Ford, queer lawyer, Simon Fisher, wet boy, and his dad, a nobody. Thanks to the writers and researchers Steve Coogan, Patrick Marber, Doon MacKichan, Rebecca Front, and David Schneider and to my producer Armando Iannucci. Thank you.

# KNOWING ME KNOWING YOU

## RADIO SHOW 5

*Alan Partridge*

*Music: 'Knowing Me, Knowing You'*

**Alan**
Ah-haa! *(Applause)* Welcome – Welcome, welcome – welcome to knowing me, knowing you, my chat show with me, Alan Partridge, knowing you, the you, my guests, and the, er, the you the audience. Before the chat show, I've got a bit of a plug I want to do with a new book I've just published. It's by Peartree Publications, the publishing wing of my company, and it's a collection of amusing sporting anecdotes, it's, it's called *A funny thing happened on the way to the stadium to Alan Partridge*, by Alan Partridge. And it's a stocking filler, you know, ha ha, I mean, it's not gonna win the Booker Prize, you know it'd be nice to be nominated,

erm, but, before I introduce my first guest, here's an extract from the book, and it's about when I bumped my car into a well-known celebrity's car, George Best's. Oh – I shouldn't have told you that actually, it's a bit of a surprise in the anecdote, anyway, I'll read it.

'I'd just finished having lunch with Geoff Capes the shot-putter at the Savoy, and I was reversing my Ford Granada out of a parking space, when BANG I'd bumped into a very flashy Lotus sports car. Who's driving that, I wondered, you'll never guess, it was none other than George Best. Sorry about that, George, I said. Oh well, he said, I suppose we'll have to swap insurance details, and I said yes.'

George Best, marvellous.

67

OK, my, er, my first, my first, nope, my first guest tonight is not George Best, he's, er, he's a bit of a handful, no, I'm honoured to say my first guest is a member of the royal family. *(Audience: oooh)* Yes, all day here at Peartree Productions we've been rolling out the
red carpets and the walls have been licked with a new coat of paint. She's regal, she's royal, please give a loyal round of applause to a very nice person, the Duchess of Stranraugh.

*Music: 'Dancing Queen'*
*Applause*

**Alan**
The Duchess –

**Duchess**
– that's right.

**Alan**
– of Stranraugh. The first question, Duchess, I have to ask, is how do I address you?

**Duchess**
Well, really there are three forms of address, formally you would call me, your grace, as, er, sorry – I'm rather nervous.

**Alan**
That's all right.

**Duchess**
As this is informal you would address me as Duchess, or just Emma, which is of course what my family or my husband would call me.

**Alan**
Of course your husband's hardly likely to call you duchess, is he –

**Duchess**
*(Laughing)* No.

**Alan**
– is my tea ready, Duchess? No, not gonna do that, is he, no, but, you are, you're a very different kind of royal because you're not like Princess Di, she's very beautiful, but you're more of an outdoor type.

**Duchess**
Yes, yes.

**Alan**
You know, and it's nice with your hair all piled up on top of your head like that, it's nice, in the royal way. Now what a lot of us would like to know, I'm sure, is – as a royal, what do you *do*? What do you *do*?

**Duchess**
Well, a lot of the time I work for charity. The rest of the time really I work on the estate. It's a large estate, as I'm sure you can imagine –

**Alan**
Hmmm.

**Duchess**
– and there is a lot of work involved, and, and it's a pleasure for me to spend my time doing that.

**Alan**
Yeah – I, I've seen a photograph of it and I – I would dearly like to come and visit.

**Duchess**
Well, well you must really, because the house and gardens are open to the public, um, three days a week –

**Alan**
Right.

**Duchess**
That's Mondays, Wednesdays and Fridays.

**Alan**
So – so if I came I'd be with like the public?

**Duchess**

Well, I hope so, yes. I mean we try to encourage all comers, we, we like to have a crowd.

**Alan**

Right, but I mean during the week's a bit difficult for me, I was thinking if I could maybe come at the weekend?

**Duchess**

We don't open at weekends, we have to have the house to ourselves.

**Alan**

Yep, um, we're getting our wires crossed here, I – I think what I'm trying to say is, I would really like to come and stay for, you know, as a guest, for a weekend.

**Duchess**

Oh, I see, I suspect you're teasing me a little bit –

**Alan**

Well, no, I mean – I – no, I would – I mean you are always welcome to Cacston Avenue in Norwich, just, you know, ring ahead, and we'll be delighted – so, I mean could I stay?

**Duchess**

Um, it would be a little difficult to arrange.

**Alan**

OK, right, fair enough – we'll – we'll talk about it after the show.

**Duchess**

Yes, yes.

**Alan**

Get our diaries out, hammer out a few dates.

**Duchess**

Yes, yes.

**Alan**

All right, now, what are your plans for next year?

**Duchess**

Well, in July next year we are planning a grand charity gala for Refuse the anti-drugs charity. And that will be at the Royal Albert Hall.

**Alan**

Wonderful, and after that?

**Duchess**

After that I think I'll be putting my feet up at home – I'll need a rest.

**Alan**

Relax, yes. So what about then?

**Duchess**

Sorry, what about then?

**Alan**

Well, can I come and stay then?

**Duchess**

Um, well I, um, think we could discuss that nearer the time.

**Alan**

Yeah, it's just that, you know, we're both busy people, you know if we discuss it nearer the time it's not going to happen, is it, I mean that's what I say when I want to put someone off, you know. Never mind, you know it's good to meet a royal like you who's got a sense of humour.

**Duchess**

Well, I have to say that as a family we have a sense of humour. I mean when we all get together we have a blooming good laugh, you know –

**Alan**

*(Laughing)* Yeah.

**Duchess**

– not to put too fine a point on it.

**Alan**

– and a dance?

**Duchess**

Absolutely, we love dancing, yes.

**Alan**

Bit of a singsong?

**Duchess**

We have many musical evenings together, yes.

**Alan**

Now and again a bit of tomfoolery.

**Duchess**

Hmm, yes, one or two practical jokes get played.

**Alan**

*(Laughing)* And I'll bet that, now and again, when you're on your own, you secretly get completely rat-arsed. *(Pause)* I'm sorry.

**Duchess**

But the point really about all this fame is that I am prepared to try to use what little fame I have for charity.

**Alan**

I'm sorry, sorry.

**Duchess**

I do a lot of work, as I've said, for Refuse – it's a drugs rehabilitation charity.

**Alan**

I think I over-stepped the mark there, before, I really am genuinely sorry about that. I went too far.

**Duchess**

Well, yes, you did. So, most of my work really –

**Alan**

Do you forgive me?

**Duchess**

– involves, erm, this kind of public relations exercise –

**Alan**

Look, let's talk about your charity.

**Duchess**

Yes, I am.

**Alan**

Right, because you were touched personally, weren't you, by –

**Duchess**

– by the drugs problem, yes, indeed. That's really what began me on this crusade, my son, Clive –

**Alan**

Yes.

**Duchess**

– had a drugs problem.

**Alan**

That's right, Clive the junkie, as he was known.

**Duchess**

Well, he's not.

**Alan**

No.

**Duchess**

Not a drug addict.

**Alan**

Ex-junkie.

**Duchess**
He *had* a drugs problem – thanks to Refuse, he no longer has one, and –

**Alan**
That was in the press, I – I don't know if – if any of the audience are – are unfamiliar with that incidence, just to sort of put you – I don't want to dwell on it, but, er, that was when, er, your son Clive was in the Café Royal –

**Duchess**
Yes.

**Alan**
– he smashed it up, didn't he?

**Duchess**
It was very unfortunate –

**Alan**
Yeah.

**Duchess**
– it was a long time ago and the point really is –

**Alan**
He trashed the place, didn't he?

**Duchess**
It, it's all in the past, because he has been able to help himself –

**Alan**
Right.

**Duchess**
– and get back, into the community.

**Alan**
Wonderful. Now, you have two lovely daughters –

**Duchess**
Yes.

**Alan**
Alicia, she's a bit of a maverick, isn't she?

**Duchess**
Oh no, she's now a performance artist and doing –

**Alan**
What, an actress?

**Duchess**
N-n-no, no, a performance artist –

**Alan**
What, you watch them paint? You watch –

**Duchess**
Well, no, it's rather more complicated than that, if I can just give you an example of a performance that she gave some time ago, in a space which I attended. She had daubed herself in paint of many colours, and accompanied by, um, a pop record, um – I think if I remember rightly it was Gary Glitter – I think it was, 'Do You Want to be in My Gang?' – I, I can't remember. She marched very purposefully, backwards and forwards, throughout the space, back and forth, back and forth, back and forth, and it was really very powerful.

**Alan**
*(Laughing)* It sounds hilarious, it really does.

**Duchess**
Well, it was witty, but it was visually –

**Alan**
Ha ha! Sounds like the Goons, yeah, very good. I don't want to press you on this but I have one of the reviews xeroxed here and it says she was seen simulating defecation on a photograph of Winston Churchill. What's all that about?

**Duchess**
I wasn't present at that performance.

**Alan**
I think it was an encore or something.

**Duchess**
I don't know, I mean you'd have to ask Alicia.

**Alan**
Get her on the show –

**Duchess**
Yes.

**Alan**
– as long as she doesn't defecate on me!

**Duchess**
I'm – I'm sure she'd only simulate it.

**Alan**
Ha – now, I'm, I'm at the top of my profession, there'd be little argument about *that*, but, you, you in a sense are not at the top of yours, you're twenty-seventh in line to the throne, that's quite a way to go.

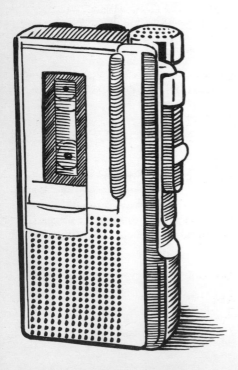

**Duchess**
Oh, well, there isn't really a career structure, you know, I mean, I have a position which I have always held.

**Alan**
Do you want to be queen?

**Duchess**
No, no I don't.

**Alan**
Hmm, deep down?

**Duchess**
No, no not at all.

**Alan**
Could happen.

**Duchess**
No, it couldn't happen.

**Alan**
Could happen, let me, let me paint a hypothesis for you. It's Christmas, Balmoral, the whole royal family are there, Edward pulls a cracker, there's a bomb in it, they're all wiped out.

**Duchess**
Oh, for heaven's sake, now really –

**Alan**
No, no, wiped out, just bear with this, right. The outer royals, the Armstrong-Jones', and that photographer bloke, they all – they are all going to the funeral in a big mini-bus, a sniper takes out the driver –

**Duchess**
No, really I must –

**Alan**
– it goes over a cliff –

**Duchess**
No, I – sorry –

**Alan**

– stay with it, stay with it, just bear with me. Now, your husband is shooting grouse, a messenger brings him the news of this tragic second event, in his excitement, he realizes he's going to be king, suddenly he loses his footing, and with his shot-gun, and this may be stressful, he blows his own head clean off –

**Duchess**

No, this is going too far –

**Alan**

Now, the prime minister knocks on your door, and says, Emma, will you be queen? What do you say?

**Duchess**

No, it's a – it's a preposterous question.

**Alan**

It – it could, I would, you know, if I was asked by the prime minister, would you be king? I'd say, I would sacrifice my career on Radio Four, and I would say, I would say YES, I will be King Alan the First. Would you, are you prepared, would you do your duty to your country?

**Duchess**

This is pure fiction. I mean –

**Alan**

In those cir— would – *(to audience)* do you think she should be queen? Do you think she should be queen? *(Audience cheers)* Yes, would you be queen?

**Duchess**

No, those circumstances would not arise. It's not a question –

**Alan**

*(Loudly)* In your people's hour of need, would you be queen?

**Duchess**

Of course, in those circumstances, yes, of course –

**Alan**

*(Interrupting)* Yes! You do wanna be queen, yes! Of course you do, you're only human, good luck, good luck, and, er, if you make it to the top job, come back on the show, tell us about it. Fingers crossed, ladies and gentlemen, the Duchess of Stranraugh.

*Applause*

**Alan**

OK, now, next guest on the show, we've got Dustin Hoffman, Sean Connery, Michael Caine and Frank Spencer. In fact we haven't really got those people on, but in a sense we have, because my next guest is a very talented young impressionist, and he can do all their voices, s-so it'd seem like they were on. My researcher spotted him in a little club, the comedy shop, and they said, Alan, he's a bit near the knuckle and I said, I don't mind that, as long as his knuckle is near his funny bone. And I'm, I'm sure – I'm sure it will be, I'm prepared to take a chance on *him*, and I hope you are too, as

I welcome, funny voice man impressionist, Steve Thompson.

*Music: 'Take A Chance'*
*Applause*

**Alan**

Make yourself comfortable, welcome to knowing me, knowing you, Ah-haa.

**Steve**

Ah-haa.

**Alan**

Ah-haa.

**Steve**

Ah-haa.

**Alan**
This is your first chat show.

**Steve**
Yeah, that's right.

**Alan**
You've not done, er, you've not done *Wogan* yet?

**Steve**
*(In his Wogan voice)* Heh, no, I haven't, yet, reached, conquered the heights, of Wogan.

**Alan**
Do – do your Wogan for us.

**Steve**
*(Pauses. In his Wogan voice)* Heh, Terry Wogan.

**Alan**
Ha ha ha, very good. Very good, well, we'll – we'll work some impressions subtly into the show, but first let's talk about this new alternative comedy thing, what is that?

**Steve**
Well, it's not really a new thing you know, it's actually been around for about ten years now –

**Alan**
Right –

**Steve**
– Yeah, a lot of people think it's new but it's not.

**Alan**
Ben Elton.

**Steve**
*(In Ben Elton voice)* Ladies and gentlemen, yes indeed, little bit of politics –

**Alan**
– no, no, I don't mean do him, I mean he's an alternative comedian.

**Steve**
Well, yeah, I mean people say, yeah, Ben

Elton he's al—, he's alternative, but I mean, you know, the distinction I want to make is between good and bad comedy, you know, it's not about alternative.

**Alan**
Right, but you hate all the old comedians.

**Steve**
Ha, no, that's another myth about, you know, us sort of newer generation, I've got a lot, the deepest respect for, you know, people like Tony Hancock, Morecambe and Wise, er –

**Alan**
Frankie Howerd.

**Steve**
Frankie Howerd, actually –

**Alan**
The Goons –

**Steve**
The Goons, brilliant –

**Alan**
Monty Python.

**Steve**
Monty Python, brilliant.

**Alan**
Bernard Manning, Jim Davidson –

**Steve**
Not, no –

**Alan**
Les Dennis –

**Steve**
Not, not so much them people, more the other people, not, not them so much.

**Alan**
Right, you hate them?

**Steve**
No, no, no, you're playing devil's advocate here, Alan.

**Alan**
I just want you to admit that you hate Les Dennis.

**Steve**
Yeah. But I mean, what, what the distinction I want to make is between sort of, you know, they're sort of joke-based comedy, and the stuff I do is more kind of truthful observational stuff.

**Alan**
Right, you, you tell observations, don't you.

**Steve**
I *make* observations.

**Alan**
Right. Do an observation.

**Steve**
Erm, er, well – this is a bad example but, um, have, have you noticed how, um, when you get in a cab and you're talking to the taxi driver, he always turns round to talk to you, so may, maybe, he, sh— he should have a steering wheel on his shoulder.

**Alan**
Is that, which bit of that's the observation?

**Steve**
First bit. The first bit.

**Alan**
Right, you're right, that's a bad example, let, let's –

**Steve**
In, in my comedy I'm trying to – trying – um, er – deal with, er, generic human truths, you know.

**Alan**
Hmm.

**Steve**
What, I want – I want to be funny *but*, with dignity.

**Alan**
(*Pause. Whispers*) Do your Frank Spencer.

**Steve**
(*In Frank Spencer voice*) Oooh, Betty, hmmm, the cat's done a whoopsy.

**Alan**
Ha ha ha! Very good. Oh, erm, do Dustin Hoffman.

**Steve**
(*In Dustin Hoffman voice*) Michael Dorssan and Dorothy Michaels –

**Alan**
(*Interrupting*) Er, great, lovely! What would Sean Connery say if he came in the door now?

**Steve**
Er, I think he'd say (*in Sean Connery voice*) my name is Bond, James Bond, your name is Partridge, Alan Partridge…

**Alan**
Ha, of course he would. Roy Hattersley.

**Steve**
Can't do him.

**Alan**
Oh, right, OK, urm, oh, oh look, Frank Spencer's come back in the door.

**Steve**
Na, I, I really don't actually do Frank Spencer, I just, I did it then 'cos, I, I need, needed to but I don't actually –

**Alan**
You, you're one of the Spitting Imagers, aren't you?

**Steve**
Well, I do voices on *Spitting Image*, yeah.

**Alan**

Right, I've been tipped off by my Spitting Images insider, that, er, deep down somewhere, they are planning to do a new puppet of –

**Steve**

Yeah, they're doing, er, Alan Hanson, 'cos he does Match of the Day.

**Alan**

Yeah, yeah, and I've heard they're doing a puppet of one Alan Partridge.

**Steve**

Ha ha! Oh, I can neither confirm nor deny that.

**Alan**

Yeah, come on, tell us the truth, let, are there, there –

**Steve**

No, I'm sworn to secrecy, Alan –

**Alan**

I'll bet, come on, are they making a puppet of me?

**Steve**

No.

**Alan**

Right, that's, that's a relief, that is, phew, close shave there, don't want to make fun of me. Urm, but you do, do an impression of me, don't you?

**Steve**

Ha, er, once I did one, yeah, at a gig, yeah, I did an impression.

**Alan**

Well, can we hear it now?

**Steve**

Well, I don't know if it's appropriate for this programme you know –

**Alan**

Come on!

**Steve**

I do it quite late night.

**Alan**

It doesn't matter, listen, you can't scare me, you talking to a man who's been de-bagged at a pharmaceutical conference. Come on, do, do your Alan Partridge.

**Steve**

No, I just, I prefer not to, I just don't want to –

**Alan**

That's why you're on the show. Do Alan Partridge. Do it.

**Steve**

*(Pause. In his Alan partridge voice)* Good evening, I'm Alan Partridge, welcome to knowing me, knowing you with Alan Partridge –

**Alan**

Ha ha!

**Steve**

– Alan Partridge, I'll just say my name again, I'm Alan Partridge, it's not that I like the sound of my own voice, it's just I enjoy hearing myself speak. I'm Alan Partridge, this is sports desk, I'm Alan Partridge, people say I make mistakes, but the only mistake I've ever made was being born –

**Alan**

What –

**Steve**

– I'm Alan Partridge, I'm the non-thinking man's Elton Wellsby, I'm Alan Partridge –

**Alan**

All right –

**Steve**

– I'm a media whore with no punters –

# Radio Show 5

**Alan**
– that's it –

**Steve**
– let me on the telly, let me on the telly –

**Alan**
I don't say that –

**Steve**
– I'm Alan Partridge, I'm the man, I'm Alan Partridge, I tell ya, I'm Alan Partridge. I'm the man who makes Jimmy Hill look like Umberto Eco. I'm Alan Partridge, Alan Partridge, urrr, Alan Partridge *(more quietly)* Alan Partridge – Alan Partridge.

**Alan**
Now that, sunshine, is libellous.

**Steve**
*(Still in his Alan Partridge voice)* Now that, sunshine, is libellous.

**Alan**
That's what I said.

**Steve**
That's what I said.

**Alan**
What are you doing?

**Steve**
What are you doing?

**Alan**
Will you just stop repeating –

**Steve**
Stop –

**Alan**
Don't –

**Steve**
Don't –

**Alan**
Stop it!

**Steve**
Stop it!

**Alan**
This is stupid.

**Steve**
This is stupid.

**Alan**
But you're making yourself look stupid.

**Steve**
You're making yourself look stupid.

**Alan**
No. Stop that now.

**Steve**
Stop that now.

**Alan**
Stop it.

**Steve**
Stop it.

**Alan**
Don't say any more.

**Steve**
Don't say any more.

**Alan**
Stop it.

**Steve**
Stop it.

**Alan**
You look ridiculous.

**Steve**
You look ridiculous.

**Alan**
That's it.

**Steve**
That's it.

**Alan**
That's it.

# Knowing Me, Knowing You

**Steve**
That's it. (*Pause*)

**Alan**
That was Steve Thompson there, the impressionist.

**Steve**
That was Steve Thompson –

**Alan**
You're not still doing it!

**Steve**
You're not still doing it!

**Alan**
Oh, it's ridiculous now!

**Steve**
It's ridiculous now!

**Alan**
You look, it's, it's ridiculous.

**Steve**
You look ridiculous.

**Alan**
Please, stop it.

**Steve**
Please, stop it.

**Alan**
I'm Alan Partridge.

**Steve**
I'm Alan Partridge.

**Alan**
What's Umberto Eco?

**Steve**
What's Umberto Eco?

**Alan**
Translate that now.

**Steve**
Translate that now.

**Alan**
What is it?

**Steve**
What is it?

**Alan**
What, what is it?

**Steve**
What is it?

**Alan**
What is it?

**Steve**
What is it?

**Alan**
(*Quietly*) What is it?

**Steve**
(*Quietly*) He's a person.

**Alan**
He's a person?

**Steve**
He's a person?

**Alan**
(*Quietly*) What does he do?

**Steve**
(*Quietly*) He's a semiologist.

**Alan**
He's a semiologist?

**Steve**
He's a semiologist?

**Alan**
What's a semiologist?

**Steve**
What's a semiologist?

**Alan**
What is it?

**Steve**
What is it?

**Alan**
What is it?

**Steve**
What is it?

**Alan**
What is it?

**Steve**
I'm not telling you.

**Alan**
What's a semiologist?

**Steve**
What's a semiologist?

**Alan**
You can't do that.

**Steve**
You can't do that.

**Alan**
Stop it.

**Steve**
Stop it.

**Alan**
*(Shouting)* I'm Alan Partridge!

**Steve**
*(Shouting)* I'm Alan Partridge!

**Alan**
*(Shouting)* I'm Alan Partridge!

**Steve**
*(Shouting)* I'm Alan Partridge!
*(Pause)*

**Alan**
*(Whispers)* If you speak again I will physically hit you.
*(Pause)*
That was, um, that was Steve Thompson there, the impressionist. A quick question before you go, Steve, what's the name of the researcher that booked you?

**Steve**
I don't know.

**Alan**
Is it Lisa?

**Steve**
No.

**Alan**
Must have been Jason then, that's all I need to know. OK, um, Steve Thompson there, thanks very much, Steve.

*Applause*

**Alan**
There's no time to clap, there's no time to clap. *(Applause continues)* There's, no, there's no time there's no time. Now, my next guest is a government minister, she made her name in the early eighties as the uncompromising leader of Norwich city council, and as an MP, she's quickly shot up the greasy pole as junior minister for housing. In the past week she's been subject to some unforgivable press rumour and innuendo, regarding her holiday abroad with two seventeen-year-old boy twins, and she's come on to my show tonight to clear her name and to tell us how she's making this country great again. Please welcome the junior minister for housing, the delightful, Mrs Sandra Peaks.

*Music: 'Gimme Gimme Gimme'.*
*Applause.*

**Alan**
Welcome. Knowing me, Alan Partridge, knowing you, the minister for housing, Mrs Sandra Peaks, ah-haa.

**Sandra**
It's my pleasure, Alan.

**Alan**
No, you say, Ah-haa.

**Sandra**
Ah-haa.

**Alan**
Thanks. Now you, you and I have something in common, don't we?

**Sandra**
We both live in Norwich, yes.

**Alan**
That's right, we both come from the little island in the bog, Norwich, and, er, you're now MP for Norwich, and you've reached, you've recently reached the dizzy heights of, er, junior ministerial office. Congratulations.

**Sandra**
Thank you very much, and thank you for your sterling work in the election with the loudhailer.

**Alan**
Yep, yeah, it was a pleasure, I don't, I don't want to disclose my political affiliations here, think that would be inappropriate, but suffice to say, that on April the tenth I think we all breathed a sigh of relief.

**Sandra**
We certainly did.

**Alan**
And of course if I may say so, a very successful leader of Norwich council.

**Sandra**
That's right, doing what had to be done, getting rates down, getting poll tax down, and, erm, not handing out money, but handing out hope, which is a lot more precious.

**Alan**
Right, and, er, getting, getting rid of those, rid of those gypsies. Er, but we're here to talk about the rumours, the sordid speculation which has blighted your life, over the past couple of days.

**Sandra**
That's been rammed down everybody's throats.

**Alan**
Yes, now, for listeners, for listeners at home, those who've, er, had the good fortune not to have seen the photographs in the tabloids, they depict the minister, quite simply on holiday, on a lounger with two young lads, just you know popping a bit of, you know, baby lotion on to your tummy and legs. Now these seventeen-year-old twin brothers –

**Sandra**
Hence the predictably smutty *Sun* headline –

**Alan**
Twin Peaks, that's right. Presumably a reference to your, er, your ample bosom there.

**Sandra**
No, that's a reference to the fact that my name is Sandra Peaks and the two lads were twins.

**Alan**
Oh right! That's clever, yeah. But it works both ways, doesn't it.

**Sandra**
Well, if you have a tawdry mind, yes.

**Alan**
Yeah. Wh-wh-what, what was actually going on?

**Sandra**
Well, look, as you well know, Alan, the only twin peaks that I'm interested in are the twin peaks of initiative and responsibility.

**Alan**
Very clever.

**Sandra**

Now these two lads, these were two homeless people, with initiative, and they wrote to me explaining the situation, which quite naturally I wanted to do something about, and we gave them a job on Brightside Constructions, my husband Brian's construction industry.

**Alan**

That's right because he's employed a lot of young boys, hasn't he?

**Sandra**

Yes, yes, two hundred and fifty in the last three months.

**Alan**

Golly, that's, that's a lot. Um, um, but why, why, did you take the boys on holiday?

**Sandra**

Well, this is the point I'm trying to make, it's very easy to lose touch with the public and Brian and I thought it would be a great idea to take Craig and Matt away, get them out of their depressing environment, get to know them at a grass-roots level. Now if a minister for housing can't get to know the very people she's trying to house, then what sort of a democracy is it?

**Alan**

Absolutely, hear hear, as they say in the House of Lords, now, now as far, as far as I'm concerned that issue is closed, we've got rid of the muck, we've hosed you down, but, er, just in case there's, er, any little bit of dirt still sticking in any nooks or crannies or, or cracks, on you, then let's get out the high-pressure nozzle, let's, let's do that by bringing on to this programme, with your consent –

**Sandra**

Absolutely, yes –

**Alan**

– the two young lads at the centre of this episode, they're here tonight, please welcome the two seventeen-year-old twin lads, they've been great in hospitality making us all laugh, please welcome Craig and Matt Bradley.

*Music: 'Gimme Gimme Gimme'*
*Applause*

**Alan**

Craig and Matt, welcome, ah-haa.

**Craig and Matt**

Ah-haa.

**Alan**
Now which, which one's Craig, which one's Matt?

**Craig**
I'm Craig.

**Matt**
And I'm Matt.

**Alan**
Right, OK, did you enjoy hospitality?

**Craig**
Yes –

**Matt**
Yeah, it's great, yeah.

**Alan**
Managed to eat the sandwiches?

**Matt**
*(Laughing)* Yeah –

**Alan**
Take a few cans home, did you?

**Matt**
Yeah, right.

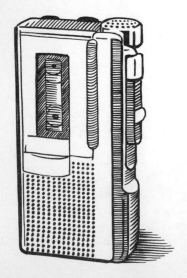

**Alan**
That's what I do. I don't really, I don't do that, I don't pilfer. Erm, now you've heard and read presumably, about the allegations, tell us about the minister, you know her better than anyone else, what's she like?

**Craig**
She's very nice.

**Matt**
Yeah, she's, she's lovely, we're just like one big happy family, ain't we?

**Alan**
And so what was your reaction when you saw the photographs in the paper?

**Matt**
I, I, I thought –

**Craig**
Very, very upset.

**Matt**
It was disgusting, you know, in this day and age, just because someone goes topless, you know, there's a big scandal.

**Alan**
She wasn't topless in the photographs.

**Sandra**
No, I never took my top off.

**Craig**
No, what Matt, what Matt means is that we, we're topless, me and Matt were topless. So Mrs Peaks was never topless.

**Alan**
Right.

**Matt**
We're just one big happy family.

**Alan**
Yes, yeah, but, er, you had a great time?

**Craig**
Yeah –

**Matt**
Yeah, brilliant.

**Sandra**
Yeah, I wish I was seventeen again.

**Alan**
Why?

**Sandra**
Just, just so that I could –

**Matt**
We were one big happy family.

**Alan**
Yeah, yeah, you've said that. *(Pause)*
OK, I've heard what you've said and I
have to say that I, Alan Partridge, think
that someone here smells deeply of fish,
and it's not Alan Partridge.

**Sandra**
Well, what are you trying to say, Alan?

**Alan**
It's all a bit too squeaky clean. Come on,
lads, bottom line, I've got a cheque book
here, how much to spill the beans?

**Sandra**
No, no no no, Alan, do not descend into
this – *(Craig and Matt murmur to each other)*

**Craig**
Twenty thousand.

**Sandra**
Don't accept this –

**Matt**
Oh, shut it, Sandra.

**Alan**
Producer's telling me you can have sixteen
thousand pounds.

**Craig**
It's not enough.

**Sandra**
I do not believe that I am sitting here, and
you, Alan Partridge –

**Craig**
It's not enough.

**Matt**
*(Quietly)* Craig!

**Craig**
*(Quietly)* Don't worry, I'll get it.

**Alan**
I'll give you four out of my own pocket.

**Craig**
Cash.

**Alan**
Yeah, right, yeah, cash.

**Craig**
After the show.

**Alan**
After the show, we'll do that.

**Craig**
Sixteen now.

**Sandra**
Right, I'm leaving.

**Alan**
Yeah, right, done. Done.

**Sandra**
I am leaving, Mr Partridge –

**Alan**
She's getting up, the minister's leaving the
show, she's walking out on my show.

**Sandra**
– I am going –

**Alan**
She's going – she's off the show *(Sandra can
be heard shouting in the background.)* Thank
you, that's all, minister. Now, dish the dirt.

**Craig**
Where's the cheque? The cheque.

**Alan**
Right, erm, there.

**Craig**
Make it out to me, Craig Bradley.

**Matt**
And Matt.

**Craig**
Na, na, that's all right, I'll sort it out.

**Alan**
There, now, come on, quick, we've got two minutes, dirt quickly.

**Craig**
We're rent boys.

**Alan**
Rent boys, right, what did you do, what did you do?

**Craig**
Everything, she got us through an agency.

**Alan**
Yep, what, what did you do? What?

**Matt**
Er, bondage, she made us dress like dogs.

**Alan**
That's disgusting, dogs!

**Craig**
She had sort of metal clanking leads.

**Matt**
Yeah.

**Alan**
Oh, that's awful, any more, any more? Quick.

**Craig**
She made us bark, and we had to eat dog food from a silver bowl.

**Alan**
That's disgusting –

**Matt**
I ate it, I ate it, Craig didn't.

**Alan**
Did, did she use a torse?

**Craig**
A what?

**Alan**
It's, er, a bamboo back leather strap, three prongs.

**Craig**
Yes, yes.

**Alan**
Right, yes, right.

**Matt**
And she made –

**Alan**
Quickly, quickly.

**Matt**
She made, she made, er, Brian wanted to be a dog as well but she wouldn't let him –

**Craig**
That's right, yeah!

**Matt**
– and she made Mr Peaks go into the bathroom and lick milk up from the shower.

**Alan**
Did he go meow, like a cat?

**Craig**
No –

**Matt**
No, no, no, no.

**Alan**
Right, OK, quickly, please, give me some physical evidence of what she did.

**Craig**
Right, all right –

**Matt**
Here, look at my bottom, look at that.

**Alan**
Look at his bottom, ladies and gentlemen, there are, look at that, look at his –

**Craig**
It's radio, Alan, they can't see.

**Alan**
I'll describe it, it's got two cheeks, it's just like an ordinary one, but it's, it's got –

**Matt**
Purple and black bits –

**Alan**
– deep welt marks –

**Craig**
He can't sit down, my brother can't sit down –

**Alan**
– inflicted by a torse, inflicted by a minister of the crown. And on that bombshell, we say, knowing me, Alan Partridge, knowing you, the you, the impressionist, the you, the Duchess of Stranraugh, the you, the rent boys, and the you, the minister of the crown. That's all from me, Alan Partridge, thanks to my team of writers and researchers, Steve Coogan, Patrick Marber, David Schneider, Rebecca Front, Doon McKichan –

*Applause*

**Alan**
Thanks also to my producer, Armando Iannucci. We'll be back at the same time next week, and, we've, we've just heard, we've just heard that Sandra Peaks, the minister for housing, has resigned, yes, a broken woman, we broke her, goodnight. Thank you.

*Music: 'Knowing Me, Knowing You'*

# KNOWING ME KNOWING YOU

## RADIO SHOW 6

*Music: 'Knowing Me, Knowing You'*

**Alan**

Ah-haaaa! *(Applause)* Welcome, welcome, welcome, welcome once again to *Knowing Me, Knowing You* with Alan Partridge *(quietly)* ah-haa, ah-haa. Now, the more observant listeners may have noticed that, that last 'ah-haa' was tinged with sadness, and that's because this is the last in the current series of *Knowing Me, Knowing You (Audience: 'Awwww –')*. No, ah-haa! Now, after the show the BBC have told me to clear my desk, pack my bags and hop it! No, of course they haven't. We are currently in negotiations for a second series, uh, basically, they say that, uh, the deal's fine as it stands, we say, things change. We say in this business, people become hot. And

when you're handling something that's hot, you don't want to get your fingers burnt, so you wear oven gloves. And you handle that hot property with kid gloves – and, and oven gloves outside, outside the kid gloves. To sum up, in case anyone's not quite sure what I'm saying, what I'm actually trying to say is, the BBC TV are on the lookout for the next big TV chat show, um, fingers crossed. TV's gain could be Radio 4's loss. OK, let's get on with the show, let's banish all talk of *Knowing Me, Knowing You* being a central component of next Autumn's BBC1 schedule. My first guest tonight is the Commisioning Director for BBC Television! Please give a warm welcome to Mr Tony Hayers!

*Applause and music*

**Alan**
Knowing me, Alan Partridge, knowing you,
Tony Hayers. Ah-haa.

**Tony**
Ah-haa.

**Alan**
Tony Hayers, Commisioning Director of
B-B-C Television.

**Tony**
Alan Partridge, presenter of Radio 4's jewel
in the crown.

**Alan**
No, no, it's *Knowing Me, Knowing You*.

**Tony**
I, I meant 'jewel in the crown' as in –

**Alan**
It's not called *Jewel in the Crown*, that's
another thing.

**Tony**
Let's move on.

**Alan**
Right, yeah, of course. Now, in a short
while, you will be taking telephone calls
from members of the public –

**Tony**
That's right.

**Alan**
– um, who want to know questions about
BBC Television. That's why you're on the
show. We look forward to that.

**Tony**
Yes, yes.

**Alan**
Now, there is an ethos behind the BBC.

**Tony**
Yes.

**Alan**
What is that?

**Tony**
We've always, and always will be,
committed to making programmes
of originality, quality and excellence.

**Alan**
I can see that because I go home, I sit
down, I turn the television on to BBC1 and
I sit and watch *The Darling Buds of May*,
and I, and I say, 'Thank God for the BBC,
this is quality.'

**Tony**
Uh, well, that's very kind, Alan. I have to
say that *Darling Buds of May* is actually ITV.

**Alan**
Is it? Oh right, um, *Inspector Morse* then –

**Tony**
ITV.

**Alan**
Right, OK, er, *The Bill*, *The Bill* –?

**Tony**
ITV.

**Alan**
Right, um, *Noel's House Party*?

**Tony**
Yes, that's us, Alan, yes.

**Alan**
Right, right, so I like to go home, sit down,
and think, 'I want originality, quality and
excellence.' I watch *Noel's House Party*
and I think, 'Thank God for the BBC.
Originality, quality and excellence!'

**Tony**
Yes.

**Alan**
*Noel's House Party*! It's interesting, actually,
you say *The Darling Buds of May*, um,
because I remember now that the BBC
was offered that show –

**Tony**
Yes, that's correct –

**Alan**
– and turned it down.

**Tony**
– that's correct, yes.

**Alan**
So, someone, somewhere along the line, let twenty million viewers slip through his fingers. He must be kicking himself now!

**Tony**
That was me.

**Alan**
It's rubbish! It's rubbish, though, isn't it?

**Tony**
Well, I thought it was very good.

**Alan**
It is, it is, it's great, it's per-fick, isn't it?

**Tony**
I'm sorry, I thought you just said it was rubbish, Alan.

**Alan**
Yeah, it is rubbish, the viewing figures, th-they're twenty million. There can't be that much, that's rubbish, that's rubbish.

**Tony**
Ri-i-ght, right, right.

**Alan**
Right. I think it's time for the first caller, which is Steve from Hornsea in North London. Steve, are you there?

**Steve**
Yeah, I am, Alan. Hello.

**Alan**
Have you got a question for Tony Hayers?

**Steve**
Yeah, er, Tony.

**Tony**
Hello, Steve, hello.

**Steve**
Um, I'm a big fan of *The Duchess of Duke Street.*

**Tony**
*(Chuckles)* Oh!

**Alan**
*The Duchess of Duke Street.*

**Steve**
I'm just wondering if you're gonna bring that back, you know, have repeats of that.

**Tony**
Um, there – I must confess – there aren't any firm plans at the moment, but I, I was a big fan of the series and I'm pleased to hear that it's fondly remembered in the public's eye and, um, yes I'll do my best to see for the fut—, actually, you could possibly get it on video.

**Alan**
Is it available on video?

**Steve**
No, I don't think so.

**Tony**
You could try the BBC shop, but I'm not sure myself.

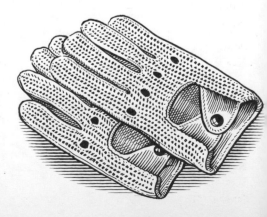

**Alan**
Well, I hope, I hope that helps you, Steve.

**Steve**
Yeah. Can I ask you a question, Alan?

**Alan**
Certainly. Fire away.

**Steve**
Why are you such a tit?

**Alan**
Um, I'm sorry, I'm sorry, we do, we can't –
we had no control of that so I apologize
in advance.

**Steve**
You haven't answered the question.

**Alan**
Why hasn't he been cut off?! He should
have been cut off – !

**Steve**
Why are you – *(he is cut off)*

**Alan**
Sorry. Um, the next is – Kelly from
Withington. Kelly?

**Kerry**
Hello?

**Alan**
Hello.

**Tony**
Hello.

**Alan**
Kelly?

**Kerry**
Kerry.

**Alan**
Kerry. Sorry.

**Kerry**
Why haven't you got more youth
programmes?

**Alan**
What? What?

**Kerry**
Why aren't there more youth programmes?

**Alan**
Why aren't there more youth programmes?

**Tony**
Um, well, Kerry, um, that's an area of
programming that we're addressing at the
moment. We have a youth controller and,
um, we hope that within the next few years
we'll really have tackled programming
for the fifteen to twenty-five-year-old
age bracket.

**Alan**
Great. And I'd like to think that *Knowing
Me, Knowing You* is in there with the youth
programmes because, um, Simon Bates is a
big fan of the show, and, um, he's certainly
got his finger on the nub of youth, and, er,
indeed Kerry's called so I imagine she's a
listener. Kerry, do you like the show?

**Kerry**
No.

**Alan**
Right, OK, all right, um, fine. Next caller
is Amanda, Amanda Southampton from
Southampton. Are you there?

**Amanda**
It's, er, it's just Amanda from
Southampton.

**Alan**
OK. Have you got a ques—, have you got
a question for Tony?

**Amanda**
Er, yes, hello, Tony.

**Tony**
Hello, Amanda.

**Amanda**
I listen regularly to Radio 4 –

**Tony**
Mm-hmm.

**Amanda**
– and I've heard all of *Knowing Me, Knowing You* as a consequence.

**Tony**
Mmm.

**Amanda**
– and, um, I just, I just want to say that, um, it's the most insidiously offensive programme that I've ever heard –

**Alan**
Right –

**Amanda**
– I don't how much of it you've heard but Alan Partridge has, on air, to my knowledge hit a child, he's gambled away his wife's car, he has taken cocaine, bribed rent boys, he was openly homophobic to a gay lawyer – I'm sorry, I can't remember his name –

**Alan**
Nick Ford.

**Amanda**
Nick Ford, thank you, and he is unfailingly patronizing to all his women guests –

**Alan**
Oh, look, have you got a question, dearie?

**Amanda**
Well, it's more, really, more of a plea, Mr Hayers –

**Tony**
Mmm.

**Amanda**
– just, p-please, don't let Alan Partridge on the television.

**Tony**
Well, Amanda, I'm not responsible for radio, so –

**Alan**
Sorry, if I, can I deal with this, please? Listen, listen, love, in the cut and thrust, in the cut and thrust of a chat show, people are going to get hit. If you can't stand the heat, get out of the kitchen. Sorry about that, I imagine that was a hoax caller, probably wife of the tit man. We've got time for, we've got time for one more call, which is from John in Norwich. Hello. John?

**John**
Hello, Alan. I listen to *Knowing Me, Knowing You* a lot. I'm a big fan, and I think it should definitely go to television.

**Tony**
Right.

**John**
It could be made very cheaply by Peartree Productions, which is Alan Partridge's company, I believe.

**Alan**
That's right.

**John**
They could make it at Anglia Studios in Norwich.

**Tony**
Yes.

**John**
Yes, very cheaply. Anglia Studios, er, I understand has excellent on-line editing facilities, and digital editing equipment as well that would be useful for television. I reckon you could probably bring in a show for about £75,000, which in TV terms is very cheap, so you'd have quality programming for a cheap budget.

**Alan**

He's got a point.

**Tony**

Mmm. Well, thank you, John, I'll bear all that in mind, that's very interesting.

**Alan**

Is that all, John? Is that all you've got to say? Anything else? *(Long pause)* Format?

**John**

Format! Because it will be transferring direct from radio, you wouldn't have to pay Peartree Productions a large development fee, you could transfer straight away, I mean, Alan could start broadcasting as of next week if he wanted.

**Tony**

Can I just ask – John, what do you do for a living?

**John**

I'm a plumber.

**Alan**

Thanks very much, er, thanks, thanks very much Jason from Norwich.

**Tony**

John.

**Alan**

John from Norwich, a plumber. OK, well, thanks very much, Tony Hayers. Give him a round of applause, Tony Hayers!

*Applause*

**Alan**

Now, my next two guests. Well, one is a TV presenter whose *bark* is worse than her bite. The other is a fashion designer whose style *leaves* a lot to be desired. And now they're both *branching* out. Why have I kept mentioning bits of trees and stuff like that? Well, this year is the Year of the Tree, and my next guests are two enterprising, stylish ladies who are launching a celebrity tree–planting event to raise public awareness about the plight of our trees. Come with me and get to know Trudy Skye and Yvonne Boyd.

*Applause*

**Alan**

Knowing me, Alan Partridge, knowing you, Trudy Skye and Yvonne Boyd, ah-haa.

**Trudy and Yvonne**

Ah-haa.

**Alan**

Now, if I can get my teeth into Trudy first. Trudy, you are known chiefly as presenter of 'The Show' on BBC2's *Def Leppard*.

**Trudy**

No, *Deaf Two*.

**Alan**

Right, you present 'Deaf Two' on *Def Leppard*.

**Trudy**

No, I present my show, 'The Show', on *Deaf Two*.

**Alan**

Right, now, for the benefit of my listeners, tell us as briefly as possible about 'The Show'.

**Trudy**

Well, it's very much a cult thing –

**Alan**

Small viewing figures, carry on.

**Trudy**

Well, it's a sort of multimedia, um, pot pourri, if you like, of, er, music, art, dance, cabaret, culture, floating sculpture, um, and it's sort of aimed at teenagers with like a four-second attention span.

**Alan**

Yeah, I have to say my teenage children, Fernando and Denise, are avid, avid watchers.

**Trudy**

Fabbo.

**Alan**

I, on the other hand, find it completely exhausting, um, it's so fast. I thought our telly was on the blink, changing all the time.

**Trudy**

Well, it's very much in-your-face television.

**Alan**

Yes, I did feel it in my face, yeah, yes. I thought my head was going to explode, like, er, like in that film – um, let me move on to you, Yvonne Boyd. You are a fashion designer but you don't design clothes that ordinary people would wear in the street. You design more, kind of outlandish, sort of funny-looking clown-type costume things.

**Yvonne**

I mean, I really think that all clothes are a statement.

**Alan**

I mean, my bank manager couldn't wear one of your clown costumes, for example.

**Yvonne**

Well, why not?

**Alan**

Because he'd look ridiculous, he'd look like a clown!

**Yvonne**

Yes, but I mean what I would say to you is, would you say that he looked ridiculous if he was wearing like, um, a long bit of striped cotton with flaps around the neck and wrist and maybe a bit of brightly coloured silk around the neck.

**Alan**

Yes, that would look silly.

**Yvonne**

Right, so you would think that he looked silly in a shirt and tie.

**Alan**

Oh, I see, very clever, OK, my bank manager looks stupid, right, and you look normal wearing what I can only describe as a shrub on your head.

**Yvonne**

It is a shrub, it's my shrub hat.

**Alan**

And the statement you're making presumably is, 'I'm wearing a shrub on my head.'

**Yvonne**

All clothes, as I said, are a statement of something, so what I'm wearing is a statement and what you're wearing now, which is, um, a sort of fuchsia and sage Pringle jumper with, um, a golf design knitted into it –

**Alan**

Thank you.

**Yvonne**

– that also is making a statement, I mean, that is saying, you know, 'I am a performer. Look, look, I'm bright and exciting.'

**Alan**

Right. Well, yes it is, it is, I mean, it's saying, 'I'm Alan Partridge, I am sports-casual.' Um, I mean, how would you describe me as a figure? What would you say I was?

**Yvonne**

I would say that you were a sort of a rococo figure, uh, a kind of a 'mock baroque' if you like.

**Alan**

Oh, thank you, thank you. Knowing me, Alan Partridge, 'mock baroque', knowing

you, Yvonne Boyd, tree lady. Now, now
the reason why you're both here is to
promote your tree campaign. Trudy,
tell us about that.

**Trudy**
Well, Treenaissance '93 is a sort of, it's
a sort of massive tree-planting eco-drive
to raise consciousness and what we're
saying, basically, is, 'Germination not
termination'. We're saying, we're saying,
'Sapling not grappling', we're saying,
'Nurture not torture'.

**Alan**
Great, I've got a good one for you, um, I
thought it up in the car on the way, on the
way down. 'Build a tree, don't cut it down,
for goodness sake!' Put that on a T-shirt.
Um, now, when, when did you first get
the idea for Treenaissance '93?

**Trudy**
Well, it was actually on one of our
hen runs –

**Alan**
Oh, yes, the infamous hen runs, tell us
about those.

**Trudy**
Well, it's once a month, about thirty of us
girlies get together and go on a coach trip,
it's sort of women only, just to sort of create
an exciting –

**Alan**
Who – what kind of people go on these
trips?

**Trudy**
Oh, just friends, you know – Yasmin Le
Bon, Annie Lennox, Katie Puckrik –

**Yvonne**
Juliet Stephenson.

**Alan**
Yeah, yeah.

**Trudy**
Yeah, Fay Weldon, Janet Street-Porter –

**Yvonne**
Pamela Stevenson –

**Alan**
Yep.

**Trudy**
All the Cholmondeleys –

**Alan**
Yeah, yeah, I get the picture, yeah, that lot –

**Trudy**
I think that, that the day that it sort of rose
in our collective psyche was –

**Alan**
When you got the idea?

**Trudy**
Uh-huh.

**Alan**
Yes.

**Trudy**
Yeah, it was an outing to Margate where
we had a wonderful day and, uh, we
actually just chanced upon this incredible
greasy cafe on the sea front –

**Yvonne**
It was really extraordinary.

**Trudy**
– it was so kitsch, it was like, uh, I can't
describe it, there were like dirty tablecloths
and the floor was filthy, and the waiter was
Italian –

**Yvonne**
The waiter had actually been born in
Italy and he'd come over here to work as
a waiter.

**Alan**
Really.

**Trudy**
– amazing –

**Yvonne**
They had these, um, on every table, they had like plastic red tomatoes, which you'd squeeze and you got tomato ketchup out of them, but they looked like a sort of Robert Rauschenberg – they were sort of, they were too big for themselves –

**Trudy**
– and they inspired Yvonne to launch her tomato collection which was sort of plastic red puffball dresses with a stomach design of a green nozzle –

**Alan**
Hmm, something else for my bank manager to wear – but to get back to the original question, tell me about Treenaissance. I suppose it was a very wacky do and everyone was all really trendy, presumably you, uh, you, you went dressed as a banana, or something like that, all bent –

**Yvonne**
No, I went wearing what I am wearing now, part of my tree collection.

**Alan**
You went wearing what you are wearing now? I hope you changed your underwear.

**Yvonne**
I don't wear underwear.

**Alan**
Of course you do –

**Yvonne**
No, I don't –

**Alan**
You do, you're just trying to be wacky.

**Yvonne**
I'm not being wacky, I don't approve of underwear. I see it as a restriction of personal freedom and I've never worn it –

**Alan**
Balderdash! Everyone wears underwear –

**Yvonne**
– not balder—, don't – I'm not lying – don't call me a liar –

**Alan**
– you do, you do – you do –

**Yvonne**
Right! I'll show you!

**Alan**
Don't, no, don't do that – don't – oh my God! – oh my God! *(Long pause)* Oh God, I can't get it out of me head! – I just, I can still see it! – that's atrocious – ladies and gentlemen, she just showed me her woman's area! Thank goodness it's radio, I never thought I'd say that! I can't believe it, that was atrocious!

**Yvonne**
If you go around calling people liars on your show then you've got to expect people to show their veracity.

**Alan**
You will not show your veracity on my show! I just want to say if anyone, if anyone's listening to this, I had no idea that they were going to be so candid and to make quite clear my abhorrence, I now will tell them to leave, and in addition to that I will ask the audience to boo them. Thank you very much to Trudy Skye and Yvonne Boyd. Goodnight. Boo them! *(Audience boos)* Boo them! Go on, boo them! *(Audience hisses.)* That's right. And hiss them!

Right. Now. My final guest tonight is an eighty-four-year-old man. *(Audience: 'Aww')* During his long, distinguished, maverick political career, he's been famous for his outspoken views and the outspoken way of speaking them. In 1963, he reduced interviewer David Frost to a gibbering wreck of tears. In a recent TV debate with feminist Andrea Dworkin he caused outrage when he told her to shut up and shave. And only, and only last week, he sensationally renounced his peerage and left the House of Lords. I better watch out, and so had you, as we get to know Lord Morgan of Glossop.

*Music: 'Waterloo'*
*Applause*

**Alan**
Knowing me, Alan Partridge, knowing you, Lord Morgan of Glossop, ah-haa.

**Lord Morgan**
*(Long pause)* Hello.

**Alan**
No, you're not going to do that? OK. Now, you just resigned from the House of Lords. Do you want to tell us about that?

**Lord Morgan**
One week ago, I stood up in the House of Lords and I said, 'My lords and ladies, you're all arses. Goodbye.'

**Alan**
Ha-ha-ha, great, um, you just published your autobiography. What's that about?

**Lord Morgan**
It's about my life, you arse.

**Alan**
Oh, you, you, you, you described your childhood in the book and I imagined your life in Glossop in Derbyshire, I imagine a life of cobbly streets, of inclement weather, a wholesome existence. Is that fair?

**Lord Morgan**
When I was five, I walked into the parlour and I witnessed my father shooting my mother. He then placed the shotgun into his own mouth and blew his brains out.

**Alan**
So, it wasn't an idyllic childhood?

**Lord Morgan**
On the contrary, I was spared the ridiculous hypocrisy of family life. The only friend a man needs is the bottle.

**Alan**
Right. No doubt then, if you're so fond of the bottle, you'll be quite pleased that we left a bottle of ten-year-old malt in your dressing room?

**Lord Morgan**
Yes. All gone.

**Alan**
Did you enjoy it?

**Lord Morgan**
Piss!

**Alan**
I can see why David Frost started crying.

**Lord Morgan**
He's an arse.

**Alan**
Well, I won't ask why.

**Lord Morgan**
You're an arse.

**Alan**
Huh. Oh, so, after, er, after childhood, what happened then?

**Lord Morgan**
Adolescence.

**Alan**
And, er, what was that like?

**Lord Morgan**
Like childhood, but with more pubic hair – ha ha! *(Coughs)* I got you there!

**Alan**
Yes, got me there – now –

**Lord Morgan**
You arse!

**Alan**
Look, please, please, now, Lord Morgan, please, people are listening. Now, in Oxford, in the 1930s, you went up to Oxford to study the Classics and it was there you met W. H. Auden –

**Lord Morgan**
Poof.

**Alan**
– Steven Spelling –

**Lord Morgan**
Poof.

**Alan**
– Cecil Day Lewis –

**Lord Morgan**
Big poof.

**Alan**
You, you, you didn't like them, did you?

**Lord Morgan**
Nancy boy, communist, poofter poets – poofy poets prancing around.

**Alan**
Right, OK. So, you didn't like them?

**Lord Morgan**
You arse!

**Alan**
Don't say that again, please, please.

**Lord Morgan**
If you don't want me to say it again, I won't say it again. I give you my word.

**Alan**
Are you a man of your word?

**Lord Morgan**
No.

**Alan**
Right, um, and er, you've been very outspoken, you're in favour of hanging –

**Lord Morgan**
Only for criminals.

**Alan**
Right, but, um, oddly, more recently, you've been an outspoken defender of pornography. Why?

**Lord Morgan**
What a man chooses to do in the privacy of his own attic is his business alone.

**Alan**
Right, but what about the feminist argument that pornography degrades women?

**Lord Morgan**
But is it not the case that sex degrades women – if it's any good? It's true –

**Alan**
Yes, yes, yes. Couldn't agree more. *(Lord Morgan coughs)* Now, now you're in *Who's Who* and, er –

**Lord Morgan**
I like those prostitutes.

**Alan**
Sorry?

**Lord Morgan**
I like those prostitutes. They were very nice.

**Alan**
Who? What prostitutes?

**Lord Morgan**
Those prostitutes you had on before –

**Alan**
They were not – they, they were guests, you can't say that, they were guests –

**Lord Morgan**
They look like whores.

**Alan**

Don't say that, don't, shh, don't!

**Lord Morgan**

They did!

**Alan**

Look *(whispers)*, look. I, you and I know they look like whores. But you can't say that.

**Lord Morgan**

*(Coughs and chokes while Alan is speaking)*

**Alan**

*(Ignoring Lord Morgan's coughing)* Now, I would love to be in *Who's Who* and I, I, we, what I've got here is my entry for *Who's Who* as follows: 'Alan Gordon Partridge, born 2nd April 1955 in Norwich. Journalist, commentator, broadcaster, and interviewer for Anglia TV's *Sport Report*, *On the Hour* BBC Radio 4, host of own chat show *Knowing Me, Knowing You* Radio 4 and others'. Is that the sort of thing that would be an acceptable form of words, with which to grace the hallowed turf of *Who's Who*'s pages? – *(long pause)* – no? I see that your own entry lists your hobbies – food, whisky and your attic – I mean, do you eat toffee? – *(longer pause)* – Lord Morgan? Lord Morgan? Could we have the chief medical officer, please? *(Quietly, in the background)* I'm very worried, is there anything at all?

**Medical Officer**

I'm afraid his pulse has completely stopped.

**Alan**

Right, I'll deal with this, I'll deal with this. *(Loudly)* Uh, ladies and gentlemen, it's, it's with great regret that I have to announce that Lord Morgan of Glossop passed away peacefully some moments ago and, and on that bombshell, on that bomb—, no we can't, I can't do that – no, this, this, this is, this is a profound moment – I suggest we perhaps observe a minute silence – in fact, I ought to cover him, um, I'm just, I'm just taking my sweater off and I'm going to drape it over his head. I drape my sweater over his head to preserve some dignity as, as Lord Morgan sits immovable beneath the hastily improvised Pringle shroud. It seems, it seems somehow appropriate to say, 'This is knowing me, Alan Partridge, knowing you, Lord Morgan, rest in peace, ah-haa. Please, please, one minute silence starting now, please, stop what you're doing, if you're in the car, pull over, if you're on the motorway, please, pull in at the next service station and observe a minute silence in your own time – er, if you're on the M1, there's Scratchwood, Toddington, and Newport where you'll find a Country Kitchen – um, if you're on the M6 you've got Knutsford, Sandback and Hill Park, so, a minute silence – *(long pause)* – I'll have to speak periodically to, so we're still broadcasting *(more silence)*. This is Radio 4 – with Alan Partridge – *(more silence)* – uh, drivers on the M4, you might, might want to pull off at Chippenham, where, if I'm not mistaken, you'll find a Julie's Pantry – uh, minute silence – *(more silence)* – in fact, I think we're running out of time, I'm sure, um, Lord Morgan wouldn't mind if I encroached on his minute silence to read out the credits, um, I'd like to thank my guests Tony Hayers, Trudy Skye, Yvonne Boyd, my team of writers and researchers, Steve Coogan, Patrick Marber, Rebecca Front, Doon MacKichan, David Schneider and my producer Armando Iannucci and, er, on this very sombre bombshell, I wish you all goodnight.

*Music: 'Knowing Me, Knowing You'*
*Applause*

# RULES AND REGULATIONS FOR
## *KNOWING ME, KNOWING YOU*
## GREEN ROOM

**1.** No food or drink to be brought into the Green Room. I realize the wine ran out before 10 p.m. the last two weeks running, but it's not like you should be partying until dawn anyway. This is a TV programme, not Stringfellow's.

**2.** No long faces! After last week's show, many people looked like they'd been working in a slaughterhouse or NHS hospital rather than making 'event' TV.

**3.** No sound crew permitted, sorry. I'd like to invite everyone, but you let the sound lads in, the floodgates are open.

**4.** No jeans or trainers. If this means bringing a change of clothes for the evening, so be it. To be honest, last week one or two people (mentioning no names, obviously) could have done with fresh 'kit'. Fair play, it's a hot studio and you have a lot of set-building to do, Chris. But this isn't *Wildlife on One* or *Time Team* – I want to be able to breathe freely after a recording. (Obviously there are very rare exceptions to this rule. See below.)

**5.** A free chair must be within 6 feet of Chief Commissioning Editor Tony Hayers at all times. Last week, the man looked distinctly uncomfortable and left after fifteen minutes, and I've only just realized why. *HE HAD NOWHERE TO SIT*. So if you're sitting and he's standing nearby, you know what to do.

**6.** A keen eye must be kept out at ALL TIMES for people from rival shows (recording on the same night). I don't want the kind of people who make Aunty's Bloomers helping themselves to the mini tikkas and making clearly sarcastic comments along the lines of 'So. Do you think you'll get a second series?' or 'I'm sure the ratings'll build', whilst sporting a massive ironic grin.

**7.** Last week, towards the end of the evening, one of the runners turned off the music tape I provided and was strumming a guitar. Although he never actually broke into song, THIS MUST NOT HAPPEN AGAIN. Josh, if you think you're more talented than Fairground Attraction, you're perfectly at liberty to go and prove it. Elsewhere.

**8.** Management between certain levels – from Producer rank up to Assistant Head of Department – are banned. Don't want all those stuffy middle-management types spoiling the post-show 'buzz'. Obviously Controllers and Commissioning Editors, and anyone from the list of celebrities I've supplied you with, are permitted. We have to be realistic.

**9.** An audience member managed to get in two weeks ago. It took seven minutes for security to get down and remove him, in which time anything could have happened. I don't care if he was in his fifties. Try telling that to Yoko Ono or Jackie Onassis. If anyone you don't know enters the Green Room, remember to ask the three test questions relating to music budget, my wife's weight and which geographical direction my dressing-room window faces.

**10.** Again mentioning no names, the Researcher and the Make-up Assistant, who are clearly having an affair (despite both already being in relationships) – please try to confine your longing looks towards each other to beyond BBC premises. My assistant Lynn is watching you like a hawk.

# KNOWING ME KNOWING YOU

*Alan Partridge* [signature]

*Music: 'Knowing Me, Knowing You'*

**Alan**
Ah-haa!

*Alan does a little run onstage and mimes pulling guns out of a holster and shooting them.*

*Applause*

**Alan**
Welcome. Welcome to *Knowing Me, Knowing You*, with me, Alan Partridge, live from BBC Television Centre. You'd better believe it, babe: there's a new chat in town.

*Drum roll*

**Alan**
Tonight is what I call a JFK kind of a night because, just as everyone can remember what they were doing when President Kennedy was shot in the head, I like to think that thirty years from now, people will

remember what they were doing when I first said, 'Ah-haa.' As tonight's motorcade of chat cruises through celebrity city, let's hope there isn't a lone sniper waiting to pick off my star guest. He arrived at Heathrow Airport ten minutes ago and is now being whisked to the studio in a black Vauxhall Carlton. He is none other than 007 James Bond, Roger Moore.

*Applause*

**Alan**
I hope you like my set. It's modelled on the lobby of a top international hotel. And, for the first time ever on a chat show, a beautiful fountain. But first, up there in their musical mezzanine, let's get to know my resident house band, Glen Ponder and Chalet.

*Music: 'Knowing Me, Knowing You'*
*Applause*

**Alan**
Knowing, knowing me, Alan Partridge, knowing you, Glen Ponder, ah-haa.

**Glen**
Ah-haa.

**Alan**
Knowing me, Alan Partridge, knowing you, Chalet, ah-haa.

**Chalet**
(*In unison*) Ah-haa.

**Alan**
Great to have you aboard, Glen.

**Glen**
Well, it's, it's great to be here. We're really –

**Alan**
Now just enjoy the show.

**Glen**
– looking forward to it.

**Alan**
Sorry?

**Glen**
Sorry.

**Alan**
Glen Ponder. Glen Ponder and Chalet! Have a good time.

**Glen**
And you.

*Applause and music*

**Alan**
Well, it's time to meet my first guest now, after I've done her introduction now. Now. Red Rum, Desert Orchid, Black Beauty, Shergar and Mr Ed. What have they got in common? Well, they're all celebrity horses. My first guest is not a celebrity horse. She's a celebrity who rides a horse. Let's see her in action.

*Showjumping video is played.*

**Alan**
(*Voiceover*) Gidee, gidee, gidee, yes! Yes! And a – yeah! Yes! Take that horse back to the stable and give it a kiss.

**Alan**
There's no finer way to start my series than in the company of World-Championship-winning, lady-showjumping horse legend, Sue Lewis!

*Applause and music: 'The Winner Takes It All', Sue Lewis joins Alan.*

**Alan**
Got a quick whiff of your perfume there, that's nice. Erm. Knowing me, Alan Partridge, knowing you, Sue Lewis, ah-haa.

**Sue**
Ah-ha. (*Laughs nervously*)

**Alan**
Right. Now. Horses. Horses. People say a dog is like its owner. Is a horse like its rider?

**Sue**
(*Nervously*) I don't know.

**Alan**
Can you speak … can you speak up a bit?

**Sue**
(*Clearly*) I don't know.

**Alan**
You don't think there's any resemblance? You don't think you look like a horse?

**Sue**
Well, I hope not. (*Laughs nervously*)

**Alan**
Speak up!

**Sue**
(*Clears throat*) I hope not.

**Alan**
Sorry, can we turn, sorry, can we turn the fountain off, please? Sorry. Sorry, Sue. Erm. Thank you. The idea of the fountain was to represent a, a fountain of knowledge, you know, to symbolize the show. Now. Now, Sue.

**Sue**
It looks lovely.

**Alan**
It, it is. Well, it cost two grand. Two grand to do that, yes. *(To camera)* That's, by the way, that's the kind of thing you'll be seeing throughout the series: lots of money spent on expensive items. Now you won the hearts of the British public when last year you trotted off with the World Championship.

**Sue**
Yes.

*Silence*

**Alan**
How did that feel?

**Sue**
Oh. Great.

*Silence*

**Alan**
Re-really?

*Silence*

**Sue**
Really great. *(Laughs nervously)*

**Alan**
Right, right, yeah. Erm and, and, and, and, and was, was the horse, was your horse, Joie de Vivre, was he aware of the excitement?

**Sue**
Oh yes.

*Silence*

**Alan**
Erm. What, what did you, erm, did you give him a treat afterwards?

**Sue**
Yes. *(Laughs)*

**Alan**
What? Did you, did you up and tickle his belly?

*Sue laughs.*

**Alan**
No, actually that's a dangerous area. I'm, er, I'm thinking of, er, that man with the dolphin. Erm. Now. Now, Sue, erm, let's move, move on to the, to the anecdotes. Do, do, do the anecdote. Do it now.

**Sue**
Well, erm, all it was was that, erm, when you transport a horse to an event in a horsebox, erm, you have to do it very carefully and it takes a lot of time and effort and so on.

**Alan**
Yeah.

**Sue**
Erm. The owner of Joie de Vivre, Maxwell Henderson, was driving –

**Alan**
Mmm. Yeah. Just a second. Just get to the bit about the horsebox on the road.

**Sue**
*(Laughs)* Right, right. Well, erm, we were driving up the motorway.

**Alan**
Yeah.

**Sue**
And, er –

**Alan**
She was driving along the motorway –

**Sue**
Sorry?

**Alan**
– with this man in a car. Sorry, I'm doing the story for you. Please –

**Sue**
*(Laughs)* Oh!

**Alan**
Sorry.

**Sue**
Erm. Right, well, we were driving up the motorway and Maxwell decided he needed a drink so we stopped off at some shops in Newbury.

**Alan**
Right. Sorry, Sue, can I just interrupt you? *(Alan presses his finger to his ear)* I've just been told that Roger Moore has just passed Heston Services – and should be with us very soon. Sorry, Sue, carry on.

**Sue**
Erm. *(Laughing)* Oh, I've forgotten where I was. Where was I?

**Alan**
I've absolutely no idea. But that's, that's not working. Abandon that. Go on to the other story.

**Sue**
Oh, I remember, I remember.

**Alan**
All right, go back.

**Sue**
Right, we, erm, we stopped at some shops in Newbury so that Maxwell could get a drink.

**Alan**
Yeah, yeah, don't, don't –

**Sue**
– water or cup of tea or something –

102

**Alan**
Yeah, mmm-hmm, yeah.

**Sue**
– and, and I wanted to buy something to read.

**Alan**
Right, so you bought a book.

**Sue**
So I bought a book and, erm, the point is that it was a very small bookshop …

**Alan**
Mmm, yeah.

**Sue**
– and they were catering for a sort of mass audience –

**Alan**
Yeah. Be quicker.

**Sue**
– so *(laughs)*, right, so I went in and I bought a book –

**Alan**
Yeah.

**Sue**
– and when I was going back out to the horsebox –

**Alan**
That's, that's, that's not quick. She bought a book, she got in the car, and the book was called *Killing Horses*. *(Sue laughs)* And the driver thought she was some, some sort of murderess. *(Sue laughs)* She explained she was just buying the book: it was hilarious.

**Sue**
It was hil—

**Alan**
Really. That's –

**Sue**
It was the only book I could find.

**Alan**

– that's, that's the end, that's the end of the story. That's the end of the story. OK. Now. It says here – it says here, 'Hawaii'. What happened in Hawaii? Exotic location. Give me spice.

**Sue**

I lost my luggage.

**Alan**

Ooh, dear. What, what happened?

**Sue**

Well, it turned up in Brazilia. *(Laughs)*

**Alan**

Oh, disaster! What, what next?

**Sue**

Well, it was fine. I mean, there was nothing missing or anything.

**Alan**

You see, that's no good. That's, that's an incident, you know. It's not an anecdote. You've got down here on your press release, 'Anecdotes'. And that's dishonest, you know. It's no good, it's no good for a chat show, you know. Just, er, just for future reference; otherwise you waste people's time.

**Sue**

Thanks.

**Alan**

Not to worry! We've got a surprise for you – in this, one of the regular features of the series, called 'Up Alan's Sleeve'. Well – well, Sue Lewis, this week I have for you, up my sleeve, a horse! And a jump! Bring on the horse and the jump!

**Sue**

Gosh!

*Music: 'Knowing Me, Knowing You', horse and jump brought on stage.*

**Alan**

It's not your horse. We couldn't get your horse, so it's, it's just a horse.

**Sue**

*(Stroking horse)* Hello, guy.

**Alan**

Now, isn't – isn't he a beauty?

**Sue**

She.

**Alan**

She. *(Looking at the rear of the horse)* Yes, you're absolutely right. Erm, Sue, we've got the horse; we've got the jump. I know I've sprung this on you, but will you rise to the challenge; will you jump the jump?

**Sue**

Oh no, I can't. *(Laughs nervously)*

**Alan**

She doesn't want to do it. Do you want her to jump the jump?

**Audience**

Yes!

**Alan**

Will you jump the jump?

**Sue**

No, I, I really, I really can't. Erm, this is a concrete, this is a concrete floor and it would – I mean, the horse, the horse has very delicate legs and it would damage the horse.

**Alan**

Well, well, well, hold on, can we gaffer-tape some sponges to the horse's hooves?

**Sue**

No *(laughing)* no, that wouldn't work. It would break the horse's legs. It really can't be done. 'Please don't break my legs,' she's saying. *(Laughs)*

**Alan**
Don't do that. All right, get rid of the horse and the jump.

*Horse craps on the studio floor.*

**Alan**
That – that's your fault.

**Sue**
She was nervous.

**Alan**
You really, you really ought to get a dustpan and brush and tidy that up. That could have been spectacular. We could have had a horse jump; now we've got a lump of dung.

**Sue**
I'm sorry.

**Alan**
Well, that's it. I've got, I've got, I've got nothing else to say.

**Sue**
No more questions?

**Alan**
No. Have you got any questions?

**Sue**
Have you ever ridden a horse?

**Alan**
Yes, I have. Yes, I, er, I went ponytrekking, er, when I, when I was a schoolboy in Cornwall.

**Sue**
Gosh.

**Alan**
It's like one of your stories, that, isn't it? *(Sue laughs)*
Ladies and gentlemen, Sue Lewis. Fame! I'm gonna live for ever. *(Sue begins to walk offstage)* Stay there, Sue. Fame! I'm gonna learn how to fly. Of course I'm not. But in … but in a sense, my next guest did.

Two years ago he was presenting the loony breakfast show on Radio Leeds. Now he's topped the ratings as the new host of *This Is Your Life*. He's a trouper; I think he's super; please welcome supertrouper Keith Hunt. Where is he?

*Applause and music: 'Superstar'; Keith Hunt jumps over the back of the sofa and joins Alan and Sue.*

**Alan**
*(Laughing)* Oh, dear. Knowing me, Alan Partridge, knowing you, Keith Hunt, ah-haa.

**Keith**
Ah-haa. Am I right?

**Audience**
You're not wrong.

**Alan**
I don't believe it. You're only on five seconds and you've got a catchphrase on already.

**Keith**
I like to slip it in early, if you know what I mean.

*Alan laughs*

**Keith**
You all right, Sue?

**Sue**
You're not wrong. *(Laughs)*

**Keith**
She's a barrel o' laughs.

**Alan**
Yeah.

**Keith**
Pity it's empty. Am I right?

**Audience**
You're not wrong.

**Alan**
Yeah, yeah.

**Keith**
We're only joking, Sue.

**Alan**
No, you really are not wrong. Erm …
now … Keith. *This Is Your Life*. That show
is a British institution. You've taken it and
you've revolutionized it … because you
now do it as a surprise party from the
celebrity's home. What a brilliantly original
idea. Where did you get it from?

**Keith**
America.

**Alan**
Great. Erm, Sue, Sue, you were on
*This Is Your Life* recently.

**Sue**
Yes.

**Alan**
Erm, was that fun?

**Sue**
It was interesting.

**Alan**
Well, we'll see for ourselves fairly soon,
but it certainly sounds like a lot of fun.

*Alan stares at the monitor.*

**Alan**
Let's see, see the clip. See the clip.

*Film clip begins; opening music:
'This Is Your Life'.*

**Keith**
Shhh. She's coming. Hold your horses; it's
Sue Lewis!

*Sue enters; partygoers in Sue's house cheer.*

**Keith**
Am I right?

**Partygoers**
You're not wrong.

**Keith**
Where's me book?

**Man dressed as a book**
Helloooo.

**Keith**
He's big, he's red, he's a book –

**Keith and man dressed as book**
– he's Big Red Booky!

*Partygoers cheer.*

**Keith**
Hey up, Sue. (*He pulls her violently towards
the camera*) This – is – your – life!

*Music: 'This Is Your Life'; film clip ends
Applause*

**Alan**
(*Laughing*) Oh, dear. Sue, Sue, how, how,
how was that?

**Sue**
Well, it was fun. I mean, I … I felt that –

**Alan**
Rubbish! Crass! Putrefying cack! Drivel!
That's … what Melvyn Bragg said about
your show. Why?

**Keith**
Because he's frightened of me. Oh, yeah. I
deliver four times as many viewers as him
and he knows that if I presented *The South
Bank Show* – which I may do, I quite like art
– then Melvyn Bragg would be stacking
shelves in Tesco's first thing Monday
morning. Am I right?

**Audience**
You're not wrong.

# KNOWING ME, KNOWING YOU

**Alan**
You know, he shouldn't, he shouldn't criticize it because it's a British institution. You couldn't get more British. It's as English as fish and chips.

**Keith**
Bangers and mash.

**Alan**
The Tower of London. Sue, do you want to mention something British?

**Sue**
Erm, Crufts?

**Alan**
Um, but you know, I mean – I would, I would, I would dearly love my show to be a British institution.

**Keith**
Oh well, you've got to change your theme tune then. I mean, Abba? Swedish.

**Alan**
Yeah, yeah. Well, that's a Swedish institution, isn't it? You can't get more Swedish. As Swedish as, er – as Ikea.

**Keith**
Volvo.

**Alan**
Sue, do you want to mention something Swedish?

**Sue**
The vegetable swede.

**Alan**
Yeah! Oh, yeah! The Swedes, the Swedes, er, the Swedish don't have a bad life really, when you think about it. I mean, they get up in the morning, have a bowl of swede, erm, hop in the Volvo, whack on a bit of Abba and zip over to Ikea, you know. I mean, I mean, you know, that's my Sunday. Er, apart from the swede. Now, Keith. I have, er, Kellogg's common sense. Er, now Keith. What's the secret of your success?

**Keith**
I'm an ordinary bloke.

**Alan**
Right. Am I an ordinary bloke?

**Keith**
Dead ordinary.

**Alan**
Good. Good?

**Keith**
It's good. It's good.

**Alan**
Right.

**Keith**
Every Saturday I go to the footie with me kid. I go down the pub with me mates, pint of bitter, game of darts: first thing I do when I fly up to Leeds.

**Alan**
Yeah, I, I, I, I'm the same. I can often be found in Norwich, you know, propping up the bar at the Pheasant Brasserie.

**Keith**
Sunday lunch. Sunday lunch: roast beef, Yorkshire pud, cup of tea. Magic.

**Alan**
I'm the same. Down the Harvester, Sunday Platter, glass of wine. Cheers.

**Keith**
We're ordinary. Ordinary, ordinary, ordinary.

**Alan**
We're ordinary, but – ah, now, the big but – Keith, you do *extra*ordinary things, because I have a local paper from Keith's –

**Keith**
Aye, what's going on here?

**Alan**
– Keith's area here. A local paper, which has a little story here –

**Keith**
Oh, no, no, no –

**Alan**
– yes –

**Keith**
– don't embarrass me –

**Alan**
– no, come on –

**Keith**
– no, no, no –

**Alan**
– a little story about, come on, now, no, no, no –

**Keith**
– I'm not here to talk about meself, no –

**Alan**
– shhhh. Now. This now is a story about Keith. Now I can either read it or you. Do you want to tell the story?

**Keith**
All right, all right. (*Holds up his hands in defeat*)

**Alan**
Right. Listen to this.

**Keith**
The headmaster of the local school where me kid goes, he knocks on me door last week, he says, 'Keith, er, we're having a raffle to raise money for a minibus for the kids. Will you host it?' I said, 'How much does this minibus cost?' He says, 'Eighteen grand.' I said –

**Alan**
Hang on, sorry, Keith, just stop you there. I – I've just been told that Roger Moore is at Chiswick roundabout. Should be with us – should be with us very soon indeed. Stay tuned. Stay tuned. Keith. Sorry, carry on.

**Keith**

He said, 'Eighteen grand.' I said, ''Ere's twenty. Buy the kids a minibus and take 'em for a fun day out at Alton Towers.'

**Alan**

What a nice man.

**Keith**

You've got to put a bit back. And it's tax deductible.

**Alan**

Yeah, well. I'm thinking – I'm thinking along the same lines. I'm thinking of, er, Alan Partridge's Espace for the Elderly.

**Keith**

Go for it.

**Alan**

Yeah, I will. Now, Keith, you like surprises. You – by the way, thanks for bringing that paper in. *(Hands the paper back to Keith, who looks embarrassed)* Thanks for that – and you – well done. And you like surprises. And we have now got a surprise for *you*, because it's time once again to go Up Alan's Sleeve. Earlier on I had a horse up my sleeve and a jump for Sue Lewis. Well, people are asking, Alan, what have you got up your other sleeve? Well, it's a child. I've got a child up my sleeve.

**Keith**

Aye, what's going on?

**Alan**

And, Keith, it's a child you know very well, because you produced him. He's here tonight, your very own son, Sam Hunt!

**Keith**

I don't believe it.

*Applause; Sam enters on steps at back of stage.*

**Alan**

Keith, Keith, Keith.

**Keith**

All right, Sam?

**Alan**

All right, Sam. Keith, Sam is, Sam is your only son from your marriage which was dissolved some years ago. Now because – because of access and custody laws you're only allowed to see him once a fortnight, so you're not allowed contact with him tonight, but I can speak to him. So you wait here while I go and talk to – Sam Hunt.

*Applause; Alan joins Sam.*

**Alan**

Hello. You little terror.

**Keith**

All right, Sam. It's Dad!

**Alan**

Right. Now. I believe, Keith, you've got something very special to say to Sam today. It's a very special day.

**Keith**

Yeah, looking forward to next weekend, Sam. We'll have a fun day out. Take you to the footie.

**Alan**

No, isn't there something else you want to say to him?

**Keith**

You see your dad on the telly last week?

**Alan**

No. Sam, do you want to tell your daddy?

**Sam**

It's my birthday.

**Alan**

It's your son's birthday!

**Keith**

Yes – yes, happy birthday, Sam.

**Alan**
What have you got for him?

**Keith**
Give him this, give him this. Quick, give him this.

*Keith moves towards Alan and Sam.*

**Alan**
No, Keith, just stay there. You know the law.

*Alan takes a banknote from Keith and gives it to Sam.*

**Alan**
There you go. Your daddy's got you – got you ten pounds. Isn't that nice? But don't despair, because we've got you a present. We've got you an Alan Partridge tie and blazer-badge combination pack. There you go. There you go. You take that. And, not only that, we've got him an all-expenses-paid trip to Disneyland with your mummy and her partner this weekend.

**Keith**
Oh, no, no, no. Oh no! No, I've got custody this weekend. She knows that.

**Alan**
No, no, no. It's been arranged.

**Keith**
No, I've got custody. She knows it.

**Alan**
Let's ask Sam. Where are you going this weekend?

**Sam**
Disneyland.

**Alan**
Disneyland! Of course you are, you little terror. That is … ladies and gentlemen, Sam Hunt. That way. That way! That way!

*Music: 'Happy Birthday To You'; Sam leaves stage and Alan returns to sofa.*

**Alan**
Great. Oh, marvellous, erm. Funny feeling that backfired a bit.

**Keith**
Well, you know, you should have checked it out with me first, Al.

**Alan**
I'm sorry. I didn't realize you were going to forget your only son's birthday.

**Keith**
Leave it.

**Alan**
Oh dear. I think I've, I think I've blown my chances of being on *This Is Your Life*.

**Keith**
Oh no, no, no. We couldn't have you on the show.

**Alan**
Why?

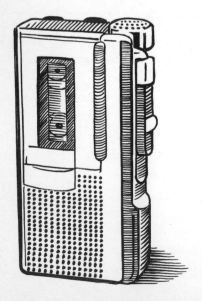

**Keith**
We only have celebrities.

*Audience hisses.*

**Alan**
Sue, you got any children?

**Sue**
No, I haven't.

**Alan**
I have, yeah. Er, Fernando – he's at Cambridge. And, er, and Denise. Yes, er, Denise's birthday is on the 27 May and, er, Fernando's is on the 6 June, so quite close together. We usually have a big family bash. All the family together. Solid as a rock. Do, er, do horses have birthdays?

**Sue**
Yes, they do.

**Alan**
Do you get them presents?

**Sue**
Sometimes.

**Alan**
Really? Even horses? Even – even horses.

**Sue**
He looks like a lovely boy, Sam.

**Keith**
Yeah, super lad.

**Sue**
How old is he?

**Keith**
Five.

**Alan**
Six. Six today. Am I right? I'm not wrong.

**Keith**
You do realize you're the only person in the country who still thinks Roger Moore's gonna turn up.

**Alan**
He'll be here.

**Keith**
Where is he now?

**Alan**
Chiswick roundabout.

**Keith**
Chiswick roundabout to TV Centre
in ten minutes?

**Alan**
Yes.

**Keith**
How's he getting here? Magic carpet?

**Alan**
If need be, yes. Ladies and gentlemen,
Keith Hunt.

*Applause*

**Alan**
(*Looking over his shoulder*) Now. Could, er –
could someone clear that shit away, please?
It's just, I, I, I, I can see it's in, it's in my
picture. I don't – you know, people may
associate it with me. I don't want that. Time
now for my next guests. If music be the
food of love, play on. That's what William
Shakespeare said. I'm not William
Shakespeare, but I say pretty much the
same thing. If music be the food of love,
let's eat it. Here with, here with her new
single, 'Monday Morning' – I know the
feeling – please welcome Shona McGough.

**Shona**
(*Dressed in floor-length dress; sings*)
Monday morning at a quarter to eight
She gives her husband his cornflakes
He mustn't be late.
She vacuums the carpets
Makes everything clean
(*background singers: 'Everything clean'*)
What would she do without Mr Sheen?

She takes the shotgun
From under the stairs
And stands in the hallway
Screaming her prAAYYERS!
*Shona removes blonde wig and dress to reveal
cropped hair, bra top, short skirt and fishnets;
starts writhing on microphone stand.*
The gasman comes
To read the meter
He writes down the reading,
Scratching his head.
It's quarter to four
And now the gasman's ... dead!

**Band**
(*Sing*) Blood bath! Blood bath!

**Shona**
(*Sings*) The postman arrives
She says, 'Hello, Ray.'
And smiles politely
As she BLOWS HIM AWAY!

**Band**
(*Sing*) Blood bath! Blood bath!

*Alan looks dismayed.*

**Shona**
(*Sings*) She's stalking the streets,
Her brain's on fire.
She guns down twenty in Vision Hire.

**Band**
(*Sing*) Blood bath! Blood bath!

**Shona**
(*Sings*) Her hubby comes home
And he gives her a kiss
She puts the gun in his mouth
And says,

**Band**
(*Sing*) 'SUCK ON THIS!'
Blood bath! Blood bath!

**Shona**
(*Sings*) Blooooood! Blooooood! Blooooood!

**Band**

*(Sing)* Blood bath! Blood bath! Blood bath!

**Shona**

*(Sings)* AHHHHH! *(She falls to the floor)*
Suck on this, sucker.

*Applause; Alan joins band on stage.*

**Alan**

No, no, no! No. No. No. No. Ladies – ladies
and gentlemen – ladies and gentlemen, I,
I must apologize. I had no idea of the full
content of that song. Let me – let me
announce this now. If any young people are
watching, let me say this: whilst it may be
all well and good for a rock band to sing
about such things, murder – whether it be
domestic or streetbound genocide – is
illegal in this country, right? What was that?

**Shona**

It was a song.

**Alan**

Well, I mean, I don't understand. You
started off so well. You whipped the skirt
off. Very like Buck's Fizz, Eurovision, that
was good. And then … and then, sorry,
do you mind standing round here as you
were told?

*A band member wanders off to sit with
Keith and Sue on sofa.*

**Alan**

Please – come back. Erm. Well. Shona
McGough's single is in the shops, if you
want to buy that. Annoy your neighbours.
Um, yes, right, sorry, I've just been told
Roger Moore – Roger Moore is at Chiswick
roundabout, so he's – so he's, so what's he
still doing there? He shouldn't be there.

*Rest of the band sit on sofa; Shona sits on
Alan's chair.*

**Alan**

I'll fill in now with a couple of minutes' chat with Shona – Shona McGough.

*Alan joins band, Keith and Sue*

**Alan**

She's beaten me to it. Oh dear. Erm. I need a – I need a chair unfortunately.

*Shona sticks her foot between Alan's legs*

**Alan**

Erm, don't do that. Don't do that. Don't do that. Please. Sue. Sue Lewis. Sorry, I need your chair. Come on. Sorry, just sit round there. Sorry.

*Sue stands at back of sofa. Alan squeezes himself between Keith and the band members. A female band member puts her legs across Alan's lap.*

**Alan**

Well, if you've just tuned in, you're watching *Knowing Me, Knowing You With Alan Partridge*. Erm, it's not quite what we planned. Erm, it's a bit crazy, but what the heck. I mean, say what you like, but – you can't say it's not interesting. Please, please don't say that.

*Female band member sticks finger in Alan's ear and wipes it on her arm.*

**Alan**

Erm. Don't do that. Get off! Stop it! Please. Erm, ah, this is interesting: a lady drummer. Erm. Very good. Close your eyes, could have been a man. Very good.

**Drummer**

Thanks a lot.

**Female band member**

I really fancy you, you know.

**Alan**

What?

**Female band member**

I think you're really sexy.

**Alan**

Really?!

**Female band member**

No.

**Alan**

Erm, Shona, do you want to put those pears back, please?

**Shona**

No.

*Shona eats a pear and throws some pears to other band members.*

**Alan**

I really would rather you didn't – you didn't mess with those pears. Please. Really, honestly, I really would rather you didn't – oh, oh, what the heck! Rock and roll! Let's all have a pear! All right, no, let me ask you this. Right. Question I've always wanted to ask a Scottish woman, right: what has a Scotsman got under his kilt?

**Shona**

His penis.

**Alan**

Oh, for God's sake. I know – I know exactly what you're thinking. You all think, right, that I'm a big square. Let me tell you something. I've seen what you – I've seen it all before. I've inhaled hashish. *(Two of the band members put two fingers up behind Alan's head)* I've – I've worn tall shoes. I had an afro haircut. I went on all-weekend binges in Prestatyn to see Wings, right? I'll tell you something else: Chris de Burgh, Mike Oldfield, Jean-Michel Jarre and the Eagles could eat you lot for breakfast. *(Turns to Keith)* You're quiet.

**Keith**

Just enjoying the show, mate.

**Alan**

Erm, let's – let's move on to the next section of the show, which is entitled 'An Audience with Roger Moore'. And to help me with that, I'm going to invite Shona, Sue and Keith – not the band – to join me in the Roger Moore room for an audience with Roger Moore!

*Music; Alan, Shona, Sue and Keith move to another set.*

**Alan**

Here we are in the Roger Moore room, er, for an audience with Roger Moore. The idea was basically, erm, that Roger could come in here and sit where, er, Sue's sitting and just chat about all these things. We're surrounded by memorabilia from Roger's glittering career in films and television. There's a little James Bond car there. See, the little man flies out; that's nice. Erm. There's a golden gun there. That's from *The Man With the Golden Gun*. Erm. There's a gold, a gold ingot there. That's from the film *Gold*, in which he co-starred with Susannah York. Erm. There's a *Saint* annual there. I was going to get Roger to read aloud from that with, er – you know, his lovely warm brown voice.

**Keith**

*(Pointing at the wall)* Al, erm, jog me memory. In which of Roger's films does it feature three ducks on the wall?

**Alan**

Ah. They are not ducks. They are wild geese from – from, from the film *The Wild Geese*, with Roger Moore playing the cigar-chomping mercenary.

**Sue**

Oh yes.

**Alan**

Sorry?

**Sue**

Oh yes.

**Alan**

Oh yes. Yes. Right. Right, now, this, this was the, er, the show opening. This should have been marvellous. Whoo, there we go: curtains, curtains.

*Music; curtains rise to show large photograph of Roger Moore as James Bond.*

**Alan**

Roger Moore! Roger Moore, the quintessential English gentleman.

**Keith**

Who's not here.

**Alan**

Erm, now, I was gonna start, I was gonna start – Roger would have loved this – I was gonna introduce myself by doing this. This is fantastic. Ah-haa, Mr Bond.

*Alan turns round in his chair, stroking a stuffed cat.*

**Alan**

I've been expecting you. You know, which I had, you know. Would have been fantastic.

**Sue**

What's that? *(Pointing to an object on the table)*

**Alan**

That's, that's a nipple. Now –

**Sue**

What?

**Alan**

That's a nipple. It's a, it's a, from *The Man With the Golden Gun*. It's a third nipple. The Scaramanga had, had three nipples. That's a gold finger.

**Shona**

Sean Connery was *Goldfinger*.

**Alan**
Well done. That was a trick object. Well done.

**Shona**
Sean Connery was the better Bond anyway.

**Alan**
Well, you know, interesting you take that position, you know, the Scottish position. I mean, in the whole, you know, in the whole Roger versus Sean debate that's been raging for the last twenty years, I, I – I have to say I'm firmly in the Roger camp, you know. I believe no one could, sort of, wear a safari suit with the same degree of casuality.

**Keith**
It's a complete shambles. You're putting a brave face on it, but he's not here. You know, you tell the viewers –

**Alan**
Sorry, Keith. Keith Hunt –

**Keith**
– he's not –

**Alan**
– let me stop you – let me stop you in your tracks there, Keith Hunt. You can eat your hat now because, ladies and gentlemen, I can confirm Roger Moore is on the show. We're having him on the show right now –

**Keith**
Where is he?

**Alan**
– live, live by telephone link-up from – from the car on a mobile phone. Hello, Roger. Hello, Roger.

**Roger**
Hello, Alan.

**Alan**
Oh, joy! Oh, Roger Moore. Oh, erm, knowing me, Alan Partridge, knowing you, Roger Moore, ah-haa.

*Phone crackles.*

**Alan**
Roger? No? All right, listen, I'm gonna cut straight to a key question, Rog, we don't have much time. Erm, a hypothetical fist fight takes place between Simon Templar, the Saint, and Roger Moore, James Bond 007. Who wins?

*Phone crackles.*

**Alan**
Any thoughts on that, Roger?

*Phone crackles.*

**Alan**
Roger? – Roger? – Roger! – ROGER!

**Keith**
Does the word 'titanic' mean anything to you?

**Alan**
Oh yeah. People go on about titanic, titanic. Let me tell you something about the *Titanic*. People forget – people forget that on the *Titanic*'s maiden voyage there were over a thousand miles of uneventful, very pleasurable cruising before it hit the iceberg. Anyway, we had him on the show. He was on the show.

**Keith**
That doesn't count. Face it, mate. He's Roger the Dodger. Am I right?

**Audience**
You're not wrong.

**Alan**
All right, point taken. Point taken. But, but let's, no, we can still rescue it. Let's turn the situation around. Let's call this section of the show 'Right to Reply with Alan Partridge'. If you've got any criticisms, let me hear them. I can deal with them.

# KNOWING ME, KNOWING YOU

**Keith**
Criticisms?

**Alan**
Yeah.

**Keith**
A horse takes a dump on your show. No manners, but what a critic, you know. You get a horse with a jump on; she won't jump it.

**Sue**
No, it wasn't that I wouldn't jump it; I really couldn't do it.

**Keith**
You, you were right not to, of course –

**Sue**
Because it would have been totally dangerous and inappropriate –

**Shona**
You get a band on. You've never heard of us. You slag us off the minute we come on.

**Keith**
Absolutely right.

**Shona**
We don't get any fold back. We're vegetarians – we get ham sandwiches. It's a shambles.

**Keith**
You get me own kid on. That is well out of order.

**Sue**
Yes, yes.

**Keith**
You just don't do that. When the Director-General of the BBC –

**Alan**
(*Gestures with his middle finger*) Up yours. Up yours!

**Sue**
You can't say that.

**Alan**
Kiss my arse!
And on that bombshell, it's time for me to say, knowing me, Alan Partridge, knowing you, Scotch lady – woman – knowing you, the Hunt, and knowing you, Mrs Mouse. And I – I've just been told Roger Moore has just checked into Claridges, where he's ordered room service. Ah-haa!

*Music: 'Knowing Me, Knowing You'*

# KNOWING ME KNOWING YOU

*Music: 'Knowing Me, Knowing You'*

**Alan**
Ah-haa!

*Alan does a little run onstage and mimes shooting and reloading a rifle.*
*Applause*

**Alan**
Welcome. Welcome to – shh – welcome to *Knowing Me, Knowing You* with me, Alan Partridge. It's a chat show, Jim, but not as we know it.

*Drum roll*

**Alan**
Well, well, it's official. This show is a smash-hit sensation. A corking copper-bottomed hit. Those aren't my words. They are the words of Mike Taylor from *TV Quick*. Of course, of course there have been one or two dissenting voices. The clever-clog papers – *Independent, Telegraph, Guardian, Observer, Mail on Sunday* – they've been a bit sniffy. One review in particular caught my eye: Philip Parsons in *The Times* called this show 'moribund'. Well, I looked up 'moribund' in my dictionary and it said 'moribund: adjective' meaning 'about to die or dying'. I ask you, is this show about to die?

117

**Audience**
NO!

**Alan**
Thank you. So, Mr Philip Parsons from *behind* the times –

*Drum roll*

**Alan**
– that proves that you are wrong. The show is very much alive. And live. Because tonight I will be bringing you another TV chat show first, as I, Alan Partridge, will allow myself to be strapped to a spinning wheel of death and have knives thrown at me. *(Audience: ooooooh!)* Is that moribund? No.

**Audience**
No.

**Alan**
No, you don't shout that. So – so please welcome my unmoribund merry band, my house band, Glen Ponder and Debonair!

*Applause*

**Alan**
Knowing me, Alan Partridge, knowing you, Glen Ponder, ah-haa.

**Glen**
Ah-haa.

**Alan**
Knowing me, Alan Partridge, knowing you, Debonair, ah-haa.

**Debonair**
*(In unison)* Ah-haa.

**Alan**
Glen, I understand you're, you're looking for a new house at the moment.

**Glen**
Yeah, that's right, Alan.

**Alan**
I bought a house this week in Mayfair for five hundred pounds.

**Glen**
Really, Alan?

**Alan**
Yes, er, I was playing Monopoly.

*Drum roll*

**Alan**
Erm. But, er, seriously Glen, you are, you are looking for somewhere, aren't you?

**Glen**
Yeah.

**Alan**
Where, whereabouts are you looking?

**Glen**
Chiswick area.

**Alan**
Yeah, Chiswick's nice. Nice. Glen Ponder and Debonair!

*Music: 'Knowing Me, Knowing You' and applause*

**Alan**
Was that chat moribund? I don't think so. So – now. My first guest is intelligent, witty, a woman of the world with a figure that would stop the traffic dead both ways on the M1 if she were to wiggle across the footbridge at Toddington Service Station. She's a quality guest from top to bottom and back up again. Please welcome the new agony aunt from *Playboy* magazine – stay tuned – the very lovely Daniella Forest!

*Music: 'Gimme, Gimme, Gimme'*

**Alan**

Ah. Isn't she, isn't she, isn't she lovely? Ay? Yes. Phuit-phew. Isn't she lovely? Ah. Erm, erm, I nearly forgot – knowing me, Alan Partridge, knowing you, Daniella Forest, ah-haa.

**Daniella**

Ah-*haa*.

**Alan**

Oooh. Oooh. Well, that's the sexiest 'ah' I think I've ever had. Oh, actually I just forgot, erm – I normally kiss my guests when they first come on. It's just a thing I do. Erm, not the men. I give them a firm handshake, but, erm, can we do that – just do the kiss quickly?

**Daniella**

Oh, sure. Where do you want to kiss me, Alan? Peachy cheek or little round mouth?

**Alan**

Little round mouth.

**Daniella**

Come on then.

**Alan**

Right.

**Daniella**

You've got to kneel down.

**Alan**

Yes.

**Daniella**

Right down.

*Alan and Daniella kiss.*

**Alan**

Mmm.

**Daniella**

Pop back on your seat. Good boy.

**Alan**

Yes, yes. Erm – right – erm, now. Dan-Daniella Forest, you are *Playboy*'s agony aunt, and you've also just published your autobiography.

**Daniella**

*Luck Be a Lady*.

**Alan**

*Luck Be a Lady*. There it is. That's the book. There we go. It's, er, it's your autobiography. It's published by Jones – never heard of them. Erm, what, what comes across very strongly is your understanding of male psychology.

**Daniella**

Well, I think I understand men because I adore them.

**Alan**

Mmmm. *(Laughs)* And what as a woman do you look for in a man?

**Daniella**

Power is attractive.

**Alan**

Mmm.

**Daniella**

Sensitivity.

**Alan**

Mmm.

**Daniella**

Sense of humour.

*Alan smiles.*

**Daniella**

I like a man who knows who he is.

**Alan**

I'm Alan Partridge, carry on.

**Daniella**

You know, I think the most important thing that I look for in a man is a fit young body like a Greek god.

**Alan**

*(Looking disappointed)* Right. Erm, now you also help people with their sexual problems.

**Daniella**

*(Whispering)* I do.

**Alan**

Let me give you a hypothetical problem. Erm – there's, there's a couple, right? They've been married fifteen, sixteen years, maybe more. And they've never slept, neither of them have ever slept with anyone else. Well, she, she has. She's – on, on one occasion she – she, um, said it was a mistake. It was her PE teacher at the local primary school. Erm, let's say. He, on the other hand, has been faithful. Solid as a rock, right? He's been tempted. Believe me, he's had offers, but – but he, he's never strayed.

**Daniella**

And he's frustrated?

**Alan**

Yes, deeply, deeply. But that's, that's only part of the problem. The real problem is that their sex life is – well, for want of a better word – moribund.

**Daniella**

People need to explore their sex lives if they're not working, you know. If it's not working in the bedroom, bring it into the living room, or the kitchen.

**Alan**

Yeah, well, they tried that but the dog just wandered in. It was very off-putting.

**Daniella**

You see, some people, they find it very sexy to be watched.

**Alan**

Not by their dog, I mean – Montgomery was frightened. He was just barking.

**Daniella**

Who's Montgomery?

**Alan**

*(Looking confused)*

*(Pause)* The man who masterminded the Battle of El Alamein. And the name of this hypothetical dog.

**Daniella**

Have you got a dog, Alan?

**Alan**

Yes.

**Daniella**

And what's his name?

**Alan**

*(Pause)* Rommel.

**Daniella**

Well, perhaps you should get Rommel involved in your sex life.

**Alan**

No, no, he's, he's too old. He's blind in one eye; he can't control his bladder.

**Daniella**

No, no. You're taking me too literally. Once again, here is a man shying away from discussing sex. When I was a man I used to have the same problem, but as a woman I find that I am liberated.

**Alan**

Well, I'm very pleased for you. Now – hang on a minute. What, who, who was a man?

**Daniella**

When I was a man.

**Alan**

*(Laughs)* What are you talking about?

**Daniella**
Well, you have read my book?

**Alan**
Yeah, yes. No, no, I never read the books. Who was a man?

**Daniella**
Who did you think Daniel was – in the photographs?

**Alan**
I, I thought that was your twin brother.

**Daniella**
I was Daniel. I used to be a man. I can't believe you didn't know.

**Alan**
I kissed you!

**Daniella**
Why did you invite me on your show?

**Alan**
I thought you were sexy. I don't now. You're a bloke. I've a good mind to knock your block off.

**Daniella**
I'm a woman. I have breasts.

**Alan**
Oh, God. You should be in a circus.

**Daniella**
Well, you'd be in the front row.

*Daniella walks off.*

**Alan**
Yeah, there she goes. There *he* goes, I should say.

*Daniella walks back on.*

**Alan**
What do you want? What – no, no, no! No!

*Daniella forces Alan to kiss her.*

**Daniella**
Ah-haa!

*Daniella leaves the stage.*

**Alan**
On your way. I knew there was something dodgy about you. Your hands are a giveaway. You've got great big flapping hands like a bloke. You could be a goalkeeper. Glen, did you know it was a man?

**Glen**
Yeah.

**Alan**
Debonair, did you know it was a man?

**Debonair**
*(In unison)* Yeah.

**Alan**
Yeah, yeah, everyone knew apart from old muggins Partridge. Ladies and gentlemen, Dan Forest. Dan 'the man' Forest.

*Applause*

**Alan**
It's, er, it's time now for a new regular feature of the series called 'Knowing Me, Alan Partridge, Knowing You, Another Alan Partridge' in which I meet an ordinary member of the public who shares my name and is therefore entitled to membership of that exclusive club, Club Alan Partridge. This week's other Alan Partridge works on a Sealink ferry. So, please welcome Petty Officer Alan Partridge!

*Music and applause; Petty Officer Alan Partridge joins Alan.*

**Alan**
Knowing me, Alan Partridge, knowing you, Petty Officer Partridge, ah-haa.

**Petty Officer Partridge**
Ah-haa.

# KNOWING ME, KNOWING YOU

**Alan**
Now, Alan, you work on the Sealink ferry from Liverpool to Dublin and, er – on, on – I imagine that that's the kind of job where there's an awful lot of camaraderie between the, er, between the – is that, is that the case? *(Laughs)* What do you – what do you keep doing that with your face for?

**Petty Officer Partridge**
Oh, it's a tic. I've got a facial tic.

**Alan**
I'm sorry. I had absolutely no idea.

**Petty Officer Partridge**
No. No, it's all right, Alan. I've had it since I was a kid, yeah.

**Alan**
Yeah, right, OK. Erm, fine, erm, now, Alan, Alan Partridge, I imagine your workmates tease you and josh with you, is that the case?

**Petty Officer Partridge**
Yeah, yeah. They call me tick-tock.

**Alan**
Why's that?

**Petty Officer Partridge**
Because of me tic.

**Alan**
No! God, no, no! I mean, do they tease you because your name's Alan Partridge?

**Petty Officer Partridge**
Oh no, no.

**Alan**
Right. I don't want to dwell on the tic. It doesn't bother me. What you choose to do with your face is, is, is your choice. Erm, it's fine, I like it, it suits you. It's good. There it is again. Erm, right, OK, erm, well, I want to present you with this now. It's the Alan Partridge tie and bla— oh, that was a big one – Alan Partridge tie and blazer-badge combination pack. There, there we go. You, you take that there.

**Petty Officer Partridge**
Thank you.

**Alan**
All right.

**Petty Officer Partridge**
Er, ay, I'll put the tie on if I can keep my head still, ay?

**Alan**
(*Laughs exaggeratedly*) What a marvellous sense of humour. What a – what a, a, a triumph for the human spirit. Ladies and gentlemen – Alan Partridge! Marvellous, yeah. Go on, go, go, go. Right, right.

*Petty Officer Partridge goes to walk off; applause.*

**Petty Officer Partridge**
(*At the stage edge*) Any chance of an aut –

**Alan**
Yeah, go, go! Last night I met a man who quite literally changed my life. He made me think, laugh and cry in wonderment. I, along with many others, witnessed his mystical powers last night at the London Palladium. Please welcome magician-hypnotist Tony Le Mesmer!

*Applause; Tony Le Mesmer enters stage in a cloud of dry ice.*

**Voiceover**
Ladies and gentlemen, enter the mysterious domain of Tony Le Mesmer. Behold the cage of Katmandu.

*Tony passes a silk handkerchief through the cage to his assistant at other side while moving his arms around theatrically.*

**Voiceover**
The void of solitude. The dance of Diabolus.

*Tony dances.*

**Voiceover**
The shroud.

*Tony and two assistants cover cage with black cloth.*

**Voiceover**
The horses turn upon their axes.

*Tony and assistants rotate cage on its wheels.*

**Voiceover**
The summoning of the spirits of Telamachus.

*Assistants pull back black cloth to reveal Tina, scantily clad, inside cage; Tony releases Tina; applause.*

**Alan**
Marvellous. Marvellous. Tony, how did you do that?

**Tony**
Simple, Alan: the power of the paranormal.

**Alan**
Right. It's not a lever or anything?

**Tony**
No.

**Alan**
Well, you tell us more about that now. Tina, I'll see you later for the wheel of death, erm, off you go.

*Tina leaves the stage; Alan looks her up and down and watches her leave.*

**Alan**
Very nice. Now that *is* a woman. OK, Tony. Tony Le Mesmer!

*Music and applause*

**Alan**
Knowing me, Alan Partridge, knowing you, Tony Le Mesmer, ah-haa.

**Tony**
Ah-haa.

**Alan**

Buddha. The Dalai Lama. Nostradamus. That man the Beatles went to see. Yu-Yuri Geller and now Tony Le Mesmer. What is it about you lot that sets you apart from mere mortal men like me, Alan Partridge?

**Tony**

We are all shaman on a spiritual quest, and we travel on this journey using the energy of the life force.

**Alan**

Right, now, this, this life force can take many forms presumably, be it transcendental meditation, bending spoons or producing a lady in a cage.

**Tony**

That's exactly right, Alan. What, what we all do, we are all channellers. We channel energy from within to without.

**Alan**

Right, now, I'm gonna try and pin you down here. Can, can you be more specific?

**Tony**

I'm a man who harnesses the harmony that is within us all.

**Alan**

Mmm, now that's, that's more vague. I want you to be more specific.

**Tony**

Let me put it like this, Alan. We have within us a consciousness, which is only partially realized. I want us to realize it fully to exploit all the hidden recesses that are within us.

**Alan**

(Looking confused) Right, now – I think, I think I know what you mean. Are you saying that if I, Alan Partridge, were to harness the harmony or spirits within me, and therefore – and, and then the beings

around me, and somehow channel that energy up, up some tubular conduit of – consciousness into – a cloud? Of – I'm sorry, I've absolutely no idea what I'm talking about. I'm, I'm really lost. Now, now, last night at the London Palladium, erm, you did a fantastic show. The highlight for me was when you hypnotized twenty people and got them to simulate sex to 'Heigh-Ho Silver Lining'.
It – it was great.

**Tony**

That's really an example of how I get people to realize their inner potential, Alan.

**Alan**

Yeah, there was a marvellous bit where you had two men in their underpants barking like dogs. Glorious.

**Tony**

It's their subconscious desire that is coming to the fore. That, that's why I'm interested in the whole world of dreams.

**Alan**

Ah, right, now, now you're being interesting because – because, because I, I often have a, I have a recurring dream in which I am an owl.

**Tony**

Erm, when you are an owl, how do you feel different?

**Alan**

Smaller. More agile. Able to fly.

**Tony**

Able to fly. Well, perhaps that means you want more freedom. And what else can you do as an owl?

**Alan**

Now, I can rotate my head 360 degrees, which, you know, is a real boon when you're driving because it eliminates the blind spot.

**Tony**

OK, OK, anything else you can do as
an owl?

**Alan**

Yes. I can emit pellets.

**Tony**

I can't help you there. Sorry, Alan.

**Alan**

No? No? Oh well. If, er, if anyone can shed
some light on that, why I, Alan Partridge,
might want to emit pellets as an owl, drop
us a line to the usual address and, er, don't
forget to mark your envelope with the word
'pellets'. We're gonna have a bit of fun
now, because, er, Tony, you are going to
hypnotize me.

**Tony**

That's right, Alan, yes.

**Alan**

OK, well, this may take, er, it may take a
few minutes, so don't worry if it –

**Tony**

Five, four –

**Alan**

– takes some time –

**Tony**

– three, two, one. Ladies and gentlemen,
Alan Partridge is now totally hypnotized.
Totally in my control. Is that not so, Alan?

**Alan**

Yes.

**Tony**

Let's just put that to the test, shall we? Alan,
when I say the word 'owl', I want you to be
that owl you mentioned a moment ago,
emitting a pellet and feeling very happy
with yourself. Owl.

**Alan**

Whoo.

*Alan grimaces twice, then smiles.*

**Alan**

Whoo.

**Tony**

Excellent. Now, now, whenever you hear
the word 'ah-haa' I want you to be a little
scary monster. Ah-haa.

**Alan**

Grrr.

**Tony**

Very good. Stop. Now, Alan, if you
could make love to any woman in the
world, apart from your good lady wife,
who would that be?

**Alan**

Ursula Andress.

**Tony**

Ursula Andress. OK, when I click my
fingers I want you to see me as Ursula
Andress.

*Tony clicks his fingers.*

**Alan**

Ursula, I've always wanted to meet you.
I can't believe it's you. I like the bikini:
very nice. I love all your films. I've got all
of them, from *Dr No* right through to all
the others.

**Tony**

Enough of this, Alan. Is there somewhere
we can go where we can make mad
passionate love?

**Alan**

Oh good. Erm, er, yes, the Moathouse
Hotel in High Wycombe. Erm, erm, they,
they know me there. They're very discreet.
Erm, you'll love it: it's got a twenty-four-
hour carvery.

**Tony**
Stop. Alan, when I click my fingers again we will be in your car on the way to High Wycombe.

**Alan**
It'll take about fifteen, twenty minutes, that's all.

**Tony**
Can we just pull over now and make love in a lay-by? Please, Alan.

**Alan**
Look, I, I, I can't stop on the motorway. That's the hard shoulder: it's illegal.

**Tony**
But Alan, I'm, I'm begging you – please.

**Alan**
Ursula, it's an offence to stop on the hard shoulder unless there's a malfunction with the car.

**Tony**
Look, Alan, I'm taking my top off – please.

**Alan**
Look, no – if I get caught in flagrante whilst violating the Highway Code, my wife will find out, I'll get three points on my licence, my insurance premium could go up by 30 per cent. That's not going to happen. Now put your top on and get out! Yeah, go, go! Get out!

**Tony**
Wake up.

**Alan**
Well, as I say, it'll take a few seconds before I'm totally, totally hypno –

**Tony**
It's all over, Alan.

**Alan**
You've, you've hypnotized me?

**Tony**
Yes. All finished.

**Alan**
Well, I hope you didn't make me look too foolish.

**Tony**
No. Of course I didn't, Alan.

**Alan**
Well, um, Tony, we'll see you later for the wheel of death. It simply remains for me to say, thank you very much, Tony Le Mesmer!

*Applause; Tony Le Mesmer leaves the stage.*

**Alan**
Now. Hollywood is much, much more than nine big letters on a hill. It's – it's a sexy, dangerous place, a hustling, wheeling-dealing kind of town where money talks and nonsense walks. I've never been there, but my next guests have, because they are a British married couple of actors who live and work in Tinseltown Stateside. I want to get to know them, I do, I do, I do, I do, I do, I do. Please welcome Gary Barker and Tanya Beaumont!

*Applause and music: 'I do, I do, I do, I do, I do'*

**Alan**
Ah. Knowing me, Alan Partridge, knowing you, Tanya Beaumont, ah-haa. Grrr.

**Tanya**
Ah-haa.

**Alan**
Grrr. And knowing me, Alan Partridge, knowing you, Gary Barker, ah-haa. Grrr.

**Gary**
*(Stares at Alan for a couple of seconds)*
Ah-haa.

### Alan

Grrr. Now – unusually, you requested to come on to my show, erm, and fortunately the scheduled guest, Ian McShane, TV's Lovejoy, erm, had to pull out at the last minute due to an emergency. He's had to fly to Spain to do a coffee advert. Now – you've asked to come on to make a public statement. This is your platform. Please be my guests.

### Tanya

Well, erm, as you know, Alan, there's been a lot of speculation in the press about the state of our marriage. *(She takes Gary's hand)*

### Alan

Well, I know, I mean I've had that kind of bad treatment in the press myself. Do you know Philip Parsons on *The Times*? He, he described the show as moribund. You know, I mean, and Philip Parsons, if you're watching, in five minutes' time I will be strapped to a wheel of death and you will have a plate with some words on it and a knife and fork. Sorry, Tanya.

### Tanya

Well, we just wanted really to –

**Alan**
Well, what I'm trying to say is you're gonna eat your words. Sorry. Sorry, Tanya.

**Tanya**
We really just want to say to the tabloid press, look, you know, we're very much married. Erm, there's a lot of real news out there. There's poverty; there's homelessness. Please, you know, report that. Leave us alone. We're just ordinary people who happen to make movies.

**Alan**
Lovely, lovely. Erm, Gary, do you want to add anything?

**Gary**
No, erm, yeah.

**Alan**
Look, are you all right? No, I'm just wondering, I'm just wondering about the, er, the glasses. You've not got a stye or anything?

**Gary**
No.

**Alan**
Erm, Tanya. Now, sorry, is he wearing those to look cool?

**Tanya**
Yes, he is.

**Alan**
I see. Right. Er, Gary, like the glasses – very cool. Where'd you get them?

**Gary**
Auction. They were James Dean's shades. He died in them.

**Alan**
Really? They look quite small. No wonder he lost control of the car. No? No. Now – you've both just flown in from Hollywood. What's it like to be back in good old London?

**Tanya**
Oh, it's, it's such a relief to be back here amongst ordinary people, you know.

**Alan**
Where are you staying?

**Tanya**
The Savoy.

**Alan**
Marvellous. Who's, er, who's paying?

**Gary**
You are.

**Alan**
Really? We – *(to crew)* is that true? Are we paying? Yes – yes, we are. Well, enjoy yourselves. Just easy on the room service. Chicken in a basket – that's your lot. No, no, seriously, have a drink, have a drink. Just don't go mad, that's all. Some people they empty the minibar into a carrier bag: that's not on. I tell you something: we had Roger Moore on the show the other week and, between you and me, if it wasn't nailed to the floor it was going back to Switzerland. He even took a towel, you know. Roger Moore is a towel thief.

**Tanya**
He's my godfather.

**Alan**
Really? He's a lovely man, a lovely man. Erm, Gary – now, but he is a towel thief. Gary, erm, you, you are known as the wild man of Hollywood. Some of the wild things you've done – I've got some here – now, Gary, believe it or not, he sawed the head off Warren Beatty's Oscar. *(laughs)* Marvellous. He drove a Harley Davidson motorcycle into Bruce Willis's er, patio doors. Erm, what else have you done?

**Gary**
Punched Jessica Tandy.

**Alan**

Yeah, that was nasty. That was nasty. Now – it says here, it says here you also threw Whoopi Goldberg's copper kettle at a cat.

**Gary**

No, no. Other way round.

**Alan**

What, you threw a cat at Whoopi Goldberg's copper kettle?

**Gary**

No, no. I threw a copper kettle at Whoopi Goldberg's cat.

**Alan**

That's what I said.

**Gary**

No, you said I threw Whoopi Goldberg's copper kettle at a cat – I didn't. I threw a copper kettle at Whoopi Goldberg's cat. It wasn't Whoopi Goldberg's copper kettle.

**Alan**

*(Looking worried)* Right. It was Whoopi Goldberg's cat. So whose copper kettle was it?

**Gary**

Jessica Tandy's.

**Alan**

Was this before or after you punched her?

**Gary**

About the same time. The incidents were related.

**Alan**

Oh. Oh, dear. Erm, Tanya, has he ever thrown a copper kettle at you?

**Tanya**

No, no. It's one of the few things he's never thrown at me.

**Alan**

Really?

**Tanya**

Joke.

**Alan**

Right. Tanya's breasts – now, sorry, that's just my notes. Sorry. Now, you're one of those great actresses who, if the role demands it, you're quite prepared to expose yourself.

**Tanya**

Well, I'm glad you value my acting so highly.

**Alan**

I do. Your name attached to a film is a seal of quality. It's a guarantee that says, come along, see the film, lads, you won't go home empty-handed, so to speak.

**Tanya**

I really think that my films are more than just titillation.

**Alan**

Mmm. I can only suggest that, er, if you wish to go and see Tanya's unexpurgated adult breast show, that, er, that you pop down to the local cinema or, erm, or marry her.

**Gary**

That's no guarantee.

**Tanya**

Grow up.

**Gary**

I am grown up.

**Tanya**

Well, act it. You're an actor, I believe.

**Alan**

Good point actually, Tanya. Erm, Gary, we were going to show a clip from one of your films, but the last film you did was an action film three years ago that starred Bill Segar. And I've never heard of him.

**Gary**
Well, I've never heard of you.

**Alan**
I'm Alan Partridge. Let's, let's talk about what you did before you went into acting – that's easier. Erm … Gary, Tanya tipped us off about this. I believe you used to be a mobile office equipment maintenance engineer.

**Gary**
Briefly.

**Tanya**
Well, three years.

**Gary**
Yeah, got the sack.

**Alan**
No, you're lying. You were awarded Mobile Office Equipment Maintenance Engineer of the Month. Well done! Now I've, I've actually got a broken photocopier at my office in Norwich. Erm, do you think you could fix that?

**Gary**
You think I'm gonna go to Norwich to mend your photocopier?

**Alan**
There's no need because Mohammed – Mohammed has, Mohammed has moved the mountain to you. It's not literally a mountain – it's a photocopier – although, coincidentally it was driven here in a white Bedford Astramax by a man called Mohammed. Ladies and gentlemen, please bring on the broken photocopier!

*Applause*

**Alan**
Gary, Gary, we've got the photocopier. Will you rise to Alan's challenge and mend it?

**Gary**
No.

**Tanya**
Just do it.

# TV SHOW 2

**Gary**
I don't want to do it.

**Tanya**
Don't make a scene.

**Alan**
Do you want him to mend the photocopier?

**Audience**
Yes!

**Tanya**
It's more embarrassing not to do it.

**Alan**
Come on, I don't believe you can mend it.

**Gary**
'Course I can mend it.

**Alan**
I don't believe you.

**Gary**
What model is it?

**Alan**
Z – Z60.

**Gary**
Mono- or multi-feed?

**Alan**
Mono-feed.

**Gary**
Easy.

**Alan**
Prove it.

*Gary gets up and walks towards the photocopier.*
*Applause*

**Gary**
It hasn't been reset after a paper jam. Basic.

**Alan**
Really?

**Gary**
Yeah. That's interesting – see this?

**Alan**
Yeah.

**Gary**
Where do you put your paper clips?

**Alan**
Just normally just around on the table
or whatever.

**Gary**
Yeah. They get lost. Stick 'em there.

**Alan**
Right. How will they stay, how will they
stay?

**Gary**
How will they stay?

**Alan**
Yeah.

**Gary**
Magnetic.

**Alan**
Well, that's interesting.

**Gary**
Yeah. Nice little feature. Worth knowing.
Yes, good machine this. There you go –
should have no trouble. I don't do that shit
any more. *(Walks off)*

**Alan**
Oh look, he's mended it! Whoa! What a
dude!

*Applause*

**Alan**
Well, Gary, Gary, not to worry. I'm gonna
put the smile back on your face because I'm
gonna present you with an Alan Partridge
tie and blazer-badge combination pack.
There we go.

*Applause*

**Alan**

Tanya, domestic tip: when you're stitching that on, it's got an adhesive behind it, so in actual fact you can simply, er, iron it on.

**Tanya**

Wonderful.

**Alan**

And then do the stitching later if you want.

**Tanya**

Labour-saving.

**Alan**

It's labour-saving.

*Gary sets fire to the tie with his lighter.*

**Alan**

What are you doing? What are you doing? For God's sake!

*Alan grabs the tie, removes some flowers from a vase and dunks the tie in the water.*

**Gary**

It just burst into flames.

**Alan**

What did you do that for?

**Gary**

Spontaneous combustion.

**Alan**

You've ruined it.

**Gary**

Sorry.

**Alan**

How much did those glasses cost?

**Gary**

Fifteen thousand dollars. You touch them, I'll break your legs.

*Tanya grabs Gary's glasses and twists them into a ball.*

**Gary**

What are you doing? You stupid bitch!

**Tanya**

I'm stupid? I'm stupid? You're sitting there with a spider on your head and I'm stupid? I mean, what a pathetic thing to do. Setting fire –

**Gary**

These are my James Dean –

**Tanya**

I don't give a toss.

**Gary**

These are James Dean's glasses.

**Tanya**

I don't care –

**Alan**

You're watching *Knowing Me, Knowing You* with Alan Partridge –

**Tanya**

– you're supposed to be a Hollywood wild man. Why don't you just go out and make some films?

**Gary**

What's your problem?

**Alan**

– Live chat as it happens.

**Tanya**

Make a bit of money. That might be quite good. Then you'd be able to afford a new pair.

**Gary**

Why don't you lighten up?

**Tanya**

I've got a problem!

**Gary**

Yeah, you've got a problem.

**Tanya**
Shall I tell people what your problem is?

**Gary**
No. No, don't –

**Tanya**
Shall I tell people what your problem is?

**Gary**
– don't, don't –

**Tanya**
Shall I tell them?

**Gary**
– don't, don't, don't.

**Tanya**
Shall I tell them? Do you know what Gary's problem is?

**Alan**
No – please tell me.

**Tanya**
Well, Gary's problem is that he's impotent.

**Alan**
What?

**Tanya**
Gary's impotent.

**Alan**
Is this true, Gary?

*Gary says nothing.*

**Alan**
I'll take that as a yes. Tanya, that explains why you sleep around. That explains why you're known as the bike of Beverly Hills. I think this is quite a serious matter. Let's change the tone and handle this in a rather more sensitive way. Let's lower the lights.

*Lights are lowered.*

**Alan**
I think, really, it's time that we ended this farcical façade of a marriage, which I presume is unconsummated – Tanya?

**Tanya**
Yes.

**Alan**
And Gary?

**Gary**
Yeah, obviously.

**Alan**
Yes, yes, of course, yes. Um, the marriage has now been rent in twain. It has been put asunder. It is moribund so, as regards the Alan Partridge tie and blazer-badge combination pack which you destroyed, don't worry about that. Um, we've got dozens of them. If you wish I'll send another one by first post to you. Would you like that? As a memento of this evening?

**Gary**
Yeah. That'd be nice.

**Alan**
Well, I think this has been a painful experience for all of us, and it simply remains for me to say, knowing me, Alan Partridge, knowing you, Tanya and Gary, ah-haa. Grrr.

*Applause*

**Alan**

Well, well, the wheel, the wheel has turned full circle for Tanya and Gary, but the wheels that turn this crazy and often unpredictable vehicle – my vehicle, my, my show – they, they keep turning, which brings me neatly on to the final section of the show, which has to happen, nothing can stop that, as I rise to meet my own challenge: *(he stands)* Alan Partridge on the wheel of death. Will you please welcome back with his wheel of death, magic man Tony Le Mesmer and Tina!

*Applause*

**Tony**

Ladies and gentlemen, every evening as part of my show at the Palladium, which runs until the end of this month, I get a member of the audience up on to the stage and I ask them to overcome their fears on the wheel of death. Tonight Alan will be that person. How do you feel, Alan?

**Alan**

*(Strapped to a vertical wheel)* Confident. I am risking my life for chat – oh, by the way, Philip Parsons, if you're watching … get a knife and fork and a plate, put your words on that plate, add a bit of humble pie and eat it. Right.

**Tony**

Commence spinning the wheel of death.

**Voiceover**

As the wheel of death commences its inexorable spin, Tony Le Mesmer prepares to unleash the deadly daggers of Damizon.

**Alan**

Er, I've changed my mind. I've changed, I'm sorry, I've changed my mind.

**Tony**

Drum roll!

**Alan**

Please. Sorry – can you – we'll do it next week. There isn't time. We'll do it next week!

*Tony begins to throw the daggers one by one.*

**Alan**

God! Please! Please! This is madness! Don't! You stupid man! Please! God! No! All right, Philip Parsons, you're right – the show is moribund! Oh! Please!

*Applause*

**Alan**

*(Still spinning)* I've done it! I've done it! I've done it! On that bombshell it's time for me to say, knowing me, Alan Partridge, knowing you, freak woman-man, knowing you, the slut actress and Mr Floppy the actor, and knowing you, Mr Loony-man with the knives. Good night and ah-haa! Grrr.

*Applause*

*Music: 'Knowing Me, Knowing You'*

**Alan**

*(In background)* Get me off. Please. Get me off now, please. Can someone get me off the wheel? I've done it. Can we get a – Naomi, Naomi. Get me off. Is Naomi there? Tell her to get me off. It's over now – They're wet. My trousers are wet!

# KNOWING ME KNOWING YOU

*Alan Partridge*

*Music: 'Knowing Me, Knowing You'*

**Alan**
Ah-haa!

*Alan does a little run onstage and mimes throwing a hand grenade.*

*Applause*

**Alan**
Ha ha. Welcome. Welcome. Welcome to *Knowing Me, Knowing You*, with me, Alan Partridge. Tonight I am a rocket. Prepare to board Sputnik Partridge and enter the stratosphere – or should I say, the chatosphere.

*Drum roll*

**Alan**
Tonight's show is *(licks his finger and holds it up)* tssss-hot. How hot, Alan? Well, imagine Debbie Harry in camiknickers, spoon-feeding a beef vindaloo to Pan's People in a sauna in Bangkok. That's half as hot as tonight's show – because among tonight's spicy guests, I've got the hottest, sexiest dance act in northern Europe: Hot Pants. And, for the first time ever on an English-speaking chat show, a Jacuzzi.

*Applause*

**Alan**

I'll be, er, I'll be getting in that later. It's plumbed in. It's thermostatically controlled and it's set on hot. But, er, first, first an apology.

*Alan clears throat and reads from letter.*

**Alan**

In last week's show I accused actor Roger Moore of being a towel thief. This allegation was untrue. Roger Moore has at no time stolen a towel, bathmat, flannel, shower curtain, sponge or any other form of hotel bathroom accessory. I, Alan Partridge, apologize unreservedly to Roger Moore for my ill-informed and ignorant comments, and I fully acknowledge that I am guilty of gross professional misconduct.

*Alan puts letter into his trouser pocket.*

**Alan**

It's time now to welcome my resident house band, Glen Ponder and Ferrari!

*Music: 'Knowing Me, Knowing You' and applause*

**Alan**

Knowing, knowing me, Alan Partridge, knowing you, Glen Ponder. Ah-haa.

**Glen**

Ah-haa.

**Alan**

Glen! If this chat show was a train, do you know what kind of train it'd be?

**Glen**

No, Alan.

**Alan**

The Chattanooga choo-choo!

*Drum roll*

**Alan**

But, er, seriously –

*Steam train whistle blows.*

**Alan**

What, what was that whistle noise? What was that?

**Glen**

Oh yeah, meant to be the train, Alan.

**Alan**

Right, well, you didn't do that in rehearsal.

**Glen**

It was meant to be a surprise.

**Alan**

Surprise me in rehearsal, Glen. Don't surprise me on a live television show. A little bit naughty that, shouldn't do that. A bit naughty. Glen Ponder and Ferrari!

*Music: 'Knowing Me, Knowing You'*

**Alan**

Ooh, this show is hot. I can really work up a thirst.

*Alan drinks from a can of drink, then holds can to face camera.*

**Alan**

Ahhh. Hah. My first guest is a singer. She's forty-one. Twenty-four years ago she was working in a shoe shop in Kansas City. One day a man came in and asked for a pair of size eight, turtle-green platform shoes. As she slipped them on him, she started singing to herself. The man said, 'I won't have these shoes – the bridge is too low and I've got wide feet.' Those were his actual words. 'They don't fit,' he said, 'but your beautiful voice fits your face like a slipper. I'm going to make you a star.' That man was Neil Sedaka. Neil's not doing so well any more, but she is. She's the biggest singing sensation in America – except for Barbra Steisland and Liza Minnelli – she requires no introduction, but, er, nevertheless, please welcome Gina Langland!

*Music: 'Thank You For the Music' and applause*

*Gina walks onstage and gives Alan three kisses on alternate cheeks.*

**Gina**
Hi.

**Alan**
Ah. Ooh dear. I got an extra kiss for free there. Not, er, not that you usually charge. Now, er, now, Gina, you, you can't stay long because in forty minutes' time you're due on stage at Earls Court for the closing night of your sell-out concert tour.

**Gina**
Mmm-hmm. It's been wonderful, Alec, you know, I mean I just had no idea that I had so many fans.

**Alan**
Well, why did you book Earls Court? It's massive.

**Gina**
Well, because it's just a wonderful venue.

**Alan**
Yeah, it is. It is. They do the Ideal Homes Exhibition. I, er, I nearly opened it, er, last year but, er, I was pipped at the post, erm, by Dave Lee Travis – again. Huh.

**Gina**
Who?

**Alan**
Who? Yes, exactly, that's what I said. Yeah. Very good. Now, Gina, it really would be great if you could stay a little bit longer.

**Gina**
Oh. You know, I'd love to, Alec, I'd really love to stay for the whole show but I just can't. *(Laughs)*

**Alan**
Well, we don't actually want you to stay for the whole show. We just want you to stay, er, er, a little bit longer, you know. I mean, we have got other guests. We've got Hot Pants – they're on later on. Stay tuned, fellas. *(Licks finger and holds it up)* Tssss. We just want you to stay for a little bit longer – please?

**Gina**
Well, I'd love to, I really would, but I'm late as it is.

**Alan**
Please?

**Gina**
I just can't.

**Alan**
Please?

**Gina**
No, I can't.

**Alan**
Ple-ease?

**Gina**
We have four minutes, Alec.

**Alan**
Right, Alan. Alan. Four minutes, OK. Now, Gina. You're such, such a busy bee, aren't you?

*Gina laughs.*

**Alan**
Buzzing from flower to flower, collecting cash pollen in, er, in the sacks on the back of your legs. Not, not literally. Not literally. That would be hideous. Um, no, I mean, I'm think— I mean if you're a bee. No, what I'm trying to say is, you're so, do you ever get time to relax? Do you ever get time off?

**Gina**
Alec, you know it's funny you should say that because tomorrow I begin a month's vacation.

**Alan**
Oh, lovely. Where?

**Gina**
Barbados.

**Alan**
I'm, I'm going there at the end of the month.

**Gina**
Really?

**Alan**
Yeah. I'm doing an advert for, er, Sprünt. Er, it's, er, it's a new, er, tropical fruit drink. From Germany.

*Alan picks up the can and holds it so the camera can see the front.*

**Gina**
I thought you weren't allowed to advertise on the BBC?

**Alan**
I'm not advertising. I'm not – that's illegal. I'm not advertising. No, no, no. No, I'm simply saying that I'm doing an advert for Sprünt. The new tangy tropical fruit drink. From Germany. Not advertising.

**Gina**
And what do you have to do in the ad?

**Alan**
Er, well, basically I, I'm on a beach and I lie on a hammock, er, sipping Sprünt, and, er, surrounded by half-naked tropical dancers.

*Alan and Gina laugh.*

**Gina**
Who are they?

**Alan**
They're called Hot Pants. We've got them on the show later on. They're on the show tonight.

**Gina**
Um, Alec, can I suggest that we –

**Alan**
Alan.

**Gina**
– we do the song now?

**Alan**
No, no! That's a surprise. No. Um, first of all there's a present I want to give to you right now. This is a new regular section of the show, called 'Alan's Big Pocket'. In this section I put my hand into my big pocket and I produce something I think my guest will like. So will you now please bring on Alan's big pocket!

*A large cardboard box is wheeled onstage. Applause*

**Alan**
Let's turn out Alan's big pocket and see what's in it. *(He opens the door and two women with dogs dressed in Victorian clothes step out)* It's two Victorian dogs.

*Applause*

**Alan**
This one's, er, this one's Sherlock Holmes; this one's Queen Victoria. Now, er, Gina, when I was on the phone to your manager in Los Angeles he, er, he happened to mention that you love collecting Victorian dogs. *Voilà*: two Victorian dogs, courtesy of Alan Partridge.

**Gina**
Victorian dolls.

**Alan**
What?

**Gina**

I collect Victorian dolls.

**Alan**

Not Victorian dogs?

**Gina**

Well, what are Victorian dogs?

**Alan**

I've no idea. We thought it'd be something like this. Do you, um, do you like dogs?

**Gina**

Well, er, I have a cat back home.

**Alan**

Does, does, does it like dogs?

**Gina**

*(Laughing)* Not really.

**Alan**

Right, that's a bit of a problem because we've got two dogs here. Listen, why don't you take them with you in the car to Earls Court. See if you like them and if you don't, um, you know, just let them out near the railway line. You know, they'll, they'll, they'll find their way back to Battersea and they'll be warm enough in all this gear. You're giving them a sporting chance, you know. No?

**Gina**

*(Laughs)* No! I, I can't. I can't do that.

**Alan**

All right, OK, we'll do it. Erm, get rid of the dogs. Ladies and gentlemen, two dogs … two dogs.

*Applause*

**Gina**

I'm so sorry, Alec, I mean, it was a lovely thought.

**Alan**

Alan.

**Gina**

Do you do Alec's big pocket every week?

**Alan**

Alan. *Alan's* big pocket.

**Gina**

Like, er, some kind of a catchphrase, I guess, as if people stop you in the street and say, 'Hey, Alec, you wanna sign my pocket?'

**Alan**

Are you deaf?

**Gina**

I'm sorry?

**Alan**

Yes, people do stop me in the street. Yes, they stop me and ask for my autograph. And do you know what I do?

**Gina**

What?

**Alan**

What I do to save time – you'll like this – I have this. It's a stamp with my autograph on it.

*Gina laughs.*

**Alan**

Yeah. And basically what I do is I give them, they give me a card, something like this, and I simply take the card and I just stamp my signature on like that. You see? It's got that there and then I give them that. That's my name. You read that.

**Gina**

Right. Alec Partridge. Great.

**Alan**

Read what it says on the card.

**Gina**

Alec Partridge.

**Alan**

No, it says 'Alan'. Alan Partridge.

**Gina**

Why?

**Alan**

Because that's my name.

**Gina**

Oh, my God. I'm so sorry.

**Alan**

It's OK, it's OK.

**Gina**

It's so embarrassing.

**Alan**

It's all right.

**Gina**

Oh God, you must have thought I was being so rude, Alec.

**Alan**

ALAN! ALAN! ALAN, ALAN, ALAN, ALAN, ALAN, ALAN, ALAN, ALAN, ALAN, ALAN, ALAN, ALAN, ALAN, ALAN, ALAN! My name is Alan Partridge. That's who I am – there.

*Alan sticks the card with his stamped autograph on his forehead.*

**Alan**

Alan Partridge. There are no excuses.

**Gina**

It's the wrong way up.

**Alan**

Right.

*Alan turns the card and sticks it back on his forehead.*

**Alan**

There.

**Gina**

Fine.

**Alan**

Now, before Gina goes, I'd like to ask her one more question: Gina, do you like Abba?

**Gina**

I love Abba.

**Alan**

Would you like to do a medley of Abba songs with me, right now?

**Gina**

*(Laughing)* I couldn't possibly.

**Alan**

Oh, why not, for goodness' sake?

**Gina**

Because, Alan, *(starts singing)*
I'm nothing special
In fact, I'm a bit of a bore

**Alan**

Ah, you're not. You're not boring. But if I tell a joke, you've probably heard it before.

**Gina**

I don't believe that.

**Alan**

No, you probably have.

**Gina**

*(Sings)* But I have a talent, a wonderful thing.

**Alan**

*(Sings)* 'Cause everyone listens when I start to sing.

**Gina**

*(Sings)* I'm so grateful and proud,

**Alan and Gina**

*(Sing)* All I want is to sing it out lou-ou-oud.

**Alan**

*(Sings)* Take-a-chance-chance-take-a-chance-take-a-take-a-chance-take-a-chance-chance-take-a-chance-take-a-take-a-chance-take-a-chance-chance-take-a-chance-take-a-take-a-chance-take-a-chance … *(continues in background)*

**Gina**

*(Sings)* If you change your mind
I'm the first in line
Honey, I'm still free
Take a chance on me.
If you need me, let me know
Gonna be around
If you got no place to go
And you're feeling down.
Take a chance on me.

**Alan**

*(Gets on one knee)*
That's all I ask, honey.

**Gina**

*(Sings)* Take a chance on me.

**Alan**

Ohhh.

**Gina**

*(Sings)* Chiquitita, you and I know.

**Alan**

*(Sings)* Can you see the stars, Fernando?

**Gina**

*(Sings)* The winner takes it all.

**Alan**

*(Sings)* Mamma mia! Here I go again.

**Gina**

*(Sings)* I have a dream.

**Alan**

*(Sings)* Gimme, gimme, gimme a man after midnight.

**Gina**

*(Sings)* Voulez-vous –

**Alan**

Ah-haa!

*Alan and Gina start to dance.*

**Gina**

*(Sings)* Take it now or leave it.

**Alan**

Ah-haa!

**Gina**

*(Sings)* Now it's all we get.

**Alan**

Ah-haa!

**Gina**

*(Sings)* Nothing promised, no regrets.

**Alan**

Ba-ba-ba-do.

**Gina**

*(Sings)* Voulez-vous –

**Alan**

Ah-haa!

**Gina**

*(Sings)* Ain't no big decision.

**Alan**

Ah-haa!

**Gina**

*(Sings)* You know what to do.

**Alan**

Ah-haa!

**Gina**
*(Sings)* La question c'est, 'Voulez-vous'.

**Alan**
Ba-ba-ba-dum.

**Gina and Alan**
*(Sing)* Voulez-voooooous
You can dance, you can ji-ive,

*Alan moves behind Gina and puts a hand under her breast.*

**Gina and Alan**
*(Sing)* Having the time of your life
Ooooh

**Alan**
*(Sings)* See that girl

**Gina**
*(Sings)* Watch that scene

**Alan**
*(Sings)* Digging the –

**Gina**
*(Sings)* – dancing queen.

*Alan runs his hand down Gina's body and holds her hand.*

**Alan**
*(Sings in a strained, high key)*
Thank you for the music,
The songs you're singing
Thanks for all the joy you're bringing,
Who could live without it
I ask in all honesty,
What would life be?
Without a song
Or a dance, what are we?
So I say
*(Alan switches to a lower key)*
Thank you for the music
For giving it to me.

**Gina**
*(Sings)* Waterloo. Knowing me,
knowing you

**Alan and Gina**
*(Sing)* Ahhh-haaaa!

*Alan tries to give Gina a kiss, but she waves and runs off stage.*

*Applause*

**Alan**
Oh. I have an announcement to make.
Last week I had naked sex with the Home
Secretary and I want to sell my story.
*(Laughs)* Of course, of course I haven't.
Ha ha ha! But, er, but, if I had, who would I
go to? Well, I'd go to my next guest, because
he is a high-profile agent and publicist who
represents both celebrities and, for want
of a better word, harlots. Please, please
welcome the man Virginia Bottomley called
'that little turd' – Laurence Noels.

*Music: 'Money, Money, Money'*

**Alan**
Laurence – you are the man they love
to hate.

**Laurence**
*(Laughs)* I prefer to think of myself as the
man they hate to love.

**Alan**
*(Laughs)* But, er, but you're not. But you're
not. You are the man they love to hate.

**Laurence**
Well *(laughs)* that's very amusing, Alan,
and some of your audience found it
amusing too. But there is a positive side to
what I do. I often help various celebrities –
if I might give you an example?

**Alan**
Please do.

**Laurence**
Let's take the Dimbleby brothers.
Supposing Jonathan and David came to
me and they said, 'Laurence, we need help.
People think of us as a little bit too serious.
A little bit dull.'

**Alan**
Yeah, I know, I know what you mean.

**Laurence**
Well, I would rectify that image problem by ensuring that the Dimbleby brothers were seen letting their hair down at a fashionable night-spot, such as Stringfellow's.

**Alan**
Right, right.

**Laurence**
Or, perhaps, sharing an ice cream at Alton Towers.

**Alan**
Or, or a can of Sprünt.

**Laurence**
Yes. Yes. Conversely, take a celebrity who is perhaps perceived as being unintelligent, someone like Paul 'Gazza' Gascoigne.

**Alan**
Or Dave Lee Travis.

**Laurence**
Yes. That's a better example.

**Alan**
Yes, it is, isn't it? Mmm.

**Laurence**
So if Dave Lee Travis was worried about looking unintelligent, I would ensure that he was seen at the opera, perhaps with a book in his hand.

**Alan**
Yes, I see. It's quite clever, yeah.

**Laurence**
Another scenario that might occur is a celebrity who comes to me and says, 'Laurence, I am a practising homosexual and I would like to keep this delicate matter private.'

**Alan**
Very wise.

**Laurence**
I would then ensure that this homosexual VIP was seen in a heterosexual context.

**Alan**
Such as?

**Laurence**
A pub. A fast car. A football match.

**Alan**
Right. You don't mean George Best?

**Laurence**
No, Alan, let me assure you that George is as straight as the passes he used to make to Bobby Charlton.

*Alan laughs.*

**Laurence**
Who, by the way, is also not a homosexual.

**Alan**
But what if someone comes up to you and says, 'Laurence, I' – how can I put it? – 'I play for both sides. I play, I play for Manchester United *(touches one side of his nose)* and Manchester City *(touches the other side of his nose)*. I'm Dennis Law.'

**Laurence**
I, I don't understand.

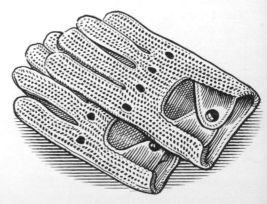

**Alan**

I'm bisexual.

**Laurence**

You are?

**Alan**

No, Dennis Law. No, not Dennis Law, no, no, God, no. Erm, sorry, Dennis, er, sorry about that. Er, if you're watching, erm, let's go for a drink sometime. As, as friends. No, actually, actually, no, let's, let's not, let's call it off. I'll just, I'll just go home to my wife. I must say, I'm, er, I'm looking forward to seeing Hot Pants later, yeah. Ooh yes, stay tuned, fellers. *(Licks finger)* Tssss. Now, Laurence, very recently you have been involved in a massive royal scandal, in which you've obtained photographs of the royal family taken from hidden cameras and, er, you, you've published these in, in a book.

**Laurence**

This book is in no way scandalous, nor salacious. The book, *Her Majesty's Pleasure (Alan holds up the book)*, is being published purely in the public interest.

**Alan**

Well, you say that, but *(opening the book)* there's photographs – there's one here: Prince Edward in the bath. Actually, it's quite interesting this. He's made himself a, er, a mock beard from the foam suds. Quite suits him.

**Laurence**

Believe me, Alan, I obtained some photos that were frankly unpublishable.

**Alan**

And are they in the book?

**Laurence**

Yes, they are.

**Alan**

OK. We've sat and listened to you present yourself with, er, with great eloquence, but … ladies and gentlemen, Laurence has unwittingly stumbled into a new section of my show called 'Eat Your Own Medicine'. Laurence, for the past four weeks you have been under surveillance from our team of *Knowing Me, Knowing You* snoopers. This is what we discovered. Show the clip.

**Alan**

Take a look at this. It's a disabled parking space. Hello, who's this parking in it? It's a big Jaguar containing able-bodied Laurence Noels. It's quite a nice car that. There you go, you get out of the car, er, look around, little pick of the nose, it's a good 'un, pop it in the mouth.

**Laurence**

Is that the best you've got, Alan?

**Alan**

No, that was merely an hors d'oeuvre. Let's, let's have a look at the main course. *(Another video clip is played)* Here you are again, emerging from an anonymous-looking black door. Another treat for Laurence Noels there. I give you this: you certainly keep your nose clean. Erm, but the question is, what's going on behind the door? *(Cut back to the studio)* I'll tell you: dermatology.

**Laurence**

Oh, come on, Alan, this is pathetic. Ludicrous.

**Alan**

Is it? Is it as ludicrous as a man with such a grotesque hairy back that he has to visit a dermatologist once every six weeks to have his unsightly and innumerable hairs removed?

**Laurence**

Alan, this is a non-story. The public are not interested in my back.

**Alan**

Aren't they? Let's ask them. Would you like to know more about Laurence's hairy back?

**Audience**

Yes!

**Alan**

There's your answer, mate. Bring on my big pocket, right now. Bring it on.

*Applause*

**Alan**

Will you please come out of my pocket, Laurence Noels's dermatologist, Clive Sealey.

*Applause. Clive joins Laurence on the sofa.*

**Alan**

*(Laughs)* Clive – Clive, just how hairy is Laurence's back?

**Clive**

It's very hairy, Alan. I mean, this is the amount of hair you'd find on an averagely haired back, yeah? *(Clive holds up a plastic bag with small amount of hair in it)*

**Alan**

Right.

**Clive**

And this – this is the amount collected at the last session with Laurence. *(Clive holds up another bag full of hair)*

*Alan laughs.*

**Clive**

I mean, it's enough to cover twelve small children.

**Alan**

This is, er, *Knowing Me, Knowing You* with Alan Partridge, smooth as an eel. Except, except in the normal areas. Unlike Dave Lee Travis – hairy cornflake. Now, the Noels's back is surely his Achilles heel. How deep are the scars?

**Clive**

Well, during the sessions he's, er, he's told me lots of the names that he was called at school.

**Alan**

Oh good. What are they?

**Clive**

Er …wolf-man, er, monkey-boy, Godzilla, King Kong …

**Alan**

Human carpet?

**Clive**

Yes, yes. Gus the Gorilla.

**Alan**

Actually, we, in the office we had a bit of fun earlier on. Um, we just came up with a list of potential nicknames for Laurence. I'll go through them very quickly, er, kiwi fruit, er, moth banquet – quite an interesting one – Furball XL5, er, Billy Furry – that's, that's Billy Fury with a different pronunciation; that's mine – er, and of course hairy Krishna. Erm, marvellous. Erm, Laurence, anything to say?

**Laurence**

You'll be hearing from my solicitor in the morning.

**Alan**

Ooh, bit prickly. Or should I say hairy? *(Laughs)*

**Laurence**

I have the same solicitor as Dave Lee Travis.

**Alan**
Big deal.

**Laurence**
And Roger Moore.

**Alan**
Oh God. Laurence Noels and Clive Sealey.

*Applause; Laurence and Clive leave the stage; Alan takes a sip from his can of Sprünt.*

**Alan**
Nice can of Sprünt, that. Now. *Schnell! Schnell! Achtung! Sieg Heil! Jawohl!* Those are just some of the comments shouted at my next guest … at the 1936 Berlin Olympics. Why? Because she won gold medal for Britain in the 4 by 100 metres women's hurdles relay. She doesn't run any more – she's seventy-eight – but she can still get up and down stairs unassisted and refuses to use the Ronstad chairlift installed by her son-in-law in 1991. Please welcome the Linford Christie of great-grandmothers, Elsie Morgan.

*Applause and music: 'The Winner Takes It All'; Elsie enters.*

**Alan**
Knowing me, Alan Partridge, knowing you, Elsie Morgan –

**Alan and Elsie**
Ah-haa.

**Alan**
No, you wait till I've said it. Ah-haa.

**Elsie**
Ah-haa.

**Alan**
That's right. Elsie, let me start by saying how wonderful it is to at last have someone old on the show. Erm, the 19, the 1936 Berlin Olympics. What did it feel like to run past the finishing line, knowing you'd just beaten the German and won the gold medal for Britain?

**Elsie**
Thrilling, because we'd stitched up the Krauts.

**Alan**
Lovely. Lovely. Is it true? Were things better in the olden days?

**Elsie**
Well, immediately after the war it was absolutely marvellous, because that time we really had completely stitched up the Krauts. But then after that it – everything got very much worse and there was a lot of immigration and, er, and inevitably crime went up.

**Alan**
Ri-right. Erm, but there must, there must, there must have been some positive things?

**Elsie**
I'll tell you a little story.

**Alan**
Please do.

**Elsie**
I brought my car in last week and, er, parked it on one of those meters, you know. I went into Debenhams very quickly, I came out very quickly again, and there was an awful man writing me a parking ticket.

**Alan**
Oh dear.

**Elsie**
I said to him, 'Now, is it reasonable to give me a parking ticket for two minutes?' Well, after a while he saw sense and admitted that it was a bit silly and he let me off.

**Alan**
Good for him. Good for him.

**Elsie**
Yes, but after I got home, I thought, 'That man let me break the law. He shouldn't have done that.'

**Alan**

No.

**Elsie**

So I rang his employers and told them what had happened. And, er, later on they rang me back and, er, I was delighted to hear they'd dismissed him.

**Alan**

Good – good riddance.

**Elsie**

Particularly as he was black.

**Alan**

Right, er, right. Er – now – er –

**Elsie**

They bend the rules, don't they, Alan?

**Alan**

– now, tell us about sport.

**Elsie**

They don't play by our rules –

**Alan**

Tell us about sport.

**Elsie**

– don't you find that?

**Alan**

Right. Shut up. You can't say those things on television. Not any more.

**Elsie**

Well, why not? They're all –

**Alan**

Shut it! Sorry. Now – now, Elsie, erm, I've got, I've got a surprise for – because it's time once again to dip into Alan's big pocket. Stay there, stay there –

*Applause*

**Alan**

And, er, it's a pocket full of emotion because tonight we reunite Britain's hurdling golden girls of 1936. They haven't seen each other for over fifty years. Sadly, er, Lindsay Farrow, who ran the second leg, is no longer with us. But the other two are. Will you please come out of my big pocket – Ann Wiley and Georgina Clarke!

*Music: 'Knowing Me, Knowing You' and applause*

**Alan**

Please, sit down. Marvellous. Knowing me, Alan Partridge, knowing you, Ann Wiley.

*Elsie, Georgina and Ann talk among themselves.*

**Alan**

Knowing me, Alan Partridge, knowing you, Georgina Clarke.

*Elsie, Georgina and Ann continue to talk among themselves.*

**Alan**

Hello? Hello? Hello! Thank you. Erm, now you're obviously, er, all feeling very emotional. If you feel the need to weep, please do, do so – you are women. Erm, no tears? No? I've got to say I was kind of banking on it. Erm, it's all right. Can I just remind you you haven't seen each other for over fifty years?

**Elsie**

Oh, no, no. We saw one another six months ago.

**Alan**

Where?

**Ann**

Sky Television.

**Georgina**

Yes, it was a programme that reunited people, called *Nostalgia* – with Dave Lee Travis.

**Alan**

I don't believe it. He's done it again. Did you cry on his show?

**Elsie, Georgina and Ann**

Oh, yes, buckets, didn't we?

**Alan**

Oh, great.

**Elsie**

Even David cried.

**Alan**

He? Oh, I don't believe it. The hairy cornflake shed a tear. Doesn't matter, doesn't matter. Let's talk about the race. 1936. In those days how did you cope with the pressure?

**Ann**

Well, I, I used to sing in the dressing-room.

**Georgina**

Oh yes, 'We'll Gather Lilacs'.

**Alan**

Probably a forgotten memory now.

**Ann**

Oh, no. *(Sings)*
We'll gather lilacs in the spring again,
And walk together down an English lane,
When you come home once more
And in the evening, in the twilight glow
I'll hold you close and never let you go.

**Alan**

Marvellous.

**Elsie, Anna and Georgina**

*(Sing)* We'll gather –

**Alan**

No.

**Elsie, Anna and Georgina**

*(Sing)* – in the spring

**Alan**

Oh God. All right. Yeah. All right.

**Elsie, Anna and Georgina**

*(Sing)* – again,
And walk together down an English –

**Alan**

*(Starts clapping)* Marvellous, marvellous, give them a round of applause. Marvellous. Lovely, lovely. That was lovely. Well … at, at this stage of the show, some of my viewers may be thinking, 'Alan, you're a liar! You promised that this show would be hot and now you're chatting to three senior citizens.' But, if I said I am now going to jump into a Tardis, go back in time and recreate the Berlin Olympics with these three old women, you would say, 'Alan, that *is* hot. We were wrong earlier.' Well, that's exactly what I'm going to do. Ladies, will you now please join me in my one-sixth scale Berlin Olympic stadium.

*Music*

**Alan**

You join us live at the Berlin Olympics on *Grandstand* in 1936 on this pleasant summer's morning in Nazi Germany. Everyone's here: Hitler's in his box; Jesse Owens' just waved at him – he doesn't like that. And we wait for the race to start. Erm, sorry, I'm just gonna, I'm gonna fire a gun. It's quite loud. Don't let it worry you, right, OK? On your marks, get set –

*Gun fires.*

**Alan**

She's off! *(Ann begins to walk slowly round the mini track)* Like a bullet. Ann Wiley. Fast as a bullet from a Luger courses ahead. Coming up to the first hurdle – she's cleared it! She's cleared it, landing like a tomcat, and off again … off again, round the bend, and puts the baton over to Lindsay Farrow – sadly no longer with us; she … she's represented by a cardboard cutout. It's a, it's a clean pass. Let's see what you're made of, Georgie girl! Put some egg on Hitler's face. Just kick that, love. Kick that over.

*Georgina kicks the hurdle over.*

**Alan**
Oh dear! The hurdle has fallen. It's all down to Elsie. Elsie Morgan. Can she do it? And she has. She's won the gold!

*Applause and cheers*

**Alan**
Ladies and gentlemen, the golden hurdlers of '36.

*Fanfare; Elsie, Georgina and Ann wave. Cut to Alan poking his face out of a small door in Alan's big pocket.*

**Alan**
Hi. I'm in Alan's Big Pocket. Why? Because I'm getting undressed. The reason I'm taking my clothes off is because Hot Pants are about to come on and raise the roof off TV Centre with their lovely legs. Then they're going to join me in the jacuzzi. Er, Glen, have you seen them before?

**Glen**
No, but I'm looking forward to seeing them. *(Licks finger)* Tssss!

**Alan**
Glen, that is my noise. Get your own sound. Move the pocket!

*Stage-hands wheel the big pocket offstage; Alan is sitting naked in the jacuzzi.*

**Alan**
Yes, I am in a jacuzzi, sipping Sprünt. It's, er, it's almost as if I'm in an advert, but of course I'm not. I'm not in an advert. It simply remains for me to thank my guests and welcome on the four gorgeous figures that fill – *(licks finger)* tsssss! Hot Pants!

*Music: 'Knowing Me, Knowing You'. Four male dancers dressed as policemen run on stage and strip to the music. Dressed in G-strings with Sprünt written across the front, they join Alan in the jacuzzi; two handcuff themselves to Alan.*

**Alan**
Ahh! They're men! They're men! And on that bombshell, on that bombshell, goodnight, ah-haa! Sprünt! Sprünt!

# KNOWING ME KNOWING YOU

*Alan Partridge* [signature]

*Shots of various traditional Paris scenes.*

**Alan**
(*Voiceover*) Paris: city of French people; home of Quasimodo, Louis XIV, Hercule Poirot and Sasha Distell; city of lovers, of artists, of the croissant, the cappuccino; city of moonlight, of dreams, of men in long coats meeting in brasseries at dawn; and the setting for the fourth show in the first series of *Knowing Me, Knowing You* with Alan Partridge.

*Music: 'Knowing Me, Knowing You'*

**Alan**
Ah-haa!

*Applause*
*Alan does a little run on to the stage and mimes pumping a machine gun.*

**Alan**
*Bonjour. Bonjour, bienvenu, tout le monde.* Why am I speaking in French? Well, it's because tonight's show is coming live from Paris.

*Audience cheer.*

**Alan**
What, what was once a pipe dream is now the Channel Tunnel: a big pipe. But tonight we're building a new construction, one that isn't vulnerable to a major terrorist attack. That's because it's a castle. A castle of chat, or a château.

*Drum roll*

**Alan**
Or, or, since we're in Paris, a chatisserie.

*Drum roll*

**Alan**
Now, when we were planning this I was asked if I would like a French co-host to help me present the show. I said, 'No! No way. *Nil point. Absolutement non.*' Then they showed me her photograph … and I said, '*Oui.* I'm happy to have this woman as my co-host, subject to certain contractual stipulations.' How can I describe her? Well, if I were mad Baron Frankenpartridge with a cellar full of pickled corpses, then I would take the clever head of Melvyn Bragg, stitch it to the torso of Edith Piaf, add some legs … er, I'm sorry, I think this is getting quite unpleasant. Erm, I'll just, I'll just bring her on. Please welcome my co-host, a delightful French madame – although she doesn't run a whorehouse, but, er, but she does have excellent organizational skills – here she is, France's answer to a younger Sue Lawley, Nina Vanyey!

*Music: 'Nina, Pretty Ballerina'; Nina enters stage.*

**Alan**
You, you won't find these at your local B & Q. *(Points to chairs)* They're, er, they're French. Knowing me, Alan Partridge, knowing you, Nina Vanyey, ah-haa.

**Nina**
Ah-haa.

**Alan**
I thought you were going to say 'oh-hoh' then, but, er, but you didn't. Now, Nina, let me start by saying that I'm delighted to have you as my co-host.

**Nina**
And I'm also delighted to have you as my co-host.

**Alan**
Er, no, no. Er, you're my co-host; I'm the host. Now, Nina, none of my, none of my British friends will forgive me if I didn't say, 'We love the Channel Tunnel, but for goodness' sake, don't send us any of your rabid dogs!'

**Nina**
No, we won't, Alan. As long as you don't send us any of your mad cows.

**Alan**
Well, I think, I think you'll find that our cows went mad because they were bitten by your dogs.

**Nina**
It's an interesting theory, if a little xenophobic.

**Alan**
No French.

**Nina**
Xenophobic's an English word. It means 'small-minded fear of other nations'.

**Alan**
It's time to meet our, our house band for this evening. They came over yesterday on the Hovercat.

**Nina**
Please welcome Glen Ponder and –

**Alan**
(*Speaks over Nina*) Glen Ponder and
Savoir Faire!

*Music: 'Knowing Me, Knowing You'*

**Alan**
Knowing me, Alan Partridge, knowing you,
Glen Ponder, ah-haa.

**Glen**
Ah-haa.

**Nina**
And knowing me, Nina Vanyey, knowing
you, Glen Ponder, ah-haa.

**Glen**
Ah-haa.

**Alan**
Knowing me, Alan Partridge, knowing you,
Savoir Faire, ah-haa.

**Savoir Faire**
(*In unison*) Ah-haa.

**Nina**
And knowing me, Nina Vanyey, knowing
you, Savoir Faire, ah-haa.

**Savoir Faire**
(*In unison*) Ah-haa.

**Alan**
Glen, erm, I was, I was taking a walk in
Paris this morning and I saw a madman
throw himself in the river.

**Glen**
Really, Alan?

**Alan**
Yes. He was quite literally insane. In
the Seine.

*Drum roll*

**Alan**
Seriously, Glen, er, seriously, are you
looking forward to, er, the high-kicking
ladies at La Folie Bergère tonight?

**Glen**
No, no, no, that was last night. Uh, we –
the plan was changed.

**Alan**
What?

**Glen**
I thought you knew. We – we left a message.

**Alan**
Well, I didn't get one. And I, I, I was
in my hotel room all night. I, I ended up
watching, er, er, *The Poseidon Adventure* on
TV. It was dubbed in French. There was
no message.

**Glen**
Well, I left one.

**Alan**
Glen Ponder and – you definitely left
a message?

**Glen**
Yes.

**Alan**
OK. Glen Ponder and Savoir Faire.

*Music: 'Knowing Me, Knowing You'*

**Alan**
Delia Smith, Keith Floyd, Fanny
Cradock and Mr Kipling are all famous
international chefs. So is our first guest –
my first guest.

**Nina**
He's the most controversial chef in Paris –
passionate about food, not so passionate
about the celebrities who dine in his
restaurant. Recently he poured rice
pudding over Bryan Ferry's head.

**Alan**

And slapped Jeremy Irons. He's wry, he's spry, he's crisp and dry, please welcome superchef Philippe Lambert.

*Music: 'Voulez-Vouz'; Philippe enters stage; Philippe kisses Nina on both cheeks, kisses Alan on one cheek, tries to kiss Alan on the other cheek but Alan shies away.*

**Alan**

Well, er, you certainly smell like a Frenchman. I mean, I mean your aftershave, it's very nice, very nice, it's a very nice smell. Was it, is it, what, Aramis?

**Philippe**

No, Alan, it's cologne.

**Alan**

Mmm. It's good. Good smell.

**Philippe**

Thank you. What's yours?

**Alan**

Er, Slazenger Sport. It's the, er, it's the stick type. I don't use the roll-on 'cause it, er, traps your hairs. Knowing me, Alan Partridge, knowing you, Philippe Lambert, ah-haa.

**Philippe**

Ah haa.

**Alan**

Now, Philippe, you have very, very kindly arranged some delicacies here for us to pick at throughout the show. Erm, now, I have to say, this, this is a whole different world to the universe of Hula Hoops, Cheesy Wotsits and Monster Munch. Tell, tell us a bit about them.

**Philippe**

It's what I call my *grande selection* –

**Alan**

*(To the audience)* Big selection.

**Philippe**

It's, er, a selection of *hors d'oeuvres* –

**Alan**

*(To the audience)* Starters.

**Philippe**

– that you might find in my restaurant. I think appetizers or –

**Alan**

*(To the audience)* Starters, same thing.

**Nina**

Philippe, these are superb. Let's talk about your restaurant.

**Alan**

Good, yeah. Good.

**Nina**

What's your fundamental approach to cuisine?

**Philippe**

Well, actually, Nina, I don't have an approach; I have a reproach, you know. I'm very bored by the whole restaurant industry. To me it seems little more than a big fat pig endlessly regurgitating and consuming that which – *(Alan takes a bite from several hors d'oeuvres, throwing each back on the plate with a look of disgust.)* – that which it eats, er, without discrimination – without taste – without joy. You know, I, I'm not interested what Egon Ronay thinks. You know, my Michelin stars, I send them back.

*Nina laughs.*

**Alan**

*(Eating a vol au vent)* You send them back? You just peel the sticker off the window and send it back?

**Philippe**

No, no, no, no, Alan.

# KNOWING ME, KNOWING YOU

**Alan**

No, I know, it is quite difficult, but it can be done. Erm, if you soak a sponge in soapy warm water and just hold it against the sticker, leave it for half an hour, come back, it will just peel away. Bob's your uncle, you've got your Michelin stars off the window.

**Philippe**

Thank you, Alan. I'll remember that.

**Alan**

Warm soapy water.

**Philippe**

Thank you.

**Alan**

It's got, it's got to be warm.

**Nina**

Philippe, the other – the other interesting thing about your restaurant, of course, is that it has no name.

**Philippe**

Yes, that's right. It's, er, if you like, er, an irony that, er, although it is called the restaurant with no name, people refer to it as The Restaurant With No Name.

*Nina laughs.*

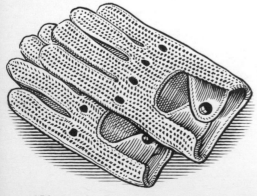

**Alan**

*(Speaks with mouthful of food)* Like Clint Eastwood.

**Philippe**

What?

*Alan chews, pointing at his mouth.*

**Alan**

Sorry. *(Keeps chewing)* I was just saying – it's like Clint Eastwood.

**Philippe**

What is like Clint Eastwood?

**Alan**

The spaghetti westerns – he was known as the, he was known as the man with no name.

**Nina**

And that's an irony that I think Jacques Derrida would appreciate.

**Philippe**

Oh, certainly, and, er, Jacques Derrida regularly dines at my restaurant and, indeed, regularly appreciates the irony.

*Nina and Philippe laugh.*

**Alan**

Who's, who's he?

**Philippe**

Jacques Derrida, the philosopher.

**Alan**

I've never heard of him.

**Nina**

Jacques Derrida, the most famous philosopher in the world.

**Alan**

Well, I wouldn't say that.

**Philippe**

Well, Alan, er, would you care to name a more famous philosopher?

**Alan**
Yeah. All the, er, all the Greek ones, yeah.

**Philippe**
Yes, but one who is alive? Who is the most famous philosopher, Alan?

**Alan**
Peter Ustinov?

**Philippe**
Yes, yes, absolutely right. Yes, I'd forgotten about that.

**Alan**
Thank you.

**Philippe**
Well, I'm lost. Your next question please, Confucius.

**Alan**
I'm not confused. All right, here's a good question. Now, you are known as the top chef in your field. You've only got one restaurant. Berni Inn has thousands. Jealous?

**Philippe**
I don't know. Who is, who is Berni Inn?

**Alan**
You've never heard of Berni Inn? He's the most famous steakhouse proprietor in the whole world.

**Philippe**
Well, I'm sorry, Alan, er, maybe Peter Ustinov should get together with Berni Inn and, er, open a steakhouse, you know. Have a steak, talk about philosophy.

**Alan**
Yeah, that's a good idea. They could call it, er, Pete and Berni's Philosophical Steakhouse. Good idea.

**Nina**
Actually, Philippe, what you were saying earlier about your restaurant having no name, I was thinking that another figure would have been amused by that. He is of course, er, René Magritte.

**Alan**
No French.

**Philippe**
He was Belgian.

**Alan**
Same thing.

*Alan starts to eat another hors d'oeuvre.*

**Philippe**
You like that one, Alan?

**Alan**
Mmmm. Quite nice. It's quite chewy. What is it?

**Philippe**
It's beef.

**Alan**
What sort of beef?

**Philippe**
Bull.

**Alan**
What – what, what part of a bull?

**Philippe**
It's a gland.

*Alan stops chewing.*

**Alan**
How – how many glands – how many of these glands does it have?

**Philippe**
Two.

*Alan spits hors d'oeuvre into napkin.*

**Nina**

Ladies and gentlemen, Philippe Lambert. *(To Alan)* Are you all right?

*Applause*

**Alan**

It's time once again for 'Knowing Me, Alan Partridge, knowing you, Another Alan Partridge', a regular feature of the series where I meet a person who shares my name, Alan Partridge. This week we had to find a French Alan Partridge. That has proved impossible, but the French for 'partridge' is '*perdris*'. So we scoured the countryside for an Alain Perdris. We found one. He's a lorry driver from Marseilles, he's visited England twice on various deliveries – I've not got the details – but he's here tonight, please welcome Alain Perdris, French for 'Alan Partridge'.

*Applause and music; Alan walks to back of stage to greet Alain Perdris.*

**Alan**

Knowing me, Alan Partridge, knowing you, Alain Perdris, another Alan Partridge, ah-haa.

*Silence*

**Alan**

Now in, in honour of the fact that you share my name, I'm very pleased to present you with an Alan Partridge tie and blazer-badge combination pack.

*Applause*

**Alan**

Well done. Well done.

*They shake hands.*

**Alain Perdris**

Er, *c'est quoi?*

**Alan**

What?

**Alain Perdris**

*C'est quoi?*

**Alan**

Oh. Er – C'est un tie – tie, tie *(Alan gestures doing up a tie)*, et un blazer, un badge pour un blazer. You st-stitch that on. No, don't take that out – please? And they come together in a boite – a box – in a combination pack.

**Alain Perdris**

*C'est pourquoi?*

**Alan**

Oh. Because it just does. Erm, now – don't know why I explained that. Erm, now, also to celebrate the new spirit of cooperation between our two nations, I have had a special painting commissioned by a Norwich-based artist. Erm, for, er, for my French viewers, Norwich is the Provence of Great Britain. Erm, it's the best of British, the best of France, it's a bulldog with frogs' legs.

*Alan gives painting to Alain Perdris; applause.*

**Alain Perdris**

*Je ne comprend pas.*

**Alan**

I don't understand. Why can't you just take it and go? *Allez*. Alan Perdris. Alain Perdris! Alain Perdris.

*Music: 'Knowing Me, Knowing You' and applause; Alain Perdris leaves.*

**Alan**

Don't like these chairs. By the way, if you're wondering where my normal furniture is, it's in Nîmes. Why? I don't know. Ask the French hauliers.

**Philippe**

Alan, er, are you growing a moustache?

**Alan**

No.

**Philippe**

Really?

**Alan**

No. Yes, yes, yes, I am. Yes, I'm growing a moustache. Is that a beard? Hmm? 'Cause I can't tell whether it's a beard or you just haven't shaved, you see. At least I'm honest. At least I'm admitting that I'm trying to grow a moustache.

**Philippe**

*(Laughing)* All right, all right. Don't get at me. Wasn't my fault you ate a testicle.

**Alan**

Er, if you remember, I spat it out.

**Philippe**

Ah yes, but there was another one.

**Alan**

No, all, no, all I had earlier was some spinach and a vol au vent – It was in the vol au vent, yeah. Very, very clever. And now it's time –

**Nina**

No, that's me.

**Alan**

Yes, sorry.

**Nina**

And now it's time for some light relief.

**Alan**

If I were to say, 'Clown time is over', I'd be lying because it's time now to send in the clowns, and I'm sure we won't be seeing the *tears* of a clown, because I'm told they're hilarious. I haven't seen them myself …

**Nina**

Please welcome this year's winner of the *Pompidou Prix de Joie, Cirque des Clowns.*

**Alan**

Circus of Clowns.

*Alan squeezes car klaxon and laughs.*

*Male clown pretends to smoke a cigarette, turns and notices female mime artist. Female clown pretends to unzip clothes; indicates that her nipples are erect.*

**Female clown**

Bing!

*Male clown pretends to screw something on to his groin, revs it up and charges round the stage, making engine noises. Clowns stand facing each other. Female clown touches her groin.*

**Female clown**

Bing!

*Male clown simulates giving female clown oral sex. Second male clown enters stage and pulls first clown away, gets on his knees and holds female clown's hands. Female clown pretends to stick knife in second male clown's eye. Male clown pretends to cut second male clown's throat. Female clown and male clown pretend to remove second male clown's penis using a chainsaw.*

**Alan**
Oh, no! No!

*Male clown pretends to swing penis round his head and throws it into audience. Male and female clown pretend to piss and crap on second male clown. Male clown pretends to wipe his bottom on tissue and stuffs it into second clown's mouth.*

*Alan stands up and walks towards clowns.*

**Alan**
No, no, no, no, no …

*Male and female clown simulate sex.*

*Alan tries to part clowns, but gets trapped between them.*

**Alan**
… no, no, no! NO! NO! NO! NO! NO!

*Alan breaks free.*

**Alan**
Cirque des Clouns! Cirque des Clouns!

*Applause; clowns applaud audience and bow.*

**Alan**
Grow up! Grow up.

**Clowns**
Shh! Shh! Shh! Shh! Shh! Shh! Shh!

**Alan**
Sh! Thank you. Cirque des Clouns, yes –

**Clowns**
Shh! Shh! Shh! Shh! Shh! Shh! Shh! Shh!

**Alan**
Cirque des –

**Clowns**
Shh! Shh! Shh! Shh! Shh! Shh! Shh!

**Alan**
Right, now, listen, listen. Right, right, hang on. *(Turns to face male clown)* I presume you're in charge. Let me tell you something, right? There's a security guard back stage called Steve, right? Now, I promise you, if you make another sound when you leave this area he will hurt you. He will hurt you physically. Cirque des Clouns.

*Clowns make farting noise, wave hands about and wrinkle noses in disgust.*

**Alan**
Cirque des Clouns. Sorry, I – I haven't broken wind. I – I haven't broken wind. That's them.

*Clowns fall to the floor, pretending to be suffocated.*

**Alan**
Cirque des Clouns will be doing a tour of art centres in Britain. I'm sure there'll be plenty of tickets available. You're a disgrace. Cirque des Clouns.

*Applause. Alan walks back to sofa. Male clown follows behind without attracting Alan's attention.*

**Alan**
Sanity.

*Alan sits down on male clown's lap and jumps up.*

**Alan**
What are you doing there? What are you doing? Get out! Why is he still here? Can we – can someone, can someone remove this clown, please? Where's Steve? Is he? He's back stage. No, he'll get him after. He'll get him after.

*Alan tries to sit down twice, but clown follows his movements.*

**Alan**

I'll do it standing up. I hope my next guest doesn't suffer from –

*Alan tries to sit down quickly, but clown grabs him.*

**Alan**

I'll do it here. I'll do it here. I'll do it here. I hope my next guest doesn't suffer from vertigo, because she's at the height of her profession.

*Drum roll*

**Alan**

She's a top international fashion designer who hails from Lancashire.

*Male clown disappears; reappears standing between Alan and camera.*

**Alan**

Let me just – let me just say – let me just say, you look stupid, you look stupid, not me. Right, I'll do it, I'll do it on three. I'll do it on three.

*Alan turns to face camera three.*

**Alan**

She's a top international fashion designer from Lancashire in the north of England.

*Clown pretends to crack egg on Alan's head.*

**Alan**

Right, no, I'm sorry, I can't, sorry – Nina, can you, can you –

**Nina**

Yes, Alan?

**Alan**

Can you get rid of him, please? Sorry about this.

**Nina**

*Alors, mon ami (Nina speaks to clown in French)*

**Clown**

*Ah, bon (he replies in French and moves away from Alan)*

**Nina**

*Ah, oui, merci.*

**Alan**

There he goes. There he goes.

*Applause; clown walks off.*

**Alan**

There he goes. Tail between his legs. Steve, he's coming out! I hope my next guest doesn't suffer from vertigo because she's at the height of her profession.

*Drum roll*

**Alan**

Sorry – sorry, what, what did you say to him to get rid of him?

**Nina**

Oh no, it's not necessary to translate.

**Alan**

No, seriously, I want, I want to know.

**Nina**

No, you don't need to know –

**Alan**

No, you know the contract: I command you to tell me.

**Nina**

Very well, Alan. I told him that you are completely out of your depth with a creative artist of his calibre and that lack of experience makes you unable to cope with a situation in a professional way.

**Alan**

*(Pause)* I hope the next guest doesn't suffer from vertigo because – because she's at the height of her profession.

*Drum roll*

**Alan**
We don't need to do it now.

**Nina**
She arrived yesterday from London on the train because she doesn't like flying.

**Alan**
She really does suffer from vertigo.

**Nina**
And she caught the train from Waterloo. Please welcome fashion guru Yvonne Boyd.

**Alan**
Who, who came from Waterloo.
*(Turns to Nina)* Right. Very important …

*Music: 'Waterloo'; Yvonne, wearing an unusual outfit and bouffant grey wig, joins Philippe on sofa.*

**Alan**
*(Sighs)* Knowing me, knowing you, Yvonne Boyd, ah-haa.

**Yvonne**
Do you want me to say, 'Ah-haa'?

**Alan**
Yes, please.

**Yvonne**
Ah-haa.

**Nina**
I'm a big fan of your clothes. I must say the outfit you're wearing tonight is wonderful. I really love it.

**Alan**
Yeah. I didn't know that as well as doing fashion you also do pantomime.

**Yvonne**
What do you mean?

**Alan**
I presume you're Widow Twankey.

**Yvonne**
No.

**Alan**
Are you an Ugly Sister?

**Nina**
Alan, these are Yvonne's clothes.

**Alan**
I'm sorry. I, I, I thought you did pantomime.

**Yvonne**
No, I don't do pantomime.

**Alan**
Well, maybe you should, you know, I mean – you've got, you've got the clothes and, er, and without wanting to be vulgar, the money is very good. It's very good. In fact, I'll tell you something, last Christmas I was in two pantomimes. I was in Norwich and Colchester as Mother Goose. And, er, in fact I had to travel from one theatre to the other in my goose suit. It was quite hectic, you know, but, er, believe me at the end of the season I quite literally laid a golden egg. It's worth considering, it's worth considering. *(Points to Nina, Yvonne and Philippe in turn)* Peter Pan, Widow Twankey, Buttons.

**Nina**
Yvonne, can you talk us through the thinking behind this magnificent outfit you're wearing.

**Yvonne**
Well, it's a sort of *fin de siècle* ghost in the machine.

**Alan**
*(Looking at her chest)* Is that the distributor cap off a Ford Mondeo?

**Yvonne**
I've absolutely no idea.

**Alan**
Let's have a look. *(He gets up and takes a closer look)* Yes, yes, it is. Do you drive a Ford Mondeo?

**Yvonne**

No. I don't drive. I don't like cars.

**Alan**

She doesn't drive. She doesn't, she doesn't fly, doesn't do pantomime. What do you do?

**Yvonne**

I design clothes.

**Alan**

Is that all?

**Yvonne**

Yes.

**Alan**

Well, that's interesting – because whereas you're a master of one trade, I like to think of myself as an Alan of all trades. And – and I've got a bit of a surprise for you, Yvonne, in this, a new regular section of the show called 'Alan's Trades', in which I demonstrate a trade that I am an Alan of. This week's – this week's Alan trade is fashion. Now, now, I'm not Giorgio Armani. I'm Alan Partridge, but – but my name has become associated with a certain look, a look I define as sports casual. Yvonne – Yvonne, tell me – tell me what you think as we look at a Partridge in Paris. A Partridge in Paris. Alan Partridge in Paris.

*Film clip – shots of Alan in Paris posing in the different outfits he is describing.*

**Alan**

The first look is what you'd wear to drive to Paris. It's called cruiser arriviste: canary-yellow shirt, horizon-blue stay-crease action slacks, a cap, Polaroids, tan stringback driving gloves. It's a look that says, 'I'm in control of my vehicle.' Who's this cool customer? Ice-white shoes, ice-white socks with navy-blue double-cadet stripe, a pair of shorts, T-shirt with chevron action flash: *l'homme du sport* – man of sport. The tossed pink sweater that says, 'I'm in Paris and nothing's gonna stop me.' That's, that's the Eiffel Tower. The classic English gentleman abroad. It's David Niven. It's Stewart Granger. It's Nigel Havers. It's a green blazer. The look: imperial leisure. Offset the look with those four old reliables: cravat, hat, summer spectacles and, for a touch of class, the Alan Partridge blazer badge. A lot of people have asked me about the blazer badge. Well, I'll describe it in – in the top right – *(badge moves out of view)* sorry, I'll do it next week. I'll do it next week. The place: Champs Elysées; the man: Alan Partridge; the look: strolling pastel. A classic summer suit with the omission of long trousers. A Partridge in Paris.

*Applause*

**Alan**

*(Nibbling on vol au vent)* Well, tell me what you think. Shoot from the hip.

**Philippe**

Alan, you are to the world of fashion what Peter Ustinov is to the world of philosophy.

**Nina**

Yvonne, is fashion a necessity of culture or a cultural necessity?

**Alan**

*(Sighs)* Hang on, hang on. I – it appears to be happy hour at Pete and Berni's Philosophical Steakhouse.

**Yvonne**

I think you're rather rude actually, because Nina's asked a very interesting question. What I think is that fashion is a necessity of culture, because really clothes are just things that cover up our mutual nakedness. I mean, you know, underneath our clothes we're all of us naked. Even you, Alan.

**Alan**

No, I'm not.

**Yvonne**
Yes, of course you are.

**Alan**
No, I'm not. I've got underwear.

**Philippe**
Yes, but underneath your underwear
you are naked.

**Alan**
No, I'm not.

**Philippe**
Of course. You have your buttocks.

**Alan**
Oh yes, here we go. I was – I was wondering
how long it would take before the show
descended into some French hidden
buttock agenda.

**Nina**
Alan, all we are saying is that underneath
your clothes, you are naked.

**Alan**
*(Clears throat)* No, I'm not. Now – now,
Yvonne, we're about to see some clothes
from your menswear collection. Now the
theme of my collection was sports casual.
Now bearing in mind that Pete and Berni's
Philosophical Steakhouse is closed, what's
the theme of your collection?

**Yvonne**
The futility of mortality.

**Alan**
Why do I bother? Bring – bring on the
models. Bring on the models.

**Yvonne**
Right, well, the first model is Tor. Tor's –
Tor's cap and shorts, erm, are made of
bandages and his linen jacket has got real
surgical stitching on it. Erm, he's also got
a little truss on, which is, erm, a sort of
ironic bumbag.

**Alan**
Is this man injured?

**Yvonne**
No. The whole collection is based on
images of hospitalization.

**Alan**
Right. So, so the idea is, you've had an
operation, you want to look good on the
ward – that, that's what you wear.

**Yvonne**
No. No, they're for wearing anywhere.
You wear them on the street.

**Alan**
He's wearing slippers. Sorry, the only man
I know who wears slippers on the street is
called Dougie. He wanders round Norwich
shopping precinct with a Cornish pastie in
his hand, shouting, 'Get away – it's a bomb.'
He's insane.

**Yvonne**
Well, maybe he's sane and we're all mad.
Anyway the next model – erm, the next one
is Numan with – Numan's got, er, a more
formal look.

**Nina**
That's beautiful, Yvonne.

**Yvonne**
Thank you. Thank you. Erm, here you see –
I've broken up the classic lines of the suit
with a saline drip attached to an umbrella,
and with a pair of brogues, one of which
is orthopaedic.

**Alan**
He looks like he's been in a car crash.

**Yvonne**
The final model, who's coming on now, is
Matt. Now here I'm playing with ideas of
constriction and freedom. So just as the
plaster boots here impede, the bandage
kilt liberates.

**Alan**
This waistcoat covered in corn plasters …

**Yvonne**
Mmmm.

**Alan**
Are they used?

**Nina**
Oh, for goodness' sake.

**Yvonne**
No, of course not. Don't be so ludicrous.

**Alan**
Sorry, I'm, I'm being told I'm ludicrous
by Mrs Whippyhead.

**Yvonne**
*(Sighs)* Well, that's the end of my collection.

**Nina**
Yvonne, it's a triumph. Thank you!

**Yvonne**
Thank you.

*Applause*

**Alan**
Sorry, er – yeah, yeah, sorry, er, I'm, I'm –
I'm, I'm confused. I've got to ask a couple
of questions. Erm, this, this man here –
what's this round his midriff?

**Yvonne**
It's a blood bag.

**Alan**
What if it bursts?

**Yvonne**
Well, you mop it up.

**Alan**
What with? What with?

**Yvonne**
With the eye patch. It's not a problem. I
mean, what if your nose bleeds, you know?
What if your, your – what if your arm bursts?

**Alan**
What?

**Yvonne**
What if your arm bursts?

**Alan**
I'm sorry. I've heard of a nosebleed, but er –
in – in my fourteen years of professional
broadcasting, including three years as a
hospital radio disc jockey, I have never had
anyone come up to me and say, 'My arm's
just burst. Could you play a dedication?'

**Philippe**
Oh, come on, Alan.

**Nina**
Alan –

**Yvonne**
You just got me on here to ridicule –

**Philippe**
You're taking things too literally.

**Yvonne**
– the clothes.

**Alan**
No, no, no, no, no. No. I'll show you. I will
show you. You with the orthopaedic shoe.
What's his name?

**Yvonne**
Numan.

**Alan**
Numan. You just walk up here and then
walk back again, easy as you like.

*Numan walks towards Alan and back –
the orthopaedic shoe makes him limp.*

**Alan**
That man has no dignity.

**Nina**
But what is dignity?

**Alan**
Right. That –

*Alan walks backwards and forwards.*

**Alan**

– that is dignity. More or less. No one will wear these clothes. They look rubbish. Ordinary people do not like those clothes.

**Philippe**

I like those clothes.

**Nina**

I like them too.

**Alan**

You're not ordinary. You're French. Glen, Glen, me old mate, Glen. Those clothes – are they rubbish or what?

**Glen**

I like them. Quite nice.

**Alan**

What? You traitor. There stands Judas Ponder. Check in his pockets, you'll find thirty pieces of silver. Except you won't because he spent them all last night at the Folies Bergère. *(Turns to face Nina and Yvonne)* What are you two staring at? You look like the Steptoe wives.

**Nina**

I think you mean the Stepford wives.

**Alan**

I thought you French were good at chatting. I thought that's all you did all day, sitting outside your brasseries, sipping your cappuccinos, chomping on onions and going, 'Oh-he-oh-he-oh.'

**Philippe**

Oh, come on, Alan, grow up.

**Nina**

Oh, now you're just being racist.

**Alan**

That is not racist. French people chomp on onions and go 'Oh-he-oh-he-oh'. That's a fact. Well, we've come to the end of the show. Erm, I've enjoyed it very much. I like to think that our two nations are perhaps slightly closer together than they were at the beginning of the show. And that can only be a good thing. It simply remains for me to thank my co-host, Nina, thank you.

**Nina**

It's been a pleasure.

**Alan**

Erm, you doing anything interesting tonight?

**Nina**

No, I don't think so. Not after last night – I'm too exhausted.

**Alan**

Why? What did you do last night?

**Nina**

I went to the *Folies Bergère*.

**Alan**

That's a coincidence – that's where Glen Ponder went.

**Yvonne**

I was there, too.

**Nina**

Yvonne.

**Philippe**

I was there.

**Nina**

Philippe.

**Alan**

You were?

**Yvonne**

My models were there.

**Alan**

Who else –

**Philippe**

Glen invited us all. Er, the clowns, they were there and, er –

**Alan**

The clowns?

**Philippe**

Yes, your security guard, Steve, he was there. He's, er –

**Alan**

I don't believe it.

**Philippe**

Yes, he's good – good friends with the clowns, I believe. He was there.

**Yvonne**

And the band were there as well.

**Alan**

The band? You! Accordion man – were you there?

**Accordion man**

Yeah.

**Philippe**

Everyone except you, Alan.

**Alan**

Glen, why didn't you invite me?

**Glen**

I left a message.

**Alan**

Right, Glen, I'm going to ask you a question, and I want you to give me an honest and truthful answer. Did you leave a message for me last night?

**Glen**

No.

**Alan**

Thank you.

**Glen**

Quite honestly, Alan, I didn't think they'd let you in, you know. There was a sign outside there saying, 'No jeans, no trainers, no sports casual wear'.

*Glen, Nina, Yvonne and Philippe laugh.*

**Philippe**

Glen.

**Glen**

Just a joke.

**Alan**

Just a joke, eh? Here's a good joke. Here's a good joke. You'll like this one. There's this bloke called Glen Ponder. He's playing jazz synthesizer in a Norwich wine bar. In walks Alan Partridge. Alan gives him a big break on national television. Glen's pleased. Glen gets lippy. Glen gets the sack.

**Glen**

What – what do you mean?

**Alan**

You're sacked. You are sacked. I'm sacking you. In fact it's happened. It's over. It's already – you are a sacked man. You've been sacked. You're the subject of a sacking. I want you off these premises in ten minutes. Knowing me, Alan Partridge, sacking you, Glen Ponder. Ah-haa. And on that bombshell, it's time for me to say, knowing me, Alan Partridge, knowing you, Monsieur Testicle, knowing you, pantomime cow, and knowing you, Ms Oh-he-oh-he-oh. Goodnight, arrividerche and ah-haa!

*Music: 'Knowing Me, Knowing You'.*

**Alan**

*(To band)* Not you, not you! Not you. *(To accordion man)* Just you.

*Glen Ponder's band stop playing; accordion man plays solo.*

*Applause*

# KNOWING ME KNOWING YOU

*Alan Partridge*

Music: '*Knowing Me, Knowing You*'

**Alan**

Ah-haa!

*Applause.*

*Alan does a little run onstage and throws some punches and kicks, Karate style.*

**Alan**

Welcome. Welcome. Welcome. Welcome to *Knowing Me, Knowing You* with Alan Partridge, or the *Alan Partridge Show*, as most people like to call it. Erm, it's easier – that's what I call it. I've got to tell you, there's so much packed into tonight's show that at the end of it I'm quite sure I'm going to be shattered. Or should I say chattered.

*Drum roll*

**Alan**

You, er, you may remember that at the end of last week's show I sacked my house band and their leader, Glen Ponder. That's TV. They had to go. So will you now please welcome my new resident house band, The Eagles! Or rather – no, don't! Don't welcome The Eagles because Glen has put a stop to that. This week he obtained a court injunction preventing his dismissal prior to an industrial tribunal to be held at the end of the series. So will you now please welcome not double-platinum-album-selling rock stars The Eagles, but Ipswich-based, hotel-lobby wine-bar band, Glen Ponder and Lazarus!

*Music: 'Knowing Me, Knowing You'*
*Applause*

**Alan**

*(Quickly and without enthusiasm)*
Knowing me, Alan Partridge, knowing you, Glen Ponder, ah-haa.

**Glen**

*(Also without enthusiasm)* Ah-haa.

**Alan**

Knowing me, Alan Partridge, knowing you Lazarus, ah-haa.

**Lazarus**

*(In unison)* Ah-haa.

**Alan**

Glen, if this show was a motorcar, what kind of motorcar would it be?

**Glen**

I've no idea.

**Alan**

Chatty-chatty-bang-bang.

*Drum beat*

**Alan**

Glen Ponder and Lazarus.

*Music: 'Knowing Me, Knowing You'*
*Applause*

**Alan**

See you –

*Band repeat last line of music.*

**Alan**

See you in court. My first guest was born within the sound of Bow Bells. He is a Cockney man. Thirty years ago he crawled out of the maggot-ridden cesspit that is the East End of London to become … to become Britain's most colourful boxing and entertainments promoter. He spends all day on the dog and bone – phone. He's about to come down these apples and pears – stairs. I'm sure we're going to have a great bowler hat – chat. So please welcome a very special antique Edwardian teachest – guest. That last one was mine. Erm, two years ago … two years ago he was cleared of garrotting a nightclub owner in Leicester Square, please welcome Terry Norton!

*Music: 'What's the Name of the Game';*
*applause; Terry joins Alan.*

**Alan**

Ah. Nice, nice, nice whistle. Whistle and toot – suit.

**Terry**

Flute.

**Alan**

Sorry?

**Terry**

Whistle and flute – suit.

**Alan**

Yeah, yeah, right, whatever. Erm, knowing me, Alan Partridge, knowing you, Terry Norton, ah-haa.

**Terry**
Ah-haa.

**Alan**
Now, Terry: sport. You have managed boxers, wrestlers, snookers – snookerers, snookerers?

**Terry**
Snooker players.

**Alan**
Snooker players. Bowling – crown green and tenpin; that didn't work – but – but you first made your name way back in the seventies with that fabulous champion boxer Billy O'Rourke.

**Terry**
Billy 'the Blitz' O'Rourke.

**Alan**
Billy the Blitz. Why did they call him 'the Blitz'?

**Terry**
Because when he come at you it was like a blitzkrieg.

**Alan**
You can say that again. Was, was he German?

**Terry**
No, he's London Irish. Out of Kilburn.

**Alan**
But, erm, he, he could take a punch, couldn't he, ay? Ay? At the end of some of those fights he looked like a bloomin' cauliflower.

**Terry**
And the other geezer looked like mashed potatoes.

*Terry and Alan laugh.*

**Alan**
Mashed potatoes! Oh. Billy 'the Blitz' O'Rourke. Sadly, of course, no longer with us.

**Terry**
Oh, Billy's still alive.

**Alan**
Well, technically. Now … now, Terry, you come from a very humble background. But now you mix with the great and the good. You're a little Cockney whelk, sitting on a plate of oysters. Do you ever – do you ever, sort of, think to yourself, how did I get here on top of this – plate of – oysters?

**Terry**
Well, well, of course I do, Alan. I mean, it's a combination of determination, perseverance and a good head for business.

**Alan**
Of course. And, if I may so, *(sings)* wi' a little bit, wi' a little bit, wi' a little bit o' bloomin' luck. Is that – is that – is that fair?

**Terry**
*(Looking annoyed)* Yeah, well, you know, if you like, yeah. No, you and me, Alan, we're the same. No, we're two working-class boys, no education, no qualifications, but through sheer determination we have made it to the top of the tree.

**Alan**
Well, I've got to pick you up on a couple of points there. I did go to East Anglia Polytechnic and I've got a couple of pretty good A levels.

**Terry**
Yeah, well, you know what I mean.

**Alan**
Yeah, I know, and very quickly, as regards working class, erm, my, my, my parents did own their home and we holidayed now and again in Spain. So I don't think that's quite right. But, erm, I imagine, er – I imagine you know Spain quite well, what with all your, er, all your connections?

**Terry**

Yeah, yeah, I've got a villa out there. It's cut into the cliff, overlooking the Med. Blindin'.

**Alan**

Lovely. Well, you would, wouldn't you, you know? Just in case.

**Terry**

Just in case what?

**Alan**

You know, just in case you need to go on holiday – quickly.

**Terry**

*(Laughs)* I think you're leading me down a dark alley.

**Alan**

*(Laughs)* I see – the last place I'd like to be with you is down a dark alley.

**Terry**

Why's that?

**Alan**

Sorry?

**Terry**

Why's that?

**Alan**

I just wouldn't. Now, Terry, you, you, you've promoted boxing, er, snooker, bowling – crown green and tenpin; that didn't work – but, er, now you're launching a new promotion, next month. Tell us about that.

**Terry**

Er, that's right, yes. I'm, er, I'm bringing back the beauty contest because, er, times may change, fashion whatever, but people will always want to look at lovely ladies. Now that is from the twentieth century right back to the Ancient Greeks.

**Alan**

Aristotle Onassis.

**Terry**

Exactly. I mean, whatever the women's libbers may say – Germaine Greer, Esther Rantzen –

**Alan**

That lot, yeah.

**Terry**

– you can't change human nature.

**Alan**

You can't, Terry. But I'll tell you something. I, er, I used to support the women's libbers.

**Terry**

Really?

**Alan**

When they said, er, 'Burn your bras.'

*Terry and Alan laugh.*

**Terry**

Yeah, well, I'm gettin' a bit of stick from the – loony left, you know, but, er, who cares?

**Alan**

Absolutely. You cannot say anything these days, Terry, I tell you. A couple of months ago I was commentating on a football match with the Cameroons. I made a harmless remark about a raindance, right? What, what happens? I get hauled over the coals. Not literally. I imagine that's the kind of thing the Cameroons do.

*Alan laughs.*

**Terry**

Well, that's right, yeah.

**Alan**

I'll probably get in trouble for that now, you know. Please, please, don't write in saying that's racist. It's not.

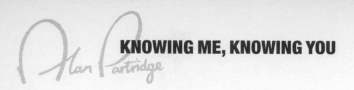

**Terry**
It doesn't matter what they say because next month live on Sky Television it's Miss Great Britain and there's nuffink can spoil that feast.

**Alan**
Oh, absolutely. And, and, we're going to, we're going to, er, eat some of that feast later, because, er, Terry has very kindly cooked up a, er, tray of lady vol au vents, if you will, which I will be eating – or compèring – later in the show. What I mean is that tonight on this programme I will be master of ceremonies for the final heat of – and it's my home town – Miss Norwich!

*Applause*

**Terry**
Yeah.

**Alan**
Now, Terry. Murderer! You killed my son! That was what the mother – of – of the garrotted nightclub owner of Leicester Square said to you as you left court, having been cleared of the murder of her son – her only son – the – garrotted nightclub owner of Leicester Square. Did, did those words hurt?

**Terry**
Well, of course. Yes, I was in Leicester Square that night, but as was proved in court, I was hailing a cab at the time it happened.

**Alan**
Absolutely. Well, we've now got a reconstruction of that night, using professional actors, some of whom have appeared in *The Bill* and *Minder*. Now, Terry. That night in Leicester Square – was it something like this?

*Man on stage wearing black balaclava pretends to strangle another man with a chain; man representing Terry faces away from them.*

**Man representing Terry**
Taxi!

**Alan**
Was that how it was?

**Terry**
Well, yeah, more or less, yeah.

**Alan**
Right, because at the time there were some people who said it happened like this.

*Man representing Terry pretends to strangle man with a chain.*

**Man representing Terry**
Taxi!

**Alan**
That's how it didn't happen.

**Terry**
What's, what's that?

**Alan**
That, that was how it didn't happen.

**Terry**
No, no. That is a couple of ponces mincing about, talking rubbish.

**Alan**
Touched a nerve there. Intriguing.

**Terry**
I could have gone down for this. It was dealt with by the law courts, the matter is finished, it's over, it's dead and buried.

**Alan**
Rather like the garrotted –

**Terry**
Now, don't muck about. You're getting out yer depth, Alan. People get out their depth, they end up drowning.

**Alan**

Calm down, it's just a chat show.

**Terry**

Do you wanna get involved? Do you wanna get involved in this world? Nightclub owners in Leicester Square who get garrotted? Ammonia in the boat? 'Cause if you wanna get involved, I'll get you involved, son. You wanna get sucked in? I'll suck you in. I'll suck you in so far you get blown out the other side. Wipe that soppy look off yer gormless face. Do you wanna get sucked in?

**Alan**

*(Looking frightened)* I don't. I don't want to get sucked in.

**Terry**

Well, then, you tell these ladies and gentlemen what that was all about.

**Alan**

That was a couple of ponces mincing about, talking rubbish.

*Applause*

**Terry**

Now, are we gonna have a beauty contest or what?

**Alan**

Beauty contest, please.

**Terry**

Thank you.

**Alan**

I'll – I'll see you later for that. Thank you for that nice chat. Erm, ladies and gentlemen, Terry Norton – an innocent man.

*Applause*

**Alan**

It's – it's time now for one of the hit bits of my show. Knowing Me, Alan Partridge, Knowing You, Another Alan Partridge, in which I meet another man whose name is Alan Partridge. It really is that simple. Two weeks ago I received a letter from an Alan Partridge in Preston, Lancashire, who asked to come on to the show. I booked him to appear tonight. One week ago he died. Well, I immediately telephoned his family and told them that I would still honour the booking if they so desired. They kindly agreed, saying, 'It is what Alan would have wanted.' So please welcome, with his widow and family, Alan Partridge!

*Music: 'Funeral March'; applause; coffin brought onstage, followed by another Alan Partridge's family.*

**Alan**

*(In a subdued voice)* Knowing me, Alan Partridge, knowing you, another Alan Partridge. Rest in peace, ah-haa. Knowing me, Alan Partridge, knowing you, Mary Partridge, ah-haa.

**Mary**

Ah-haa.

**Alan**

Knowing me, Alan Partridge, knowing you – I'm sorry, I've forgotten your name.

**Liam**

Liam.

**Alan**

Liam. Liam Partridge, son of Alan, ah-haa.

**Mary and Liam**

Ah-haa.

**Alan**

No, no, not you. Just you.

**Liam**
Ah-haa.

**Alan**
Ah-haa. Tell us, what was he like?

**Mary**
Well, he liked to drink.

**Liam**
He didn't suffer fools gladly.

**Mary**
Oh no, he'd got quite a temper on 'im.

**Alan**
Right.

*Silence; Alan knocks on coffin lid.*

**Alan**
But, he, he, he, he, he did, he did, he did like this show, didn't he?

**Mary**
Oh yes. It was his – what? Second favourite television programme.

**Alan**
Right. So, so what, what, what was his first?

**Liam**
*Baywatch.*

**Alan**
Right. About the beach people?

**Mary**
He liked the girls.

**Alan**
Don't we all. Don't we all. Er, let's hope there are girls in heaven, erm, if – if that's where he's going, you know. From what you say, it seems a little unclear. But, er, who knows? Perhaps, perhaps there are girls in purgatory or, or, or hell. Erm, but no one leaves this show empty-handed, so I'm very glad – I don't know know why I'm doing it in that voice – *(speaks in a cheerier voice)* no one leaves this show empty-handed, so I'm very pleased to present Alan this lovely headstone for Alan's grave. It's a granite marble mix in Normandy grey and, er, it's covered in Duboseal, which means any graffiti from vandals can just be wiped clean. Do you like it?

**Mary**
It's lovely.

**Liam**
He was actually born in 1931.

**Alan**
Right. What, what have, what have we got?

**Liam**
'32.

**Alan**
Right. One year out – not bad. I mean, if, if, if it's a problem, we can, we can regrind it. We can take it away and get it reground.

**Liam**
Yes, that'd be great.

**Alan**
Right. Erm, the problem is, I mean, we can do that, it's just that it will take a couple of weeks and, erm, it's only one year out.

**Liam**

He'd like the right date.

**Alan**

He would like the right date.

**Liam**

He would like the right date.

**Alan**

Right.

**Mary**

He'd got quite a temper.

**Alan**

Well, he's hardly likely to display that now, is he? But, er, if – you know, if you want it reground we'll get it done.

**Liam**

Thank you. It's what he would have wanted.

**Alan**

Well, we'll do it! It's not a problem.

**Liam**

Thank you.

**Alan**

Thank you.

**Mary**

Sorry.

**Alan**

What?

**Mary**

Sorry.

**Alan**

Sorry, right. Well, er … ladies and gentlemen, Alan Partridge, his son Liam and his lovely widow, Mary!

*Music: 'Funeral March'. Coffin wheeled off. Applause*

**Alan**

Well, as we heard, Alan was quite fond of pretty ladies, so it seems entirely appropriate that in his presence we hold now the grand final of Miss Norwich. Mary, you've agreed with Liam and your uncle Pete *(Pete joins them onstage)* there, to, er, to stay a little bit longer and judge tonight's contest.

**Liam**

Yes.

**Alan**

So take up your positions, please. Glen, would, er, would you like to judge Miss Norwich?

**Glen**

I'd love to.

**Alan**

Well, you can't. Now – now if you're watching this at home in your Parker Knoll armchair, hit the recline button, sit back, relax as we go girl-crazy with a bit of harmless fun – that's all it is. Please – please welcome the finalists for Miss Norwich!

*Applause; first finalist enters stage.*

**Alan**

The first contestant is Susan Atkinson. She's twenty years old. Her vital statistics are 34, 24, 33, so she's slightly bigger at the top. She's a shop assistant for Saxone Shoes, and she tells me the most popular shoes are plain black lace-ups with six eyes. Contestant number two is Donna Cookson.

*Applause and whistles; Donna enters stage.*

**Alan**

Donna – Donna is twenty. Come on! Keep it down. Donna used to – Donna used to dance in a nightclub, but it was closed down after a fire. Contestant number three is 21-year-old Lisa Thornton.

*Applause; Lisa enters stage.*

**Alan**

Lisa – Lisa is a nanny for a professional couple, whom she tells me make adverts and live in a converted barn. Sometimes she has the whole house to herself and she likes to use the CD system to dance around the living room to pop music. She's the shortest of tonight's contestants. Contestant number four is Maria McNulty.

*Applause; Maria enters stage.*

**Alan**

Maria is an Irish Roman Catholic. She tells me that before each beauty contest she says a quick prayer. She has a 36-inch bust. Ave Maria! And our final contestant tonight is Siobhan Glokowski.

*Applause; Siobhan enters stage.*

**Alan**

Siobhan works in William Hill bookmakers. So, what are her odds tonight? I'll tell you. They're fifty to one – she's a rank outsider. Siobhan also has a Polish grandmother who doesn't speak any English. And those are tonight's finalists.

*Applause – models stand in a line across the stage.*

**Alan**

Well, we've looked at their bodies. Now let's, let's look at their minds. Erm, Susan Atkinson, you work at Saxone Shoes?

**Susan**

Yes.

**Alan**

And I imagine, do you get a lot of competition from Dolcis?

**Susan**

Mmm, yeah. We do.

**Alan**

Great. Lovely. Erm, Donna – Donna Cookson.

*Applause and whistles*

**Alan**

You, er – you certainly, er, seem to have a lot of fans out there. Er, are you enjoying the competition?

**Donna**

Yes, I am.

**Alan**

Mmm. And, er, do you watch this show at all?

**Donna**

No.

**Alan**

No. That's all right. That's OK. No, that's fine. Lisa Thornton, do you have, er, do you have any hobbies?

**Lisa**

Yes, I like swimming and dancing.

**Alan**

Right. Lovely. Very nice.

**Lisa**

I've always wanted to meet you.

**Alan**

Really? Oh.

**Lisa**

I like your moustache.

**Alan**
Really?

**Lisa**
Yeah. It, like, really suits your face.

**Alan**
I keep it trimmed with nasal scissors, yes.

**Lisa**
Oh. Makes you look like Rhett Butler in
*Gone With the Wind*.

**Alan**
Well, thank you, my dear. I don't give
a damn.

*Lisa laughs.*

**Alan**
Of course I do. Of course I give a damn.
You're, you're lovely. What's, what's, what's
your ambition?

**Lisa**
Well, I'd like to work in television.

**Alan**
Really? Great, great. Well, we – we should
have a chat. After the show. What – you're
all staying at the Holiday Inn?

**Lisa**
Well, the other girls are, but I'm staying
here at home with my mum.

**Alan**
Right, OK. Right. *(Walks over to next
contestant. Turns back to Lisa)* You could just
go back to the hotel for a drink, you know, a
quick drink and, you know, we'd get you a
taxi home afterwards. I'll speak to your
mum if you want.

**Lisa**
OK.

**Alan**
Right.

**Lisa**
Lovely.

**Alan**
Yeah, we'll have a chat afterwards.

**Lisa**
Thank you.

**Alan**
Good luck!

**Lisa**
Thanks.

**Alan**
Right, OK. Now, do you like animals?

**Maria**
Yes.

**Alan**
Do you?

**Siobhan**
Yes.

**Alan**
Right, OK. Fair enough. Right, erm – well,
we've, we've done them all, so, while the
judges make up their minds I'm afraid
you're just gonna have to listen to Glen
Ponder and Lazarus.

*Applause; Music: 'The Winner Takes It All'.*

**Alan**
*(Talking quietly to panel while music plays)*
Number three has got the best personality,
and I think that's, that's what matters.

**Mary**
No.

**Alan**
Number three?

**Mary**
No.

**Alan**

All right, yeah. Number three, because it's the best personality. Right, now look, it's a majority decision. Say it's all three. Just leave it at that. Right. Shut up. Shut up. Shut up. Right.

**Alan**

*(Talking out loud)* OK, right, Glen, Glen, Glen – thank you, Glen.

*Music stops.*

**Alan**

Well, we – we have a unanimous decision. The winner of this year's Miss Norwich beauty pageant is contestant number three, Lisa Thornton. Ah-haa!

*Applause. Tommy puts tiara and sash on Lisa.*

**Alan**

*(With his arm around Lisa)* Lisa, are you pleased?

**Lisa**

Oh, yes. *(Giggles)* Oh. I didn't think I'd win.

**Alan**

Why not, for heaven's sake?

**Lisa**

Well, I thought number two would win.

**Alan**

Well, you shouldn't think that. Well, I think this could be the start of a glittering career in television. I'll see you later for that chat. Who – who're you waving to?

**Lisa**

That's – that's my fiancé, Andy.

**Alan**

Right. *(Taking a step away from Lisa)* Hi, Andy. Hi. Erm, well, Miss Norwich, soon to be Mrs Norwich. Don't wave any more. Well, I said before that if this show was a car, it would be Chatty-chatty-bang-bang. So now –

*Drum roll*

**Alan**

So now let's slip that car into another pig's ear – gear – a more serious pig's ear/gear in a new regular feature of the series in which I tackle the big contemporary political issues of the day in 'Partridge Over Britain'. *(To Lisa)* You can go now.

*Applause; music: 'Knowing Me, Knowing You'; Alan joins four people sitting at a table.*

**Alan**

Next week the voters of West Chalfont in Buckinghamshire go to the polls for a by-election caused by the death of the sitting Conservative MP, Sir Maurice Christopher, who tragically died last month after choking on scampi. So let's meet the candidates. Firstly, knowing me, Alan Partridge, knowing you, sitting on my left, and I imagine to the left of the majority of the people in West Chalfont, the Labour Party candidate. She's a teacher, she's divorced, she is Charlotte Fraser. Ah-haa.

**Charlotte**

Ah-haa.

**Alan**

Knowing me, Alan Partridge, knowing you, the Liberal Democrat candidate. He's a practising lawyer, he sits on Chalfont Council's Education Committee and he's black. Ronald Biggs. Ah-haa.

**Ronald**

Ah-haa.

**Alan**

In the middle, me, Alan Partridge, ah-haa. And, er – and on my right the Conservative Party candidate, Adrian Finch. Adrian and his wife, Rosemary, have been married for fourteen years and together they have three lovely children. Adrian, I believe you're also a big fan of steam engines.

**Adrian**

Yes, that's right, Alan. It's, er, full steam ahead for the by-election.

**Alan**

(Laughs) Lovely. Lovely sense of humour. Erm, Adrian Finch. The Partridge meets the Finch. Ah-haa.

**Adrian**

Ah-haa.

**Alan**

Lovely. And the final candidate, who we had to have on – he's paid his deposit and that's democracy – is Lieutenant Colonel Kojak Slaphead III of the Bald Brummies Against The Big-Footed Conspiracy Party. Ah-haa.

**Lt. Col. Slaphead**

(Wearing a clown's wig, big nose and spectacles and huge bow tie) Bald Brummies!

Whistles from audience member wearing the same outfit

**Alan**

Come on! Please, there's a time and a place for fun and enjoyment, and it's not on this show. Right, erm, we're going to open it up

to my studio audience. Throughout the questions I will be remaining impartial at all times. I will remain Pontius Partridge. So, erm – so any questions for the panel, please? Yes, the woman with the high head.

**Audience member**

Yeah, I'd, erm, like to ask the panel, in view of the rising crime rate, would they consider the reintroduction of capital punishment?

**Alan**

Fair point. Charlotte Fraser, Labour. We see these pictures of old women's faces in the paper. Surely the best way to deal with hooligans is to hang them by the neck until the spinal column is severed, thus starving the body of oxygen. Isn't that the best, most sensible way to deal with them?

**Charlotte**

Absolutely not. No, hanging really is brutal and barbaric and the hallmark of an uncivilized society.

**Alan**

OK. All right. What about lethal injection? Gas chamber, electric chair, you know. We're spoilt for choice.

**Charlotte**

That's not really the point, Alan. Erm, I mean all the indications –

**Alan**

Firing squad.

**Lt. Col. Slaphead**

The head slap.

**Alan**

The head slap. Sorry, sorry, please. Please don't, erm – please don't do that Lieutenant Colonel Kojak Slaphead III.

**Charlotte**

There's no evidence to show that capital punishment would reduce the crime statistics.

**Alan**
Well – it'd reduce it by one, wouldn't it?
Erm – Adrian Finch. Capital punishment.
There's a gibbet – will you pull the lever?

**Adrian**
Well – whether I pull the lever or not is not
the question.

**Lt. Col. Slaphead**
Yes it is.

**Adrian**
Erm – the, the, the, whole issue – the whole
issue of, of capital, capital punishment of,
of hanging is, is one which, which must be
addressed, erm, on a moral level by the, the
public in general, erm, before we can make
any absolute moral decision.

**Alan**
Good point. Very good point. Very – very
good point. You see, er – Charlotte Fraser,
it's not simply yes or no. Ronnie Biggs, it's
not yes or no, is it?

**Ronald**
Well, yes, it is.

**Alan**
Good.

**Ronald**
No, I'm – I'm disagreeing with you –

**Alan**
Fine.

**Ronald**
– er, it is a yes-or-no question.

**Alan**
Right. No one really cares, I mean, I mean,
yes, no, maybe. You know, it's not life or
death.

**Charlotte**
Well, yes, it is.

**Alan**
Yes, but it's boring. Right, erm. OK, well,
the phone – the phone lines are open. We
have a call. Erm, David Silk from Leeds.
David, are you, are you there?

**David**
Yes, I am.

**Alan**
Are you wearing any silk?

**David**
No, I'm naked.

**Alan**
What's – what's your question.

**David**
Erm, which of the candidates would
have the bottle to tighten up the laws on
immigration?

**Alan**
Immigration. It's a political hot potato.
Charlotte Rampling, catch.

**Charlotte**
Fraser.

**Alan**
S-sorry, yes.

**Charlotte**
Erm, yes, immigration is one of those
questions that comes up time and time
again at meetings like this –

**Adrian**
(*Talking at same time as Charlotte*)
Yes, I think there's a reason for that.

**Charlotte**
And you know it's interesting –

**Adrian**
Sorry.

**Charlotte**
– because it always seems to be mostly
when other social –

**Alan**
Sorry. Excuse me! Excuse me. He's trying to speak. You're such a rude woman. Go on. Go ahead.

**Adrian**
Yes, erm, what, what, what we must do, erm, absolutely is, is put in place a, a system of, erm –

**Lt. Col. Slaphead**
Head-slapping?

**Adrian**
No, erm – a system of , er –

**Lt. Col. Slaphead**
Head-slapping?

**Adrian**
No, please – I'm trying to answer the question. Do you mind? Er – a system of –

**Lt. Col. Slaphead**
Head-slapping?

**Adrian**
You're putting – you're putting me off. Please.

**Lt. Col. Slaphead**
I know.

**Adrian**
Er, er, a system of –

**Lt. Col. Slaphead**
Head-slapping?

**Adrian**
A system of –

**Lt. Col. Slaphead**
Head-slapping?

**Adrian**
System of –

**Lt. Col. Slaphead**
Head-slapping?

**Adrian**
System of –

**Lt. Col. Slaphead**
Head-slapping?

**Adrian**
System of –

**Lt. Col. Slaphead**
Head-slapping?

**Adrian**
System of –

**Alan**
Ignore him! Ignore him! Erm, the Government, aren't they bringing out a White Paper or something?

**Adrian**
Sorry?

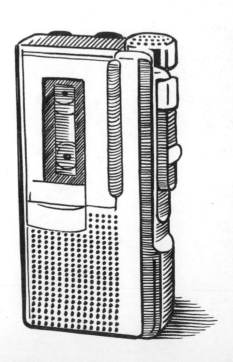

**Alan**
Aren't the Government bringing out
a White Paper?

**Adrian**
Are they?

**Alan**
Yes, they are.

**Adrian**
Right. Erm, yes, yes, we're, we're bringing
out a White Paper which, which should end
all, all discussion.

**Alan**
You're going to have to do better than that.
I'm trying to help you out here, mate. You're
in danger of losing the safest Conservative
seat in the country. Get a grip.

**Adrian**
Full steam ahead.

**Alan**
No, you made that joke earlier and it wasn't
funny then.

**Lt. Col. Slaphead**
He's run out of steam.

**Alan**
You see, he's quick. Get on the ball. Erm –
Charlotte – don't tell me, don't tell me. No,
it's gone.

**Charlotte**
Fraser.

**Alan**
Fraser, right. Erm, do you want to talk
about, I don't know, women or something?

**Charlotte**
No, I'd like to carry on talking about
immigration as I was before you
interrupted me.

**Alan**
Fine.

**Charlotte**
Erm, it's interesting, you know, that
people very rarely mention the fact that
the immigration laws in this country are
actually –

*Alan builds a tower of marker pens while
Charlotte continues talking.*

**Charlotte**
– some of the most stringent anywhere in
the world. I'm sure, Ronald, you'd bear me
out on that.

**Ronald**
I'm afraid that is the case. There are
statistics showing that more people
emigrate from the country than immigrate
into it.

**Charlotte**
Exactly.

**Alan**
Shh, shh, shh, shh, shh, shh, shh. Shhh. I've
never done five. Great! Six. Oh. *(The tower
collapses)* All right, let's, let's, let's have
another question. Erm, from the studio.
Yes, the woman – yes, that, the woman up
there with this business *(flaps his hands
around his head, indicating her hair)*.
Yeah, yeah.

**Audience member**
Erm, what would the panel do to create
more cycle lanes in –

**Alan**
Oh, that's a terrible question. Erm, the
gentleman with the spectacles there.

**Male audience member**
*(Bald)* Yes, yes, I'd like to ask a ques—

**Alan**
Hang on, hang on. Are you a Slaphead?

**Male audience member**
I'm sorry?

# TV SHOW 5

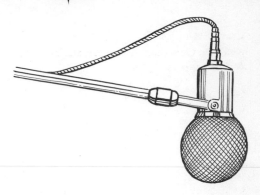

**Alan**
Are you a Bald Kojak Big-Foot Hater?

**Male audience member**
Look, I just want to ask a question about sport.

**Alan**
I'm sorry. My mistake. Please, please do go ahead.

**Male audience member**
Thank you. Er, I'd like to ask the panel their views on, on the possibilities of *(talks in Birmingham accent)* of the bald Olympics coming to Birmingham!

*Lt. Col. Slaphead cheers.*

**Alan**
Oh God. Very good. Very good.

**Bald Brummies in audience**
*(Whistling and shouting)* Bald Brummies!

**Lt. Col. Slaphead**
Bald Brummies!

**Alan**
Quite –

*Bald Brummies in audience blow whistles.*

**Alan**
Quite – who are you?

*Bald Brummies in audience blow whistles.*

**Alan**
Who are you?

**Lt. Col. Slaphead**
I am Lieutenant Colonel Kojak Slaphead III.

**Alan**
No, you're not. You're not at all. *(Alan pulls off his wig and glasses)* I'll tell you exactly who you are. Your name is Martin Dwyer. You're entertainments officer for Warwick University Students Union. And he's not your – he's not your father. Who's he?

**Lt. Col. Slaphead**
David Harrison.

**Alan**
Don't – don't do that voice any more. It's not funny. Who's he?

**Lt. Col. Slaphead**
*(Talking without Birmingham accent)* David Harrison.

**Alan**
And what does he do?

**Lt. Col. Slaphead**
He's a tutor in political science.

**Alan**
And what – and what are you studying?

**Lt. Col. Slaphead**
Law.

**Alan**
What do your parents think of this?

**Lt. Col. Slaphead**
Not that keen.

**Alan**
You're just – everyone likes a bit of fun, but you're just – you're just wasting people's time. Get yourself a girlfriend. *(Turning to Charlotte and Ronald)* Well, erm, I think we know a little bit more about – thank you for coming along. We know more about –

# KNOWING ME, KNOWING YOU

**Lt. Col. Slaphead**
*(grabbing his wig back when Alan isn't looking)* Bald Brummies are back! *(Taps Adrian's head)* Whoo, he's a slaphead! Look at his slaphead!

**Adrian**
You – you are a bloody shit!

**Alan**
*(Quietly)* Oh, God.

**Adrian**
You're a bloody buggering shitting bugger head.

**Alan**
*(Quietly)* Don't, please. Don't do that.

**Lt. Col. Slaphead**
I think he's just lost the safest Conservative seat in the country. Full steam ahead *(blows whistle)*.

**Adrian**
You bugger! Buggering –

*Lt. Col. Slaphead runs to back of stage with Adrian chasing him; Adrian grabs his wig and starts hitting Lt. Col. Slaphead with it. Alan joins them.*

**Alan**
Don't! Please! This is not political debate! If you're going to fight, do it in the car park!

**Lt. Col. Slaphead**
Ow!

**Alan**
*(Trying to break them up)* Just stop it. Please.

*Two Bald Brummies run on stage, blowing whistles, naked except for rosette attached to their posing pouches.*

**Alan**
Get security! Get security! Right. I'll have you.

*Alan chases Bald Brummies round stage.*

**Alan**
I'll have the both of you. Come here. Come here. I'll have you. I'll have you both. Right, I'll have you. Right.

*Alan rugby tackles one of them to the ground and lies half on top of him, staring at his buttocks.*

**Alan**
Right. Right. And on that – on that bombshell, it's time to say, knowing me, Alan Partridge –

*Bald Brummie struggles; Alan attempts to cover Brummie's buttocks with his hand.*

**Alan**
– knowing you, my guests. If you want to write in, then do so. Goodnight and ah-haa!

*Music: 'Knowing Me, Knowing You'; Bald Brummie escapes and runs off stage.*

# KNOWING ME KNOWING YOU

*Music: 'Knowing Me, Knowing You'*

**Alan**
Ah-haa!

*Applause. Alan does a little run onstage and mimes setting off an explosive – there is a bang and lots of smoke.*

*Music: 'Knowing Me, Knowing You'; women wearing Alan Partridge masks perform dance routine with Alan.*

*Applause*

**Alan**
*(Licks finger and holds it up)* Tssss!
Welcome, welcome to *Knowing Me, Knowing You*, with Alan Partridge. It's not the talk of the town: it's the chat of the town.

*Drum roll*

**Alan**
Tonight we're going to climb the mountain of conversation. Yes, I'm going to get my grappling hook and scale the north face of Chatmandu.

*Drum roll*

**Alan**

And as usual I'm going to cause quite a stir. I'm going to put the *chat* amongst the pigeons.

*Drum roll*

**Alan**

But suffice to say, tonight's show is an exciting stew of exotic vegetables – or guests – in a tomato-based – a tomato-based sauce of entertainment. Yes, you've guessed it, I'm serving up Chatatouille.

*Drum roll*

**Alan**

But, er, first an important announcement. You may remember that my dance troupe, The Alan Partridge Playmates, were wearing Alan Partridge masks. These masks *(takes mask)* – thank you very much – are official merchandise available in all good novelty shops and Welcome Break service stations in the South-East. However, last week these fun items were abused. Take a look at these pictures from a security camera. *(Black and white footage of men in Alan Partridge masks holding up a bank)* Natwest, Sycamore Road, Corby, on Tuesday last, when three masked gunmen, wearing my rubber face, burst in. Then they ran off with £15,000 in a copper-coloured sports holdall. I wish to disassociate myself from this act. My face was designed as a leisure accessory. When people rob, maim, pimp, ram-raid, smuggle, stalk or peep with my face, they drag it through the mud. And I don't like it. And if necessary will take action, either through the courts or by other means, believe me. That said, erm, if you do want to buy one, they really are great fun, and, er, they're available in the shops right now, and at service stations. I'm told they're particularly popular with students – that's lovely. So, er, buy one

today and give your neighbours a fright. Sneak up on them. But, but don't stalk them – or mug them. Just frighten them in a friendly way. Well, it's time now to meet and greet my resident house band: Glen Ponder and Bangkok!

*Music 'Knowing Me, Knowing You'*

**Alan**

Glen, erm, I'm pleased you've seen sense and decided to, er, cancel your court action. Very impressive. Erm, and it means that –

*Alan rises towards Glen on a movable platform.*

**Alan**

I've, er, I've no fear now of saying, knowing me, Alan Partridge, knowing you, Glen Ponder, ah-haa.

**Glen**

Ah-haa.

**Alan**

And knowing me, Alan Partridge, knowing you, Bangkok, ah-haa.

**Bangkok**

*(In unison)* Ah-haa.

**Alan**

Glen, erm, I'm in a bit of bother this week. I've got a confession to make. I actually stabbed a senior academic to death in my kitchen.

**Glen**

Really? Who was that?

**Alan**

Professor Plum. I was playing Cluedo.

*Drum roll*

**Alan**

But, erm, but seriously, Glen, I believe you've just had a new kitchen fitted. Is that right?

**Glen**
Yeah, yeah, that's right, yeah.

**Alan**
What, what prompted that?

**Glen**
Well, er, my boyfriend's a bit of a cordon bleu and, er *(Alan looks uncomfortable)* it was his idea really. His idea.

**Alan**
I didn't – I didn't know. Take, take me down, please.

*Alan's platform descends.*

**Glen**
Well, he needed a bit more space, you know, and, er, I thought what the hell. Let's splash out.

**Alan**
Thanks a lot. Conversation's finished now.

**Glen**
You could come round for a meal some time.

**Alan**
No thanks. No thank you.

**Glen**
You'd be very welcome.

**Alan**
No. It's all right. Can we get this quicker? Sorry – I'm gonna, I'll jump, I'll jump the, er, last couple of feet, that's all right.

*Alan jumps to floor.*

**Alan**
Glen Ponder and Bangkok!

*Music: 'Knowing Me, Knowing You'*

**Alan**
Ba-ba-ba-ba-ba-ba-ba-ba-ba-ba-ba! Ba-ba-ba-ba-ba-ba-ba-baaaaa-ba! Hah. That – that was the music for Pearl and Dean. We all know it. We all love it. We all admire it. My next guests are not Pearl and Dean. They're called Scott and Dean. But they are connected with cinema. That's why I just sang the, er, Pearl and Dean song. They are two brothers who produce, write, direct and star in their own movies, and who swept through Hollywood like a plague of locusts shouting, 'Action' – if you can imagine such a thing. They're two of Tinseltown's big-shots, which is quite ironic really, since they're both under four foot ten. You'll see what I mean when I welcome Scott and Dean McLean.

*Music*

**Alan**
Ahhh. Brrrr. Yabba-dabba-doo. *(Laughs)* Ay? Can you do that? *(Pulls funny face and laughs)* Marvellous. Lovely. Erm, knowing me, Alan Partridge, knowing you, Scott McLean, ah-haa.

**Scott**
Ah-haa.

**Alan**
Good lad! He's done it. Well done. Well done. And, er, and, er – see if you can do it now, Dean, hmm, get ready? – knowing me, Alan Partridge, knowing you, Dean McLean. Ah-haa.

**Dean**
Ah-haa.

**Alan**
By George, he's got it! Good lad. Marvellous. Lovely. OK. You've just flown in from LA. Did you enjoy the flight?

**Scott**
It was a pain in the ass.

**Alan**
Right, erm, let's move on. Next question: er, Dean, how old are you?

**Dean**

I'm eleven.

**Alan**

Eleven? Hmm, big lad. Big lad. And, er, Scott, how old are you?

**Scott**

I'm nine. Just coming up for the big one-oh.

**Alan**

What?

**Scott**

Ten. One zero. I'm gonna be ten.

**Alan**

Great. Lovely. And, er, are you looking forward to your birthday?

**Scott**

I guess when you hit double figures you gotta take time out to look around. Ask yourself some pretty serious questions.

**Alan**

Right. Like what?

**Scott**

Am I satisfied? Where am I going? What do I want?

**Alan**

Er, and what do you want? A space hopper? A Meccano set? Or do you want a Batmobile?

**Dean**

Believe me – this guy, he wants it all.

**Alan**

Well, I can't get you that. But I can get you a da-na-na-na-na-na-na-na-na-na-na-na-na-na-na Batmobile! *(Holds up the toy)* There you go. Lovely. And, er, I don't want Dean to feel left out. He's looking a bit grumpy there. Whooor – why haven't you got anything for me? *(Laughs)* So there you go: Alan Partridge mask. All right? Lovely.

*Scott and Dean laugh.*

**Alan**

What – what are you laughing at? My face? You shouldn't laugh at my face.

**Dean**

No. It's not the mask. It's the Batmobile.

**Alan**

What's wrong with it?

**Dean**

We don't mean to be rude, it's just that last week Tim Burton – he directed *Batman* –

**Alan**

Yeah, I know who he is.

**Dean**

Well, he gave us the actual Batmobile used in the movie.

**Alan**

What the full-size –

**Dean**

With all the gadgets.

**Alan**

Well, you can stick that on the dashboard.

**Scott**

The Batmobile is so cool and we drive it all around the estate.

**Alan**

Right, yeah. When I was ten I got, er, a bat and a ball. I used to play with that round the, er, estate. It was attached by a piece of elastic, so you could kind of bat it and it'd sort of bat back and forth. You know, it really was quite … in the bat and ball world it was state of the art, it really was.

**Scott**

And do you still have it, Alan?

**Alan**

No, erm, it was – it was taken off – stolen from me by a boy called Steven

McCoombe. A big lad. He used to bully everyone. He just threw it in the canal. Just threw it in – and I remember, I told the teacher, I said, 'Steve McCoombe threw it in the canal.' And she said, 'Don't tell tales. Don't be a sneak.' Where's the justice in that? Where, where is the justice in that?

**Dean**
You gotta let these things go, Alan.

**Alan**
Yeah, you're right. Right, where was I?

**Dean**
Er – our new movie.

**Alan**
Yes, thank you. Thanks, Dean. I like you.

**Scott**
What about me?

**Alan**
Yes. Now, er, the new movie – you're shooting it here in Britain at the moment. It's an action thriller called *Interface*. Tell us about that.

**Dean**
That's right. It's dealing with that whole – virtual reality, um, CD-ROM paranoia.

**Alan**
Yeah, yeah, that whole paranoia, yeah. And, er, so this bloke, Seedy Ron, how seedy is he?

**Scott**
What?

**Alan**
Seedy Ron, how seedy is he?

**Scott**
CD-ROM.

**Alan**
What?

**Dean**
CD-ROM. It's a computer process which allows you to, um, interface with visual information on compact disc format.

**Alan**
Right, right. Seedy Ron's got a compact disc player.

**Scott**
Jesus Christ.

**Alan**
Excuse me, can I ask you to watch your language, young man? So, er, tell us about Bruce Willis. I understand you fired him only three weeks into filming.

**Dean**
Yeah, that's right. We had a difference of opinion.

**Alan**
What was that?

**Scott**
He thought he was cool; we thought he was an asshole.

**Alan**
OK, w-w-well, all right, what about me? Am I, I –

**Scott**
Yeah, you're an asshole too.

**Alan**
No, no. No, yeah, OK. No, I mean, Bruce Willis – do you think I could take over from Bruce Willis? I can do, I can do an American accent. *(In American accent)* I'm Seedy Ron. I'm gonna gun you down.

**Scott**
Sorry, Alan. We've just cast Harrison Ford.

**Alan**
Yeah, it was a joke.

**Scott**

Hang on a minute. In the movie Sharon Stone's got a British husband.

**Dean**

Oh yeah, that's right. Maybe he could do it.

**Scott**

Yeah.

**Alan**

What, what, really?

**Scott**

Sure. Fly over to LA next week.

**Alan**

Yeah, well, yeah, I, I could do that. I mean, I'm supposed to be doing a – a sales conference for, er, Nabisco at the Birmingham Metropole, but, er, I could get Nick Owen to do that. He owes me one.

**Scott**

But you got to understand. It's only a supporting role.

**Alan**

I – I have done acting. I was, er, I was Mother Goose in Ipswich and Colchester. And, and, er, I've done – I did do a commercial for, erm, Fords of Norwich. I don't know if you've seen it?

**Scott**

Really?

**Alan**

Yeah, it was – a thirty-second commercial. It was on at the garage forecourt, erm, surrounded by, er, Ford Granadas, and I simply stand up – I'll do it for you – I simply stand up and say, erm, 'I'm Alan Partridge and Fords of Norwich are driving me crazy!' *(Alan stands up and starts spinning around)* You know …

**Dean**

That's good. That's good.

**Alan**

It's only – it's a bit of fun, but it shows that I can handle big-screen action.

*Scott and Dean laugh.*

**Scott**

Alan, it was a joke.

**Dean**

We were only joking. You can't be in an action movie.

**Scott**

You're too old.

**Alan**

I'm younger than Harrison Ford.

**Dean**

You look older.

**Alan**
Yeah, well, I was joking too. So the joke's on you. I started the joke.

**Scott**
No, we started the joke.

**Alan**
No, I started it. I started the joke.

**Scott**
Right, one big happy joke.

**Alan**
Yeah, one big happy joke that I started.

**Dean**
No, you didn't.

**Alan**
Yes, I did.

**Scott**
You didn't.

**Alan**
I did.

**Dean**
Look, this is getting childish.

**Alan**
Yeah, why don't you, why don't you grow up?

**Scott**
What, like you?

**Alan**
No, just act your age.

**Dean**
He's only nine years old.

**Scott**
Just coming up to the big one-oh.

**Alan**
Yes, very good. Very clever. Look, the point is, I started the joke and now I've finished it. The trouble, the trouble with you Americans is you haven't got a

sophisticated sense of humour, quite frankly. Have you heard of *Robin's Nest*? Not got a clue. You haven't got a clue.

**Scott**
Look, you're three times as old as us, and we're fifty times as rich as you, and a hundred times as talented, and you don't like it.

**Alan**
Why don't you get a life? I've got a life. Why don't you get one? Why don't you go and play Tig or something?

**Scott**
What kind of a life have you had?

**Alan**
I've had a very successful one. Last month I was voted Man of the Moment by *TV Quick* magazine.

**Scott**
Whooo.

**Alan**
Yeah. Shut up, right? In 1998 I was Sports Reporter of the Year for Radio Norwich.

**Dean**
Oh, big time, huh?

**Alan**
Yeah, it is big time actually, yes. And ten years ago I was broadcasting highly complex traffic information to the whole of the East Anglia region when you were just a foetus. Think about that.

**Scott**
Oh, your breath is gross.

**Alan**
I have not got bad breath.

**Scott**
It's like something's died in your mouth.

**Alan**
Nothing has died in my mouth.

# KNOWING ME, KNOWING YOU

**Dean**

*(Puts on Alan Partridge mask and leans towards Scott)* I'm Alan Partridge. My mouth's a chemical dump.

**Scott**

Oh, gross breath. Aaaaarrrggghh!**Alan** Right. That is it. I'm confiscating that. *(Pulls mask from Dean)* I'm confiscating that.

**Dean and Scott**

You can't do that. Give it back! *(They jump around Alan while he holds the mask over his head)*

**Alan**

I can. No, you're not having it.

*Dean stamps on Alan's foot and punches him in stomach; Scott knocks Alan to floor; Dean grabs mask.*

**Alan**

Oh God, God. Get security. They shouldn't be doing this.

*Alan tries to stand up; Scott and Dean trip him up.*

**Alan**

Christ.

**Scott**

Sorry.

**Alan**

You should be in a bloody Borstal.

**Scott**

Any further questions?

*Alan stands up and sits in his chair.*

**Alan**

No.

**Dean**

*(Wearing the Alan Partridge mask)* Can we go now?

**Alan**

Yes. Scott and Dean McLean.

**Dean**

I'm Alan Partridge.

*Applause; Scott and Dean leave stage, making vomiting noises.*

**Alan**

Sorry about that. Now – women. What are they? To some women you can say, 'That's a nice dress. Would you like to have dinner?' With other women you've got to keep your distance. Best not get involved; just be pleasant. I'm talking about those women who until the last century were confined to the island of Lesbos. In other words, lady lesbians. That's what my next guests are. Yes, next week this show will be replaced by a new series for lesbians called *Off the Straight and Narrow* – quite clever, that – and it will be hosted by my next guests. I've been told by the BBC to have them on to promote their show, which I think is a good idea. I can't – I can't tell you what's going to be in their show – that's their job – so let's hear it from the horses' mouths. Please welcome, Wanda Harvey and Bridey McMahon.

*Music: 'Honey, Honey'; applause; Wanda and Bridey join Alan.*

**Alan**

Diddley-de-dee-dee, two ladies. Diddley-de-dee-dee, two ladies. Diddley-de-dee-dee, and I'm the on-ly man, yah. Diddley-de-dee-dee, I like it. Diddley-de-dee-dee, they like it. *(Chuckles)* Diddley-de-dee-dee, this two for one. Ba-dom-ba-dom-bom. Bom. *(Wanda and Bridey stare in silence)* I'm sorry, that was, that was misjudged. I'm sorry about that. Erm, knowing me, Alan Partridge, knowing you, Wanda Harvey, ah-haa?

**Wanda**
Ah-haa.

**Alan**
And knowing me, Alan Partridge, knowing you, Bridey McMahon, ah-haa.

**Bridey**
Ah-haa.

**Alan**
*(In exaggerated Irish accent)* Bridey McMahon. Bridey McMahon. *(In English accent)* Lovely name that. It's – the kind of name you'd imagine an, er, er, Irish flame-haired fiery woman to have in a film with John Wayne, isn't it? You can just imagine him saying, *(in American accent)* 'Bridey McMahon, I'll have you over my knee and give you six of the best.' And you'd be saying, you'd be saying *(in Irish accent)*, 'Oh, I'll have nothing to do wi' yer. Keep yer hands to yerself.' *(Sighs)* You know, but of course, in the end, you marry him – and, er – well, of course that's not going to happen: you're a lesbian. And, er, you're, you're Wanda. Erm, Wanda, I was just thinking actually, if you married Glen, you know what your name would be, don't you? Wanda Ponder. But, erm, that's, that's not going to happen because, er, you're, er, you know, and so's he – I don't, I don't want to get bogged down in this whole nest of gay vipers.

**Wanda**
Have you, er, have you got a question?

**Alan**
Yes, yes. First question: what's it like to be a lesbian?

**Bridey**
Well, you're asking us to sum up the experience of millions of women in one media-friendly soundbite.

**Alan**
If you could.

**Bridey**
Well, I can't.

**Alan**
Well, you're gonna have to, love, if you want to make it in the TV business.

**Wanda**
Well, with all due respect, considering we have a series which runs for twenty-four weeks, I think we've –

**Alan**
Twenty-four weeks? I only got six.

**Wanda**
Well, perhaps the BBC think our show's going to be four times as good as yours.

**Alan**
*(Laughs)* No they don't. Now, you two. You're both lesbians – we know that. I don't mind. It's not a problem. Does it bother you when you hear people use these slang expressions?

**Bridey**
What slang expressions are you referring to?

**Alan**
You know, the usual: er, lesbos, lezzers, lezby friends, dykes, bulldykes, dick van dykes … spare-rib ticklers, erm, catflaps, pussy-footers, knicker-pickers, men, er, back-packers, tent-peggers, trout-fishers, er, melon farmers, quick-fit fitters, baggage handlers and, er, left luggage. Do those names hurt?

**Wanda**
Where are you getting all these names from, Alan?

**Alan**
Just names.

**Wanda**

Yeah, that you and the guys thought up in the office?

**Alan**

No. We didn't think them all up. I mean, er, lezzers and dykes – can't take the credit for those. Erm, but, er, OK, now let's talk about your show – because I've *got* to. Erm, now, tell us. What, what is, what's it about?

**Wanda**

Well, next week Jeanette Winterson will be reviewing the latest gay fiction, and, er – this should interest you, Alan – we have a woman's football team. And also in the next show we have Kitty Mayhew from the British Museum. She'll be looking at some Etruscan earthenware depicting early gay iconography.

**Alan**

*(Looking at his clipboard)* Fantastic!

**Wanda**

Are you interested in gay ico –

**Alan**

No, no, no, no. I just realized an anagram of, er, 'Alan Partridge' is 'great drain pal'. Amazing.

**Bridey**

You can get the word 'prat' out of Partridge, too.

**Alan**

Yeah, I know.

**Bridey**

And 'Alan' is an anagram of 'anal'.

**Alan**

Yeah. I'm well aware of that.

**Bridey**

So, er, 'anal dirge prat'.

**Alan**

I didn't know that. That's a good one. That's a very good one, that, yeah. I've, er, I've been trying to think of one for, er, 'Glen Ponder'. So, er, if you could help me out there that'd be good. Er, now, your new show.

**Bridey**

Porn legend.

**Alan**

Sorry?

**Bridey**

Porn legend. It's an anagram of 'Glen Ponder'.

**Alan**

Yes, you're absolutely – yes, you're absolutely right. Glen, er, are you a porn legend?

**Glen**

Well, my boyfriend thinks so.

**Alan**

Yeah, all right. I don't want to – don't want to get bogged down in that whole gay hornets' nest. Erm, tell us a bit more about your show.

**Bridey**

Well, we're also having features on, er, gay holidays, on Virago Press. Er, we'll be looking at mortgages for lesbian couples.

**Alan**

Are you, are you a couple?

**Wanda**

I hope that you're not assuming that because we're both lesbians we're an item.

**Alan**

No. No, no, no. But, er, are you?

**Wanda**

No. Absolutely not.

**Bridey**
We used to be.

**Alan**
Ooh! Ooh.

**Wanda**
We went out for while.

**Briday**
We were passionately involved for three years.

**Alan**
Now we're cooking. Turn it up!

**Wanda**
It was, it was fun while it lasted.

**Bridey**
It was as if the surf rolled over us and we were sheltering beneath the wings of a great bird.

**Alan**
Lovely. Lovely. Now, of course, you're sheltering beneath the wings of a great partridge. Not – not literally. That would be hideous. Like something out of *Jason and the Argonauts* – quite frightening. Erm, your new programme's called *Off the Straight and Narrow*. That's a bit of a mouthful, isn't it?

**Wanda**
Well, we call it O. T. S. A. N. or Otsan for short.

**Alan**
Nearly an anagram of 'satan'. Carry on.

**Wanda**
Yeah, Alan, it's just an abbreviation like you abbreviate this show to K. M. K.Y.

**Alan**
No, no, that's not its full title. Its full title is K. M. K.Y.W. A. P. or Kmkywap as someone in the office said the other day. It's the kind of thing you might expect a Red Indian to say to Kevin Costner in *Dances With Wolves*, isn't it? Kmkywap. *(Laughs)* Me big chief chatting partridge. Kmkywap. Ah-haa.

**Wanda**
It also sounds a bit like a moist toilet tissue: a kmkywap.

**Alan**
Yeah, yeah, can't argue with that. Yeah. I could, er, I could wipe myself with a kmkywap and, er, throw it down my great drain pal. *(Laughs)*

**Bridey**
After cleaning your anal dirge prat.

**Alan**
Yeah, that's just offensive.

**Wanda**
I wouldn't worry about it, Alan. No one's watching.

**Alan**
Yes, they are.

**Bridey**
You've been losing one million viewers a week.

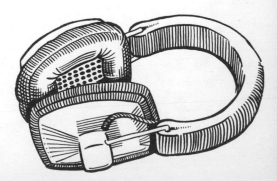

**Alan**

(*Getting agitated*) Yes, all right, I admit it. There's been some sort of a conspiracy to deprive me of viewers. And I'll tell you who's behind it: your mates. That lot upstairs. The Mr and Ms of BBC2. They don't like me. They've all been to Oxbridge University, wherever that is. They all wander round in their baggy linen suits and their flip-flops, saying, 'Ooh, look at me. I work for BBC2. Do you like my glasses? They're like John Lennon's.' I loathe these people. Every week, just before I'm about to go on air, a whole bank of them come into the studio and say, 'You can't do that. You can't say this. You can't say that.' Get out! I wish all of you BBC2 people would get on a bus and just drive over a cliff. I'd happily be the driver.

(*Calming down*) That said, erm, good – good luck with the series. Please sit around for my next guest. Er, ladies and gentlemen, please thank Wanda Harvey and Bridey McMahon. Two ladies, diddley-de-dee-dee!

*Applause*

**Alan**

Well, let's take a break from, er, all this chat and have a little light relief. Fifteen years ago I was on a Hoseasons holiday in Bournemouth and I went to the summer cabaret. It was pretty mediocre. Then one man came on and raised the roof. He made me laugh quite literally like a drain. After the show I went backstage and I said to him, 'I'm Alan Partridge. If I ever get my own TV series, I promise to give you a big break.' Remember this is fifteen years ago. Well, tonight I intend to honour that pledge by introducing a very special entertainer. Hold on to your sides, they might just split, as I welcome on Joe Beazley and Cheeky Monkey!

*Applause; music; Joe enters stage with monkey hand-puppet.*

**Joe**

(*Laughs*) Good evening, ladies and gentlemen, boys and girls. My name's Joe Beazley and –

*Joe wiggles monkey and taps it on head.*

**Joe**

Aye. This is Cheeky Monkey, ladies and gentlemen. Well, it's a great privilege to be here on the Alan Partridge show, *Knowing Me, Knowing You*, and I was thinking to myself in the dressing room, that's an Abba song, in't it, ladies and gentlemen. So here's a little joke – right? What do you get if you cross Fred Flintstone – no, not what if you cross – er, what do you – what do you get if you, er, what does a Swedish, what does a Swedish Fred Flintstone say? Yabba-dabbo-dooo! No, he says, 'Abba-dabba-doo!' Abba-dabba-doo, that's what he says. Erm, so, then, er, ay, other week –

*Joe wiggles monkey.*

**Joe**

Pack it in, you – the other week – stop it – the other week me and Cheeky Monkey, we went to Blackpool Pleasure Beach, right? And at Blackpool Pleasure Beach – I don't know if you know this, ladies and gentlemen, boys and girls – but they've got the biggest rollercoaster in the world. It's massive, in't it?

*Joe wiggles monkey.*

**Joe**

And we went up the big – up the big dipper –

*Monkey's hands, attached by Velcro around Joe's neck, come unclasped.*

**Joe**

Oh God. We went up the big dipper –

*Joe tries to fasten monkey's hands round his neck.*

**Joe**

 – and, er, we were on the big dipper, right? And we were going about 200 m-miles an hour. Two hundred miles an hour on, on, on the big dipper.

*Joe fails to fasten monkey's hands round neck and places one of monkey's hands on his chest instead.*

**Joe**

And, erm, we got on the big dipper, right? And we come round the corner and Cheeky Monkey, right? 'E – *(silence)* We're on the big dipper, right? No. That … ooh, you cheeky monkey. 'E's made me forget … it's his fault, ladies and gentlemen *(laughs)* he's made me forget. He ma— oh. Ooh. *(He hits the monkey)* He's always doing that, ladies and gentlemen. Forget, forget – forget the joke there. Chee— you cheeky monkey. Cheeky, cheeky monkey. Chee–

**Alan**

*(Joining Joe onstage)* Ladies and gentlemen, Joe Beazley and Cheeky Monkey!

*Applause*

**Alan**

Thank you. Well done. Joe, I think you, we – I think you've been, er, I think you've been very brave.

**Joe**

There's more jokes, Alan.

**Alan**

Ay –

**Joe**

There's plenty more.

**Alan**

It's fine –

**Joe**

Just a little mistake there.

**Alan**

I don't think, I don't think it's working –

**Joe**

Just a little mistake. You should apologize to Cheeky Monkey. Look –

*Joe wiggles monkey in Alan's face.*

**Alan**

Don't do that. It's not real.

**Joe**

You've upset – oh, look, he's upset him, ladies and gentlemen.

**Alan**

He's not real.

*Alan goes to take monkey.*

**Joe**

Don't touch it! I'm sorry. I'm sorry.

**Alan**

You've got a big problem. If you've got any sense of dignity – this is – look, your act is, your act is really poor. You – you – if you've got any sense of dignity, you'll leave the stage. I'll make sure you get a round of applause. Now, come on, quit while you're ahead. Come on. Ladies and gentlemen, the wonderful Joe Beazley and Cheeky Monkey!

*Applause; music; Joe and Cheeky Monkey leave.*

**Alan**

Erm, my final guest in this show – and of the series – has dined with Fidel Castro, President Kennedy, Mikhail Gorbachev and Bing Crosby. He's one of the most feared, respected and opinionated men in Great Britain. He is, of course, the restaurant critic of the *Spectator* magazine. He's had more free dinners than I've had hot dinners. In *Who's Who*, under his list of hobbies, it really does say, 'Food, food, glorious food – and wine.' He's just recovered from a double heart-bypass operation, please welcome raconteur and bon viveur Forbes McAllister!

*Music: 'On and On and On'; applause; Forbes McAllister walks onstage and sits on sofa.*

**Alan**

This is the last time I'm ever going to do this, so you – you know the form.

**Forbes**

Yes. I've seen the show.

**Alan**

Right. Er, let's make it a good 'un. Knowing me, Alan Partridge, knowing you –

**Forbes**

Ah-haa.

**Alan**

You've just ruined it. It was the last one.

**Forbes**

Hello, lesbians.

**Alan**

Right, now, you were in the papers –

**Forbes**

Where's your moustache?

**Alan**

What?

**Forbes**

You had a moustache last week. Made you look like a spiv.

**Alan**

Yeah. Yes, I shaved it off: it didn't suit me.

**Forbes**

No, no, it made you look like a Lebanese pimp.

**Alan**

Yes, as I said, it didn't suit me.

**Forbes**

It did.

**Alan**

Right. Now, Forbes, erm, you, you were in the papers yesterday because you were at Sotheby's for an auction, in which you paid over £100,000 for the personal effects of Lord Byron, which we've got here. I'm gonna bring them forward.

*Artefacts brought onstage and passed to Forbes.*

**Alan**

Erm, these are the personal artefacts of Lord Byron – £100,000 worth. That's a lot of money. You must be a big fan of Byron's.

**Forbes**

No, can't stand him. Big ponce with a club foot.

**Alan**
So why've you bought all his bits?

**Forbes**
Because Michael Winner was bidding for them. And I hate him even more than I hate Byron. Ended up with all this junk. Got Byron's lock of his stupid hair. You want to look at that, lezzer? And, er, manuscript of some of his rubbish poems. Want to look at some rubbish? Be careful: they're valuable. But this is what Michael really wanted to get his greasy hands on. *(Opens the box)* Lord Byron's duelling pistols. *(Waves pistols in air)* Michael, I've got the pistols.

**Alan**
Yeah. Can I ask you a question? *(Alan takes one pistol)* Are you entirely motivated by hatred?

**Forbes**
Yes, I think I am. It's rather perceptive of you.

**Alan**
Thank you.

**Forbes**
I hate *you*.

**Alan**
Erm, Wanda, Bridey, do you like Byron?

**Forbes**
Hate him.

**Bridey**
Yes, actually I adore Byron. I find his work powerful and moving. It, it, it speaks to me like the, the sea in a shell.

**Alan**
Lovely. You really do have a lovely voice.

**Forbes**
Yes. It's very beautiful, if I may say so. I could fall in love with you. If you put a bag over your head.

**Alan**
Please, Forbes.

**Forbes**
*(To Bridey)* I hate you. *(To Wanda)* Not as much as I hate you, though.

**Alan**
Forbes, we have a bit of a surprise for you. Er, we know that when you were a child, growing up in Scotland, you used to love the sound of the bagpipes. So will you please welcome the Balmoral Highland Pipers!

*Applause; Balmoral Highland Pipers play for couple of seconds; applause.*

**Alan**
Forbes, what do you say? What do you think?

**Forbes**
I used to throw stones at pipers. I hate them.

**Alan**
They're Scotland's number one bagpiping combo. I mean, they, they've been on *How Do They Do That?*

**Forbes**
Do you want me to lie and say I like the bagpipes?

**Alan**
*(Fiddling with the pistol)* Yes, yes, I would, if you don't –

**Forbes**
All right, I love the bagpipes. I love the screeching, wheezing, rasping din they make. Be careful with that.

*Alan accidentally shoots Forbes in the chest; screams.*

**Alan**
Oh my God!

**Floor manager**
Get the gun, get the gun.

*Runner takes gun from Alan. Programme cuts for two seconds then returns to set.*

**Alan**
Er, what happens now? What happens now?

**Floor manager**
Ladies and gentlemen, is there a doctor somewhere?

*Wanda screams.*

**Alan**
It's not my fault. It wasn't my – I didn't know it was loaded.

**Floor manager**
Can everybody stay calm, please –

*Wanda and Bridey are led from stage; doctor examines Forbes.*

**Alan**
Didn't know it was loaded.

**Floor manager**
– there is no need to panic.

*Producer walks on stage.*

**Producer**
*(Whispers)* Tosser!

**Alan**
Sorry. It's just, I didn't know it was loaded. It's not my fault.

**Producer**
I'm gonna kill you.

**Alan**
Is – is he all right?

**Doctor**
I'm afraid he's dead.

**Alan**
Give it – cover him up! Cover him up with this. *(Picks up an Alan Partridge mask;*

*Producer snatches mask from Alan and stamps on it)* Right. I'm the Executive Producer. You're fired. You're fired. Go on.

**Producer**
What? You just killed a man and I'm fired?

**Alan**
Yes, yes, you're fired. Go on.

**Producer**
I'm fired?

**Alan**
Yes, you're fired.

**Producer**
I'm fired?

**Alan**
Yes.

**Producer**
I'm fired?

**Alan**
Yes.

**Producer**
Wanker!

**Alan**
Yeah, right. Right. Get the pipers! Get the pipers back on! We're carrying on. Get the pipers back on!

**Floor manager**
Back on?

**Alan**
Back on. Ladies and gentlemen, this is *Knowing Me, Knowing You, with Alan Partridge*. It's a live show, erm, in, in a live televis— anything can happen. I, I, I don't know if you remember *Blue Peter* when the elephant, erm – made a mess on the studio floor. Ironically it was in this very studio. Tonight I've made a mess. I can't deny it. You saw it there. You saw, saw it here first. Another exclusive for *Knowing Me,*

*Knowing You, with Alan Partridge*, or Kmkywap. Just as a packet of Kmkywaps help clear up a mess, I'm *(gulps)* I'm gonna help clear up this mess, so – may I be the first to offer my condolences to the family of Forbes – Glen – *(clicks fingers)*

**Glen**

McAllister.

**Alan**

McAllister. Forbes McAllister. But he's at peace now. He went out like a light. He wouldn't have suffered. He wouldn't have suffered: I shot him straight through the heart.

*Guests and the Alan Partridge Playmates join Alan onstage.*

**Alan**

Well, it's time to close the show and the series in the way that Forbes would have wanted, with the Balmoral Highland Pipers playing us out, together with my wonderful, wonderful guests and, of course, The Alan Partridge Playmates, and very lovely they are. Erm, I'll – I think I'll have to speak to the police. They're here, they're here now. They're waiting for me in the wings. Erm, knowing me, Alan Partridge, knowing you, the police, ah-haa. Be chatting – chatting with you, er, in a short while. Erm, in the meanwhile, enjoy the rest of the show – what's left – officers. So on that fatal bombshell it simply remains for me to say goodbye for the last time. By the way, if any of you are in Manchester on the seventeenth of next month, I'm opening a new Texas Homecare, so why don't you, er, pop along? It should be a lot of fun. Erm, for now this is me, Alan Partridge, saying knowing me, Alan Partridge, knowing you, whoever you may be, ah-haa!

*Balmoral Highland Pipers play 'Knowing Me, Knowing You'; everyone waves at the camera. Police walk onstage.*

**Alan**

Right. Do I have to go right now? Right. OK. OK.

*Alan, still waving, is led away by police.*

# KNOWING ME KNOWING YULE

A CHRISTMAS SPECIAL

*Alan Partridge*

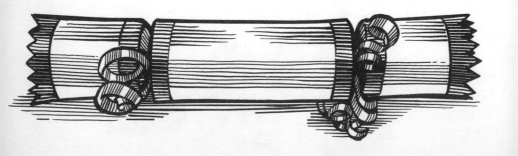

*Alan outside studio in the snow, with choirboy.*

**Choirboy (Stanley)**
*(Singing)* Knowing me, knowing Yule
Ah-haa, there is nothing we can do
Knowing me, knowing Yule
La la la la la la – *(continues while Alan is speaking)*

**Alan**
Ah-haa. What is Christmas? It's a little robin redbreast, petrified by the wind. It's an orphan in a blanket, being helped into a shed. And it's a snowman whose nose carrot has been stolen and subsequently eaten by a gypsy thief. But more than that it's me, Stanley, three stunning hostesses, some Santa chat, and quality poultry. I.e. *Knowing Me, Knowing Yule,* with Alan Partridge. I bid ye good tidings. Now!

*Music as Alan enters house from the snow.*

**Alan**
Ah-ho-ho-ho! *(Applause)* Don't, don't worry, don't worry. That stuff you saw me brushing off earlier wasn't dandruff, it was just fake snow. It's just a polyurethane composite…the kind of thing they used to use in *Doctor Zhivago.* Welcome to *Knowing Me, Knowing Yule,* with Alan Partridge. There's no need to shop around for your festive entertainment. Simply put your feet up and peruse my chatalogue.
*(Drum roll)*
And I mean that chategorically.
*(Drum roll)*
Tonight's show, tonight's show is coming live from BBC Television Centre, where we've built an exact replica reproduction of the interior of my house.

**Audience**
Wooo-oooooo!

**Alan**
Please, don't take that as a green light to go to Norwich and burgle my actual house … as happened during my television series six times. Because sitting at my home right now are two men from Securicor, Mike and Ted, with their two Alsatians, Tin-Tin and Pickles. So, er, if anyone out there is thinking of burgling me then don't bother. No, in fact *do.* Have a go. Because, because quite frankly you'll be picking up your teeth with a broken arm. So just think about that before you trespass on my property. Because you people are scum. *(Points to camera)* Let's meet the bell ringers of Norwich Cathedral.

*Applause; bell ringers ring hand bells.*

**Alan**
Knowing me, Alan Partridge, knowing you, the bell ringers of Norwich Cathedral, ah-haa.

**Ringers**
Ah-haa. Ah-haaaa.

**Alan**
Christmas, I imagine, a very busy time for bell ringers?

**Mary**
Yeah it is, it's very busy but it's very lovely for us to be able to celebrate, through bell ringing, the birth of Jesus Christ our saviour.

**Alan**
Fair enough. It's nice to have you on the show.

**Mary**
Thank you, it's nice to –

**Alan**
Great.

**Mary**
Oh, sorry.

**Alan**
No, carry on, sorry.

**Mary**
No, I was just going to say it's nice to be on a television show that's not all about, you know, swearing and child pornography.

**Alan**
Look, have you seen *Noel's House Party*?

**Mary**
Yes.

**Alan**
That's the kind of show this is. Keep it light. All right? Right. Have you had a mince pie?

**Mary**
No.

**Alan**
Have a mince pie.

**Mary**
I, I was just saying –

**Alan**
Have a mince pie.
*(Walking away)* Next. Next!

**Mary**
All I was saying was that –

**Alan**
Mince pies! Later on, Mick Hucknall from Simply Red will be singing 'Ding Dong Merrily On High'. Mick will be backed on a Korg M1 synthesizer by my musical man with fingers like a centipede, Glen Ponder!

*Applause*

**Alan**
Knowing me, Alan Partridge, knowing Yule, Glen Ponder. Ah-haa.

**Glen**
Ah-haa.

**Alan**
Well, Glen, did you, did you have a nice Christmas?

**Glen**
Oh, quiet. We just stayed in, didn't we?

**Andy**
Yeah, yeah.

*Laughter as Alan looks at Glen and Andy, shocked.*

**Glen**
What about you, Alan?

**Alan**
Ooh, very pleasant, very pleasant. Except on Boxing Day, when I chopped a man's head off and stuck it on a spike.

**Glen**
Really, Alan?

**Alan**
Yes. I was playing Mortal Kombat on my nephew's video game.

*Drum roll*

**Alan**
But, er, seriously – the, the highlight of my Christmas was receiving a brand-new Rover Vitesse fastback. Which, I don't mind admitting, is the best executive car I've ever had. And, what, what, what did you get, Glen?

**Glen**
*(Smiling at Andy)* Andy bought me a silk kimono.

**Alan**
*(Walking away)* Glen Ponder. And Andy.

*Applause and music*

**Alan**

Now, now the idea of this show is that there's a party atmosphere in my home, my mock-up home. And what party would be complete without three lovely hostesses hired for the evening? *(Alan walks towards three girls dressed as 'Mrs Santa Claus')* They'll be circulating with mulled wine and Boaster biscuits. Um, they're – they're, they're an assortment of chocolates and hazelnuts compacted on to a sweet oatmeal base. Quite buttery, um. Anyway, there they are, Yvette, Martine and Sam. They are my three Christmas crackers. And, er, I wouldn't mind pulling one of those. *(Alan watches them walk away)* Now, while the girls whet our appetite, who's going to provide us with the meat? Well, it's a TV chef with a difference. So let's go and see what *she* is up to, as we go over to my kitchen, my mock-up kitchen, to join daytime TV's favourite chef, the rude Fanny Thomas.

*Music and applause. Alan walks over to Fanny at kitchen station.*

**Fanny**

*(Holding a meat cleaver)*
Alan, you've caught me with my hand wrapped around me enormous chopper. Ooh, pardon!

**Alan**

She's outrageous. K. M. A. P. K. Y. F. T. Ah-haa.

**Fanny**

You what?

**Alan**

I'm saying: knowing me, Alan Partridge, knowing you, Fanny Thomas, ah-haa.

**Fanny**

What for?

**Alan**

I'm, I'm just trying to save time. We worked out during my last TV series that we wasted two minutes during every show saying my catchphrase so –

**Fanny**

Why don't you cut the catchphrase then?

**Alan**

Can't do that. I mean, that would be like JFK not saying 'Ich bin ein Berliner'.

**Fanny**

But he only said that once.

**Alan**

Yeah, and look what happened to him.

**Fanny**

Alan, are you saying that if you don't say your catchphrase, you might be assassinated by someone?

**Alan**

N-n-n-no, I'm not saying that. Although I can never completely eliminate the threat of assassination. I mean, I live daily under the shadow of a gunman. But saying the phrase may cause the assailant to abort the mission in the confusion. Anyway, I was, I was trying to save time. I could have been shot four or five times in the time it's taken me to say this. I'm going to have to drop one of the guests. *(Turning to production crew)* Cut Zola Budd. Pay her off. Stick her in a cab.

**Fanny**

Shall I show you what I'm cooking?

*Alan walks away.*

**Alan**

No, there isn't time, but – er, we'll come back to you later. Basically, just to explain, we all know what Fanny Thomas does. She cooks lovely food and she makes innuendos. Fanny, what are you cooking?

**Fanny**
Oh. Roast partridge. Do you want stuffing?

**Alan**
Yes, please.

**Fanny**
You don't look the type, oooh pardon!

**Alan**
That sort of thing. Anyway … more of that later.

**Fanny**
You'll be lucky!

**Alan**
Ooh, outrageous. Don't talk with your mouth full.

**Fanny**
Ooh, reminds me of my boyfriend last night.

**Alan**
No, please, that's too many. Now, on with the party. My house is open, my mock-up house, is open to all comers … *(to Fanny)* don't … from … from the rich man and his Rover to the poor man in his Vauxhall Corsair. So let's see, let's see who's here. Can we just have you for a second? *(Approaches male guest.)* Now this man looks like a clerk, or possibly someone who works in a bank, but in fact he's my new boss. The new chief commissioning editor of BBC Television. Mr Tony Hayers.

*Applause; Alan and Tony sit down.*

**Alan**
K. M. A. P. K. Y. T. H. Ah-haa.

**Tony**
A.

**Alan**
Sorry?

**Tony**
An abbreviation for ah-haa.

**Alan**
No no, I, I, I don't want you to do that. I, I, I, I don't want anyone to abbreviate the ah-haa's. *(To the crew)* By the way, when I greet anyone else on the show I want you to utter the full response, OK? Only *I* will be using the abbreviated form. *(To camera)* This is eating into the show much more than I ever intended. This was actually meant to save time. I, I think I'll abandon it. No, no, I'll stick with it; I'll stick with it. Tony – er, welcome to the show. Before you came to the BBC you were chairman of Euro International Airlines, and whilst you were there you sacked over 2,000 people. Will you be doing the same at the BBC?

**Tony**
*(Laughing)* Well, I don't know about that, Alan, but, if I can borrow an image from your very wonderful musical opening there, I, I hope to ring some changes.

**Alan**
My show is your bell. Please – please peal it. Peal my bell. I, I'm sorry. Just tell us what you're going to do at the BBC.

**Tony**
All right, well, I will be looking at our output very carefully. We live in a market economy and the BBC should be no exception, that's how I see it. So, every programme will have to justify itself, and you know, if it's a lame duck it may have to go.

**Alan**
Well, let me assure you that *Knowing Me, Knowing You, with Alan Partridge* is a very healthy duck. With … with plenty of legs. So, um, so you can axe any show you like as long as you tell me I'm going to get a second series. *(Pleading jokingly)* Please, please tell me I've got a second series, boss.

*Tony laughs.*

**Alan**

*(Nervously)* Do you want to do that? Just to, to clear the air? I know this is not really the, the time …

**Tony**

No, no, it's not really the, the time, no.

**Alan**

No, you're absolutely right. I'm sorry, I'm sorry, I put you on the spot there, I'm sorry. I've embarrassed you. Everyone's embarrassed.

**Tony**

It's gone. Gone.

**Alan**

What's gone?

**Tony**

That moment. The moment's gone.

**Alan**

Oh good! I thought you meant the second series. Now … now Christmas at home is … I'm sorry, just all that faffing around, it won't, it won't affect my chances of a second series?

**Tony**

No, it, um, won't affect the decision.

**Alan**

You mean the decision's been taken?

**Tony**

Decisions are made and unmade all the time, Alan.

**Alan**

Right, so the decision might not have been made?

**Tony**

The decision is pending.

**Alan**

What you're saying is, if tonight's show goes well I *will* get a second series?
*(Silence)* Don't say anything. Don't, don't say a word.
*(Silence)* Now – Tony, what kind of a Christmas did you have?

**Tony**

Well, you know, traditional: Christmas tree, turkey, all the children together –

**Alan**

Midnight mass?

**Tony**

No, I'm Jewish.

**Alan**
Are you?

**Tony**
Mmm.

*Silence*

**Alan**
*(Searching for words)* Jews are good – Jews are good. Knowing you, Tony Hayers, Jew. Knowing me, Alan Partridge – Jew-liker. By, by, by the way, by the way, all that stuff, you know, before – that's all water under the bridge.

**Tony**
What the, the second series?

**Alan**
No, the crucifixion. No, no, no I didn't, no I didn't. No, I meant the second series, not the crucifixion, I meant the second series. Let's talk, let's talk about moral standards at the BBC.

**Tony**
I think that a lot of people now are worried about moral standards. Like the young bell ringer was saying earlier, I think people are afraid that the media can tend to –

**Mary**
Sorry, I wasn't talking about the media. I meant people in general are worried by sex and violence and –

**Alan**
*(To Mary)* Listen, love, we chatted earlier, but you must remember, you, you are a peripheral guest. Right, so –

**Tony**
No, I think that's a salient point. It's worth hearing.

**Alan**
Good idea! Good idea! L-l-l-let's – let's hear her salient point. Bring her on!

Come and join us. Can we get a drink for the Christian? Sorry, love, I didn't catch your name.

*Mary joins Alan and Tony on the sofa.*

**Mary**
Mary.

**Alan**
Mary. Like the Virgin Mary. Are you, are you –? Oh it's none of my business.

**Mary**
Yes, I am actually.

**Alan**
Oh. Well done. Um, er – Fire away.

**Mary**
I'd like to ask Mr Hayers why he allows on the BB –

**Alan**
How did this happen?

**Mary**
What?

**Alan**
Nothing. Carry on.

**Mary**
Yeah, I'd like to ask Mr Hayers why he allows on the BBC the graphic depiction of, of such sordid practices as swearing, fighting, masturbation –

**Alan**
Listen, love, sorry, if you're going to talk about a subject, can you just avoid using – using that word.

**Mary**
Masturbation?

**Alan**
Yes, that's the one.

**Mary**
Well, I do object to the graphic depiction of onanism.

**Alan**
What's onanism?

**Tony**
It's masturbation.

**Alan**
Thank you, thank you. Look, love, what's – what's your problem with it?

**Mary**
Well, I don't like it.

**Alan**
Well, don't do it.

**Mary**
(*To Tony*) I'd just like to ask you really what you intend to do about all the filth?

**Alan**
It's not his fault, leave him alone!

**Tony**
No, no, I'd like to deal with this.

**Alan**
Let him speak!

**Tony**
The BBC has a brief, and part of that brief is to provide an opportunity for provocative, innovative, experimental drama.

**Alan**
*Crime Watch UK.*

**Tony**
Now obviously this can't be to everybody's tastes.

**Alan**
*When the Boat Comes In.* Terrible.

**Tony**
But if you look at it within its own context –

**Mary**
What I object to is that some of these programmes are nothing short of pornographic, really.

**Tony**
(*Laughs*) I think to call the BBC's output pornographic is, if you don't mind me saying, is being slightly hysterical.

**Alan**
(*Laughs*) Slightly hysterical, very good.

**Mary**
I'm not being hysterical. The BBC broadcasts pornography.

**Alan**
Listen, love, the BBC might be many things but porn it ain't. The only way you can get access to hardcore pornography is if you mail off for a satellite smart card decoder. Then you're in business.
(*Pause. Mary and Tony stare at Alan*)
Let's talk about Christmas. Anyone got any thoughts on Christmas? Fanny?

**Fanny**
Me spatula's stuck under me flapjack. Oooh, pardon!

**Alan**
Outrageous. Hang on a sec, that, that doesn't make sense.

**Fanny**
Oh, um. You know spat— No. No it doesn't work does it?

**Mary**
I'd just like to say that I think it's really nice that we're here to celebrate Christmas, this is a Christmas show and it's celebrating the birth of Jesus Christ and his incarnation as a human being.

**Alan**
No, it's not, it's, it's – it's *Knowing Me, Knowing Yule with Alan Partridge*.

**Mary**
And Christ.

**Alan**
Christ isn't in the title. It's, it's not *Knowing Me, KnowingYule with Jesus Christ.*

**Mary**
Do you believe in God, Alan?

**Alan**
Yes.

**Mary**
What is he?

**Alan**
God is – a, a, a gas.

**Tony**
What does that mean?

**Alan**
Well, you know, I mean, he's not a small, he's not like sort of – Calor Gas, or something. He's something big, you know, like, like, like oxygen, or – or carbon dioxide. No, no, that's bad, isn't it? No that's the devil. I don't really want to get bogged down in this because I haven't thought it through quite as much as I wished I had. *(Points at the door)* Oh look, there's someone at the door!

**Mary**
Is there?

**Alan**
Yes there is, there's someone at the door! *(Under his breath to someone offstage)* Santa, Santa –

*Door bell rings; Alan jumps up to answer it.*

**Alan**
Ooh let's see who it is, let's see who it is, oooooh. Oh, I've got a good feeling about this. Yes! Oooh, it's Father Christmas!

*Music and applause. Father Christmas enters.*

**Mike**
(As Santa) Ho-ho-ho-ho-ho. Ho-ho-ho-ho-ho. Hooooooooo –

**Alan**
All right. All right, Mike, that's enough – Father Christmas is in actual fact none other than Mike Taylor of the Norfolk Rover dealer network. Mike, thanks very much. Thanks very much for being Father Christmas. Thank you.

**Mike**
It's a pleasure, Alan.

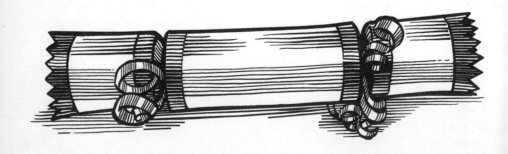

**Alan**

Mike, I heard recently that Norfolk Rover are offering nought per cent finance on selected models this season. Is that true?

**Mike**

Well, that's absolutely true, Alan. The snowy weather has enabled us to freeze the prices on the whole of the Rover 600 series.

**Alan**

Right.

**Mike**

But, Alan, I understand you have a Rover Vitesse Fastback?

**Alan**

Yes, I do.

**Mike**

And what is it you particularly like about it?

**Alan**

Well, apart from the walnut and leather interior, which I think really does give it luxury car status, the thing that impressed me most was the overall economy. I mean 38.4 miles to the gallon at a constant 56 miles an hour, I think, makes it a class leader.

**Mike**

That's absolutely right.

**Alan**

Father Christmas!

*Applause*

**Mike**

Ho-ho-ho-ho.

*Applause. Alan walks to sofa.*

**Alan**

Let's meet a few of my other guests at tonight's party. Over there that's WPC Kate Fraser. She patrols my area.

**Fanny**

And I bet she takes down your particulars. Ooh pardon!

**Alan**

It's getting quite tiresome now – And, and I want you to meet this character. His name is Alan. This is the man responsible for getting me where I am today. Quite literally, he's my chauffeur.

*Drum roll*

**Alan**

*(To Glen)* Yeah, he did deserve one of those, yeah. Alan. Did you get here all right tonight?

**Alan 2**

Yeah, fine. Bit of a snarl up at Shepherd's Bush there. A lot of those Asian blokes out on the street having a party or something. What is it you call them again? Ram, ram-a-dam-a-ding-dong?

**Alan**

No, not now! It's, it's, it's Ramadan, Alan.

**Alan 2**

No, no, but you said, you said ram-a-dam-a-ding –

**Alan**

Yeah, all right, not now, Alan. Now, the conversations, the conversations I've just had I think successfully recreate the conversations I have with my ordinary friends in my real home. Once again, if you've just tuned in, this is a mock-up. However, this *is* real. This is my favourite piece of furniture. *(He opens up a cabinet)* It's a genuine eighteenth-century Queen Anne wardrobe, hollowed out to include a 36-inch television with companion video. And, I'll just unwrap this and, it's for all those people who ask me, 'Alan, what do you get up to at Christmas in Norwich?' Here's the answer: it's Christmas in Norwich with Alan Partridge.

# KNOWING ME, KNOWING  YULE

*Music. Alan puts on a video; action turns to video footage of Norwich.*

**Alan voiceover**
Norwich. City of mustard, and shoes. After the bombing of Dresden, Norwich became the city with the largest number of pre-reformation churches in Europe.

*Footage of Alan posing in jogging gear.*

**Alan voiceover**
I love to jog around Norwich, but I can still make calls to the office via my digital telecom headset communicator.

*Views of Norwich*

**Alan voiceover**
Norwich Cathedral is breathtaking, and its beautiful golden stone cloisters are the perfect place to go jogging every morning, whilst making those last-minute budget decisions.
*Footage of Alan jogging, speaking on hands-free mobile.*
300 K, 300 K or we take it to *Sky*. If Raquel Welch doesn't want to stay in a Trusthouse Forte, then we'll stick her at a youth hostel and see if she likes that.

*Views of Norwich*

**Alan voiceover**
Four hundred years ago, this serenity was shattered by a bloody big fight between the townsfolk and the cathedral monks. Six friars were beheaded on this site, which is now a Dorothy Perkins. The blood runs deep. Many say the ghosts of that carnage still haunt the town square. *(Camera shakes violently)*

*Footage of Alan driving.*

**Alan voiceover**
It's three days before Christmas, and I drive the Rover Vitesse Fastback to the Royal Norwich Hospital.

*Alan parks and removes a box from the boot of his car.*

**Alan**
*You* can't park here. *I've* got special permission because I'm distributing a large box of second-hand toys to the sick children.

*Alan in the children's ward.*

**Alan**
*(To children)* Hello. I'm Alan Partridge.

**Alan voiceover**
I love kids. The things they say.

**Alan**
*(To children)* There you go. Right, let's have a toy. It's second-hand, but it's in quite good condition. Well, basically shop-soiled, you know, but it is, it is, as you can see, it's still in pretty good condition. There's nothing technically wrong with it. Does anyone watch my show? *Knowing me, Knowing You with Alan Partridge*? No? No?

*Children all shake their heads.*

**Child**
No.

**Alan**
No? No one knows it? Does anyone –

**Child**
I've never heard of you.

**Alan**
You've never heard of me?

**Child**
No.

## Alan

Right. It's very rude to say that actually. In the studio, well basically what it is is a building, is an enormous mock-up of my house! In a studio. It's great. I mean, the budget is about two eight, two eighty K. Er, I don't believe you are familiar with TV budgets, are you? *(Pause)* Are you looking forward to Christmas?

## Child

Yeah.

*Silence. Alan looks around and pats a girl on the head.*

## Alan

*(Singing)* Jingle bells, Jingle bells Jingle all the way.

*Alan sitting in his car.*

## Alan

The good thing about the automatic transmission on these things is that you don't have to do those tricky hill starts. Right, now I just hit the gas and away we go. *(Drives off)*

*Footage of Alan entering Tandy's.*

## Alan voiceover

It's been a busy few days. What better way to unwind than at Tandy's. I've got a special arrangement with their Norwich branch, who let me into their store after they're closed to the general public. If you are a well-known celebrity, Christmas shopping can be an absolute nightmare. So, it's always nice to mooch around without fear of being threatened or pick pocketed. *(Touches a CD player)* Nice action. Very nice action.
*(Presses eject button on CD player)* Mm, that is a very nice action.
*(Presses eject again)* It's a, it's a quality action. *(Walks away)* I've got one though. *(Picks up a Traffic Master)*

Right. Aaah, Traffic Master. Can these be dash-mounted?

## Assistant

*(Holding lots of boxes)* Yeah, that will stand up.

## Alan

Excellent, excellent. It's like *Crackerjack* this, isn't it, all these presents – *(Alan attempts to put the Traffic Master on top of the assistant's pile, but drops it)* Ooh, Jesus Christ! Sorry – sorry.

*Footage of Alan looking at telephones.*

## Alan voiceover

It's at times like these, simply browsing among electrical goods at Tandy's, that I know who I truly am. I'm Alan Partridge.

*Cut to Alan walking towards his house door; turns to camera.*

**Alan**

Well, it's Christmas Eve, all the good deeds are done. And the Rover's in the garage along with the Espace, and the Toyota Starlet, a little run-around for Denise when she's home. Um, parked there safely in the garage, it's a triple garage, it's quite large. We'll show you a cutaway of that, now. *(Shot of a three-door garage)* I'm about to go into the house and tuck into a turkey. That's all from me. You can't come in my house, it's private, but I will see you later in the mock-up. Goodnight. And Merry Christmas.

*Alan trips over doormat. Camera closes in.*

**Alan**

Seriously, seriously, a bit of privacy. Thanks a lot. Goodnight.
*(Steps inside, closes front door and peers through window at camera.)*

*Back to studio; applause.*

**Alan**

*(With his mouth full)* You caught me chomping on a mince pie. Do they taste a bit off? A bit sort of minty, sort of fermented? Everyone, the mince pies are off. Don't eat the mince pies. Tony, I hope you're going to sort out the BBC catering?

**Tony**

I'll make it my top priority, Alan. Although, there are other things that I will be addressing –

**Alan**

Sorry, sorry, can I just interrupt you there? Mary, can I ask you to eat less noisily. *(Alan gets up and puts microphone to Mary's mouth)* I, I'm not being rude but if I, if I hold my microphone close to your mouth … now chew …
*(Chewing noises over mic)*
Yes, you see now, that, that's what people are hearing at home, you see? I, I'm not

being rude, it's just that you, you sound like a pig. So, Tony …

**Tony**

Yes, there are other things apart from catering that I will be looking into. Um, for example, product placement.

**Mary**

What's product placement?

**Tony**

It's when a presenter abuses his or her position to advertise a specific product. I see that as a severe breach of contract and it'll be punished with instant dismissal.

*Father Christmas enters, handing a present to Tony.*

**Mike**

Ho-ho-ho, Merry Christmas, Tony.

**Tony**

Oh thanks, a little present, thank you.

*Tony starts unwrapping present.*

**Alan**

Don't open that now. Don't open that now. You don't have to open that now.

**Mary**

What is it?

*Tony unwraps a miniature car.*

**Tony**

Oh. It's a Rover.

**Mike**

It was on special offer. It was last –

**Alan**

Mike, Mike, Mike, not now. Not now, Mike. I'm going to have some mulled wine. Glen. Glen, do you want some mulled wine?

**Glen**

No thanks, Alan, I'm fine.

**Alan**
Right. Does your friend Andy want some?

**Andy**
No, I'm fine, thanks.

**Glen**
No, Andy's fine.

**Alan**
Right, well, if he wants some, you know, you just let me know, all right?

**Alan 2**
I'll have some, Al.

**Alan**
Get your own.

**Alan 2**
Ram-a-dam-a-ding-dong.

**Alan**
Yeah. *(Turns to hostess)* Oh, hello again. Hello. How are you? All right? I'm looking for the mulled wine. Oh, oh, Boasters. Yeah, *(bites into one)* mm, mm. Quite nice, these. Have you had a Boaster? You should have one yourself. They're quite interesting, Boasters. I mean, three years ago, Hob Nobs were probably the number one biscuit. I mean, it *was* digestives, then Hob Nobs came along and blew them into the weeds. And so I mean, you know, until recently in the oatmeal kingdom, Hob Nobs ruled the biscuit roost. But … I mean, you know, then Boasters came along. I would love to have been a fly on the wall at the Hob Nob factory when Boasters, when Boasters hit the streets. I'm not implying that there are flies, by the way I'm not, I'm not implying that flies are on the wall at a Hob Nob factory. I was talking about hypothetical flies. But on the real Hob Nob wall. I'm loving this chat with you. You're doing very well; I've been watching you. *(Waitress walks away. Alan turns to camera)* Don't forget, Mick Hucknall coming up

later on, but time now for my star guest, erm, apart from Mick Hucknall. That's contractual. Now, if you've been reading your *Radio Times*, you may be expecting Raquel Welch at this point. She cancelled, this afternoon. I can't say anything beyond that. Five o' clock she cancelled. However, we've got something better, I think. We've got two very lovely golfers who are going to step into Raquel's shoes. One in each. The story has touched the nation. *She* used to be *his* caddy, and now *he* is *her* caddy. Why? You will see for yourself as I introduce a married pair of top professional golfing people, Liz and Gordon Heron.

*Music and applause. Liz and Gordon enter. Liz pushes Gordon down a ramp in his wheelchair.*

**Alan**
Watch, watch the Queen Anne cabinet. Watch Glen's friend Andy. You better not hit him. In you go. If you just want to park in there. Great. Lovely. You'll be doing three-point turns next. K. M. A. P. K. Y. Gordon and Liz Heron, ah-haa.

**Gordon and Liz**
Ah-haa. *(Liz laughs – a high-pitched squeaky giggle)*

**Alan**
That's a nice laugh. It sounds a bit like a big bird, doesn't it?

**Liz**
*(Laughs)*

**Alan**
Yeah, it really does. Now, as I said, your story is a Christmas fairy tale isn't it? You're Gordon Hansel and Liz Gretel. Allow me if you will to be Hans Christian Alan Partridgeson.

*Applause. Alan picks up a book and pretends to read from it.*

# KNOWING ME, KNOWING  YULE

**Alan**

'Once upon a time in November 1993, a young golfer was on the eighteenth hole. He was about to putt his way to victory in the Colgate Cup. As his flaxen hair blew in the wind, it started to rain. And then, disaster. A bolt of lightning struck him down and he was paralysed.' *(Turns to Gordon)* How did that feel?

**Gordon**

It sort of felt, it felt a bit like *(yells and screams)*.

*Liz and Gordon laugh.*

**Alan**

Wonderful. Wonderful. Wha-w-w-w-w-w-what a lovely sense of humour. Anyway, if I can just, just finish the fairy story. *(Alan pretends to continue reading from book)* 'Gordon the golfer didn't lie down like a dog and become a bitter and twisted hateful lunatic. He picked himself up, and in the tradition of many other heroic disabled people – Lord Nelson, Napoleon, Ironside, Daniel … Daniel Day Lewis, Captain Hook and Dave Allen – he became Liz's golfing coach and caddy, in a special motorized cart. And two years later, Liz Gretel putted her way to glory in the Colgate Cup. And just last week she was named Ladies Sports Personality of the year by the readers of *SHE* magazine. The End.' It's a fairy story. Gordon, you were robbed of the use of your legs. In a sense, you were a victim of a leg thief. If you could speak to that leg thief now, what would you say?

**Gordon**

Well, I suppose I'd say to him, you know, 'Why didn't you pick on someone who had more legs than they need?'

**Alan**

A centipede.

**Gordon**

Exactly, a centipede with ninety-eight legs could still get about.

**Liz**

What about a millipede? A millipede's got a million legs.

**Gordon**

No, a thousand.

**Liz**

What's got a million legs then?

**Gordon**

A thousand millipedes.

**Alan**

It, it doesn't seem fair, does it, the way that God gives some things a thousand legs? I mean, I really can't believe a millipede has the intelligence to appreciate just how lucky it is. And then God gives other things, like people, only two legs.

**Liz**

Well, God's probably got lots of legs himself.

**Alan**

Yeah, except God's a gas. Probably got gas legs. That, that'd make sense, yes. Now, Liz. Lovely Liz. Much as I respect professional golfers, I have to say I do find the sport incredibly dull. Is it?

**Liz**

Ooh, isn't he rude? No, golf's a great sport. It's actually one of the world's most traditional sports because it dates back to King Henry VIII. Now he was the fat king with the six wives, do you remember, lucky bloke *(laughs)*. He used to play croquet on the village green outside Buckingham Palace, because in them days London was like a sort of big village. Um, I think they

called it Londinium. *(Alan looks bored. He puffs out his cheeks)* And anyway, so through the centuries the sticks became the golf clubs that we know and the balls became smaller. They became the golf balls that we know and love. So you see, it's a very traditional and exciting sport, and dull it is *not*.

**Alan**
*(Uninterested)* Hmm. Gordon, do you get out much?

**Gordon**
When I can.

**Alan**
I mean, do you have any hobbies, now you have all this time on your hands?

**Gordon**
Yeah, I like, like making maps.

**Alan**
Oh what, Ordnance Survey maps, *A to Z*s, what …

**Gordon**
No, maps of imaginary places, you know.

**Alan**
What do you mean?

*Gordon smiles to himself and draws images with his hands.*

**Gordon**
I create them, you know, like a mountain or a pond, maybe a little stream.

**Alan**
Right. I mean do, do you hang them on the wall?

**Gordon**
No, I don't draw them. They are in my head, they're imaginary.

**Alan**
Right. Are, are they any use?

**Gordon**
Not really.

**Alan**
Good. Well, well, I'd love to have a walk round your head sometime. I'm sure it's very picturesque.

**Gordon**
No, you can't, it's private.

**Alan**
All right. I wasn't going to book an appointment.

*Liz laughs.*

**Alan**
Liz, Liz. Lovely Liz with your lovely bird laugh. Um, now in the past, before the *(makes lightning-striking noise)* I, I believe Gordon was a bit of a ladies' man. In fact he was, he was known quite simply as randy Gordon.

**Liz**
That's right. Well, now I like to call him Chairman Mao. I say, 'Morning Chairman Mao.'

**Alan**
*(Laughs)* Is he a communist?

**Gordon**
No, I'm in a wheelchair.

**Alan**
Yes, of course, chairman Mao. I'm sorry. Yes, um, right, well, Gordon, in the past, you know before the *(makes lightning noise)*, you, you, I mean, what I mean is, do you still have an eye for the fairer sex?

**Gordon**
*(Laughing)* Oh yes, still chase the ladies. But I stop when they get to the stairs.

*Liz laughs.*

**Alan**

Yes. A bit like a Dalek. Can't, can't go up the stairs. I'm not, I'm not comparing you, I'm not comparing you to a Dalek. You're, you're more like Davros, the leader of the Daleks. You're half-human half-Da… I'm sorry, I'm deeply sorry, I'm, I'm in the, I'm sorry. Now you're married to Liz, there's no escaping that. Um, but, in the words of Dr Hook, when you're in love with a beautiful woman, you watch your friends. Do you watch your friends?

**Liz**

Was Dr Hook a *real* doctor?

**Alan**

Do you know, I've absolutely no idea? *(Turns to production crew)* Can we find out? Can we find out if Dr Hook was a fully qualified GP? By the end of the show? Yeah, fine, they'll let us know.

*Gordon points to a painting on the wall.*

**Gordon**

Is this you, Alan?

*Alan jumps up to the picture and points proudly.*

**Alan**

Yes. Now that, this is a portrait I commissioned by a local Norwich artist, David Morton. He has done quite a few famous people. He did Sebastian Coe, the celebrity Conservative runner. And, uh, but –

**Liz**

I think your mouth looks a little bit big.

**Alan**

Yes, that's intentional. That's intended. He takes the facet of his subject which is most significant, and then exaggerates it. So with me I'm obviously a professional chatter. I don't know what I'd do if my mouth was struck by lightning, I have to say.

**Gordon**

Sure you can find another hole to talk through.

*Liz laughs.*

**Alan**

Lovely, lov-lovely sense of humour.

*Alan kicks Gordon's wheelchair as he walks past.*

**Alan**

You should put the brakes on that. Or drop anchor, whatever you do.

**Liz**

It's nice that you've got all these ramps everywhere for us.

**Alan**

Do you like those? I mean, I've installed them for you in my mock-up home. I don't have, actually have ramps in my real home, you know, but …because, well frankly I don't actually know that many disabled people. But, if you and I were to become friends then, you know, I would happily purchase a set.

**Gordon**

Don't get your chequebook out just yet, Alan.

**Alan**

No, I would. It's the least I could do. You know. I mean it would be nice if you chipped in, you know, made a contribution. I mean, you *would* be the major user. I'm sorry, I would fund them exclusively, I'm sorry. *If* we were friends. Right now, it, it says here 'announcement'. What's that about?

**Liz**

Oh, that's me. I'm pregnant! Ladies and gentlemen, in five months I shall be giving birth to a little baby Heron. *(Liz and Gordon hold hands)*

**Alan**
Not literally, that would be hideous. But congratulations. Congratulations.

**Gordon**
Yes, I used to say she caddied me clubs, now I say she's caddying me baby.

**Alan**
Well, congratulations and best wishes to both of you. And a special congratulations to, to you, Gordon. Well done.

*Alan touches Gordon's arm.*

**Gordon**
What do you mean?

**Alan**
Well, I was just saying, you know, well done. Best, good wishes.

**Gordon**
I *can* have sex.

**Alan**
Yes, I know. Look I'm not saying –

**Gordon**
I can *still* shag.

**Alan**
Please – it's Christmas.

**Gordon**
*(Talking over Alan's protestations)* Just because I'm in a wheelchair doesn't mean that I don't feel sexual desire any more. I actually feel more sexual desire now, ever since I've been in a wheelchair than before. I'm a better lover as well, aren't I?

**Alan**
Please, I don't –

**Gordon**
But people don't want to talk about it. They don't want to hear about people feeling lust because they're disabled –

**Alan**
Please! Please!

**Gordon**
Don't give me *(mimicking Alan)* 'please, please' –

**Alan**
Look, look, I, I, I –

**Gordon**
La-la-la –

**Alan**
*(Exasperated)* Don't do … Listen, I'm on your side! I had those wheelchair ramps installed at three hours' notice. Do you know something, there's no disabled access at the Strand Theatre tonight, because *we've* got the ramps. If you're in a wheelchair and you want to see *The Buddy Holly Story* tonight, you can forget it because of you. *(Points fiercely at Gordon)* This, this, this lot didn't want to have you on the show. They said you'd be a fire hazard. I've got a fire extinguisher under my chair in case you go off.

*Liz laughs.*

**Alan**
Anyway. Thank you for sharing your fairy story. Stay around, enjoy some mulled wine. Ladies and gentlemen, Gordon and Liz Heron, a fairy story.

*Applause; Alan walks into another room.*

**Alan**

Now – now I, now I know what you're saying. You are saying to yourselves 'Alan, this show *is* a success. Granted there were one or two hiccups, but we're sure they can be ironed out if this show went to a second series.' I hope you're listening, Tony, this, this is the viewers speaking. 'However, Alan,' you're saying, 'you are a spiv. You're a rip-off merchant. You say it's a Christmas special but you haven't even pulled a cracker.' And to those people I say 'Right, bring on the biggest Christmas cracker in the world!'

*Music; giant cracker with Alan's face on the side is wheeled on by studio crew.*

**Alan**

The cracker is – the cracker is five feet high –

*Applause*

**Alan**

The cracker is five feet high, the height of a large cow. And it's, it's twenty-three feet long. That's about the length of a small Chinese restaurant. Our, our thanks for construction go to Hilary Simpson of White City Pyrotechnics.

*Applause. Shot of Hilary acknowledging applause.*

**Alan**

Thank you, Hilary. Hilary, of course, can be a man's name, just like Lesley or Vivian. So, so thank you, sir, for donating your services for free. This a charity pull. Fanny, I ask you not to comment. Inside the cracker is a kidney dialysis machine. If we break the world record, the dialysis machine will be winging its way to the Royal Children's Hospital in Norwich, and here to pull the cracker are the Royal Plymouth Sea Cadets.

*Music; cadets march onstage.*

**Alan**

Now, we were going to have Zola Budd to blow the whistle. She can't do that, obviously, so Gordon, perhaps you'd like to join me and blow the whistle instead. In your own time. On your marks, get set *(blows whistle)*. The force required to split the cracker is the equivalent of a Land Rover winching a small sapling up from its root. It's –

*Cracker ignites as cadets pull each end.*

**Alan**

Right, the, the cracker's on fire! Abort the pull! Abort the pull! Get Gordon! Where's the fire extinguisher?

**Gordon**

It's under your chair, Alan.

**Alan**

It's under a chair! It's under my chair; it's under his chair!

*Crew extinguish fire.*

**Alan**

Put my face out! Put my face out! Ladies and gentlemen. We, we have had a cracker fire in the studio. Yes, I'm being told the split in the cracker does not constitute a complete snap, and we haven't broken the world record. I suppose the lesson to be learnt from this is, don't ever get your props and special effects made by White City Pyrotechnics. Because, and I'm quite happy to go on record with this, White City Pyrotechnics are run by twits. *(Points at Hilary)* And there's one over there. There he is. And he's got a girl's name. And he makes pyrotechnics like a girl.

*Mike enters and picks up the joke from the giant cracker.*

**Mike**

Shall I do the joke, Alan?

*Knowing Me, Knowing Yule*'s guest cook, 'Fanny'. I've never really understood his/her sort. But recently I saw *Priscilla, Queen of the Desert*. Brilliant film – and a real insight into why certain types of gay men in make-up like to shout so much. There's a scene where this bus full of drag artistes turns up in a little Australian town full of macho men. Funniest thing I've ever seen. Genius.

Me in the foreground with Mick Hucknall in the background – which is how things once were, albeit very briefly. Pleasant enough chap. To your face. Hasn't had a hit in a while.

Presenting *Knowing Me, Knowing Yule*, a show broadcast to celebrate the birth of the greatest man ever, who was born in a barn, died for our sins and ascended to Heaven. Anyway enough about me, it was also a Christmas show! Only joking. I'm not Christ. I'm just here to do his work.

Me in my favourite exercise shorts. I bought them two years into my marriage. Like the wife, long gone now. The underpant containment area finally perished forever back in '99. My head ruled my heart and I got a new pair rather than attempt a repair for sentimental reasons. A bit like the marriage!

Lynn Anne Benfield. There are probably better PAs around – as I jokingly remind her from time to time – but who else knows what size floppy disks I need or where to track down a fresh pair of boxers at 7 p.m. in Dundee? If I'm a jumbo jet, she's the pilot. The co-pilot. She knows where the bodies are buried – as she jokingly reminds me.

The Linton Travel Tavern, my home for perhaps a little too long. I still drive past it occasionally. I've considered checking in for a night, just to remind myself how lucky I am now to have my own house and a girlfriend. But that would be mad and not a little depressing. And I'll bet their room rates have gone up. They had a refit in March.

Inmate 3768 Partridge of Cell 7 at the Linton Travel Tavern, wrongfully convicted of being a bad broadcaster and a failed husband. Horrible time, to be serious. No amount of excellent full English breakfasts can fill a man's empty soul. Only joking.

Dave Clifton, ace DJ, whose brave battle with the bottle suffered another setback recently. He was arrested in Pizza Express after a row over wanting to play his own tape as he ate. I really must sit down and talk to him about it. Over a pint! Only joking, Dave. You're clearly in a dark place. And I don't mean your studio!

Making hay while the sun shines: Linton Travel Tavern receptionist Sophie and the boy who used to work there. These days she's apparently 'making a go of it' with a Greek chap she got pregnant by on holiday. I bumped into the boy – Dan, I think he was called – in the covered market in March. He now works for Weatherspoon's, going around the country chalking up their pub menus. Seemed a bit down. We chatted for a few minutes but I had to go.

A woman I paid to 'be' my wife for a Hamilton Waterbreaks video. Ironically, at the time this was taken I was paying rather heavily for my actual wife Carol to not be my wife. I mean we were getting divorced! It's weighted against the man.

Cap'n Popeye Partridge welcomes you aboard the Skylark!*

*Thanks to Hamilton Waterbreaks.

I was actually wearing jogging bottoms when this one was taken! I'd overslept that day and hadn't even showered! (It was about now I was starting to bottom out.) But the studio door was open so hopefully it wasn't too unpleasant for people. You should smell it after Clifton's been in there! The stench of beer is phenomenal.

December '99. I had put on so much weight, I was unsure if I was going to fit into the new millennium. Not that I cared – all that mattered was getting my next Toblerone hit. The darkest time was in Dundee. I was in the deepest hole imaginable. I don't mean Dundee. (Although that's hardly hula-hula land. Little tip: don't try asking the staff of Ryman's there if they have a lavatory you can use. They will freeze you out – however badly events unfold.) A terrible bleak empty period about which I can now laugh.

My good friend Michael. A damn good friend who's usually there for me. Michael has a great fund of tales from his army days, although I'm becoming increasingly convinced that they're fantasies. I had a researcher at Radio Norwich run a few background checks and not a single regiment in Britain has a record of him.

My pride and joy – Lord House – under construction. It's looking a bit better these days! The caravan, scaffolding and dusty lads with bricks and accents are long gone. Where the cement mixer stood there's now a bag of peat.

My girlfriend Sonia – who's taught me to smile again. Of course, that's not all she's taught me! (Although a lot of smiling is involved!) They say you can't teach an old dog new tricks. Well, she's taught me a lot of new tricks. Sex ones!

Another lazy summer night with Michael, watching the world go by or stop on the forecourt, setting the world to rights over a Flavia machine coffee and a microwaved Ginsters' Steak and Onion Slice. It's the simplest pleasures in life that always win out.

Don't forget to put the batteries in or it won't work! Or the torch! (As well as Lynn.)

**Alan**
No, don't do the joke, Father Christmas.

**Liz**
Yeah, go on, Father Christmas, give us all a giggle. *(Laughs)*

**Mike**
What make of car goes 'woof woof'?

**Tony**
Is it a Rover?

**Alan**
Mike, please, Mike. Mike, Mike, please. Help me out here, please, please.

**Mike**
No, it's not a Rover. It's a – a Vauxhall Labrador.

**Alan**
*(Laughs)* Oh, hilarious.

**Gordon**
There's no such car.

**Alan**
Yes, yes there is. My dad had one in the sixties; we had great times in the Vauxhall Labrador. Right, can we clear this up? Well, while they're clearing up that mess, let's have some breakfast bar chat. A new section of the show. What would you like to talk about?

**Mary**
What's going to happen about that dialysis machine?

**Alan**
Um, it will just go back to the suppliers.

**Liz**
How much does a dialysis machine cost?

**Alan**
About £20,000.

**Mary**
Oh. And how much does this programme cost?

**Alan**
That's none of your business, that's confidential information.

**Tony**
£300,000.

**Alan**
That's correct, yes.

**Gordon**
So you could have got fourteen dialysis machines instead of making this programme.

**Alan**
I think if you asked the British public whether they would prefer fourteen kidney dialysis machines or an Alan Partridge Christmas special, the answer would be pretty unanimous, wouldn't it, Tony?

**Tony**
Yes, I think it would.

**Alan**
Thank you. And thanks, thanks to everyone for a very entertaining breakfast bar chat. Quite a good section, that. That could be a regular feature in my show if, *if*, we got a second series.

*Music; Alan lip-synchs to a song he has pre-recorded.*

**Alan**
On the first day of Christmas, my true love gave to me, a Partridge in a pear tree. On the second day of Christmas my true love gave to me, two turtledoves, and a Partridge in a pear tree. That's me. On the third day of Christmas my true love gave to me, three French hens, two turtledoves –

*People dressed as doves and hens descend from ceiling on ropes.*

*Alan stops singing to backing track and points at giant cracker.*

**Alan**
This should have been, this should have been moved
*(Singing)* – Alan Partridge in a pear tree. This should have been moved. Can we, can some –
*(Singing)* On the fourth day of Christmas my true love gave to me, four calling birds, three French hens … *(Backing track continues)*
Can we just stop, just cut the music! This is, we can't do this –
*(Backing track)* – two turtledoves, Alan Partridge in a pear tree.

*Alan helps a bird down from a rope.*

**Alan**
Are you all right? Keep flapping, it looks good. There we go. We got you there; I've got you there. I'm just going to put this turtledove down. I'm sorry; this is the French, French hens … Are you all right there? You don't have to flap any more, love, it's OK. Come down. I just want to keep you away from the dialysis machine. I don't want you to damage it. It's got to go back to the suppliers.
*(Alan points to cracker)*
This really should have been cleared, it should have been cleared. I, I'm sorry, I've had to abandon my big number, which is shame because there's still twenty-eight people backstage in funny costumes that were going to come on and dance. But, what the heck. The show, the show's still going well and I believe that. Let's go back to Fanny Thomas and her Christmas partridge.

*Music*

**Fanny**
Well now, Alan, I've basted the bird now, now what we need to get sorted out is the trimmings. Now I don't know about you, but there's nothing I love more than a hot spicy stuffing. Ooh pardon! Anyway, I'd like you to help me out now, right, by grasping this *(hands pepper mill to Alan)* very firmly and giving the top a good hard tug.

**Alan**
What does your mother think of you?

**Fanny**
Very proud.

**Alan**
Very proud. Go on, say something about proud now.

**Fanny**
Sorry?

**Alan**
You know, about standing proud or something.

**Fanny**
I don't get it.

**Alan**
You know, I mean, like a, like a man's member or something. I don't know. I mean I don't want to encourage you; I just, I'm just surprised you missed that one, that's all.

**Fanny**
I don't know what you mean. Go on, *(points at peppermill)* twist it, twist it.

**Alan**
It's quite stiff.

**Fanny**
That's what they all say. Ooh pardon! No, no, leave it alone, leave it alone. Now, Alan, look, here's the stuffing, right? And what I want you to do is grab a great big fistful.

*Alan grabs a handful of stuffing and begins to stuff the turkey.*

**Fanny**
Ooh, he's not shy! Now, stick it right up, go on. Stick it right up; go on, that's it. Further. Further.

*Liz and Gordon laugh.*

**Fanny**
*(Touching her mouth provocatively as she watches Alan)* Right up to the neck.

**Alan**
*(Pointing at Fanny)* Now that's enough!

**Fanny**
It's rude to point, Alan. No, I'm not talking about your finger. Ooh, pardon!

**Alan**
I'm not, I am not aroused.

**Fanny**
Ooh. Methinks the lady doth protest too much.

**Alan**
Oh, put a cork in it!

**Fanny**
Oh well, I tried it but it doesn't help.

**Alan**
Knock it on the head.

**Fanny**
Oooh. I didn't know you were into the rough stuff, honestly. It's enough to make a girl blush.

**Alan**
You're, you're not a girl. You're not a girl, are you? Your name's Peter Willis, you're a failed disc jockey who dresses up as a woman for cheap laughs.

*Fanny removes wig and resumes male role. Pulls Alan's face close to his.*

**Fanny**
Right, this is Peter, right? Now what do you want? Do you want Peter, or do you want Fanny?

**Alan**
Fa-Fanny, I want Fanny.

*Fanny replaces wig and reverts to female voice.*

**Fanny**
Now I think you pulled out too soon. Go on, pop it back in. That's right.

**Gordon**
Oi, Alan, what do you do for an encore? Shag a robin? *(Laughs)*

*Alan swings towards Gordon and punches him, with turkey still intact on his hand. He then punches Tony with the turkey.*

*Tony gets a nosebleed.*

**Alan**
*(Desperately)* I'm sorry, I'm sorry, I'm sorry. I need help. I'll get help. Listen, my wife left me on Christmas Eve. I spent Christmas Day all on my own here. Well, not here, this is a mock-up.

**Tony**
This is a disgrace. I'm going to make sure you never, *never* work on television again!

**Alan**
Please, please don't take my chat away from me. Is there anything I can say or do that will make you change your mind?

**Tony**
No *(Pause)*

*Alan punches Tony again with the turkey, then turns and gestures to Mary.*

**Alan**
Do you want some, eh? I'm handy! I'm handy! *(To Mary)* Do you want some?

**Mary**
No thank you.

*Alan turns to Liz.*

**Alan**
What about you, Mrs Potter? Do you want some, big bird? Eh?
*Alan turns to cameras, shaken.*
Arrrggghhhhh! I will never work in broadcasting again. And on that bombshell, it's time for me, Alan Partridge, to say Knowing Me, Alan Partridge, Knowing Yule, wherever you are, and who'st … is who'st a word, I don't know? And, um, and I have just been told that Dr Hook is not a qualified medical doctor. Er, happy Christmas, and, oh, and here's Mick Hucknall to sing 'Ding Dong Merrily on High', ah-haaaaaaaa!

*Applause. Mick Hucknall enters.*

**Mick Hucknall**
(*Sings*) Ding Dong Merrily On High

*Alan walks dejectedly across the screen, turkey still on hand.*

## CLOSING TITLES
## PROGRAMME ENDS
3 seconds black

*Footage of Alan in country gear, walking through the countryside.*

**Alan**
Hi, I'm Alan Partridge. I'm a busy man. One day I can be recording a TV show, and the next I can be shuttling up to Harrogate to host a debt-motivated weekend for the Bostik sales force. But when I go back to Norwich, I like to relax by rambling. I switch off my mobile phone, put my pager on mute, and enjoy the stillness of the Norfolk countryside.

*Music and title: A Christmas Ramble with Alan Partridge.*

**Alan voiceover**
I always like to go for a walk on Christmas morning for two to three hours. Alone. I do ask the others. My wife Carole, son Fernando – he's at Cambridge – and Denise, but they always make their excuses. It's as if they know that I, Alan Partridge, require solitude. So I hop in the car and hop along the A47 to Swaffham. Swaffham was our stalking ground when we were young. We'd all pile into the back of a friends mustard-coloured Triumph Dolomite and we'd head over to Swaffham and have a picnic. And then drive home again. Great days. And not just Swaffham, I don't want Swaffham to get all the credit, it was the whole area. I'm talking about North Pickenham, Necton, Great Palgrave, Spall, we even went as far as East Walton. I mean, there was no stopping us. There's a caravan site down there. It's, it's quite a good one. There's not gypsies, I mean there's proper toilets and proper amenities.

*Alan in a field, talking to camera.*

We're, we're actually on the grounds of Mike Oldfield's country estate. We're not actually on his ground, this is common ground. That's Mr Oldfield's, over there (*points with his walking stick*). Hergest Ridge, the name of one of his albums. We did ask Mr Oldfield if we could film there but he said, being Christmas he'd want a bit of privacy. That's understandable. It would have been nice, you know. Bit small-minded really, a bit nasty. Anyway, on with the ramble. Can't go over there, got to go over there.

**Alan voiceover**

Oldfield hosts a celebrity clay-pigeon shoot every Christmas. He invites round Paul Eddington, Adam Faith, Danny Baker, Moira Stewart, Edward Heath and Mr Motivator. And Francis Rossi of Status Quo.

*Footage of Alan skimming stones across river.*

**Alan**

That was my watch! Ha ha! I just lost my blooming watch. Ha! Actually keep that bit in; it, it's nice. It gives it a human touch. Nice. Keep it in.

**Alan voiceover**

I used to come here as a child on my own. I would skim stones. On one occasion I hit a duck and it disappeared beneath the water. To this day I don't know whether it was dead or just badly concussed. I love birds and I like to come here and make bird noises. (*Makes bird noises towards treetops*) I'm no Dr Doolittle, but there are times when I think birds are the only ones I can really talk to. Maybe that's because I'm a partridge. Alan Partridge.

*Footage of Alan walking through leaves. Talks to camera.*

**Alan**

Someone should clean up these leaves. In the same way that I'm having a Christmas ramble, two thousand years ago the holy family had a ramble from Nazareth to Bethlehem. In much the same way that I'm having a ramble from Norwich to Swaffham, um, although I'm not comparing myself with Jesus. I don't want to get bogged down in that whole controversy again. Right? So I'm not Jesus. And I want to make that absolutely clear, right? I am not Jesus.

*General views of countryside.*

**Alan voiceover**

It's beautiful here. The nearest shop is over two miles away. You know, which is a problem. Erm, somebody suggested building a small snack bar, but there was a meeting at Swaffham village hall and the planning people said it would spoil the beauty of the area. So, I suggested a compromise, which was to be a series of vending machines placed in hedges. They could give out Kit-Kats, Mars bars, chunky soup, slices of ham, 5-Alives, but, er, they voted it down. So, you've just got to come prepared. I pack a finger of fudge – about the size of a slim panatella.

*Alan leans on a gate and talks to camera.*

**Alan**

I used to, er, come here when I was at East Anglia Polytechnic. Erm, they weren't particularly happy days, but, er, I'd come down here on my own. Transistor, sing my favourite, er, pop songs.
(*Sings*) I'm a one-man band Nobody seems to understand Is there anybody out there who'll lend me a hand? (*Morosely*) I'm a one-man band.

*Alan turns from the camera and retreats across field.*

(*Upset*) Thank you for joining me on a Christmas ramble with Alan Partridge, gonna go, I'm gonna go back to my wife now. Thank you. Bye bye.

*Closing music.*

re: Anoraky Iraqi

Mike, Hi!

I've been trying to speak to you in person, but Caroline keeps telling me you're out of the office all week. That's clearly a lie, unless Radio Norwich have come up with some kind of GM robot clone of you! (Though one programmed to avoid eye contact with me in the car park.)

Joking apart, it's now three weeks since your bizarre decision to insist I drop my comedy character, Baghdad-based trainspotter, the Anoraky Iraqi. Amazingly it only went out once and I'm still getting letters about it.

When you told me to drop the sketch, you said that it risked offending listeners, and was especially sensitive material given that it was transmitted on the night the bombing of Iraq began. With all due respect, I don't have a direct line to the Oval Office and was unable to know that 'Shock and Awe' would fill the living rooms of the world that night. You then went on to comment that me shouting the numbers of trains in an Arabic-style voice was not funny. Frankly, I thought that was both below the belt and beyond the pale.

Mike, I went to a great deal of effort to produce this item, the first in a series of thirty-six sketches. I recorded the background 'atmos' myself at Norwich station with a recordable mini-disc player, edited out the British platform announcements for accuracy, then added the bombing sound effects and mullah wailing the call to morning prayers. (I get Al-Jazeera free with my digital package and it's a great fund of material for this kind of thing.)

I don't know if you've seen *Good Morning Vietnam*. I watched it on Sky MovieMax 2 last week and, while Robin Williams is fundamentally irritating throughout, a very good point was made about censorship in times of war. This was a man who dared to do impersonations of the President and Vietnameses while all around him bombs were going off and young, distressed naked women were running down long roads – and for that was thrown off the island and replaced by a small idiot playing polkas. Ring any bells? You don't need me to tell you how the Vietnam war went, Mike. What I'm saying is, at times like this, we need the Anoraky Iraqi more than ever. Characters like 'Bebop Bill' on Danny Franchetti's Jazz Cupboard may not have had a single complaint in eleven years but it doesn't exactly generate headlines either. An ageing DJ doing a deep voice into a paper cup is hardly satire, is it?

Anyway, all I want to say is, If you're still too scared to transmit these sketches, that's your call (and a bad one, might I add). I only ask that I am compensated for the mini discs, time taken and petrol expenses.

Love to Sue. She's going to pull through, you watch.

Yours

Alan

# I'M ALAN PARTRIDGE

## EPISODE 1:
## A ROOM WITH AN ALAN

*Radio Studio*

**Alan**
That was 'Big Yellow Taxi' by Joni Mitchell, a song in which Joni complains they 'Paved paradise to put up a parking lot', a measure which actually would have alleviated traffic congestion on the outskirts of paradise, something which Joni singularly fails to point out, perhaps because it doesn't quite fit in with her blinkered view of the world. Nevertheless, nice song. It's 4.35 a.m., you're listening to *Up With The Partridge*.

**Jingle**
Cock-a-doodle-dooo! Ah-haa!

**Alan**
And now it's time for Alan's 'Fact of the Day'. Crabsticks do not actually contain any crab, and from 1993 manufacturers have been legally obliged to label them 'crab-flavoured' sticks. Another one of those same time tomorrow.

**Jingle**
*(Elderly male voice)* Radio Norwich, the best music.

**Alan**
Pray silence, please, for the Electric Light Orchestra.

*Back in the studio, later that morning.*

**Alan**
Time now to hand over to mine breakfast host, Mr David Clifton. Good morning to you, sir!

**Dave**
And good morning to you, Mr Alan Partridge, sir! And I heard your phone-in, and I liked your chat with the guy from Swaffham. Er, he was a wacky fella!

**Alan**
Yeah, yeah, he was. I – I actually think he was a bit simple.

**Dave**
Er, heard you laying into the criminals again there, Alan. Vandals got to your car again?

**Alan**
'Fraid so, third time. Scum. Sub-human scum.

**Dave**
OK! It's 7 a.m., wakey wakey, it's the breakfast show. Here's Yazoo.

*Music*

*Alan is driving. His car is graffitied with the words 'Cock', 'Piss' and 'Partridge' in large, black lettering.*

**Alan**
*(In car, speaking on hands-free headset)*
Lynn, message from Alan. Something to pitch to Tony Hayers at BBC lunch, Friday. Idea for film extravaganza. Plot, thus: Malcolm McDowell is trapped in the future. He's being pursued by a cyberpunk from the past, played by Rutger Hauer. Erm, terrible idea. No one will watch that. I've not thought it through, Lynn. I'll call you back.

*Car pulls into the forecourt of the Linton Travel Tavern. Alan jogs up the steps, into the lobby, and up to reception desk.*

**Alan**
*(Singing loudly)* Guaranteed to blow your mind!

**Susan**
Good morning, Alan! How are you today?

**Alan**
Classic Queen! I'm very well, thank you, how are you?

**Susan**
I'm fine.

**Alan**
I like the, I like those earrings. Are they gold?

**Susan**
Yes, they're rose gold.

**Alan**
Well, that's not really gold, is it? But, er, they're very nice. Like little tears, little wax tears dripping from your ears because they're sad. Don't cry, ears! You're on the side of a lovely head!

*Susan giggles and Alan sighs.*

**Susan**
Good show this morning?

**Alan**
It was a belter! Did you hear it?

**Susan**
No.

*Alan's face falls.*

**Alan**
Oh. Any messages?

**Susan**
Just the one. From Bill Oddie.

**Alan**
Oh, did he leave a message?

**Susan**
No.

**Alan**
No, he never does. Right, well, I'm afraid, Susan, I've got some very bad news.

**Susan**
Oh?

**Alan**
*(Shouting)* I'm leaving you, you cow!

*Susan looks a little frightened. There is an awkward pause.*

**Alan**

Sorry, bit of a joke there. Backfired. Um, no, I'm basically just saying that I'm going to be checking out at the end of the week.

**Susan**

Are you going back to your wife?

**Alan**

No! No, God, Carol? No, God, no. No no. She's, er, living with, er, the fitness instructor. He provides all her, er … sexual, er … intercourse.

*Alan picks at the back of his ear.*

**Alan**

Sorry, I'm, er . . . dry skin. I'm flaking again. I'm sorry about the cow earlier, by the way. You, you're not a cow. And if you were you'd be a lovely Jersey, ripe for milking.

*Sophie appears behind reception.*

**Alan**

*(To Sophie)* Sorry, just talking about cows. D-do you like milk?

**Sophie**

No.

**Alan**

Oh. *(To Susan)* Actually can, can I talk to you? There's rather a delicate matter …

*The phone rings.*

**Susan**

Oh, excuse me. Sophie, could you deal with this?

*Sophie looks worried.*

**Alan**

Er, Sophie …

**Sophie**

Mr Partridge?

**Alan**

As you know, at the end of the week, I'm meeting Tony Hayers, at the BBC. And, he is Mr Numero … one … And, er, the problem is I've got some rude daubings on the side of my car.

**Sophie**

Can you still drive the car?

**Alan**

Well, yeah, yeah, obviously. I mean that's not … do you know what it says on the side of my car?

**Sophie**

Tosser?

**Alan**

No. No it's, well, you're in the right ballpark. No it, it, erm, actually says, 'Cock', 'Piss', 'Partridge'.

*Sophie turns away, trying not to laugh. Susan returns.*

**Susan**

*(Brightly)* Is everything all right?

**Sophie**

Mr Partridge, erm – has got, has got some rude – graffiti – on –

227

*Sophie tries to control her laughter and runs out the back.*

**Susan**
*(Alarmed)* Graffiti? What, in the hotel?

**Alan**
No, no, God. There's never any graffiti in the hotel. Although in the Gents a couple of weeks ago I did see someone had drawn a lady's part. Quite detailed. The guy obviously had talent, that's the tragedy. But no, it's not the, it's not the … it's on the side of my car; it says 'Cock', 'Piss', 'Partridge'.

*Sophie attempts to return, but turns away again to hide her laughter when she hears Alan.*

**Alan**
*(Distracted by Sophie)* Which is … er, which is illegal. Is she new?

**Susan**
Yes, she is.

**Alan**
I mean, I'm basically driving around in an obscene publication. I'd love to get my hands on the bastard. Or bitch, might be a lady. *(Smiles)*

*Sophie returns, still grinning.*

**Sophie**
Susan, can I take five minutes?

**Susan**
Yes, of course.

**Alan**
*(Disapprovingly)* Nipping off for a fag?

*Alan walks towards the lift, shaking his head.*

**Susan**
*(Shouting after Alan)* Don't worry about your car, Alan. I'll get Michael to sort it out for you.

**Alan**
OK.

*Michael comes out of the lift.*

**Alan**
Oh! Talk of the devil!

**Michael**
Morning, Mr Partridge.

**Alan**
Yeah, Michael, I was just saying to Susan. Bit of a job for you. Er, unfortunately some vandals have sworn all over my car again.

*Michael shakes his head and sighs.*

**Michael**
*(In a thick Geordie accent)* Vandals, eh, Mr Partridge? You know, it makes you wonder what it's all about.

**Alan**
Aboot?

**Michael**
Aye. You know, vandals. You know, what is it all about?

**Alan**
Oh, about. Sorry, sometimes it's difficult to understand the, er, the Geordie … people.

**Michael**
You know, what I reckon is, if they had themselves proper jobs, they wouldn't be up to all this, you know, larking every night.

**Alan**
*(Irritated)* What?

**Michael**
What I'm saying is, like, if they had themselves proper jobs, you know, for them to go to, they wouldn't do it. You know, a lot of them's from broken homes.

**Alan**
I'm sorry, that was just a noise. All I got there was broken homes. And a broken home is not an excuse for evil. You, look at you – do you go around drawing, I don't know, peephole bras on the wall?

**Michael**

Aye, but it was different for me, like, 'cause, you know, I was in the army when I was seventeen.

**Alan**

*(Stepping into the lift)* Well there you go. They taught you a trade. Minor repairs.

**Michael**

Aye. That and killing.

*Alan jams the lift open with his arm and pokes his head out.*

**Alan**

Really?

**Michael**

Oh aye. I've seen some terrible things, mind.

**Alan**

What, like three men burning in a tank, going 'uuurghhh'?

**Michael**

You wouldn't want to know, Mr Partridge.

**Alan**

I'll be honest, I'm pretty curious. Wh—, I mean, I'd basically like to understand man's inhumanity to man … and then make a programme about it. Anyway, uh, regarding the graffiti, if you could … *(mimes shooting a handgun)* kill that, then *(attempts a bad Geordie accent)* I'll see you reet, me old fishy on a dishy.

*Alan steps back into the lift.*

**Michael**

I'll tell you what I'll do, I'll do, just like, a quick fix on it for now, and –

**Alan**

You've gone again!

*In Alan's room. A close-up shot of an article in the* Guardian *newspaper, headline reads 'Hayers to sweep away "dead wood" at BBC'. Alan is sitting on the side of his bed, reading the article. He sighs.*

**Alan**

*(Speaking into dictaphone)* Idea for a programme, er, Ladyshapes with Alan Partridge. I look at the changing shape of ladies through the ages, from fat, chubby ladies of the Renaissance, to hard-faced Cromwellian sourpusses, right up to twentieth-century well-toned women like Sharon Davies *(picks up framed photo)* and Jet from Gladiators.

*Alan sighs and lies on his bed.*

**Alan**

Jet from Gladiators to host a millennium barn dance at Yeovil aerodrome. *(He puts the dictaphone down. Looking worried, he picks it up and speaks into it again)* Properly policed. It must not, I repeat not, turn into an all-night rave.

*Alan switches the dictaphone off. As he lies on the bed he begins to daydream. Alan, dressed in platform shoes, Pringle sweater and leather thong, dances and gyrates onstage in a nightclub. Tony Hayers sits at a table in front of the stage.*

**Alan**

*(Dancing towards Tony)* Would you like me to lap-dance for you?

*Tony Hayers offers the gyrating Alan a ten-pound note.*

**Alan**

*(Shaking his finger)* Uh-uh. I want a second series.

*In hotel room. There is a knock at the door.*

**Lynn**

*(Calling)* Alan!?

**Alan**

*(Clenching his fist, still half asleep)* Mmm –
fight you! *(Alan suddenly sits up, startled)*
Sorry – Come in! Door's open.

*Lynn enters.*

**Lynn**

Just me.

**Alan**

There's tea in the pot.

**Lynn**

Oh good.

*Long pause – they look at each other.*

**Lynn**

Do you want a cup?

**Alan**

Thank you. What have you got for me,
Lynn?

**Lynn**

Well, I've arranged for you to see a show
house at ten o'clock.

**Alan**

Good. Got my fungal foot powder?

**Lynn**

Oh, yes.

*Alan takes the powder from Lynn and dusts his
feet with it.*

**Alan**

Ah, it's a lifesaver, you know. I'd effectively
be disabled if it weren't for these.

**Lynn**

I also rang all the companies on the product
list you gave me. Um, Foster's Menswear
said yes, if you get the second series, and
you wear one garment a week on air.
Monza said 'no' to a free caravan and 'yes'
to a towbar.

**Alan**

I'll take it. Er, Dolphin Bathrooms?

**Lynn**

No, they said they didn't do that sort
of thing.

**Alan**

That's rubbish. I know for a fact Martin
Lewis got two power showers out of them.
One for him and one for his brother-in-law.
Right, dry skin cream. I'm having an attack
of the old flakes again. This morning,
my pillow looked like a flapjack. *(Goes to
bathroom and applies cream to his face)* OK,
Lynn, er, quick practice for this meeting
with Tony Hayers this Friday. So, you be
Tony Hayers. Hello, Tony! How are you?

**Lynn**

I'm fine. How are you?

**Alan**

Um, oh, very busy. I've been working like a
Japanese prisoner of war. But a happy one.

**Lynn**

Good. Would you, would you like a second
series of your chat show?

**Alan**

*(Poking his head around the bathroom door)* I
think he'll be a bit tougher than that, Lynn.

**Lynn**

We might give you a second series.

**Alan**

Yeah, that's about right. OK, small talk.
Er, would you like a Cuban cigar, Tony?

**Lynn**

Yes, please.

**Alan**

Rolled on the thighs of a virgin.

*Lynn looks embarrassed.*

**Alan**

I'm being bawdy, Lynn. Enjoy it.

*Lynn grunts. Alan comes back from the
bathroom with cream on his face and sits
on the bed.*

**Alan**

Well, he might make that noise. Be a bit weird. Right, er, you said you might give me a second series. Why is there any doubt?

**Lynn**

Things have to be compartmentalized, Alan. You know, for example, in this drawer you    *(Lynn opens a drawer and freezes)* You, erm, you have, erm … things … *(Alan slowly gets up from the bed, looking embarrassed)* And, erm, those um, sometimes you can have too many things …

**Alan**

*(Shutting the drawer abruptly)* Er, abandon that, Lynn, it's not working. OK, doomsday scenario. You, Tony Hayers, have decided not to give me another television series. Why? Be tough.

**Lynn**

Well, Alan, the ratings for the first series started poorly and went downhill from there.

**Alan**

*(Looking unhappy)* Are you being Lynn or Tony?

**Lynn**

Tony.

**Alan**

Be Lynn again. Can I have a second series?

**Lynn**

Well, who am I?

**Alan**

*(Agitated)* Just say yes!

**Lynn**

Yes!

**Alan**

Thank you. *(Points at the drawer)* They were there when I moved in. *(Walks out)*

*Alan and Lynn drive along in Alan's car, listening to the radio.*

**Radio Norwich jingle**

*(Elderly male voice)* From Swaffham to Cromer on 106.5 and now in Hensbury on 106.9, this is Radio Norwich.

*Alan's car pulls up outside a large house with a 'For Sale' sign outside. The graffiti on his car has been changed with purple paint and now reads 'cook', 'pass' and 'Babtridge'. Inside the house, Alan is being shown round by the estate agent.*

**Estate Agent**

Living room …

**Alan**

Oh, I like this, yes. Certainly enough room to swing a cat in here, isn't there?

**Estate Agent**

Swing a tiger in here, really!

**Alan**

You could, couldn't you! *(Taking off his jacket)* Wouldn't want to, though. Not unless it had been stunned. Even then it's going to weigh the best part of a ton.

**Estate Agent**

Yeah, um *(looking past Alan to Lynn)*, do you like the room?

231

**Lynn**
Oh, it's very nice.

**Alan**
Lynn's not my wife. She's my PA. Hard worker, but, er, there's no affection.

**Estate Agent**
So, you'd be living alone, then?

**Alan**
Yes. In fact, you know, the best thing I ever did was getting thrown out by my wife! *(Snorts)* She's living with a fitness instructor. He drinks that yellow stuff in tins. He's an idiot! Erm, is there a neighbourhood – sorry, I'm very close to you there *(steps back)* – is there a neighbourhood watch system?

**Estate Agent**
I think so, yeah.

**Alan**
Right, well, I'll do my stint. I'd, er, want expenses, though. Otherwise people start taking liberties, before you know it you're mowing their lawn.

**Estate Agent**
Shall we have a look at the rest of the house?

**Alan**
Yup.

**Estate Agent**
Uh – huh *(moves off towards the door)*.

*Alan pushes Lynn out of the way and steps in front of her.*

**Alan**
One more question. I – On the way here, quite nearby, I did see a community centre with a mural on the side.

**Estate Agent**
School for the deaf.

**Alan**
Right. That mean, there will be noise or there won't be noise? Difficult one to figure out, that. But they're just deaf, they're not deaf offenders?

**Estate Agent**
They're just deaf. *(He opens the door)*

**Alan**
After you.

*Alan follows the Estate Agent out of the door. Lynn tries to follow but Alan turns around and holds his hand up to her face.*

**Alan**
Er, not you, Lynn. Stay here, get on the phone, pester Debenhams for free lamps, free lampshades, whatever you can blag. *(Shuts door)*

*In the kitchen*

**Estate Agent**
This is the kitchen, obviously …

**Alan**
Oh lovely. Has this kitchen been distressed?

**Estate Agent**
Yep, it has, yes.

**Alan**
Right. What's this? It's a cast-iron egg-tree, lacquered. Is that included? I mean, it's not a deal-breaker but I would like to know.

**Estate Agent**
Everything you want to keep here could be kept. Or not …

**Alan**
Optional.

**Estate Agent**
As you wish, certainly.

**Alan**
What's this, er, this little sink here?

**Estate Agent**
That's a rinser.

**Alan**
Yeah. Get rid of it.

*In the bathroom*

**Estate Agent**
Bathroom …

**Alan**
You know what this bathroom says to me?
Aqua. Which is French for water. It's like
being inside an enormous Fox's Glacier
Mint. Which, again, to me is a bonus.

*In the dining room*

**Alan**
*(Pulling at the table)* Yes, it's an extender!
Fantastic. That is the icing on the cake.
Do you know, if King Arthur had had an
extender on his table …

**Estate Agent**
It'd have been a different story, really,
wouldn't it?

**Alan**
Well, it wouldn't have been round!

**Estate Agent**
No.

**Alan**
… for kick-off.

*Alan and the Estate Agent walk upstairs.*

**Alan**
It's very Cluedo this house, isn't it? Colonel
Mustard in the en-suite bathroom with
a lead pipe. Battered.

*In the upstairs bathroom*

**Alan**
I do like that toilet. It's very futuristic, isn't
it? Very, sort of, high-tech, space age. I can
imagine Buck Rogers taking a dump on

that. In the twenty-first century. Mind if I
… have a go?

**Estate Agent**
Sure. Help yourself.

*Pause*

**Alan**
Can I have a go on the loo?

*Another short pause*

**Estate Agent**
Oh! Sorry, sorry.

**Alan**
I'd prefer to go alone.

**Estate Agent**
Sure, sure. *(Leaves)*

**Alan**
Most times. Thanks. *(Closes the door)*

*In the lounge downstairs, Lynn and the Estate
Agent are sitting in silence. Alan bursts in
through the doors.*

**Alan**
It flushed on the first yank! I love this
house!

**Lynn**
Alan?

**Alan**
One yank, gone!

**Lynn**
Alan, that was Tony Hayers' office on the
phone. They've put the meeting forward
to 12.30 today.

**Alan**
When did you get this call?

**Lynn**
Three minutes ago.

**Alan**
So why didn't you tell – what have you
been doing for three minutes?

**Lynn**
You were on the toilet.

**Alan**
Was I on that long? *(Lynn and Alan both turn to the Estate Agent)*

**Estate Agent**
*(Looking a little flustered)* It, it was in that area.

**Lynn**
We're going to have to zip.

**Alan**
Right, OK. *(Lynn helps Alan put his jacket on)* One more question about the house. Um, petrol stations nearby?

**Estate Agent**
Shell, about a quarter of a mile away.

**Alan**
Right, has it got a mini-mart?

**Estate Agent**
Mini-mart?

**Alan**
Scaled-down supermarket, fits inside a petrol station. Sells pies, anti-freeze ...

**Estate Agent**
Yep, it's got one of those.

**Alan**
In that case, you've got yourself a deal! I'll take the house.

**Estate Agent**
Well, are you going to make an offer?

**Alan**
Oh, yes, of course. Erm, how much is it?

**Estate Agent**
It's on at three hundred and twenty-five thousand.

**Alan**
Ooh. Will you take three hundred and twenty ... four?

**Estate Agent**
Yeah.

*They shake hands.*

**Alan**
How many bedrooms has it got?

**Estate Agent**
Five.

**Alan**
Five, cor. My five-bedroomed bastard house. Great, Lynn, let's, er, go off to the BBC. *(To the Estate Agent)* I'm going to be back on TV, I don't know if you – did you use to watch my TV show?

**Estate Agent**
Oh yes.

**Alan**
Did you like it?

**Estate Agent**
I loved it.

**Alan**
*(Opening his arms wide)* Ah-haa!

*The Estate Agent looks confused. Alan and Lynn leave.*

*Alan's car enters the car park at BBC Television Centre.*

**Lynn**
What if Tony Hayers sees 'Cook', 'Pass', 'Babtridge' painted on your car?

**Alan**
Don't worry, Lynn, I'll play it down.

*Alan and Tony walk into the BBC restaurant. They are greeted by a waiter.*

**Alan**
... and it says Partridge, I can understand, but then it says 'Cock', and 'Piss'.

**Waiter**
A table for two, sir?

**Alan**
Yes … no, sorry, you … *(gestures towards Tony Hayers)*

**Tony Hayers**
Yes, in the name of Hayers.

**Waiter**
If you'd like to follow me.

*They follow the waiter to their table.*

**Alan**
*(Loudly)* We managed to rectify it, though, because it now says, by adapting it, it now says 'Cook' where it once said 'Cock', and it says 'Pass' now where it once said 'Piss', so it's slightly less rude.

*The two sit at their table. The waiter hands them their menus.*

**Waiter**
Would you like a drink first?

**Alan**
Um, I'll have a pint of bitter.

**Tony**
Just a mineral water for me, please.

**Alan**
Actually, I'll have a mineral water, too.

**Waiter**
Will you be having wine with your meal?

**Tony**
Not for me.

**Alan**
No, no. *(Sighs)* All this wine nonsense! You know, you get all these wine people, don't you? Wine this, wine that. Let's have a bit of red, let's have a bit of white. Ooh, that's a snazzy bouquet. Oh, this smells of, I don't know, basil. Sometimes you just want to say, sod all this wine, just give me a pint of … mineral water.

**Tony**
I don't think wine's an elitist thing any more, you can get good wine in Tesco's now. I'd love to make a genuinely popular wine programme.

**Alan**
Can I just shock you? I like wine. Despite what I just said earlier. At any one time I have nine bottles of wine in my house.

**Tony**
Really?

**Alan**
Interesting fact.

**Tony**
Well, it's my weakness, I'm afraid. I've got a cellar.

**Alan**
So have I. There's no wine in it, just a couple of bikes, some smokeless fuel, and an old bag of cement. Gone hard.

**Waiter**
Are you ready to order?

**Tony**
Um, yes. I think I'll have the Fettucini a'la Arabiata, please.

**Alan**
And … can I have the same, please? But with different shaped pasta. What do you call those pasta in bows? Like a bow-tie but, but miniature? Like an Action Man bow-tie.

**Tony**
Farfalle.

**Alan**
Yeah, that with Action Man bow-tie.

**Waiter**
Anything else?

**Alan**
Yeah, I think I'll have some wine, actually.
Yes, erm, just give me half a bottle of Blue
Nun, please. *(Turns to Tony Hayers)* I loved
your article in the *Guardian*, by the way.

**Tony**
Really?

**Alan**
I loved that phrase you used, it was very
very clever – 'Revolution not evolution'.

**Tony**
No, it was the opposite. 'Evolution not
revolution'.

**Alan**
Well, whatever, you know, because that is
me. I 'evolve', but I don't … 'revolve'… Or
vice versa, you know. I suppose what you're
trying to say is, you don't want another
Chris Evans on your hands.

**Tony**
No, that is what we want.

**Alan**
I'm your man.

**Tony**
That's, that's what I wanted to talk about,
Alan. Your career. I can see a lot of very
exciting opportunities ahead for you, really
I can.

**Alan**
Oh, can I just say this is music to my ears.

*The waiter starts to pour Alan's wine.*

**Alan**
Whoa, whoa, whoa! What are you doing!?
What are you doing?

**Waiter**
Pouring the wine out.

**Alan**
*(Indignantly)* I want you to pour a little bit,
let me sip it, then pour the rest.

**Waiter**
Well, I've already poured half.

**Alan**
It – it's all right.

*Alan drinks the whole glass in one gulp.*

**Alan**
That's fine, fill her up. *(Turns to Tony)*
Oh – Here's to our future relationship
at the BBC.

*Alan lifts his glass and touches Tony's empty
wine glass on the table.*

**Tony**
You know, I don't think you should see your
future just at the BBC, Alan. I just think it's
time for you to consider moving on to new
pastures.

**Alan**
Have I got a second series?

**Tony**
There's so many opportunities for a man –

**Alan**
Can – Let, let, let me rephrase that. Can
I … no, in fact I'll just repeat the question.
Have I got a second series?

**Tony**
No.

**Alan**
*(Quietly)* Thank you. That's all I wanted to
know.

**Peter**
Tony! *(Peter walks over to their table)*

**Tony**
Oh, Peter! Hello, how are you?

**Peter**

Fine, fine.

**Tony**

Um, Alan, this is Peter Linehan, he's revamping our current affairs output.

*Alan shrugs.*

**Peter**

We, er, we haven't met, but I liked your chat show.

**Alan**

Thank you very much.

**Peter**

Has he given you another series?

**Alan**

No, he won't give me one.

*Tony and Peter laugh, Alan forces a smile.*

**Peter**

*(To Tony)* Give him another series, you swine!

**Alan**

Yeah, give me another series, you shit.

*Tony's smile freezes. Alan looks anxious and Peter stands in awkward silence.*

**Tony**

Look, Alan, I don't want you to feel that the – I'll see you later, Peter *(Peter walks away)* – I don't want you to feel that the doors have all closed here at the BBC. If you come up with anything else, then please, I don't want you to hesitate to call …

*Close-up of Alan's worried face. He begins to daydream. Alan is dancing onstage in his leather thong and Pringle jumper. Tony Hayers sits at the table in front of him with a bottle of Blue Nun.*

**Alan**

*(Moving towards Tony)* Would you like me to lap dance for you?

**Tony**

*(Laughing manically)* Blue Nun! Ha ha ha!

*Each shot of Tony shows him with less and less hair; he is finally nearly completely bald. Cut back to the restaurant, and an anxious Alan.*

**Tony**

…don't hesitate, if you have any other ideas. I'd be very interested …

**Alan**

Got them here, got them here! *(Alan reaches down and picks up a file)*

**Tony**

Right …

**Alan**

Right, OK. 'Shoestring', 'Taggart', 'Spender', 'Bergerac', 'Morse'. What does that say to you about regional detective series?

**Tony**

There's too many of them?

**Alan**

That's one way of looking at it. Another way of looking at it is, 'people like them, let's make some more of them'. A detective series based in Norwich called 'Swallow'. Swallow is a, is a detective who tackles vandalism. Bit of a maverick, not afraid to break the law if he thinks it's necessary. Um, you know, he's not a criminal, but he will, perhaps, travel 80 m.p.h. on the motorway if he, for example, he wants to get somewhere quickly …

*Tony Hayers shakes his head.*

**Alan**

Think about it. No one had heard of Oxford before *Inspector Morse*. I mean, this will put Norwich on the map.

**Tony**

Why would I want to do that?

**Alan**
Yep, fair point. OK, um, right. 'Alan Attack!' Like *The Cook Report*, but with a more slapstick approach.

**Tony**
*(Shakes his head again)* No.

**Alan**
Er … 'Arm Wrestling with Chas and Dave'.

**Tony**
I don't think so.

**Alan**
Pity, because they were very keen on that one. Right, ah, now you'll like this one. 'Knowing M.E., Knowing You'. I, Alan Partridge, talk to M.E. sufferers about the condition. Um, you know, we intersperse it with their favourite pop songs, make it light-hearted, you know, give them a platform, you, you, you've got to keep the energy up, because …

*Tony shakes his head, horrified.*

**Alan**
You don't like it?

**Tony**
No.

**Alan**
That's all right, that's OK. 'Inner-City Sumo'.

**Tony**
What's that?

**Alan**
We take fat people from the inner cities, put them in big nappies, and then, er, get them to throw each other out of a circle that we draw with chalk on the ground.

**Tony**
No, no, it's a bad idea.

**Alan**
Very cheap to make.

**Tony**
No.

**Alan**
Do it in a pub car park.

**Tony**
*(Laughing)* No.

**Alan**
If you don't do it, Sky will.

**Tony**
Well, I'll live with that. Is that it?

**Alan**
Well, no, no. Um, cooking in prison.

**Tony**
*(Laughing)* Oh, no.

**Alan**
*(Desperately)* 'A Partridge Amongst The Pigeons'.

**Tony**
What's that?

**Alan**
Well, it's just a title, I mean … erm, well, no, erm, opening sequence, me, in Trafalgar Square, feeding the pigeons, going, 'Oh God!'

**Tony**
*(Holds his hands up)* No, I'm sorry, no! Stop!

**Alan**
Whoa, whoa, whoa, erm, 'Youth Hosteling with Chris Eubank'.

**Tony**
*(Laughing and shaking head)* No!

*Pause*

**Alan**
'Monkey tennis'?

**Tony**

*(Seriously)* There is to be no second series, and I've listened to your ideas, I've listened to them all, and I haven't liked a single one.

**Alan**

Tony, I've, look I've just bought a house. It's like, it's got a Buck Rogers toilet. One yank, all gone!

**Tony**

We don't owe you a living. You are someone who has a proven track record for making mostly bad television programmes.

**Alan**

That's – that's – that's bollocks, but carry on.

*Alan plays nervously with his lower lip.*

**Tony**

It's not bollocks. Your, your programmes were appalling. The ratings were a ninth of what we could have expected, they started badly, they got worse …

**Alan**

*(Imitating childishly)* They started badly, they got worse … ooh, your programmes, your programmes …

**Tony**

Alan, you're making a fool of yourself.

**Alan**

*(In a high-pitched whine)* Who-oo … who-oo … *(almost normally)* who do you think you are?

**Tony**

Well, unfortunately for you, I am the Chief Commissioning Editor of BBC Television.

*The two men stare at each other for a second.*

**Alan**

*(Forcing a smile)* Oh, let's forget about all this!

*Alan takes his fork and stabs it deep into a large block of cheese. He holds it up.*

**Alan**

Do you want some cheese?

**Tony**

*(Sitting back, looking worried)* No, thank you.

**Alan**

*(Sniffs it)* Mmm. Quite nice. Smells. Do you, do you want to smell it? *(Alan offers the cheese, still on the end of his fork, to Tony)*

**Tony**

No, thanks.

**Alan**

Smell the cheese.

**Tony**

No, I don't want to.

**Alan**

*(More forcefully)* Smell my cheese!

**Tony**

Alan, please.

*Alan gets up from his seat and thrusts the cheese into Tony's face.*

**Alan**

*(Shouting)* Smell my cheese, you mother!

*A waiter attempts to restrain the hysterical Alan.*

**Waiter**

*(Angrily)* I think that's quite enough, thank you!

*Alan charges out of the restaurant, holding the cheese aloft in front of him.*

**Alan**

I've got cheese! This is cheese!

*Alan runs outside to the car park.*

# I'M ALAN PARTRIDGE

**Alan**

*(Muttering to himself)* … bloody BBC …
*(to some people sitting outside)* What are you
sitting around for? Haven't you got
programmes to make? No, you're all on the
BBC gravy train. I wish I was. *(Getting into
the car)* Take this cheese *(hands the cheese
and fork to Lynn)*.

**Lynn**

How did it go?

**Alan**

I've been bad, Lynn.

**Lynn**

Ooh, smelly.

**Alan**

It's got walnuts in.

**Lynn**

Right.

**Alan**

*(Quickly puts his seatbelt on and drives off)*
Let's go.

*It's dark. Alan and Lynn talk in the car outside
the house they viewed earlier.*

**Alan**

I wasn't expecting that, Lynn. That was
a negative, and right now I need two
positives, you know. One to cancel out the
negative and another one, you know, just
so I can have a positive. Oh my God.

**Lynn**

You know, one can find some strength,
when you're at your bleakest moment, if
you open yourself up to new choices …

**Alan**

Lynn, I'm not coming to your Baptist
church! They always get people when
they're down. I don't want salvation, I just
want to be able to say, 'I'm Alan Partridge.
Join me tonight when my guests will be,'

I don't know, 'Chris Rea.' Actually, he lives
in the area. I could have had him over. 'All
right, Chris!', 'Hello, Alan, I didn't know
you'd moved in', 'Yeah, just moved in, last
week. I'm having a barbecue, fancy coming
over?', 'I'd love to! Do you mind if I bring
my guitar?', 'I'd rather you didn't, it's not
that kind of area'. 'Do you like Mini
Kiev's?', 'I love them! But my wife's
vegetarian', 'Doesn't matter. She can have
fish', *(gradually getting irritated)* 'No, she
won't eat that either', 'Oh forget it!'. You
people. Go on, Lynn. These people are
starting to annoy me. I'll tell you
something, you know. They may have very
nice Tudorette-style housing but can they
order an Irish Coffee at 3 a.m. in the
morning and get it delivered to their
bedroom?

**Lynn**

Nope.

**Alan**

Nope. I can. Come on, I'll drop you at a
cab rank.

*In hotel room. Alan puts 'Jet' by Wings on the
hi-fi and picks up the phone.*

**Alan**

Hi. Um, can I have an Irish Coffee
delivered to the room, please? *(Pause)* No?
Er, right. Tea? Er, right. Can of Fanta?
Minibar, right. No, I'll get it myself. *(Alan
puts the phone down and jumps on to the bed.)*
*(Singing)* Jet! Jet! Jet!

*He begins gently jumping up and down on
his bed.*

**Alan**

Right, minibar.

*After a few warm-up jumps, Alan tries to jump
off the bed, but falls awkwardly, and knocks a
lamp off a table. The room goes dark.*

*Radio Station. Close-up of Alan's profile.*

**Alan**

Kate Bush, there, the lovely Kate Bush with 'The Man With The Child In His Eyes' – which brings us on very neatly to my next guest, Mr Stephen Brai, whose father invented Cats Eyes.

*Alan turns to his guest, revealing a large black eye.*

**Alan**

Stephen, what was it like living with, er, being the son of the man who invented cats eyes?

**Stephen**

Well I, I remember he came home from work one night very excited, and he, erm –

**Alan**

Did, erm, do people, er … did he ever turn all the lights off in the house and, sort of, run towards you with a torch hoping to catch the reflection in your eyes?

**Stephen**

Well, the idea of reflection of course is what Dad was interested in, the idea of –

**Alan**

*(Looking uninterested)* Can I just interrupt you there, Stephen, it's time now for Alan's Fact of the Day. Most cornflakes come from the USA, we'll have another one of them tomorrow. I remember I hit a fox once. Yes, in the Peak District. I remember seeing the reflection in its eyes just before I hit it. It was, it was too late, of course. But I didn't kill him, that was the tragedy, I had to go back and finish him off with a jack. This is Huey Lewis and the News. *(Music starts)* No it's not, it's Kate Bush. What am I doing? Sorry. Huey Lewis, there we go. *(A radio jingle plays)* Oh Christ. I'm sorry –

*Alan's car is outside. Added to the words 'Cook', 'Pass', 'Babtridge' is now a fourth, in red – 'Twat'. Another jingle plays as the camera fades.*

**Alan**

– no, sorry about that –

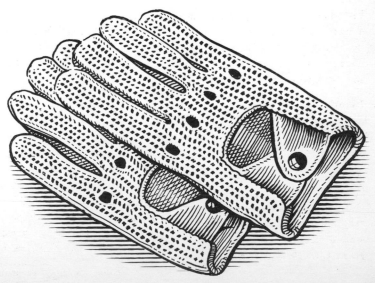

# I'M ALAN PARTRIDGE

## EPISODE 2: ALAN ATTRACTION

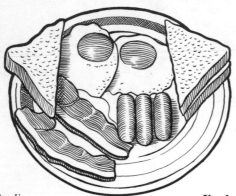

*Radio Studio*

**Alan Partridge**

Mmm! A nice big thick slice of 'Thin Lizzie'. That was for my tireless PA, Lynn, fifty, who is as dilligent and hard-working a creature as ever graced this world we call … um, earth. It's 4.39 a.m. Time to run yourself a big bath – it's Chris Rea.

*Opening music*

**Alan**

*(In opening sequence drinking a pint of bitter)* Very malty.

*Radio Studio*

**Alan**

OK! There will be no telephone Cluedo today because of a threat of a court injunction from the makers of Cluedo. It's 6.58 a.m.

**Jingle**

Cock-a-doodle-do! Ah-haa! Mwwwha!

**Alan**

Ha ha ha ha. That kissing sound wasn't someone kissing me, or kissing a cock, it's simply – a cockerel, I mean – it's simply a way of saying it's Valentine's Day, er, a day on which Mr Al Capone ruined a romantic night out for many diners by massacring them. Died of syphilis, he did, so there is some justice. Anyway, time for me now to hand over to a man who will hopefully not be massacring anyone this evening *(Dave Clifton smiles)* or indeed killing them with syphilis *(Dave's smile fades)*, is Monsieur David Clifton.

**Dave**

*Ah, Bonjour Monsieur Partridge, comment allez-vous, Monsieur?*

**Alan**
Yeah, whatever. Did you get any Valentine's cards this morning?

**Dave**
Actually, Alan, I have to say, I came down this morning and I couldn't open my door …

**Alan**
Lose your key?

**Dave**
I couldn't open my door because I'd lost my key!

**Alan**
Yeah, well, I did just say that. Anyway, chocolate oranges –

**Dave**
OK! It's 7 a.m, and we've got a good show lined up for you this morning –

**Alan**
*(Loudly)* Do you like chocolate?

**Dave**
Pardon?

**Alan**
Do you like chocolate?

**Dave**
Yeah, love it!

**Alan**
I've really got to say this, Dave.

**Dave**
Yeah?

**Alan**
Um – Chocolate oranges are available from Rawlinson's … *(quietly, almost mouthing)* that's all –

**Dave**
*(Looking irritated)* Yeah. OK! It's 7 a.m, and first of all we got China Crisis.

*Linton Travel Tavern. Alan enters hotel lobby. It is decorated for Valentine's Day.*

**Alan**
Morning!

**Ben**
All right.

**Alan**
Sorry?

**Ben**
Good morning.

**Alan**
That's the one. *(To Susan, behind reception desk)* Susan, is he new?

**Susan**
*(Cheerfully)* Yes, he started yesterday.

**Alan**
Yeah, he just said 'good morning' with his back to me.

**Susan**
Oh, he's OK.

**Alan**
No, it's just I've never seen that done before. Anyway, Happy Valentine's Day. How are you?

**Susan**
Oh, I'm a bit tired. I need my beauty sleep.

**Alan**
Oh, you don't need beauty sleep. Well – forty winks. *(Susan forces a smile)* Did you get the chocolate orange?

**Susan**
Oh yes, thank you.

**Alan**
Good. You might find some superficial damage to the box, but the chocolate's perfectly edible. I, er, I give them to all the ladies I know aged fifty and under. Over fifty just seems sarcastic.

**Susan**

Well, I'm afraid I need to watch my figure.

**Alan**

I'll watch it for you! With my little binoculars – wooo! *(Mimes looking through binoculars)* Mind you, I can't talk. I've got a fat back.

**Susan**

What's that?

**Alan**

It's a build-up of fatty deposits just above the belt-line. It's fairly well concealed in casual clothing, but, er, you don't want to see me in my underpants!

*Sophie walks into reception and turns her back to conceal her smile. Susan leaves.*

**Alan**

Sophie, did you get your chocolate orange?

**Sophie**

Yeah.

**Alan**

I got you a dark chocolate one because I know you don't like milk.

**Sophie**

I do like milk chocolate.

**Alan**

Oh, right, well I could exchange it. I could talk to my chocolate people.

**Sophie**

Oh, yes, please. *(Produces the box from beneath the counter and places it on the counter)*

**Alan**

Right. Er, have you tampered with the wrapping?

**Sophie**

No, but there is a bit of superficial damage to the box.

**Alan**

Don't bother about the damage. They're all damaged. Er, right. Have you kept it below room temperature?

**Sophie**

I don't think so.

**Alan**

Ah, right. In that case *(pushes the box back over the counter towards Sophie)* I'm afraid you've invalidated the warranty. Above room temperature it all congeals into one big dark-chocolate cricket ball. Um, so, I'm afraid consumer rights no longer apply. I mean, you could try *Watchdog*, but I think they've got bigger fish to fry.

*Ben approaches Alan.*

**Ben**

Excuse me, are you Alan Partridge?

**Alan**

*(With mock-weariness, and a smug smile)* Yes …

**Ben**

You dropped this, your ID card. Radio Norwich?

**Alan**

Oh, right, thanks. *(Mimics Ben)* Awroight?

**Ben**

*(Jokily)* Good morning.

*Alan turns back to Sophie, looking irritated.*

**Alan**

Um, actually, Sophie, er, there's an issue I've been meaning to raise for the last two weeks. You know those little soaps you leave in the shower room? Well, they will withstand, at best, one aggressive body scrub. They start up the size of mini-Frisbees, and they, they end up like actual-size Paracetamol.

**Sophie**
Can't you use two?

**Alan**
I suppose that *might* work –

*Alan mimes washing himself with two hands, paying attention to his bottom and genitals.*

**Sophie**
I'll just write that down.

*She turns away, shaking with silent laughter. Susan returns.*

**Susan**
Hello!

**Alan**
Hello, Susan. Sorry, have I upset her?

**Susan**
No, she's fine.

**Alan**
Right.

**Susan**
Erm, Alan? Did you send Sophie a Valentine's card this morning?

**Alan**
Oh God, no, no. I'm old enough to be her father! Well, her older brother. Either way it's incest!

**Susan**
Ben, did you send Sophie a Valentine's card?

**Ben**
*(With a large grin)* Um, well, I'm not at liberty to divulge that information.

*Susan and Sophie giggle. Ben walks away.*

**Alan**
You know, the fact that he made that jokey remark doesn't necessarily mean that he actually sent you the card.

**Sophie**
*(Suddenly serious)* Did you send it?

**Alan**
No, I sent you a chocolate orange, but I had the decency to admit it.

**Susan**
Oh, come on, Alan. It's just a bit of fun.

**Alan**
A lie is a lie.

**Sophie**
*(Looking over Alan's shoulder)* Your PA's here.

**Alan**
Oh. Oh, hello, Lynn. Shall we grab a pew?

*Alan and Lynn sit down on some chairs at the other end of the lobby.*

**Lynn**
Thanks for my dedication this morning. Very nice.

**Alan**
You're welcome. You realize it was nothing to do with Valentine's Day.

**Lynn**
Oh, of course.

**Alan**
Right. What have you got for me?

**Lynn**
Do you want to hear the good news or the bad news?

**Alan**
The good news?

**Lynn**
Well, Rawlinson's have said you can have another fifty of the shop-soiled chocolate oranges if you plug them again tomorrow.

**Alan**
Excellent. And the bad news?

**Lynn**

The accountants say that since you've definitely not got a second series from the BBC you're going to have to sack everyone at Peartree Productions and close the office down; otherwise they're going to declare you bankrupt on Friday.

**Alan**

Right. *(Pause. Weakly)* Still, good news about the chocolate oranges.

**Lynn**

Now, Alan, you're going to have to trade down your Rover 800 for a smaller car.

**Alan**

Go on.

**Lynn**

I picked up these brochures for the new Metro. It's, it's a lovely car. And if you do –

**Alan**

*(Interrupting)* Lynn, I'm not driving a mini-Metro.

**Lynn**

But you do have to make substantial savings.

**Alan**

Lynn, I am not driving a mini-Metro.

**Lynn**

But if you do, you can keep Peartree Productions going with a skeleton staff of two, and –

**Alan**

There's no point finishing the sentence, Lynn, because I am not driving a mini-Metro.

**Lynn**

But if you'd –

**Alan**

Lynn! I'll just speak over you.

**Lynn**

But I –

**Alan**

No! Go on, try and finish the sentence and see what I do. Go on.

**Lynn**

With a skeleton staff of two –

**Alan**

*(Speaking over Lynn)* I'm not driving a mini-Metro, I'm not driving a mini-Metro, I'm not driving a mini-Metro.

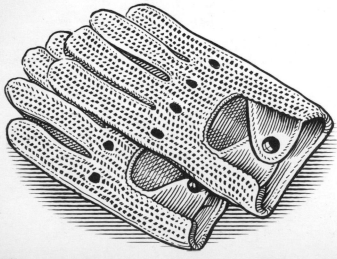

**Lynn**
No, no, it's different. It's called a Rover Metro now.

**Alan**
They've rebadged it, you fool!

**Lynn**
*(Sternly)* Well, Alan, if you want a Rover 200 you're going to have to sack everyone at Peartree Productions.

**Alan**
Fine.

**Lynn**
Including Jill.

**Alan**
Jill. Lovely Jill. She's my favourite – but fine, I'll sack her.

*Lynn smiles faintly.*

**Alan**
You smiled, then, Lynn.

**Lynn**
No, I didn't.

**Alan**
Yes, you did. I can read you like a book. And not a very good book. Certainly not *Bravo Two Zero* by Andy McNab. Which actually improves with every read. No, you smiled because you don't like Jill because she's younger than you.

**Lynn**
No she's not. She's fifty.

**Alan**
Well, so's Helen Mirren.

**Lynn**
So's Benjamin Netinyahu.

**Alan**
You're always going on about Benjamin Netinyahu. Let it go, Lynn, you're never going to meet him. *(Lynn looks crestfallen)*

Right, I'm gonna get a spot of breakfast. Oh, quick tip, Lynn. You know the breakfast buffet? Eat as much as you like, but from an eight-inch plate? See that? *(Opens his bag to partially reveal a dinner plate)* Twelve inches. Keep it in my room! See you later.

*Lynn leaves. Alan heads for the restaurant.*

**Michael**
*(In a thick Geordie accent)*
Aye-aye, Mr Partridge! Morning! Valentine's Day today, eh? Love is in the air!

**Alan**
It's Valentine's Day today, and love is in the air?

**Michael**
Aye! Aye!

**Alan**
Oh! I'm getting the hang of this! Mind you, I have been here ten weeks.

*Michael leads Alan to his table.*

**Michael**
So, are you having the full English breakfast?

**Alan**
Yes, please. Can I have my sausages burnt to a crisp, please?

**Michael**
Oh, right.

**Alan**
So that they can only be identified by reference to their dental records.

**Michael**
OK. Either that or their fingerprints, eh?

**Alan**
Can you fingerprint a sausage?

**Michael**
Yeah, well, I suppose technically you could, aye.

**Alan**

I suppose if I was a burglar and I wanted to avoid detection, er, I could strap sausages to my fingers. Probably survive a couple of break-ins before it started to fall apart.

**Michael**

Aye. Maybe it just have, like, a beefburger for your palm, you know?

**Alan**

No I think that's a bit too far-fetched. I do enjoy these chats in the morning.

**Michael**

Oh aye.

*Michael leaves the table. Alan shiftily produces the twelve-inch plate from his bag.*

**Alan**

*(Singing)* Eighteen 'til I die, I'm gonna be eighteen 'til I die …

*Peartree Productions. A number of employees are waiting in the boardroom. Alan and Lynn enter.*

**Alan**

Morning, everyone. Morning, Jill.

**Jill**

Ahh. Thanks for the chocolate orange, Alan.

**Alan**

You're welcome. Did you notice anything about the box?

**Jill**

No.

**Alan**

Exactly. All the others had superficial damage. I paid for yours. All your segments were intact.

**Jill**

Well, they were when I looked this morning!

*Alan and Jill snigger.*

**Employee**

Alan? Have we got a second series?

*Alan looks worried. He looks at Lynn who nods encouragingly.*

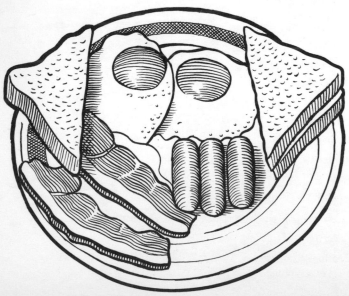

**Alan**
Yes.

*Lynn looks horrified. The employees cheer.
Jill gets up and hugs Alan, who steals a glance
at Lynn.*

**Jill**
Why didn't you say?!

**Bill**
I knew it! Well, I'll go and, er, get some
champagne, shall I?

**Alan**
Actually, Bill, sparkling wine will be fine,
I think.

**Bill**
Well, whatever. *(He leaves)*

**Jill**
I'll go and get some crisps and things.

**Alan**
Actually, Jill, pipe of Pringles will suffice.

**Jill**
*(Teasingly)* Unless there's anything else
you fancy?

*Alan leers at Jill and leans towards her.*

**Alan**
Yeeeeeah – No, just a pipe of Pringles
is fine.

*Jill leaves. Lynn looks at Alan disapprovingly.*

*Alan starts daydreaming. He is dancing
onstage in a nightclub wearing platform shoes,
a leather thong and a pringle sweater. Tony
Hayers is seated at a table.*

**Alan**
Would you like me to lapdance for you?

*Tony Hayers holds up a ten-pound note.*

**Alan**
*(Shaking his finger)* I want a second series.

**Tony**
I like your thong.

**Alan**
*(Matter of factly)* Yeah, it's vulcanized
rubber, which means it won't perish.

*Into the boardroom. Alan is looking anxious.*

**Young employee**
*(Leaps up to Alan and puts a party hat on
him)* Wahaaaay!

**Alan**
*(Knocking the hat off forcefully)* Bash
your arse!

**Alison**
Any more news, Alan?

**Alan**
Uh – No, he just said, 'Second series in the
bag, you're all on board, details to follow,'
and erm … and, and who left this coffee
cup here?

**Young employee**
Sorry, Alan, I meant to clean it last night.

**Alan**
Yeah, well, that's not good enough.
You're sacked.

*Employees laugh.*

**Young employee**
*(Laughing)* What?!

**Alan**
I will not have uncleansed coffee cups in
Peartree Productions. The plague started
from a mal-attended surface.

**2nd Employee**
What are you doing, Alan?

**Alan**
You're sacked, too.

**2nd Employee**
Why?

**Alan**

Because, you do this all the time *(throws his head back and tuts)*.

**2nd Employee**

What? *(Throws his head back and tuts)*

**Alan**

Yeah, see? You did it again! Yeah, you're definitely sacked. Now, Alison, you're a lady, I don't want this to be unpleasant –

**Alison**

Are you sacking me as well?

**Alan**

Yes, I am.

**Alison**

You rotten shit.

**Alan**

Yeah, well, you're a rotten shit, too. Get your coat.

*Alison leaves. Alan moves towards the door.*

**Alan**

*(Quietly, to Lynn)* Go go go go go go. *(He discreetly passes her the keys)* Start the car.

*Lynn and Alan leave, closing the door behind them. In an adjacent office, Alan dials through to the loudspeakers in the boardroom and speaks to the hands-free phone.*

**Alan**

Hello, it's Alan again. I've locked you all in the boardroom so you don't get me. But you can leave by the fire escape. *(The employees begin to put on their coats and leave by the fire escape)* We haven't got a second series; I just didn't have the guts to say that earlier. Um, bit like doing my radio show, this, isn't it? You're listening to *Up With The Partridge*. Ah-haa. Bye!

*Employees follow each other down an emergency spiral staircase on the outside of the building. Back inside Alan meets Jill trying to get into the locked boardroom.*

**Alan**

Ah, hello, Jill!

**Jill**

Why is this door locked?

**Alan**

To keep you out, you thief!

**Jill**

What?

**Alan**

I'm being light-hearted. Shoot your chuff through that door.

*Alan and Jill enter the boardroom.*

**Jill**

Ooh. Right, I got the Pringles, and that's for you. *(Hands Alan a Lion bar)*

**Alan**

Oh, thanks.

**Jill**

Where's everybody else?

**Alan**

*(Hesitating)* They've … gone … to … Longstanton Spice Museum.

**Jill**

Why?

**Alan**

Pfff … I said, congratulations, you've got a second series, uh, we can't celebrate with the Spice Girls, so why not get your arses down to the, er, spice museum in Longstanton.

**Jill**

Oh.

**Alan**

I mean, you know, it's, er, it's not just spices. No, it's all about the spice trade. *(Alan starts backing out of the door)* Yeah. They've got a model of a slave boat. It's very big, and you press a button and you hear all the slaves going 'uuurgh'. *(Peeking through a crack in the door)* Because, you know, they packed them in too tight. Listen, Jill, I really like you, but –

**Jill**

Oh, I like you as well. Hmmm.

**Alan**

Oh, thanks.

**Jill**

You're packed in a bit tight! Ha!

**Alan**

*(Gives a leering groan)* Listen, just – just clear something up. You know when you make those sort of risqué comments, um, are you just flirting in that sort of crude way that er, middle-aged divorcees do, or do you genuinely like me, sex-wise?

**Jill**

Well, you know. You're a man, I'm a woman …

**Alan**

That's a relief. Your mind plays tricks.

**Jill**

You're quite successful. You've got a second series …

**Alan**

*(Looking disappointed)* Oh. Carry on.

**Jill**

You've got needs.

**Alan**

Yes I have.

**Jill**

I've got needs.

**Alan**

Good. Jill, um, is the answer to my original question, 'Do you like me sex-wise?', is the answer to that yes, or no? Quickly.

**Jill**

Yeah.

*Alan now steps into the room, a big smile on his face.*

**Alan**

I'm Batman!

*Jill giggles. Alan leers at her and sighs deeply.*

**Alan**

Lion bar?

**Jill**

No. I prefer fingers.

**Alan**

Uh! Chocolate ones?

**Jill**

I don't mind, really!

*Alan makes a long, drawn out leering groan.*

**Alan**

Jill, you are so dirty! *(Jill giggles)* It's quite refreshing. You call a spade a spade. Actually you probably call it a big tool.

**Jill**

So what are we going to do together, then? Norwich is our oyster.

**Alan**

Hmmm … Jill, do you like owls?

**Jill**

They're quite nice, I suppose, yeah.

**Alan**

I know a cracking owl sanctuary. How about it? Unless you can think of anything better?

**Jill**

We could go shopping.

*Close-up of an owl. Alan and Jill are strolling beside tethered birds.*

**Alan**
I like the Astroturf they, er, place on the wood, there. It's basically zero-maintenance grass. Useful stuff.

**Jill**
Mmm.

**Alan**
You know, when I used to see you in reception –

**Jill**
Yeah?

**Alan**
Do you know what I used to, er, used to think?

**Jill**
No.

**Alan**
I used to think, 'Ooh, she's nicer than my wife!'

**Jill**
Ah! That's terrible! That's a terrible thing to say, Alan!

*Alan strikes an exaggerated pose, hands on his hips and legs apart, and blows a raspberry.*

**Jill**
You're mad, you are!

**Alan**
I know, I am a bit mad!

*Alan growls like a monster, and pretends to attack Jill. She screams playfully and leaps away.*

**Jill**
(*Squealing*) Get off!

**Alan**
(*Calling off-camera*) It's all right. No, it's all right. I was just portraying a madman. All right.

*Close-ups of various birds. Lynn and Alan are looking at birds of prey, all tethered in a row.*

**Alan**
It looks a little like death row, doesn't it? I'm sorry, Mr Hawk. Your pardon has been turned down. You have been found guilty of premeditated homicide of a mouse, er – and you'll be hanged by the neck until dead. And don't try to hover up so that the rope goes slack. Because they could do that, couldn't they? If you tried to hang a hawk, they could always hover so the rope went slack. So, er, I suppose if you were going to execute a bird of prey the, the most human way would be death by firing squad. (*He looks serious*)

*Alan and Jill in Alan's car.*

**Alan**
Ah, that is the best Valentine's Day I've had in eight years.

**Jill**
What did you do eight years ago?

**Alan**
You know, I just had a better one.

**Jill**
What did you do?

**Alan**
Went to Silverstone. Shook Jackie Stewart's hand. Superb. My marriage fell apart soon after that. Listen, Jill, um, there is a romantic buffet-supper at the hotel tonight. As much as you can eat for six pounds. I've got a scam going with a big plate. Do you, er, do you fancy being my er ... co-eater ... lady?

**Jill**

Oh! Yeah, Alan I'd like that, yeah.

**Alan**

Here, listen to this, it'll blow your socks off.

*Alan puts on the car stereo, and sings along enthusiastically. In the restaurant. Alan and Jill have finished their meal, and Alan is wiping his twelve-inch plate with a piece of bread while Jill smokes.*

**Alan**

Just give that a quick clean. Saves me doing it later.

*Ben appears at the table, carrying a bucket of roses.*

**Ben**

Bonsoir. Would you like to buy a rose for the lady? It's two pounds for Norwich Children's Hospital.

**Alan**

*(Reluctantly reaches into his pockets)* I've already done something for them. Did an after-dinner with Bill Oddie.

**Ben**

*Voilà. (Hands a rose to Jill and leaves)*

**Jill**

Ah, thank you, Alan. That's really lovely.

**Alan**

Keep it, keep it. You can, er, you can always get me something of equivalent value. A pint of bitter, big marker pen, whatever.

*Michael walks over to their table.*

**Michael**

Have youse all done? Maybe like to order a dessert? *(Hands Jill a menu)*

**Jill**

I'll have – chocolate mousse.

*Michael goes to clear Alan's plate. Alan grabs it back.*

**Alan**

Whoa! Leave that there.

**Michael**

*(Takes the menus back)* Two chocolate mousses. On its way.

**Alan**

I'm just going over there for a bit …

*Alan walks on to a small stage where a live band are playing. He takes the microphone.*

**Alan**

Ah, this is a romantic tribute … *(band begins to play)* … to a lovely lady over there with orange hair and a cigarette in her mouth. *(Singing)* Why do birds *(Alan struggles to reach the high note)* suddenly appear – That's too high – *(Singing)* Every time … every time … time, you are near *(an octave lower)* near? Just like me … *(an octave higher)* just like me… they long to be… *(lower again)* close to you … *(tries various notes)* why do … why do … No that's not working. *(Replaces microphone)* Well you get the general idea, you know. Thank you.

*Alan walks back to the table looking apologetic.*

**Jill**

That's great actually! I didn't know you could sing.

**Alan**

Yeah, I, er, I used to be in the choir at primary school. Before it all dropped. In my, er, pre-hair days.

**Jill**

It's all fallen into place now though, innit? Ha ha ha!

**Alan**

Yup, I've been pubic for thirty-one years. I was, I was one of the first in my class, actually.

**Jill**
Mmmm.

*Michael arrives with the dessert.*

**Michael**
Here you go. Two chocolate mousses.

**Jill**
Ah, thank you.

**Alan**
Marvellous.

**Jill**
I love chocolate. *(Alan and Jill lean closer together, face to face)*

**Alan**
Yeah, so do I.

**Jill**
Whispers.

**Alan**
Aeros.

**Jill**
Ripples.

**Alan**
Flakes.

**Jill**
Caramac.

*They both groan.*

**Alan**
It's good this, isn't it? Even though we're basically just listing chocolate bars. *(Looking over Jill's shoulder)* Oh my God, Lynn's here.

*Lynn walks over.*

**Alan**
Lynn, what are you doing here?

**Lynn**
Oh, Alan, more good news. I managed to negotiate a walnut gear-knob for your smaller Rover.

**Alan**
And you've come all the way out here to tell me about a walnut gear-knob?

**Lynn**
Yes, well, I've been ringing you all day but your mobile was switched off.

**Alan**
Lynn, if my mobile's switched off it's switched off for a reason. I was at an owl sanctuary. I was worried that the ringing may have sounded like a mating call. I can't have a bird trying to have sex with my phone. Why are you wearing that snazzy cardigan?

**Lynn**
Oh, I just threw it on.

**Alan**
If you think you can upstage Jill by wearing that you're very much mistaken. But thanks very much for the gear-knob, and er, good night.

**Lynn**
*(To Jill)* We're in the same area, I wondered if you'd like to take a taxi back with me, you know, make a saving?

**Jill**
*(Reluctantly)* Well …

**Alan**
No, er, Jill will be sleeping with me tonight.

**Jill**
I don't recall saying that!

**Alan**
Oh, come on.

**Jill**
Yeah, all right then.

*Alan looks at Lynn smugly.*

**Lynn**
OK. Have a good night, then.

**Alan**
I will.

*Lynn leaves.*

**Alan**
I'll go and get another half-bottle of champagne.

**Jill**
Yeah, go on, then.

*Alan leaves the table. Lynn returns, carrying a small bottle.*

**Lynn**
Could you give this to Alan? *(Gives bottle to Jill)* It's fungal foot powder. Now, he's got a condition, so make sure he rubs it in his feet last thing at night and first thing in the morning. Only it just gets a little bit … smelly.

*Lynn leaves. Alan returns with the champagne.*

**Alan**
They've got some goat's cheese out there.

**Jill**
Oh.

**Alan**
They've left it out a couple of hours so it's had a chance to breathe. *(Notices the foot powder)* Oh, she remembered, great. *(He puts the bottle in his jacket pocket)*

*Alan and Jill lean together again, face to face.*

**Jill**
*(Indicating the desserts)* Why don't we take these to your room?

*Alan grins inanely. They both get up.*

**Alan**
My room! It's over there, by the lift.

**Jill**
*(Stumbling)* Oopsie!

**Alan**
Right, you link my arm, we'll try and leave with some dignity.

*Alan grabs his big plate and they walk together out of the restaurant. Jill staggers drunkenly.*

**Michael**
Night night, Mr Partridge.

**Alan**
*(Looking embarrassed)* Night.

**Michael**
And your good lady!

**Jill**
Michael.

**Ben**
Good night.

**Sophie**
Good night.

**Alan**
Night.

**Jill**
*(Giggling)* Good night!

**Susan**
Good night.

**Alan**
Good night.

**Susan**
Got your big plate, Alan?

**Alan**
*(Irritated)* Yes.

*Alan emerges from his bathroom in a white dressing gown. He attempts to wrap a rolled-up hand-towel around his shoulders but it's too small and springs back. He notices Jill lying in bed in her underwear.*

**Alan**
Ah. I wouldn't go in there *(indicates bathroom)* for a bit. Leave it about fifteen, leave it about fifteen minutes. I must say, I'm, er, tremendously excited by all this.

**Jill**
My sister's got this bed linen.

**Alan**
Oh yeah? Does she live in a travel tavern?

**Jill**
No, she'd like to. It's nice, innit?

**Alan**
No, it's a bloody nightmare.

*Alan places some loose change on the bedside table.*

**Jill**
Is that for me, Alan?

**Alan**
That, oh God, no! No, I always put my money there in the evening. No, it's, it's, if it was for you you could add a zero to that. It's seven pounds six.

**Jill**
Seventy quid?

**Alan**
Well, no, double it.

**Jill**
It's still cheap!

**Alan**
I'm not haggling! I mean, I was trying to pay you a compliment, unless I've grossly misread the situation. It was my understanding in the lift that, er, no money would change hands.

**Jill**
I'm all yours.

**Alan**
Er, do you mind if I turn the light out?

**Jill**
Well, can't you just dim it a bit?

**Alan**
Yeah, OK. *(Slowly dims the light)* Bit more … bit more … how's that? *(Room is in darkness, we can only hear their voices)*

**Jill**
Yeah, that'll do.

**Alan**
Right, let battle commence! *(Slightly muffled)* Do you like me doing that? Shall I, shall I do it more quickly or shall I maintain the same speed?

**Jill**
That's fine.

**Alan**
Right. Shall, er, shall I move on to the other one? Right. Oh, that's lovely. That's first class. That is superb. Ooh, there you go, it's all happening! Um, Jill, I'm afraid I have no sheaths.

**Jill**
No what?

**Alan**

Sheaths, er, prophylactics, you know, rubber johnnies. Actually, er, being your age and everything there's probably no need for them. I'm talking about the menopau— whoooo! Jill, you know your onions! Ooh! Do you mind if I talk? It helps me keep the ... wolf from the door, so to speak.

**Jill**

Mmmm.

**Alan**

Jill, what do you think about the pedestrianization of Norwich town centre? I'll be honest I'm dead against it. I mean, people forget that *(sounding breathless)* traders need access to *(louder)* Dixons! *(Regaining his composure)* Yes, they do, they do say it'll help people in *(half-sighing)* wheeeeelchairs –

**Jill**

Oh hang on, I've got an idea.

**Alan**

Jill, whoa whoa. Jill ... Jill! What are you doing!? For God's sake, Jill, what are you doing!?

*Jill laughs.*

*The lights come back on. Alan is standing by the bed. Chocolate mousse is smeared all over his face and dressing gown.*

**Alan**

Jill, for God's sake!

**Jill**

*(Also covered in chocolate)* Well, I just thought I'd pour chocolate mousse over you.

**Alan**

You've got it on the bedsheets, you've got it on my dressing gown, you've got it on the valance ...

**Jill**

On the what?

**Alan**

The skirt thing round the side of the bed.

**Jill**

I thought it'd be erotic.

**Alan**

Oh, Jill. Mousse from a bowl is very nice, but to put it on a person is demented!

**Jill**

Come on, it's only a bit of chocolate!

**Alan**

It may be chocolate to you, Jill, but to an unwitting member of staff this could look like some sort of ... dirty protest against the standard of service in the hotel, which I happen to think is very good. I mean, it's not five-star but it's certainly competitive.

*There is a knock at the door.*

**Alan**

Oh God. *(Alan opens the door. It's Michael)* Yes?

**Michael**

Is everything all right, Mr Partridge? I heard a bit of commotion.

**Alan**

No, no, it's fine.

**Michael**

Oh, right. Erm, do you know you've got chocolate on your face?

**Alan**

Yeah, I've just been eating some mousse.

**Michael**

Oh. Right, right, fine.

*Alan wipes a little bit off his cheek and licks it.*

**Michael**

Aye, well, you've missed a bit.

**Alan**

*(Pause)* I'll deal with it later.

**Michael**

Right, hey, it reminds me of this time, you know, we'd camouflaged ourselves up 'cause we were doing jungle exercises, right, out in Belize, but –

**Alan**

Michael, can we talk about this in the morning?

**Michael**

Well, no, I won't be on in the morning 'cause I'm doin' lates now, right, so I don't come on until about two o'clock. So, you know –

**Alan**

Well, you know, 'when de boot comes in'.

**Michael**

Oh.

**Alan**

Now, er, booger off.

**Michael**

Aye, OK. *(Saluting)* Message understood, sir!

**Alan**

Stand down, at ease … *(irritated)* you're not in the army any more.

*Alan closes the door and turns, looking ill.*

*Radio Studio*

**Jingle**

*(Elderly male voice)* Across the Ouse to the Waveney, this is Radio Norwich

**Alan**

And now it's time for Alan's Love Bud.

*Jill in a taxi. It's dark outside. She is listening to Alan on the radio.*

**Alan**

This is a story of a woman, fifty, and a chap in his early forties. *(Jill begins to pay attention and smiles)* This woman enraptured this man, made him feel sixteen again. He thought – 'I'm going to wear a T-shirt with Crowded House written on the front of it'. He thought, 'Yes, I *will* buy that copy of *Punch* magazine'. But then, she committed a gross act upon his person, which was tantamount to vandalism, and he realized that not only must they part company but that he must also *sack* her from her job as his receptionist. *(Jill's smile fades)* Er, I didn't mention that earlier, but part of the problem was that she did work for him and he had to sack her anyway. Anyway, he thanks her for that stolen afternoon, but, you know, even then it was stolen. It's not your property, love. You've got to give it back. So just to re-emphasize one more time, her contract has been terminated. This is Hot Chocolate, 'It Started With A Kiss'. *(Music starts)* In three minutes' time I'll be talking to Norvert's youngest butcher.
*(Singing)* It started with a kiiiiiis
Never thought it would come to thiiis
It started with a kiiiiis
Never thought it would come to thiiis
Do you!
Don't remember me do you!

*Music fades. The taxi drives on into the night.*

# PARTRIDGE'S EYE
## The columnist they all fear

One of the many things I don't miss about London is the homelessness. They say London's paved with gold, but these days I think they'd say it's paved with tramps. Picadilly is bumper to bumper with sleeping bags.

But the homelessnessness plague is spreading fast. I saw a young tramp in town today. As I hurried past, not breathing in, he just said 'smile'. And I thought, he's got so many more problems than me and yet he's the one saying 'smile'. Actually, to be honest, he's got less. But whereas I have lots of smaller problems, he has the one very big one – where am I going to sleep tonight? – which is equivalent to about six of my problems. Remember – for every ten tramps who are going to spend it on drink or drugs there is one who is genuinely trying to better himself.

**I saw the *Rocky Horror Show* the other day. It wasn't frightening at all.**

Why can't more rockers behave like Ronan Keaton? This multi-talented Irish lad has both sung on stage, produced and sniffed out new young talent like The Westlife. Such a shame that others, with even more money – and perhaps a little less talent (I'll be frank, I'm talking about Robbie Williams) – can't show such professionalism offstage. Which brings me to 'Name-alike of the week' which comes from John Carr of Flitwick. John has spotted the similarity between the names of Robbie Williams and Robin Williams. 'Imagine if they got mixed up!' writes John. ' . . . And Robin Williams turned up on *Top of the Pops* crooning a no doubt hilarious version of "Angels Instead", while Robbie Williams starred in *Flubber*.' John wins a free copy of my new book, *Bouncing Back* which comes out on 14 January.

**I actually think gays should be allowed in the forces. Apart from the RAF. You don't want two gay men in a Swing-wing Tornado having an argument over clothes. Twenty million pounds of aircraft – and, smack, you've hit a pennine. There goes a low-level fighter jet and two perfectly nice chaps. You do the math.**

Martin Sharland of Terrington St Clement has sent me an idea for a political cartoon. He says he can't draw but somebody else may like to have a go. Martin suggests a cartoon of Gordon Brown with lots of pockets where he can put taxpayers money, a pair of trainers so he can run away with the money, rose-tinted spectacles through which to view past policy initiatives, and a pair of dracula teeth (these aren't explained). Leave it to the professionals, Martin. Please don't send any drawings in.

**Eddie Murphy. Now there's a man I've changed my mind about.**

We all want to be able to get into the middle of Norwich. Drivers, white goods deliverers, police, drinkers – and pedestrians. I have nothing against pedestrians – I myself am one when it suits me.

All I feel is that in the kingdom of the blind councillor, the one-eyed pedestrian is king. My point here is that the burghers of Norwich City Council are 'blind' to the needs of everyone except pedestrians – and, given their almost fascistic devotion to the rights of the disabled – one-eyed pedestrians probably would be king. (Or rather president, given the anti-royal people that the council probably are.)

**Warning!! Don't book into Choristers Country Club today because the Maitre D's put little spy-holes in all the rooms so he can look at all the lovely lady guests and do a 'numero uno' or 'numero dos'. Only joking. To the best of my knowledge, he's not a sex pest.**

Watch out for my new book *Bouncing Back* which hits the shops on 14 January. Well, the big one people get as presents anyway.

# I'M ALAN PARTRIDGE

## EPISODE 3: WATERSHIP ALAN

*Radio Studio*

**Farmer**
… er, then we bring the cows in, get them milked by 6 a.m., so all the –

**Alan**
You're listening to 'This Morning's Farmer'.

*Pause*

**Alan**
Go on, you were … talking about cow bringing-in.

**Farmer**
Yeah, we bring them in for milking, and then all that can go –

**Alan**
Pop the strait jackets on them?

**Farmer**
*(Pause)* What?

**Alan**
Thanks very much for being 'This Morning's Farmer', Robert Moon. Robert, er, did you have your breakfast this morning?

**Farmer**
Well I, I reckon the way things are going, I –

**Alan**
Can you just answer yes, for the purposes of a joke?

**Farmer**
Yes?

**Alan**
In which case, you must be a full moon!
*(Pause)* Hello?

**Farmer**
I'm still here.

**Alan**
Yeah I was, er, making a pun on your name.

**Farmer**
Oh, right.

**Alan**
*(Shaking his head)* Anyway, thanks very much for being 'This Morning's Farmer'.

**Jingle**
*'Old Macdonald' tune.*
Mooooo!

**Alan**
Sorry about that. Robert a bit slow on the uptake, there. I don't know what he had for breakfast. Presumably an infected spinal column in a bap. Just making a quick joke there about how infected cattle feed can attack the central nervous system. It's just coming up to 5.35 a.m., *Kommen Sie bitte, und* listen to Kraftwerk.

*Opening music.*

**Alan**
*(In opening sequence)* Put that in the bin.

*Radio Studio*

**Alan**
Let's get back to 'Cock-a-doodle who'.

**Jingle**
Cock-a-doodle who! *(Echo)* Whoooo.

**Alan**
And I asked 'who' invented the skip. Jack on line two.

**Jack**
Morning, Alan.

**Alan**
Morning.

**Jack**
Er, look. I just wanted to, er, say your comment earlier about farmers was ignorant and offensive.

**Alan**
Who invented the skip?

**Jack**
*(Pause)* I don't *care* who invented the skip. I think it's way out of order –

**Alan**
*(Speaking over him)* Who invented the skip?

**Jack**
– you speak like a man who has no knowledge of his subject –

**Alan**
Who invented the skip?

**Jack**
– that you're talking about, right?

**Alan**
Who invented the skip?

**Jack**
I don't know who invented the bloody skip. Bobby Moore, I don't bloody know, do I?

**Alan**
*(Quietly)* That's wrong.

**Jack**
I'm just sick and tired of you slagging farmers off. Are you going to apologize to them all on your show, are you, eh? Are you going to apol—?

**Alan**
Come on, I mean, you must know some of the rotten rubbish you produce, I mean, tongue, for example. Who eats tongue, for goodness' sake? Ever seen a tongue sticking out of a sesame seed cob?

**Jack**
Listen, you make these comments without any real knowledge about the pressures that we're under. I just didn't find it very funny, that's all.

**Alan**
Well, I wouldn't eat one of your tomatoes if it came up and said, 'Eat me,' which is not unlikely considering all the rubbish you stick in 'em.

**Jack**
Oh, listen, you ignorant shit –

**Jingle**
*(Cuts off the caller)* Cock-a-doodle-doo!

**Alan**
Caroline, line four. Hello?

**Caroline**
Hello, Alan.

**Alan**
Hello.

**Caroline**
Hello, yeah. Have you got a brain or is your head just full of shit?

**Jingle**
*(Cuts caller off)* Moooooo!

**Alan**
OK, Mike from Polgrave, are you there, sir?

**Mike**
Oh, you ignorant cu—

**Jingle**
*(Cuts caller off)* Fanfare music

*Linton Travel Tavern. In his room, Alan is doing exercises, dressed in extremely small blue shorts and a thick jumper. Michael is in the corner fixing the air vent.*

**Alan**
*(Singing)* Take a pinch of white man, wrap him up in black skin … what's the next bit?

**Michael**
*(In a thick Geordie accent)* Add a dash of blue blood.

**Alan**
*(Singing)* Add a dash of blue blood.

**Michael**
And a little biddy bit of a Red Indian boy.

**Alan**
And … something else in Geordie.

**Michael**
This hasn't been cleaned out for years. Hey, there's a little Japanese soldier in here still fighting the war!

**Alan**
Ha ha. You daft racist. *(Singing)* Curly black and kinky, mixed with yellow chinky … can you still say that?

**Michael**
Oh, aye. You're all right with that, like, because it's a race of people, and it's a food.

**Alan**
*(Thoughtfully)* Chinese. Yeah, you're absolutely right, yeah.

*The phone rings.*

**Alan**
Partridge? Yes, I'll hold. *(To Michael)* I'm possibly up for presenting a Hamilton's Water Break video.

**Michael**
Oh.

**Alan**
Yeah, you know, the Norfolk Broads?

**Michael**

Aye.

**Alan**

I'll tell you how I found out about this job. Bill Oddie was – sorry – *(into phone)* hello, yes. Well, no, the last, the last corporate job I did was for a company that makes toner for photocopiers. Um, no, I was dressed as an exclamation mark. Well, no, I walked out after five minutes, it was demeaning. I had to flag a cab dressed up. Which helped, actually. Well, I'd be delighted to do the job. Well now, hang on, you can't book me and ask me to pull out when Cliff Thorburn becomes available again. Well, no, look; you've got a choice. You can either book me now or wait for Cliff Thorburn. But if Cliff Thorburn goes AWOL you're up slack alley. Now who's it to be, me or Cliff Thorburn? *(Crosses his fingers and looks to Michael)* Thank you very much indeed. *(Puts the phone down)* Kiss my face! *(Strokes his cheek)*

**Michael**

Yay!

**Alan**

I am going to present a corporate video for Hamilton's Water Breaks.

**Michael**

Champion.

*Alan starts doing tai chi style exercises with accompanying sound effects.*

**Alan**

Wai-aye – that sounds Geordie, doesn't it? Wai-aye …

*Michael looks confused. Alan walks into the bathroom.*

**Alan**

You ever been to the Far East, Michael?

**Michael**

Well, only Manila, Hong Kong and Bangkok, like.

**Alan**

*(Interested)* Bangkok?

**Michael**

Aye.

**Alan**

Erm, so what did you see in Bangkok?

**Michael**

Oh, I saw the Golden Temple, man. Beautiful, it was.

**Alan**

Yeah, wh-wh-what else?

**Michael**

Er, well there was the river market, like. All the little boats come up and they've got all the fresh produce on them, and –

**Alan**

*(Walking out of the bathroom)* Michael, Michael, Michael, Michael. Come on … tell me about the ladyboys.

**Michael**

Oh, you mean those transsexuals? Aye, I seen them, but, you know, they're disgusting. I kept away from them.

**Alan**

Oh God, yeah, yeah … Fascinating creatures, though. Looks like a lady, but really it's a man. I don't find them attractive, it's just confusing. I don't suppose you've got any army stories about them?

**Michael**

I, I did hear about this corporal, right?

*Alan lies down on the bed, looking fascinated.*

**Michael**

And he's in the third battalion this lad, but he's right mean, OK? And he goes out in Bangkok, right? And all the prostitutes is comin' up and saying 'How much?' and he's going 'Oh I'm not paying that', right? And then this beautiful lassie comes up –

*There is a knock at the door.*

**Michael**

– she's gorgeous, man. And she's half the price of the others. And they're getting down to it –

*Lynn enters the room.*

**Michael**

– he puts his hand up her skirt, gets a hold of the old meat and two veg, right? Thinks, hang on, I've paid my money, I'm going to have something, so he flips him over, and he fu—

*Michael suddenly notices Lynn.*

**Michael**

F— And funnily, and funnily enough, it lands on its wheels, and it starts first time and they just drive away.

**Alan**

*(Looking confused)* Strangest story I've ever heard. *(Gets up)* Oh, hello, Lynn. Oh! I see what you were … ah, right, yes. No, erm, hello. Michael was just telling me an army story about a friend of his who slept with … a Landrover. Lonely nights in the desert.

**Michael**

That's all fixed, now, Mr Partridge. I'll be on my way.

**Alan**

Right, OK.

**Michael**

*(To Lynn)* Morning.

**Alan**

*(Quietly to Michael)* Just check, that wasn't the real ending to the story, was it?

**Michael**

No.

**Alan**

You were just saying that because Lynn's here?

**Michael**

Aye.

**Alan**

Right, fine. *(Closes the door behind Michael)*

**Lynn**

Just a few things, Alan.

**Alan**

Right.

**Lynn**

We've had a call from Norwich Radio. There've been more complaints from farmers about … well, what you've said.

**Alan**

Right, how many?

**Lynn**

Fifty.

**Alan**

Oh, your age. *(Alan sits on the side of his bed)* Well, Hamilton's have –

**Lynn**

*(Looking shocked)* Alan, you've, er, come free at the side.

**Alan**

*(Looking down and adjusting himself)* Oh, sorry, sorry. It was a genuine mistake. Anyway, I got the Hamilton's job.

**Lynn**

Yes, I've been speaking to them. They're coming over this afternoon.

**Alan**
Right.

**Lynn**
Er, did they say that you have to have your wife on the shoot?

**Alan**
*(He stands up, irritated)* Oh, Lynn, did you tell them that my wife has left me and she's living with a narcissistic sports pimp? *(He sighs, and sits back down)*

**Lynn**
You've … you've popped out again.

**Alan**
Oh. *(Adjusts himself again, with a sigh)* Sorry, that wasn't deliberate, I promise you. It's not a cry for help. It's just I've had these shorts since 1982. They did have an underpant lining, but er, it's perished. Yeah, they've taken a bit of a pounding over the years. In fact, can you get me some new ones, please?

**Lynn**
Of course.

*Lynn writes his request down on her notepad.*

**Alan**
I'm going to have to ring Carol *(starts dialling)* and ask if she'll do the corporate video. Lynn, Lynn, you speak to her, you speak to her, please. *(Gives the phone to Lynn, who groans)*

**Lynn**
Oh, hello. Yes, he is. *(Hands the phone to Alan)* It's a man.

**Alan**
Oh, that's, that's her boyfriend. Hello? Yeah, it's Alan, your lover's husband. The immersion heater? *(Alan sits behind Lynn, pulling the telephone cord around her neck)* It's underneath the stairs. You only really need to press that if you're having a

deep bath. Well, put it on an hour before, Bob's your uncle, you've got a deep bath. Yeah, well if you would, please, yes. *(To Lynn)* He's gone to get Carol. You speak to her, you speak to her.

*Alan twists round and hands the phone back to Lynn, wrapping the cord around both their necks and tying their heads together.*

**Lynn**
Hello, Carol, how are you?

*Alan gestures with his hand.*

**Lynn**
Oh, er, Carol, would you like to be in Alan's corporate video? Right. *(To Alan)* She says no and she wants to speak to you.

**Alan**
Tell her I'm not here.

**Lynn**
He's not here. *(To Alan)* She says she can hear your voice.

**Alan**
Erm … call her a fat cow then hang up.

**Lynn**
Fat cow!

*Lynn slams the phone down, pulling her and Alan's heads down towards the bed.*

**Alan**
Well done, Lynn. Now, before we get up, I'm just going to warn you, I have popped out again. Um … It, it's in no way connected with our proximity, so just don't turn round.

*Alan untangles himself from the phone and adjusts his crotch.*

**Alan**
Right, the boys are back in the barracks! *(Singing)* Take a pinch of white man …

*Alan and Lynn in the lift. Lynn is smiling slyly.*

**Alan**
(*Singing*) What we need is a great big melting pot / big enough to take the world and all it's got / keep it turning—

**Lynn**
I could pretend to be your wife.

*Long pause. Lynn's smile slowly fades. Alan leaves the lift, shaking his head at Lynn, and walks to reception.*

**Alan**
Morning.

**Susan**
Hello, Alan!

**Alan**
Lynn's a good worker, but er, I suppose she's a bit like Burt Reynolds. Very reliable, but she's got a moustache. Bit like er, ladyboys. Look like a, a woman, but really it's a man. I mean, I don't find them attractive, it's just confusing.

*Sophie appears behind reception.*

**Alan**
Morning, Sophie. You're not a man, are you?

**Sophie**
No. Would you settle this month's bill, please?

**Alan**
(*Reading the bill*) Right. Eight pounds 'Miscellaneous Services'. That sounds disconcertingly vague.

**Sophie**
(*Smirking*) You used this pay channel. (*Writes something down*)

**Alan**
Ah, right, yeah. It's very confusing.

*Sophie turns away to hide her laughter.*

**Alan**
Sophie, I find the pay channels very confusing. C-can I just explain? I was trying to access *Driving Miss Daisy*.

**Sophie**
(*Turning back*) Oh, right. And that's why you only watched it for fifteen minutes?

**Alan**
Yes, because, because it was the wrong, wrong film. Have you seen it, is it good?

**Sophie**
What, *Driving Miss Daisy* or 'Bangkok Chick-boys'?

**Alan**
(*Sternly*) *Driving Miss Daisy*. Is it a good film?

**Sophie**
I don't know, I haven't seen it. Was 'Bangkok Chick-boys' good?

**Alan**
I don't know, I didn't see it. I couldn't see it because I was … I was in the bathroom.

**Sophie**
Oh, Ben. Mr Partridge was just saying that he couldn't see 'Bangkok Chick-boys' from his bathroom.

**Ben**
Well, you can if you angle the mirror by the door. Do, do you want me to show you?

**Alan**
No! I only watched it for five minutes. The remote control's confusing.

*Sophie smiles at Ben.*

**Ben**
Oh, what you will have done is, when it flashed up on your screen, 'Do you want to watch Bangkok Chick-boys?' you must have pressed the button that said 'yes'.

**Alan**
Yeah, well, as I say, it's very confusing.

**Ben**
Do you want me to come up and show you how to press the button that says 'no'?

**Alan**
Yes. I mean, yes, I want you to show me the button that says 'no'.

**Ben**
Oh, and I'll show you that mirror thing.

**Alan**
No. *(To Sophie)* Look, er, do you want me to settle this bill?

**Sophie**
Er, no. I mean, yes! Ha ha! You're right, it is confusing, isn't it?

**Alan**
*(Sternly)* Yes.

*At the bar, where Michael is serving.*

**Michael**
Oh, hello, Mr Partridge. Drink?

**Alan**
No, no. Have you got any tonic water?

**Michael**
Aye.

**Alan**
With some ice *(Michael follows Alan's directions.)* … and … a segment of lemon … yeah, and could you top it up with some Gordon's Gin.

**Michael**
A gin and tonic.

**Alan**
Yeah, that's right. Yeah, fine.

*Alan looks through a brown folder. Lynn arrives.*

**Lynn**
Hello, Alan.

**Alan**
Oh, hello.

**Lynn**
The gentlemen from the corporate video are on their way.

**Alan**
Excellent. Well, I've done my homework. Would you like a drink?

**Lynn**
Oh, thank you. Well, I'll have a Baileys.

**Alan**
One small Baileys, please. Lynn, I was thinking about getting a substitute wife, and I would really love you to *(Lynn perks up)* go down to Sol Dangerfield's casting agency *(Lynn's face falls)* and tell them to get me a forty-year-old scorcher. And, and do use that word.

**Lynn**
Right.

*Lynn leaves just as the two Hamilton's men arrive.*

**Steve**
Er, are you Alan Partridge?

**Alan**
Yes.

**Steve**
Hi! I'm Steve Bennet. I'm the director of the Hamilton's Water Breaks video.

*Alan and Steve shake hands.*

**Alan**
Oh, right. We spoke on the phone?

**Steve**
Yeah. This is Hugh Morris, he's the marketing director for Hamilton's. He's going to be coming along with us, sort of keeping an eye on us.

**Alan**

Make sure I don't sink the boat and drown everyone like a big twit!

**Hugh**

*(Using a voice box)* No, I'll be down the pub, probably.

**Alan**

What?

**Hugh**

I'll be down the pub, getting the beers in!

*Hugh and Steve laugh.*

**Alan**

Why are you speaking like that?

**Hugh**

Oh, it's a voice box.

**Alan**

That's great fun! Do you get those at a toyshop?

**Hugh**

Alan, I haven't got any vocal cords.

**Alan**

You sound like the girl in *The Exorcist*.

*Hugh and Steve laugh.*

**Alan**

I've got to say, I love the script, it's superb.

*Hugh and Steve snigger.*

**Alan**

There's a lovely phrase in it, which says, 'Boating appeals to both friends and family alike.' Lovely phrase, very simple, very moving.

**Steve**

Alan, it's, it's a boat video. You know, we're not making a James Bond movie.

**Alan**

Interesting, because you do sound like a baddie in a James Bond film. *(Points at Hugh)* Dr. No ... vocal cords.

*Steve and Hugh look bemused for a second, and then laugh. Hugh sighs deeply into his voice box. The noise he creates makes Alan very uncomfortable.*

**Steve**

No, Alan, we want to keep it simple. That's why we hired you – you're a local fella, you know, that means good communications with, with tradesmen, with landlords, with farmers – *(Alan winces slightly)* – and at the end of the day, you know, the pubs are open, and we'll be in there getting pissed, really!

**Alan**

Sounds good to me! Michael, do you want to pop that in the bin? *(Hands him his folder)*

**Michael**

Aye.

**Alan**

Just some notes I made last night, for a laugh. I was drunk, you know. Yeah, I mean, I woke up this morning asleep on the sink, just like this – *(leans on the bar, with his eyes closed)*. I'd been asleep for eight hours like that. Got up, walked downstairs, straight downstairs. Had breakfast, didn't even wash my hands. 'Cause I'm a bloody bloke!

*Hugh and Steve cheer.*

**Alan**

Yeah. Anyway, there's the bar, gentlemen. Choose your weapons.

**Hugh and Steve**

What?

**Alan**
I, I'm offering you a drink.

**Steve**
Oh, right.

**Hugh**
Now you're talking my language!

**Alan**
I hope not.

**Steve**
Pint of lager.

**Hugh**
Pint of lager.

**Alan**
Two lagers. Three. Three lagers.

**Michael**
Three pints of lager, righty-ho.

**Steve**
You're having a lager and these two drinks here?

**Alan**
Yes, yes. These … are … they're chasers.

**Steve**
I've never had one of those.

**Hugh**
God.

**Alan**
You've never had a lager and gin and tonic and Baileys Irish Cream chaser?

**Steve**
No.

**Alan**
You big girls' bras!

**Hugh**
Has that got a name, that drink?

**Alan**
Yeah, they're, they're called, er, Ladyboys.

**Steve**
Right, because gin and tonic and Baileys are, like, a lady's drink, and lager's a boy's drink?

**Alan**
That's why I said that. Yeah. Cheers.

*Alan takes a gulp from his three drinks.*

**Alan**
*(In a high-pitched voice)* Ooh, ladyboys. Do you want one?

**Steve and Hugh**
Yeah, yeah.

**Alan**
Great! Three, three no, four ladyboys.

**Michael**
Four ladyboys, righty-ho.

**Alan**
How much is that?

**Michael**
That'll be, er, thirty-three pounds.

*Alan grimaces.*

**Alan**
Well, here's to a good corporate video, and um, lots of being men.

*The three men clink their glasses and drink their lagers. Hugh puts on his voice box while he swallows. Alan looks worried. Camera fades.*

*Alan is leaning on the bar with his eyes closed, asleep.*

**Steve**
*(Prods him)* Alan?

**Alan**
Oh! I'm confused. What time is it?

**Hugh**
Six o'clock.

**Alan**

Uh … How long have we been drinking?

**Steve**

Three-quarters of an hour.

**Alan**

I think I'll, erm, go to my room and, er, lean on the sink. And have a little bit of … sick.

*Alan wanders off.*

**Michael**

Mr Partridge, that's the kitchens!

**Alan**

Yeah, I'm going to … cook all the food.

**Steve**

Alan, this is a hotel.

**Alan**

Three star.

*In Alan's room. Alan is sitting on the bed, dialling the phone.*

**Alan**

Hello, Carol? It's Alan. How are you? Me? I'm having a fantastic time, yeah. I'm having the best time since … sliced bread. How's, er, how's Mr Planet of the Apes man? Oh. Is he still driving that Renault Megane? Yeah, can I just read you something from er, *Top Gear* magazine? No, it's all right, I've got it here, I've got it here. *(Opens the magazine on the bed and reads)* 'With a mere ninety break-horse-power available, progress is too leisurely to be called fast, but on the motorway in fifth gear the Megane's slow pace really becomes a pain. Uphill runs become power-sappingly mundane, while overtaking National Express coaches can become a long-drawn-out affair.' Not my words, Carol. The words of *Top Gear* magazine. *(Click)* Hello?

*Alan puts the phone down. There is a knock on the door.*

**Alan**

Come in.

*Ben enters.*

**Ben**

Hiya. I've come to show you how to use your telly.

**Alan**

Oh, oh, yes, yes. Very confusing.

**Ben**

Yeah. *(Picks up the remote control and flicks through the channels)* So that's Sky Movies … Sports … CNN … Adult Channel. That's your dirty movies.

**Alan**

Yeah. Not really my cup of tea.

**Ben**

Well, I can disconnect it. Put a scrambler on it, just lock it out the system.

**Alan**

Pfff … Er … that'll probably be a lot of trouble, won't it?

**Ben**

Not really. It's just, um, just a switch.

**Alan**

Erm …

**Ben**

Look, it's up to you, yeah? You're the boss. What you get up to in here, it's your business.

**Alan**

I don't get up to anything!

**Ben**

Do you want me to disconnect it?

**Alan**

Yes.

**Ben**
OK. *(Flicks a switch on the back of the TV)*
There, that's disconnected.

**Alan**
Good.

*A small riverside harbour. Alan walks over
with a pint and joins Steve and some other
men at a table.*

**Alan**
All right, lads?

**Men**
All right, Alan.

**Alan**
Yeah … I got really drunk last night. I was
sick everywhere. Were you sick?

**Men**
No, not really. No.

*A couple of attractive young women walk past.*

**Steve and men**
Look at the legs on that! Hello! All right?

**Alan**
Mmm. She was certainly, er, first in the
queue when God was handing out …
chests, or, mammary glands. Ooh! I'd
love to have it off with her. Urrr! Sex.

*The harbour; 'Hamilton's Water Breaks' flashes
on screen.*

**Alan**
*(Voiceover)* For a British holiday with
a difference on a boat, always choose
Hamilton's Waterways. With the melting
of the polar ice-caps, most of East Anglia
will be underwater in the next thirty years.
So make the most of her stunning fens
before the floods come, causing a little
concern for these local farmers I chatted to.

*Alan is followed by four menacing farmers.
The video then cuts to Alan with his arm
around a woman, pointing at something.*

**Alan**
*(Voiceover)* This is my wife and I going off
to the local marketplace, where we could
buy anything from plimsolls to posters of
famous Hollywood stars.

*Alan inside a holiday barge.*

**Alan**
This chemical toilet is a Saniflow 33. Now
this little babe can cope with anything, and
I *mean* anything. Earlier on I put in a *pound*
of mashed-up Dundee cake. Let's take a
look. *(He opens the lid)* Not a trace. Peace
of mind, I'm sure, especially if you have
elderly relatives on board.

*Profile shot of Alan steering the barge down
the river.*

**Alan**
*(Sighs)* Try pedestrianizing this!

**Steve**
*(Off-camera)* OK, can you hold that pose,
now, Alan?

*In the background, the angry farmers follow
the barge, shouting insults. Alan maintains his
broad smile.*

**Farmer**
Partridge, you wanker!

**Alan**
Ahhh! *(Once the farmers are out of shot)* We'll
dub that out. Play some music over it.

*Inside the barge kitchen. Alan is having
breakfast with his wife.*

**Alan**
How are your, er, how's your friends?

**Wife**
Fine.

**Alan**
(*Voiceover*) It might look a bit poky from
the outside, but a Hamilton's boat is
deceptively large. My wife and I found
it actually offers the kind of luxury and
comfort you'd normally associate with
a good quality static caravan.

**Alan**
You're not having any bacon?

**Wife**
No, I'm vegetarian.

**Alan**
Yes … I know. Just a joke.

*At the harbour. Alan is interviewing
a young woman.*

**Alan**
I'm joined by Alice, who's not going to
shrink me into a little bottle. She's going to
tell me about Hamilton's Holiday Breaks.
You regularly book, don't you?

**Alice**
Yep.

**Alan**
And do you do that with your boyfriend,
or …?

**Alice**
No, I do it alone.

**Alan**
What, you book alone?

**Alice**
Yep.

**Alan**
How old are you?

**Alice**
Twenty-five.

**Alan**
What do you do on a boat, alone?

**Alice**
Read a book, relax, look at the scenery.

**Alan**
(*Turns to someone off-camera*) No, she
sounds weird. We can't use that. Sorry
(*to Alice*), thank you, love. Thank you.
(*Alice walks off*) A bit odd.

**Steve**
(*Off-camera*) Cut!

*Radio Norwich. Alan is in the interview
room with another man.*

**Jingle**

*(Alan)* Up with the Partridge.

**Alan**

You're joining me, Alan Partridge, and Peter Baxendale Thomas of the Norfolk Farmers' Union. Uh, now, yesterday I, sort of, trod in a rather large farmer's pat when I made some comments about, um, intensive farming. Where did I go wrong?

**Peter**

Well I think your comments were ill founded. They were deeply ignorant, they showed a complete lack of understanding of modern agricultural methods, and simply served to highlight the sort of intense stupidity that farmers encounter from armchair pundits who forget to think before they open their mouths. *But* with a full and frank apology that you're about to give us this morning I'm sure you can dig yourself out of this rather ugly hole.

*Alan looks increasingly irritated during this speech. He forces a smile.*

**Alan**

Yeah. Erm, sorry. Er, do you have any requests, anybody you want to say hello to, or …?

**Peter**

Look, I'm just trying to say that when you make ignorant comments like you did the other day, you serve simply to alarm the public and to inflame the farmers, which is exactly what you've done. Why don't you just apologize and make it nice and simple –

**Jingle**

Mooooo!

**Alan**

Thought that, thought that'd fool you. You could talk the hindlegs off a donkey. But your donkeys are probably born without

hind legs because of all … all the chemicals you put in their … chips.

**Peter**

Alan, I don't have donkeys. And even if I did I wouldn't feed them chips. This is exactly the sort of rubbish you came up with the other day when you talked about putting a spine in a bap.

**Alan**

I, I admit that, that was a mistake. I shouldn't have said bap.

**Peter**

Well, good. Well, that's a start.

**Alan**

Well, no, I should have said baguette. Because a spinal column would fit in a baguette.

**Peter**

Lis-listen, you've upset half the farmers in this community. You seem to alienate everybody you come across, including, I gather, your wife, which is why you end up living like some bloody tramp in a lay-by.

**Alan**

It's a travel tavern.

**Peter**

I don't care what you call your sordid little grief-hole. It makes no difference to me. The fact is that an awful lot of my colleagues are –

**Alan**

Are farmyard animals, yes.

**Peter**

You're talking about my friends, here.

**Alan**

I, I, I've probably got more friends than you've got cows.

**Peter**

This is ridiculous.

**Alan**
How, how many cows have you got?

**Peter**
I've got a hundred cattle.

**Alan**
Yeah, I've got a hundred and four friends.

**Peter**
I don't see what this is going to gain you. Why don't you just issue a frank and full retraction of what you said, and you'll get yourself out of a lot of silly bother.

**Alan**
Yeah, you are a big posh sod with plums in your mouth.

**Peter**
I don't think it's got anything to do with class –

**Alan**
And the plums have mutated and they've got beaks.

**Peter**
Beaks?

**Alan**
Yes, beaks.

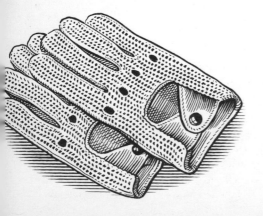

**Peter**
Have you got any more of this, or do you want to stop at quacking plums?

**Alan**
No, no. You, you make pigs smoke.

**Peter**
I want to know where you think you earned the right to go swanning off on these ludicrous flights of –

**Alan**
Ah, swans, swans. You feed beefburgers to swans.

**Peter**
Do I?

**Alan**
Yes, you do.

**Peter**
All right, well, perhaps you can tell me what's wrong with feeding beefburgers to swans?

**Alan**
Uh … What?

**Peter**
Well if you fill a swan's stomach up with beefburgers it's full of fat and it'll float better. That's why we do it.

**Alan**
Really?

**Peter**
No, you complete cretin. I'm just contributing to this total farce. What else are you going to accuse me of?

**Alan**
I'll tell you what. You, you farmers, you don't like outsiders, do you? You like to stick to your own.

**Peter**
What do you mean by that?

**Alan**

I've seen the big-eared boys on farms.

**Peter**

Oh, for goodness' sake. This is all –

**Alan**

If you see a lovely field with a family having a picnic, and there's a nice pond in it, you fill in the pond with concrete, you plough the family into the field, you blow up the tree, and use the leaves to make a dress for your wife who's also your brother.

**Peter**

Look, have I got anything else to say here or shall I go?

**Alan**

Well, listen, I'll tell you what the point is. You have big sheds, but nobody's allowed in, and inside these big sheds are twenty-foot-high chickens. Because of all the chemicals you put in them.

*Peter, shaking his head, gathers his stuff and leaves.*

**Alan**

And these chickens are scared. They don't know why they're so big. They go, 'Oh why am I so massive?' And they're looking down on all the other little chickens, and they think they're in an aeroplane because all the other chickens are so small … do you deny that? No. Uh, his silence, I think, speaks volumes.

*Lynn enters. Alan gestures at her to take Peter's seat.*

**Alan**

And … and basically, do you agree that everything I've said thus far is completely correct?

**Lynn**

Yes.

*Alan mouths 'lower', and gestures.*

**Lynn**

*(In a deep voice)* Yes.

**Alan**

And do you also run over badgers in your tractor, for fun?

**Lynn**

Yes.

**Alan**

Thank you, Peter Baxendale Thomas. This is T'Pau.

*Music plays.*

**Lynn**

How, how did it go?

**Alan**

Oh, you know. Up and down.

**Lynn**

Hmm. More bad news, I'm afraid. The actress playing your wife can't do the filming today.

**Alan**

Oh, for good—, why not?

**Lynn**

She's got a part in *The Bill*. She's playing a shoplifter.

**Alan**

Oh, that's quite good. Oh well, we'll just have to think of something.

*Alan is on the deck of the holiday barge. A clapperboard is held up to the screen.*

**Female voice**

Scene thirteen, take two.

*The clapperboard is removed, to reveal the back of a woman's head, sitting opposite Alan.*

**Alan**

One of the benefits of global warming and international terrorism is that more and more people are holidaying in England. I'll drink to that, cheers!

*Alan and the woman clink glasses.*

**Alan**
*(To Steve, off-camera)* How was that, OK?

**Steve**
No, it's not working. You can tell.

**Alan**
Really?

*The woman turns around – it's a large man in a black wig and dress.*

*Alan is on the barge again. The woman is represented by a dummy, dressed in the same black wig and dress. The clapperboard is held up.*

**Female voice**
Scene thirteen, take three.

*Clapperboard removed.*

**Alan**
*(Holds his glass up and smiles)* One of the benefits of global warming and international terrorism is –

*The dummy falls forward.*

**Alan**
You all right there, love?

*Alan pushes her back up.*

**Alan**
Is that –

**Steve**
*(Off-camera)* No, no, no.

**Alan**
No.

**Steve**
Cut it.

**Alan**
No, right.

*Alan stands on the bow of the barge, the dummy sitting next to him. A row of farmers are standing on a bridge in the distance.*

**Alan**
*(To the dummy)* Absolutely! *(To camera)* The Norfolk Broads offer the true peace and tranquillity of the English countryside. A million miles from the urban decay of the Manchester Ship Canal, and the pot-smoking, whore-ridden waterways of Amsterdam. Indeed, disused cotton-mills and legalized hardcore pornography are a million miles away from your thoughts as you negotiate the Norfolk Broads. In fact, the very fact that hardcore pornography is not on the agenda –

*A large Friesian cow falls on Alan from the bridge above. The camera moves around frenetically. Everyone talks at once.*

**Alan**
Jees! –

**Hugh**
What's going on? What's going on?

**Steve**
It's a cow. It's a dead cow! Where the bloody hell did that come from?

**Hugh**
Where did the cow come from?

*The farmers on the bridge run away. Alan is groaning with pain, flat on his back underneath the cow.*

**Hugh**
Farmers! It's not funny!

**Steve**
I know it's not funny. I know it's not funny.

**Alan**
*(Slowly)* Can you hear me? I'm trapped under a cow.

**Steve**
All right, he's OK. Look, get the cow off the boat, please.

**Hugh**
Get the cow off the boat! Get that cow off the boat!!

**Alan**
I'm not OK. I'm not OK. Help! I can feel an udder on my leg.

**Steve**
Can you call Cliff Thorburn now, please.

**Alan**
Cliff Thorburn is not, primarily, a presenter. He is a snooker – ex-snooker player – and is, is an unknown quantity.

**Hugh**
Yeah, but he's not under a cow.

*Close-up of Alan's head, speaking to camera.*

**Alan**
So book a holiday with Hamilton's 'Water-way' to have a good time. Cheers!

*Alan sips from a pint of bitter.*

**Steve**
*(Off-camera)* Cut! OK, stick him in the ambulance.

*Camera pulls back to reveal Alan, tied on to a stretcher, which has been held vertical by two paramedics. The beer glass is held by someone wearing the same jacket as Alan.*

**Steve**
Lovely, great, well done.

**Hugh**
*(Off-camera)* Cheers, Alan!

**Alan**
Thank you.

**Hugh**
Well done.

**Alan**
Good luck with the edit.

*Linton Travel Tavern, at night. In his room Alan, moving stiffly, is positioning a mirror outside the bathroom door. He takes off his jumper, revealing a neck brace. Alan sighs and lies down on his bed. He switches the TV on.*

**TV**
*(Female voice)* Hello, and welcome to 'The Learning Zone', Thursday night into Friday morning on BBC2.

*Alan looks bored. He leans over and picks up the phone.*

**Alan**
Hello, is that reception? Susan? Oh, hi. Can you, er, make pornography come on my telly, please? Oh, that's very nice of you. Thank you.

*Alan puts the phone down. He looks at his right hand, which is bandaged up, and groans.*

# I'M ALAN PARTRIDGE

## EPISODE 4: BASIC ALAN

*Radio Studio*

**Alan**
That was one of the biggest stadium bands in the world, R.E.O. Speedwagon, and the time, for those who like to tell it in a slightly wacky way, is fifty to six. Or, if you'd like to develop the idea, seventy past four. Um, or even, er …

*Alan writes something down on a notepad, then uses a calculator.*

**Alan**
… bear with me … one thousand, two hundred and thirty to twelve. I'm joking of course, but the time is ten past five. Er, let's say hello to my new comedy character, Camp David. Hello, Camp David!

**Camp David**
*(Alan, with disguised voice)* Well, hello, Alan!

**Alan**
Ha ha ha! And, what did you have for breakfast this morning?

**Camp David**
Ooh, mince!

**Alan**
Mmm. Yes, indeed. Er, more from Camp David tomorrow. The time is – well, let's not get bogged down in the time again. Simply time to say, 'Ruddy hell, it's Softcell!'

*Opening music*

**Alan**
*(In opening sequence, drinking a pint in the pub)* Yeah, well, they're scumbags, aren't they? Yeah.

*Alan emerges from the lift at the Linton Travel Tavern.*

**Alan**

*(Singing)* Out on a winding, windy moor we roll and fall in green, you had a temper like my jealousy, too hot, too greedy …

*Furniture in the hotel lobby is covered in cloth. Alan walks up to reception.*

**Alan**

*(Singing loudly)* How could you leave me when I needed you, possessed you, I hated you – I loved you too.

**Susan**

*(Sings in a high-pitched voice)* Bad dreams in the night, You told me I was –

**Alan**

Dear oh dear oh dear. That is, that is extraordinary. I mean, to look at you, you'd think you'd sing like an angel, but, er, in actual fact you sound like a trapped boy.

*Susan giggles good-humouredly.*

**Alan**

What a lovely smile. You, you could have been throwing up all night for all I know, and yet, and yet your smile wouldn't show it. I don't know, perhaps that's how you keep your figure.

*Susan's smile fades.*

**Alan**

Ahh. You could tell me anything with that smile, and it'd seem like … Christmas.

**Susan**

Well, we are having some major repairs done to the lobby, so I'm afraid all this is going to be out of bounds for the weekend. We decided to go ahead, seeing as you were the only guest staying in the hotel.

**Alan**

*(Singing)* Ding dong merrily on high, in heaven the bells are ringing.

**Susan**

*(Singing)* Ding dong merrily the sky –

**Alan**

*(Holding his hands up)* Don't sing, Susan! It sounds bad. Just stick to your smile. It's a lovely smile. You know, you could work on the *Titanic*. You could say, 'I'm terribly sorry, we've run out of life-jackets.' And people wouldn't mind. They'd say, 'Thank you for the information, I'll take my chances. Can I get a coffee?' Presumably the buffet's a bit of a free-for-all. Does the rule about women and children first –

**Susan**

Alan, why don't you go and talk to somebody else?

**Alan**

See, I don't mind that, you know. Because of the smile. Yeah, you'd make a very good Judas. Betray me and then kiss me.

*Alan smiles intensely at Susan.*

**Susan**

All right, then – I mean, I just don't want a kiss. I want to go the whole way.

*Alan looks uncomfortable.*

**Susan**

If you want me I'll be round the back.

*Susan leaves. Michael, Sophie and Ben are playing Charades in the lobby.*

**Michael**

No, no. Look, right, four words.

**Sophie**

Four words.

**Ben**

Four words.

*Michael flaps his arms around, growling.*

**Sophie**

Big bird, big bird – Eagle? Er … hawk?

**Ben**
Albatross? Bat?

**Sophie**
Eating?

*Alan walks over.*

**Alan**
'The Eagle Has Landed'.

**Michael**
Aye, it's 'The Eagle Has Landed'.

**Alan**
Michael, can I have a drink, please?

**Michael**
Aye, sure. What would you like,
Mr Partridge?

*Alan follows Michael to the bar.*

**Alan**
Er … I'll have a mineral water, please.

**Michael**
Aye. Still, or fizzy?

**Alan**
Er, half and half.

*Michael makes the drink and hands it to
Alan as he rushes back to Ben and Sophie.
Alan hovers in the background.*

**Michael**
Hey, I've got another! Right.

**Sophie**
First word, 'the'.

**Michael**
The … er …

**Ben**
Second word.

*Michael mimes going to sleep and waking
up again.*

**Sophie**
Second word is … 'sleep'?

**Michael**
No, er …

**Ben**
'Sleeping'?

**Sophie**
'Awake'? No. Er …

*Michael starts barking.*

**Alan**
'Day of the Jackal'. 'Day of the Jackal'.

**Michael**
Aye, it's 'Day of the Jackal'.

*Alan starts doing his own mime.*

**Michael**
Oh, er, three words? Er … wash … my …
car. Oh, aye! Wash my – oh, I'm sorry, Mr
Partridge. I'm on my, on my way now.

*Alan smiles and walks back to reception.*

**Michael**
*(To Ben)* I've got to go and wash his car.

**Sophie**
*(Behind reception)* Is everything all right,
Mr Partridge?

**Alan**
Yeah, yeah. Erm … what's round the back?

**Sophie**
A couple of traffic cones and an old
mattress.

**Alan**
Oh, right, uh –

**Sophie**
Would you like me to book you in for
Christmas dinner?

**Alan**
It's May! Sophie, if I'm still here in seven
months' time I think I'm going to be a
rather sorry individual.

**Sophie**
(*Smirking*) Well, why don't I book it now, and you can always cancel later?

**Alan**
Yeah, that's fine.

*Sophie grins. Alan walks to the lift. Ben leans over reception and kisses Sophie.*

**Sophie**
Why don't you come round the back?

*Alan hears and jams the lift doors open to listen to their conversation.*

**Ben**
Round the back?

**Sophie**
Yeah, it's quiet. Come on, fifteen minutes.

**Ben**
All right, fifteen minutes.

*Alan walks out of the lift, smiling.*

**Alan**
Er, Ben?

**Ben**
Yep?

**Alan**
Could I have a sandwich, please?

**Ben**
Yeah, sure.

**Alan**
Er, cheese. A cheese sandwich.

**Ben**
Right, OK.

**Alan**
And cooked meat. And a hot egg. And a crescent of crisps, please. And a side clump of cress.

**Ben**
Right. And you want that now?

**Alan**
No, no. Any time. Any time in the next fifteen minutes.

*With a smug smile, Alan strolls back into the lift.*

**Alan**
(*Singing*) Oh it gets dark, it gets lonely …

*In Alan's room. His uneaten cheese sandwich is on the table. Alan puts a tape on his hi-fi and lies back on the bed.*

**Alan on tape**
(*Accompanied by pan-pipe music*) Welcome to Tape 2 of 'Let Go', with Alan Partridge. A sequence of easy exercises to relieve stress, enhanced by the tropical music of the pan-pipes. First, find a quiet place to recline – a bed, or a big chair. I want you to imagine you're lying on the beach, divested of all the trappings of the twentieth century. No mobile phone, batteries out of your pager …

*Alan has been glancing at his shoes by the side of the bed. He gets up and straightens them into a neat pair, then lies back on the bed.*

**Alan on tape**
… no clothes. You're completely naked, or with undergarments perhaps made from bark. You're all alone, the waves gently licking at your feet, your bark trunks soaking up the water like a sponge …

*Alan, looking increasingly agitated, gets up again and pushes the shoes under the bed. He lies back down.*

**Alan on tape**
Your head loosens from the torso and bobs into the distance. (*Seriously*) Remember the breathing techniques from Tape 1. Please relax. I can't emphasize that enough. All of us experience stress –

*Alan leaps up and shuts all the drawers in the room. He straightens a stack of CDs, then lies back down on the bed.*

**Alan on tape**
– whether you're a heart surgeon making vital incisions, or just Dave Bloggs queuing for a rail ticket behind a man who's buying a travel pass which involves photographs, scissors, forms being filled in, and his access won't wipe. Y-you get the picture. But stress like this just won't go away, and it has to be combated.

*Alan gets up and switches off the tape.*

**Alan**
Sod off.
*(He picks up a dictaphone and speaks into it)*
Idea for a programme entitled 'Yachting Mishaps'. Er, some funny, some tragic. Presented by that man who was trapped upside-down in his hull eating chocolate.

*Alan looks out of his window. Sophie and Ben emerge from the bushes and kiss. Sophie notices Alan spying on them and they run off laughing.*

**Alan**
*(Into dictaphone)* Idea for a programme called 'Free Spirits'. No, actually change that to 'Bad Attitude'.

*He walks over to the phone and dials.*

**Alan**
Hello? Oh, hello. Um, I'd like to speak to Fernando Partridge, please. *(Irritated)* It's his father. *(Calmer)* It's his father. Ah, hello. Who's she? Is she your, your latest … ah, right. You both sound exhausted, have you been running? I was just wondering if you wanted to go for a drink. Yep *(sighs)* Fernando, you're twenty-two years old and you're spending Saturday afternoon in bed with a girl. You're wasting your life. It's a

beautiful day. Take her out to a local fort or a Victorian folly. Yeah, of course. Look, look, your mum and I, believe me, we did it everywhere. You know, in the lounge … in the hall … behind a large boulder on Helvellyn on my birthday. Actually, that is where you were conceived. Well, we just, we just didn't take precautions. No! No, we were delighted. Well, I mean, at first I was mortified, you know, but, then you were born and we, er, grew to like you. I remember I left a tartan flask up there. Yeah, one of those very fragile ones with the screw-on cup stroke cap. These days they're much more resilient. They took the technology from NASA, basically, which is extraordinary. Modern, modern flasks today are directly linked with the Apollo 11 space mission. Hello? Oh, sod him.

*Alan puts the phone down. A moment later he picks it up again, dials, and lies back on the bed.*

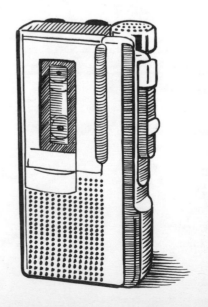

**Alan**
Hello, is that Curry's? I'd like to make an enquiry about two er, supplementary auxiliary speakers to go with my midi hi-fi system, apro po achieving surround sound. Apro po. I mean, it's Latin, isn't it? Well, *(sighs)* you ought to have a basic grasp of Latin if you're working in Curry's. Oh, you've got them. Excellent, good. Um, one last thing, what time do you knock off? *(Looks at his watch)* Uh, fancy going for a drink? No, OK, just thought I'd ask. Thank you.

*Alan walks into the lobby.*

**Alan**
Hello?

*He stands in the middle of the lobby, looking around.*

**Alan**
*(Calling out)* Just going for a walk. The, er, petrol station. Get some, er, windscreen washer fluid. *(Louder)* Anyone, er, anyone want to join me? *(Quietly)* No. *(Shouting)* Breath of fresh air?

*Alan strolls down the hard shoulder of a busy dual carriageway.*

**Alan**
*(Singing)* Goldfinger, he's the man, the man with the Midas touch, A spider's touch –

*Outside the petrol station shop. Alan enters, we hear the conversation but don't see him.*

**Alan**
*(Singing)* Such a cold finger ... hands up! Give me all your petrol.

**Attendant**
Pardon?

**Alan**
No, just a joke. Have you got any windscreen washer fluid?

**Attendant**
Yeah.

**Alan**
I'll have, er, twelve bottles, please.

**Attendant**
OK.

**Alan**
Nice, er, nice array of pasties you've got today.

**Attendant**
Oh, thank you.

**Alan**
I don't want one, I'm just making small talk.

**Attendant**
That's, er, thirty-one twenty, please.

**Alan**
Fancy a pint later on?

**Attendant**
No, thanks.

**Alan**
*(Quickly)* No, neither do I. Thank you.

*Alan emerges from the shop.*

**Alan**
*(Singing)* Such a cold finger, Pretty girl, beware of his web of sin. But don't go in.

*Alan skips occasionally as he walks back down the hard shoulder.*

**Alan**
*(Singing)* And the golden girl knows when he's kissed her, It's the kiss of death from Mr Goldfinger – do doooo doo!

*Close-up of Alan on the phone, in his room.*

**Alan**
Oh, hello, Susan. Slight problem. I was a bit bored, so I dismantled my Corby trouser press.

*Pieces of the dismantled trouser press are strewn across his bed.*

**Alan**

I, er, I can't put it back together again. Um, will, will that show up on my bill? Great, thanks.

*He puts the phone down and looks out of his window. Michael is in the car park rubbing his head agitatedly. He notices Alan, who mimes shooting Michael from the window. Michael half-heartedly clutches his chest in response. Alan mimes putting the gun in his mouth and blowing his head off. He beams at Michael, and laughs. Michael walks inside.*

*Alan drives slowly with another car following closely behind. Alan speaks on his hands-free headset.*

**Alan**

Hello, Lynn, message from Alan. Idea for a television programme based on Michael Palin's *Pole To Pole*. Except I circumnavigate the globe only driving through countries where they drive on the left. And I do it in a lovely old Bullnose Morris. We could call it 'Around The World With Alan Partridge In A Bullnose On The Left'. Oh, I'm sorry, Lynn. *(Sighs)* I think that is possibly the *worst* idea I have *ever* had.

*A long queue of cars has developed behind Alan.*

**Alan**

I'm going nowhere, Lynn. Quite literally, I'm on the ring road. Third time round. I've just been into B&Q for a bag of tungsten-tipped screws. Never gonna use 'em. Never gonna use 'em … meet me in the car park in half an hour, Lynn.

*Hotel car park. Alan and Lynn sit in his car.*

**Lynn**

Sorry I'm a bit late; I, er, got caught in a taxi that broke down over there. Couple of miles back. I had to walk.

**Alan**

Was that a lie?

**Lynn**

No. I'm very hot.

*Alan sighs deeply.*

**Alan**

You know, these are inertia-reel seatbelts. They were developed in the sort of late-sixties, early-seventies basically to, er, enable you to lean forward for things. *(Alan leans forward to demonstrate. Lynn copies him)*. But in a crash, they do stop you because … *(Alan yanks hard on the seatbelt)* Impact! Bang! Lock! I mean, you get bruises, but er … I'd love to feel an airbag go off in my face. It would be *(leans forward again, sharply, then mimes an airbag going off)* Brrr, boosh! Boosh! A really cushioned effect on the face. Ohh. I'll be honest, Lynn, I'm at a loose end, today. That's, that's why I'm, er … that's why I'm, er … talking … talking … that's why I'm talking …*(He sighs)* Could you cool me down with a hand fan, please?

*Alan looks out of the window as Lynn holds up the hand fan close to his face.*

**Alan**

You know, when I met Damon Hill – *(Alan turns his face and collides with the fan)* Ow! Lynn! Be careful with it!

**Lynn**

Sorry. I didn't realize I was so close.

**Alan**

You'll take my lip off.

*Inside the hotel lobby Susan, Ben and Sophie are playing cards. Susan calls over as Alan and Lynn enter.*

**Susan**
Lynn! Lynn! Come and join us, Lynn. Make the numbers up, come on.

**Sophie**
We need you, come, sit down and play rummy.

*Lynn joins them and they chat happily.*

**Alan**
I'll er … Lynn, I'll, I'll just go up to my room. Got a bit, got a bit of work to do, so, er …

*Alan walks off, his briefcase falls open and a small wallet and a biro fall out on to the floor. He stoops to pick them up.*

**Alan**
I normally have files in here, but, er, I've got some in the room to put in later. *(He zips up the bag and throws it over his shoulder)* Strap's optional …*(he walks off)*

**Susan**
*(To Sophie as she deals)* Oh, no no no. Show, show Lynn.

**Ben**
Oh, yeah, do it! Do it!

**Sophie**
*(Impersonating Alan, hands held stiffly by her sides)* Morning, Susan! Ah-ha!

*They all laugh. Alan reappears. He swipes his bag over their heads and hits a barstool. He then picks up a packet of crisps from the table and throws it on the floor.*

**Alan**
Watch it!

*Alan runs for the lift.*
*In his bedroom, there is a knock on the door.*

**Alan**
Come in.

*Lynn enters.*

**Lynn**
Would you like a mint?

**Alan**
*(Annoyed)* No. Ye– yes.

*Lynn gives Alan a mint. Lynn eats one too.*

**Alan**
I don't think you should have one, Lynn. Considering what's happened.

**Lynn**
Right. *(She removes the mint from her mouth)*

**Alan**
I tell you, it's a good job you weren't here five minutes ago. Listen to this. Listen, listen. *(Alan picks up his dictaphone and plays it)*

**Alan**
*(On dictaphone)* Sack Lynn for being unloyal – disloyal, and for joining in fun in a, in a way that excludes her employer. And, and sack her for being an absolute idiot, and, and inefficient. Then, can you call Bill Oddie and –

**Alan**
*(Stops the dictaphone)* That's something else. I've calmed down, now.

**Lynn**
Why don't you come down and play, then?

**Alan**
Play? Lynn, they were doing impersonations of me.

**Lynn**
Well, they were doing impersonations of everyone, Alan. Even me. It was quite savage.

**Alan**
Were, were they really savage? Were they going, 'Ooh, shall I sit there? Ooh, shall I sit there? Ooh I'm, er, like a little mouse.' *(Alan hunches himself up with his hands in front of him)*

**Lynn**
*(Annoyed)* No, actually. It was a little bit like this – 'Shall I let you walk all over me? Sorry, mother, I can't get you out of the bath, I've got to pop down to Linton Travel Tavern to sort out Alan's problems.'

**Alan**
That's very good.

**Lynn**
Thank you.

**Alan**
Tell them I'll, er, I'll join in, and to show that I'm not a stick-in-the-mud I'm just preparing a little joke for them, which should be a lot of fun.

*In the lobby. Susan walks behind reception. Alan leaps up from under the counter and growls. He is dressed in a shower curtain and mat, with food stuck to his face.*

**Alan**
Waaahhh!

*Susan screams and runs away. Michael runs in, fist held high.*

**Alan**
I'm a zombie! I'm a zombie, I'm dressed as a zombie! I'm Alan Partridge!

*Sophie, Ben and Lynn arrive in the lobby.*

**Michael**
Would you come out, please, Mr Partridge, because guests are not allowed behind reception.

**Alan**
All right! All right. It was just a joke, all right, it's backfired.

**Ben**
Is that blood?

**Alan**
It's tomato ketchup.

**Susan**
Why have you got a shower curtain round your neck?

**Alan**
I don't – I'm a zombie, I don't know! It's supposed to be a flap of skin or something.

**Susan**
Did you pull that off one of the showers?

**Alan**
No, I checked all the rings to make sure I could re-attach them afterwards. Nothing has been damaged.

**Michael**
Why have you got, er, biscuits sellotaped to your face?

**Alan**
They're complimentary, they're supposed to be flaky skin. I'm a zombie.

**Sophie**
What's that hanging down between your legs?

**Alan**
It's a flex off a mini-kettle. Supposed to be a tail.

**Sophie**
Zombies don't have tails.

**Alan**
All right, it's inconsistent! Zombies, by their very nature, are inconsistent. They're a mish-mash of different bits.

**Ben**
No, that's Frankenstein.

**Alan**
Right, you've made two glaring errors *(raises his finger)*.

**Ben**
What's that on your fingers?

**Alan**
They're tungsten-tipped screws, claws. Right, error one – actually is, they're quite good for making a point, aren't they? Error one, right, Frankenstein right, the name of the creator, not the monster. Error two, right, Frankenstein is a zombie. He's a type of zombie. It's like people who say Tannoy when they mean public-address system. Tannoy is a brand name. Why are you all staring at me? I'm not having a go at anyone, I'm having a pop at the undead. Do you see any upset zombies around?

**Sophie**
Just the one.

**Alan**
This country. *(He sweeps his shower curtain and walks off)*

*Later, at the bar. Alan is drinking a pint of bitter. Michael is serving.*

**Alan**
Ah. It's so depressing, isn't it?

**Michael**
Aye.

**Alan**
You ever thought that suicide might be the answer?

**Michael**
Well, sometimes, aye.

**Alan**
Really? When?

**Michael**
Well, when I've seen you looking all depressed and that, you know.

**Alan**
Not, not me, you! Have you ever considered suicide?

**Michael**
Oh, no. Pff, that's the coward's way out, man.

**Alan**
You must have got up to a few pranks in your time.

**Michael**
Wai-aye. Hey, I mind this one time, right. I was stationed out in Belize, right, and I had this little macaque monkey as a pet, right? And one day, I came back to my tent, right, and it'd eaten all my fags. *(Alan laughs)* So I picked it up and I threw it in the sea.

*Alan's face falls.*

**Alan**
You threw a monkey in the sea?

**Michael**
Well, it had eaten all my fags, man. It was a big packet of two-hundred duty-frees, like.

**Alan**
You threw a monkey in the sea? That's awful. I mean, I was fishing for some sort of funny story. That's just upsetting.

**Michael**

Well, you know, I wasn't thinking straight, right. I just, kind of, got the red mist in front of my eyes and I just grabbed the monkey and hurled it in the sea.

**Alan**

Will you stop saying you threw your monkey in the sea? All I can see is a monkey spinning towards the water.

**Michael**

Well, it didn't go straight in the water. It bounced off a rock.

**Alan**

Oh, Michael. That is such a pointless death. At least when they experiment on them they sort of get something out of it, a nice perfume or something.

**Michael**

Aye. You know, I've often wondered, right, why is it that they put the perfume in the monkey's eyes, right? Why not just put it on its wrist, like, you know, posh ladies in the department stores?

**Alan**

It's just cruel, isn't it. I mean, mind you, if you've been to Knowsley Safari Park and they're pulling the wipers off your windscreen and nicking your hub caps, you lose sympathy.

**Michael**

Aye. I'll tell you what, maybe the monkeys is trying to collect enough parts together to make a complete car, right? And they'll all just pile in it and break through the gates and escape.

**Alan**

(Nods in agreement) It's a frightening thought.

**Michael**

Aye. Is this, er, making you feel any better?

**Alan**

Not really, no. Yeah, you, you've done some crazy things in your life.

**Michael**

Aye.

**Alan**

I, I wish I'd been a bit more spontaneous, you know. Sometimes I feel like just going out and, I don't know, stealing a traffic cone, putting it on my head and saying, 'Look at me, I'm a giant witch!'

**Michael**

Aye. Aye. You should just do it, you know. Go and steal a cone, man.

**Alan**

Oh, I can't. That's outrageous.

**Michael**

I'll come with you!

**Alan**

Yeah?

**Michael**

We can be like Thelma and Louise, eh?! We'll just steal a traffic cone and then just go off somewhere!

**Alan**

I don't want to go off anywhere. I just, I just want to steal a cone and sort of wave it around a bit, you know.

**Michael**

Aye, I tell you what, I could hold it up to my mouth like a Tannoy, right –

**Alan**

No, no – it's a speaker system.

**Michael**

Sorry. I could just hold it there and shout: 'STOP TELLING ME WHAT TO DO!'

**Alan**

Ha ha … *(Alan looks uncomfortable, then smiles)* No, it's a good idea. I mean, I could get Lynn to drive us there. She's fully comprehensively insured, she's a named driver! Let's go!

**Michael**

Away the lads, man! Come on!

**Alan**

Right!

*Michael leaps over the bar and runs off. Alan puts down his drink and follows him.*

*Alan is questioned by two policemen next to his car.*

**Policeman**

*(Talking into his radio)* Yeah, we're questioning one bloke. The other bloke … he seems to have disappeared. There's a, er, a woman in the car. Out.

*Lynn is sitting in the driver's seat, looking very worried.*

**Policeman**

*(To Alan)* So, let's get this straight. Your wife was driving?

**Alan**

Yes.

**Policeman**

You felt a bit sick?

**Alan**

Mmm-hmm.

**Policeman**

So you asked her to pull over so you can get a traffic cone to be sick into?

**Alan**

Yes.

**Policeman**

Why?

**Alan**

I didn't want to be sick on the road. The cars might, you know, skid on it and crash.

**Policeman**

There was another fellow with you. Where's he gone?

**Alan**

He ran off over there *(points at the side of the road)*. He got scared and ran away. He was in the army and I think he saw people being blown up, all *(makes a face)* like that, and, erm …

**Policeman**

Do you want to know what I think? I think you've got a very vivid imagination.

**Alan**

*(Suddenly very worried)* I wasn't trying to steal a traffic cone!

**Policeman**
I'm not saying you're stealing it. I've not said that. Why are you saying that? Why are you saying 'steal'?

**Alan**
Because … to an innocent bystander, it could – may – look like traffic cone theft. And I am an innocent bystander, and, you know, to me it looks like traffic cone theft.

**Policeman**
But it's not.

**Alan**
But it's not *(he scratches his chin nervously)*.

**Policeman**
What's your name?

**Alan**
*(His voice wavers slightly)* Bill.

**Policeman**
Bill?

**Alan**
Caarr. Bill Carr.

**Policeman**
Bill Carr. Where do you live, Bill? What's your address?

**Alan**
King Road … King Road …

**Policeman**
Is there a number?

**Alan**
Ten! King Road in … Ipswich.

**Policeman**
Where are you going now?

**Alan**
I'm going to go home, and just probably go straight to bed and just keep out of trouble.

**Policeman**
Good, good. We'll let this go … but I don't want to see you here again, all right?

**Alan**
OK, thank you.

*The policemen walk off. Alan gets into the back of the car.*

**Alan**
*(To Lynn, quietly)* Right, go. Just drive away. Drive away normally.

*Lynn panics. She struggles to start the engine.*

**Alan**
Stop panicking! Start the engine.

*Lynn puts her face in her hands for a second, then tries again. The car alarm goes off.*

**Alan**
Oh *(shouting above the noise)* you've set the alarm off! Lynn! *(Alan leans into the front seat)* Lean back. What are you doing? Stay still. *(Alan switches the alarm off and starts the engine. Then he sits back.)* I was technically in charge of a motor vehicle, then. I could have been done for drink driving.
*(Lynn sobs)* Be careful.

*They drive off.*
*At the hotel, Alan and Lynn walk into the lobby. Close-up of Alan's miserable face – he starts daydreaming that he is dancing on the stage in his leather thong and platform shoes. His Pringle jumper has holes cut in where his nipples are. Tony Hayers watches him from a table.*

**Alan**
Would you like me to lap dance for you? Ooh, my peephole Pringle is modelled on an SAS balaclava. Sweet feet.

*Close-up of Alan's feet as he twirls on stage. The next time we see his torso two traffic cones are filling the holes in his jumper.*

**Alan**
Do you like my cones? They're little ones, I got them from a cycling test centre.

*Tony Hayers drinks out of a mini traffic cone.*

**Alan**
I've got a clean licence. Yours is dirty!
You've got six points, I've got two *(he
places two fingers on the points of his traffic
cones)* … points.

*Alan wakes up and turns to Lynn.*

**Alan**
Oh dear. Tonight I was *that* close – *that*
close to being infamous. I don't want to
be infamous. I want to be … famous.
*(He pronounces it as in infamous)* Famous.
*(Normally)* Like the Rudyard Kipling
poem, 'If'. You know that? 'If' you do X,
Y and Z, Bob's your uncle. Oh, do you
want a lift to the cab rank?

**Lynn**
Oh, yes, thank you, I would.

**Alan**
Mind you, it's only a fifteen-minute walk,
isn't it?

**Lynn**
Yes. Hm.

**Alan**
Right, well, be careful because there's no
lights on the dual carriageway.

**Lynn**
Right.

*Lynn walks out. Alan sees Michael.*

**Alan**
*(Friendly)* Ahh, there you are! Ha ha ha.

**Michael**
Ha! Aye-aye, Mr Partridge.

**Alan**
That was a bit of a close shave, wasn't it?

**Michael**
Aye, it was a bit, eh?

**Alan**
You disappeared pretty sharpish.

**Michael**
Aye. Scalded cat, man. I was away!

**Alan**
Erm, can I have a couple of eggs for
breakfast tomorrow?

**Michael**
Aye, certainly.

**Alan**
Yeah. And I'd like you to lay them,
you chicken!

*Alan storms off into the lift. Susan joins him.*

**Susan**
Oh, hello, Alan.

**Alan**
Hello, Susan. Third floor?

**Susan**
Third, yes, thank you.

*Alan and Susan stand side by side in silence.
Alan glances furtively at Susan, who stares
ahead. After a few seconds, the lift arrives
at Alan's floor. He starts to walk out.*

**Alan**
Right, well.

**Susan**
*(Smiling)* Are you getting out here,
or are you going all the way with me?

**Alan**
*(Anxiously)* I'm getting out here.

**Susan**
Right. Good night, Alan.

*Pause. The lift doors close.*

**Alan**
This country.

*Radio Norwich.*

**Alan**

That was The Police with 'Doo Doo Doo Daa Daa Daa', their gibberish classic, and my tribute to Her Majesty's police. It's nearly seven o'clock. This is Dave Clifton.

**Dave**

Yes, indeed! Good morning, my name's Dave Clifton, and there goes Alan Partridge, cone but not forgotten!

*Alan forces a groan, and laughs.*

**Dave**

Uh, you off to see a film, like Cone-an the Barbarian?

**Alan**

*(Looking annoyed, but still playing along)* Yeah, good one.

**Dave**

Then watch a bit of TV, eh? Like Cone Dancing?

**Alan**

Yeah. Not, not so good, but fine.

**Dave**

Oh, come on, Alan. What's the matter with you? Cone you take a joke?

**Alan**

Oh, fuck off.

*Dave stares in shocked silence, then regains himself.*

**Dave**

Actually, I am *speech*less. Dave *Clifton* is actually speechless. I don't believe you just said that.

**Alan**

You don't sound it. I wish you were.

**Dave**

Well I am. Now, I really don't know *what* to say. I find it really difficult to find a way –

**Alan**

Try saying nothing!

**Dave**

You and I both know that dead air is a crime, and I think it's terrible that you have to fill it with swearing on your show.

**Alan**

Unfortunately, Dave, you are bang wrong. It's one minute past seven, it's your show, you're responsible for the output, I am technically a guest and you've failed to control me. Read the small print on your cone-tract.

*Dave looks annoyed.*

**Dave**

From 'Go West' –

**Alan**

– Fanny –

**Dave**

This is 'Call Me'.

*Music plays. Fade and cut to securicam footage of Alan pulling up by a line of traffic cones. Alan and Michael jump out and grab a traffic cone each. A police van pulls up, Michael drops his cone and dashes off, but Alan carries his slowly towards the car, where he places it on the ground. He backs off as the police approach him.*

**Linton** ▶**Travel Tavern**

3 June 1997

Dear Alan

This is to address your queries regarding your bill.

Firstly, neither I nor Sophie have any record of a conversation in which you were told that the *Daily Mail* left outside your door was complimentary. It is not the policy of Traveltaverns PLC to provide a free newspapaper other than the *Daily Express* throughout the week or the *Independent on Sunday* on Sunday.

The line marked 'Repairs to dressing table': You have pointed out that you are not responsible for the damage to the dressing table and that it must have been another guest. However, the table was unharmed before you moved into the hotel, and nobody else has stayed in the room in your four months here, apart from your friend who left in the middle of the night after the incident with the chocolate on the sheets. Of course if you have had other guests, that is your business (though we normally charge a supplement), but could they have been responsible for the damage? If so, unfortunately we would still have to insist on payment for repair.

Regarding your request for an overall room discount given the length of your stay, you have indeed been offered a lower monthly room rate, but have responded that there would be no point, as you would be out of the hotel within days. Given that you've now been here for five months, I wonder if you would wish to reconsider?

Yours

Susan Foley
Manager

4 June 1997

 *A Partridge*

Dear Susan

Can I start by commenting on your addressing me as 'Dear Alan'. I'm aware that you call me Alan during our daily encounters on the premises of the hotel. To be honest, these little moments of familiarity – however forced – have helped me through one of the darkest times of my life. However, I am still a paying guest, and the use of my Christian name in a letter simply oversteps the boundary and sets a poor example. (Michael the handyman started calling me Alan about a month ago, which I'm a bit uncomfortable with. Perhaps you could have a quiet word with him?)

I take your point about the *Daily Mails*. However, I was unaware of this fact, and would not have been ordering the paper if I knew I was paying for it. Please cancel my order; I'll just have to start the day with the *Express*. Not a nice thought, but I am forced to make economies. However, I draw the line at the *Independent on Sunday*, so please continue to supply me with the *Mail on Sunday*.

I accept that the dressing table was not in any way harmed when I moved into the hotel. Perhaps I should be a little more forthright. It was me who 'damaged' it, though ultimately the blame lies elsewhere. I had something in the drawer which was very dear to me. Because I was concerned that my possession might go missing, I locked the drawer. I then had a day of meetings in Cardiff, and when I returned to the room late that night, wanted to open the drawer. I found that I no longer had the key. In the cold light of day, the only rational explanation is that I was pickpocketed – quite probably at Severn View services. As ever, there were several suspicious characters in the cafeteria, including a fat family who kept looking at my car keys.

On my return, I realize I could have telephoned reception and asked for Ben to come and open the drawer with a master key, but it was past 10 p.m. and I didn't want to disturb anyone. To be honest, the meeting in Cardiff hadn't gone well – it was a job presenting a new local magazine show on BBC Choice Wales and it was down to myself and some chap called Gaz Top – and it was clear from the moment that I walked into the room that I was from the wrong side of Offa's Dyke (I wasn't Welsh). This may have added to the exertion I applied in attempting to open the drawer. Please apply the repair cost to my bill and hopefully we can draw a veil over this affair.

As for your discount offer, it is indeed true that I have been offered a monthly rate before. However, it has always been Sophie making the offer, in a half-taunting voice which seems to imply I'll still be here when I'm drawing a pension. I know I can't prove that, as she's very clever about the ambiguous way she does it. I will accept your offer for the next month, though I think it's extremely likely I'll be checking out before then, especially given rumours of a rift between my wife and her body-builder lover.

In return for my commitment, I would accept the following gestures of goodwill:

The sachets of shampoo left in my room, which deliver, at best, one serving, to be replaced by opaque plastic mini-bottles as supplied in Stakis rooms. These are easier to open when in the shower, as opposed to the sachets, which, despite the 'tear here' section, can only actually be opened by biting down on the corner and pulling at the rest of the sachet, an act which on four occasions has led to my having shampoo in my mouth. I feel here like I'm writing some kind of Bill Bryson (a very amusing American author who writes about going on holiday from a gently wry perspective) skit, but the underlying point is a deadly serious one.

One daily bottle of Lowland Glen still mineral water in the mini-bar, clearly marked as complimentary.

A laptop in my room to check emails. To be frank, the year is 1997. It is laughable for a modern business hotel such as yours to not supply a laptop in every room able to download the Internet at the flick of a switch. I had a conversation in the bar last night with a 'dotcom entrepreneur' who was telling me that this is all the next big thing so I suggest you 'web up' – or get left in the 19th century.

Yours

*Alan Partridge*

Mr Partridge

# I'M ALAN PARTRIDGE

## EPISODE 5: TO KILL A MOCKING ALAN

*Radio Norwich*

**Alan**

That was Orchestral Manoeuvres In The Dark with some classic electro-rock from their album *Architecture and Morality*, two subjects I'm sure we could discuss all night. Indeed, the lines are open if you want to call, make a comment on either architecture or morality, two equally hot but differently shaped potatoes. Chips, and … crinkle-cut chips. So, give me a call. Please! Seriously, though, do give me a call. It's 4.50 a.m. The Queen is dead, long live the King's Singers!

*Opening music.*

**Alan**

(*In opening sequence, sitting in his car next to Lynn*) Just pop your elbow on there – (*Alan presses the door-lock down with his elbow*) you've locked the door. Sometimes you don't want to.

*Radio Norwich*

**Alan**

Now, we've had several calls during, er, the last few hours about a humorous comment I made some time ago. Just to reassure you, the Queen is not dead. It was a humorous intro into a song which seems to have been taken a bit too literally by one or two listeners … and a newspaper. Um, so, just to repeat, Queen Elizabeth the Second is not dead … er, unless she went in the night and is yet to be discovered by the maid. Just coming up to seven o'clock. Gadzooks! It's the noble Sir David Clifton of radioshire! *(Dave laughs)* Good morning to you, sir.

**Dave**
Arise, Sir Alan of Partridge!

**Alan**
Yeah. Shall we stop talking in this medieval way?

**Dave**
Yes.

**Alan**
What's on your show today, Dave?

**Dave**
Right! Get dialling if you want to try and cross the Clifton Suspension quiz, the prize money has soared to an incredible eleven thousand pounds. So, just to remind you of …

*As Dave talks, Alan starts daydreaming. He is dancing on stage, dressed in a leather thong and Pringle jumper.*

**Alan**
*(Groggily)* Sexy … *(Dave is silent. Alan suddenly wakes up)* Er, sorry …

**Dave**
Yes, I didn't know you cared, Alan! *(They both laugh)* That was OAP, Old Alan Partridge.

**Alan**
*(Smiling)* I'm not old! I'm forty-three, you cheeky git. *(His smile fades)*

**Dave**
And this is 'Blue Oyster Cult' from the album 'Agents Of Fortune'.

*Alan takes off his earphones and leaves.*

*Linton Travel Tavern. Alan emerges from the lift.*

**Alan**
*(Singing)* The chances of anything coming from Mars / Are a million to one

*Michael is sticking letters into a noticeboard, advertising Alan's presentation.*

**Michael**
Morning –

*Alan raises his finger.*

**Alan**
*(Singing)* But still they come.

**Michael**
*(In a thick Geordie accent)* Morning, Mr Partridge. Hey, 'War Of The Worlds'.

**Alan**
W-Wild woods?

**Michael**
No, 'War Of The Worlds'. I'm playing guess the tune.

**Alan**
Oh, 'War Of The Worlds', that's right, yes.

**Michael**
So, what do you reckon? '3 p.m., An Afternoon With Alan Partridge, with Special Celebrity Guest Star Sue Cook'.

**Alan**
Yeah, can you just put 'plus Sue Cook'? I suppose the good thing about this is, er, you can't hear your Geordie accent on the board. You should turn this into a sandwich board, and you could press on to your chest what you're trying to say. *(Michael nods)* Sort of a primitive form of Stephen Hawkings' voice box. I mean, the good thing about Stephen Hawkings is, he is clear.

*Alan walks over to reception.*

**Jed**
It's you, isn't it? You're Alan Partridge!

**Alan**
*(With a pleased smile)* Yes I am.

**Jed**
Oh, I don't believe it! I'm your biggest fan! Look, I'm coming to your afternoon, I've got my ticket. Shake my hand!

**Alan**
There you go.

*They shake hands while they talk.*

**Jed**
Well what's it about, then, Alan?

**Alan**
It's basically a TV show that's, er, not on TV.

**Jed**
Really?

**Alan**
It's like Kilroy, but with tea, Wagon Wheels and Sue Cook.

**Jed**
Oh, brilliant! I can't tell you what a pleasure it is to shake your hand.

**Alan**
Oh I can see that. You're obviously enjoying yourself!

**Jed**
Yeah! Ha ha!

**Alan**
You're not going to let it go, are you!?

**Jed**
No!

**Alan**
Can I have it back?

**Jed**
Yeah …

*Alan pulls his hand away.*

**Alan**
Thanks.

**Jed**
It's so nice that you let your fans have a chance to meet you, you know. A lot of them don't. No, They forget that it's fans like us that make you what you are.

**Alan**
I don't actually agree with that, but, er … I know some people do, but I – I don't.

**Jed**
I couldn't ask you for your autograph, could I?

**Alan**
Yes, certainly.

*Alan picks up a pen on the counter and starts writing.*

**Alan**
What's your name?

**Jed**
Jed. Jed Maxwell.

**Alan**
Oh, Jed Maxwell. You're no relation to Robert Maxwell?

**Jed**
No.

**Alan**
You're not going to go all fat and steal my pension?

**Jed**
*(Shocked)* No.

**Alan**
Just a joke.

**Jed**
This is so exciting!

*Alan turns away before he's finished writing.*

**Alan**
Actually, could you ask me for this later in front of some important people?

**Jed**
You've done it now.

**Alan**
Yeah, but it just says 'To Jed Maxwell from Alan', you know.

**Jed**
That's better! It sounds like you know me.

**Alan**
Right, OK, well, there you go …

*Alan writes on the paper.*

**Alan**
There. 'To Jed Maxwell from Alan Smith.' Who's he? Never heard of him. *(Jed looks anxious)* I'm expecting two television executives from RTE, who are coming over from Dublin. We're going to be brunching in there *(points to the restaurant)*.

**Jed**
Can I shake your hand again?

**Alan**
No, you've had enough of that. Now, it would make me look very important if you would ask for my autograph in front of them, you know, and shake my hand. *(Jed puts out his hand)* Later.

**Jed**
Never you mind, Alan. You can rely on me.

**Alan**
Thank you.

**Jed**
*(To Susan, behind reception.)* It's Alan Partridge! I can't believe it! Oh, you haven't lost it, Alan. *(Jed hits Alan playfully on the shoulder. Alan looks horrified)* I don't care what they say! *(To Alan)* See you later.

**Alan**
Right. Er, Susan – mm! That's a nice smell. Is that new perfume?

**Susan**
Yes, it is.

**Alan**
Oh! That's very nice. What is it?

**Susan**
My fiancé bought it for me.

**Alan**
Yeah, I didn't ask you who bought it for you. I just asked you what it is.

**Susan**
It's Ralph Lauren.

**Alan**
Can I have a sniff?

**Susan**
Yeah, sure!

*Susan puts out her wrist. Alan grabs hold of it and hoists himself over the counter to sniff her neck. Susan looks embarrassed.*

**Alan**
Mmm. Actually, I shouldn't touch members of staff. Unless I'm reprimanding them, and then I'll put you across my knee and smack your bare bottoms.

*Sophie arrives in reception.*

**Sophie**
Oh, there was a call for you. A Mr Nesshead rang.

**Alan**
Right. Never heard of him. Did he leave a first name?

**Sophie**
No, it was just a Mr P. Nesshead.

**Alan**
Sophie, that, that's a crank call. That's another crank call.

**Sophie**
*(Smirking)* Is it?

**Alan**
Read it back to yourself.

**Sophie**
*(Looking at the piece of paper she's holding, still smirking)* Oh yeah, I can see what he's done now. Shall I put it on the list with all the others.

**Alan**
If you would. Actually, can I have a look at that list. I want to get to the bottom of this. *(Reading)* Mr G. String … Mr Nick Hers …Y. Front … Mr T. Osser? That doesn't even work. T. Osser. Mr B. Ody – this is Bill Oddie. It's not a prank call. Why, why have you put it on there?

**Susan**
Well, we thought it looked like 'body'.

**Alan**
What's rude about a body?

**Sophie**
Tits?

*Alan looks at Sophie, annoyed. Ben arrives.*

**Ben**
Good morning, Sophie.

**Sophie**
Good morning, Ben. Did you sleep well?

**Ben**
*(Smiles at Sophie cheekily)* Yeah. It was a good night last night, wasn't it?

**Alan**
*(Flicking through a magazine)* Of course, if you're professional and you know you're working in the morning then, er, you would have got your head down about midnight.

**Ben**
Oh *(looking at Sophie)* I got my head down all right.

**Alan**
I've had some pretty late-night sessions myself, yeah. In 1976 I er, saw E.L.O. at the Birmingham N.E.C. I was there shouting with everyone else – 'Come back on, E.L.O., and carry on playing.'

**Susan**
Alan, your PA has arrived.

*Lynn appears in the lobby, struggling with a heavy box.*

**Alan**
Oh, right. Lynn! Oh, let me take that. *(Takes the box from Lynn and examines its contents)* Alan Partridge tie and blazer packs and the Wagon Wheels. Excellent. There you go.

*Alan hands the box back to Lynn, who staggers towards the lift.*

**Ben**
Can I take that for you?

**Lynn**
Oh, how very thoughtful! *(She hands the box to Ben)*

**Ben**
You're welcome.

**Alan**
*(With a stern look at Ben)* I'll take it, I'll take it.

*He takes the box off Ben, buckling under the weight.*

**Alan**
This'll happen to you when you hit forty. *(He walks towards the lift)* It's cutting into my fingers.

**Lynn**
Oh, I'm so sorry.

*Alan hands the box back to Lynn.*

**Alan**

Erm, can you smell my breath? *(He breathes into Lynn's face)*

**Lynn**

Ugh. It smells a bit like gas.

**Alan**

Oh. You know what that is, don't you?

**Lynn**

No.

**Alan**

It's those scotch eggs we had at the petrol station.

**Lynn**

*(Breathless, under the weight of the box)* Oh.

**Alan**

What time was that?

**Lynn**

Ooh, about quarter to eleven.

**Alan**

*(Looking at his watch)* Yeah. It, it's going to be in the system till about four.

**Lynn**

Right, well I, I'll buy a packet of mints.

**Alan**

Great.

*The phone rings at reception.*

**Susan**

Excuse me, Alan, there's an urgent call for you.

**Alan**

Right, you go on up, Lynn. *(Alan walks to reception and takes the call)* Hello? Well, right. Well, where are you? *(Angry)* Oh, come on! Oh, this is – oh that, that's bang out of order! Oh, w— I – take a look in the mirror! What? Pardon!? No, no, I've got a better idea. Why don't you shove it up *your* arse?

*Alan slams the phone down and sighs.*

**Alan**

*(To Susan)* Sue Cook's pulled out. Michael, change that to 'An Afternoon with just Alan Partridge'.

**Michael**

Oh, OK. Roger and out.

**Alan**

Yeah, we're not on short-wave radio. Actually, that is quite eye-catching. I suppose that's the opposite of what you were taught in the army. You know, camouflage.

**Michael**

Aye. Well, I also done this course at the army school of commando training, and what we had to do was target identification, right? You had to go into this big building, right, full of people, and you had to identify the hostages and the terrorists, and take out the terrorists. I've sort of employed it here, like *(indicates the writing on the noticeboard)*.

**Alan**

Do you know, I know exactly what you mean, because a couple of weeks ago I was doing a corporate for Allied Dunbar, and, er, afterwards a bunch of us went down to Laser Quest. And in there it's very scary. Seconds count.

**Michael**

Aye.

**Alan**

But, er, you know, really quick-on-the-draw, quick-on-the-draw *(he mimes drawing a gun from a holster)*.

**Michael**

No look, you see, look, here. If you ever find yourself in a situation with a concealed weapon, right, what you want to do is, when you draw your weapon, make it –

*Michael turns away from Alan, his hand by his side. Alan copies him.*

**Alan**
*(Smiling broadly)* It's great, I love this.

*Michael turns to Alan, looking serious. Alan's smile fades.*

**Michael**
It's no laughing matter. *(Resumes his stance)* When you draw your weapon, right, make it as smooth as you possibly can. *(Michael mimes pulling a gun from its holster and points it in front of him. Alan copies)* So draw, hold, fix, and fire. And then just move, and fire, and move, and fire –

*The two men stalk across the lobby firing their guns, Alan copying Michael.)*

**Michael**
– And move, and fire, and move, and fire –

*Lynn steps out of the lift.*

**Alan**
*(Shouting above Michael)* Get back in the lift, Lynn!

*Lynn retreats, looking shocked.*

**Michael**
Get down! Quick, reload! And fire!

*Michael gets up, to find himself pointing at Susan, who has appeared behind reception.*

**Susan**
*(Angrily)* Michael! What do you think you're doing?!

**Michael**
I'm sorry. *(He walks away)*

*Alan moves away to the other end of the lobby looking guilty. He joins Michael at the noticeboard.*

**Michael**
So, do, er, do you want us to take out Sue Cook for you?

**Alan**
God, no! Oh, I see. Er, yeah, fine.

*Michael adjusts the noticeboard. In the restaurant Alan and Lynn are sitting at a table with two men.*

**Alan**
Now I must say I'm very grateful you've come over – big fans of all the Irish … stuff. Um, yep. Love your pop music, Enya, and er, the other one – ripped up the Pope, bald chap? And I think … that's it.

**Aidan**
Well, there's U2, of course.

**Alan**
Yeah, oh, well, yeah. Fantastic. 'Sunday Bloody Sunday'. What a great song. It really encapsulates the frustration of a Sunday, doesn't it? You wake up in the morning, you've got to read all the Sunday papers, the kids are running round, you've got to mow the lawn, wash the car, and you think 'Sunday, bloody Sunday!'

**Aidan**
Yeah, I really hate to do this to you, Alan, but it's actually a song about –

**Paul**
Yeah, bloody Sunday is actually about a massacre in Derry in 1972.

**Alan**
A massacre? Ugh. I'm not playing that again.

**Aidan**
I must say this is a really horrible hotel. Who, who stays in a place like this?

**Paul**
Terrible.

**Aidan**
It's so sterile here.

*Alan looks worried.*

**Lynn**
*(Quietly)* Yes it is.

**Aidan**
The staff are polite but it's as if their smiles are …

**Lynn**
… painted on.

**Aidan**
Yeah, exactly.

**Alan**
Yeah, they are. It's very false, isn't it? Yeah, I mean, the great thing about this hotel is it's situation. It's equidistant between London and Norwich. That's the genius of its location. Even though I do hate it and I don't live here. I just pop in for breakfast.

*Susan arrives at the table.*

**Susan**
Hello, Alan!

**Alan**
Which is why she knows my name. Hello, Susan. *(To Aidan and Paul)* Just clocking the name tag, there. *(To Susan)* Can we have four full British-Isles breakfasts, please.

**Susan**
Certainly. *(She leaves)*

**Alan**
*(Calling after Susan)* You robot! *(To Aidan and Paul)* I wouldn't be surprised if she went into the kitchen, opened her chest up, and er, stuck in a screwdriver and turned her smile up. It's a nice chest, but … full of wires.

*Alan sighs deeply.*

**Aidan**
*(To Paul)* Do you smell gas?

*Alan looks at Lynn.*

**Lynn**
Do you want a mint?

**Alan**
The food'll probably …

**Lynn**
Well, it'll break it down.

**Alan**
It'll break it down, yeah. Actually, I'll pop over and get some ruby grapefruit juice. That'll help, too.

*Alan leaves the table.*

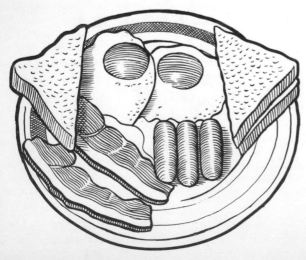

**Lynn**
Where are you from in Ireland?

**Paul**
Well Aidan is from Selbridge, which is near Dublin, and I'm originally from West Cork.

**Lynn**
Oh? Whereabouts?

**Paul**
You know Skibbereen?

**Lynn**
*(Excitedly)* Skibbereen! Oh, I, I used to go there as a little child!

**Aidan**
Really?

**Lynn**
I used to go on nature trails! I used to spot flowers, and Mummy used to say to me –

*Alan returns, carrying a big jug of grapefruit juice.*

**Alan**
There we go! Ruby grapefruit juice. I thought I'd take the whole jug in case it's all quaffed by R2-D2 over there.

*Susan returns to the table.*

**Susan**
Tea? Coffee?

**Alan**
*(With robot voice and hand gestures)* Tea or coffee – tea or coffee … four teas please.

*Alan grins at Aidan and Paul. Susan walks off, looking confused.*

**Aidan**
You ever been to Ireland, Alan?

**Alan**
No, no. I'd love to go.

**Aidan**
It amazes me when people say that and it's only forty-nine quid on a plane.

**Alan**
Yeah, I think that's what puts me off. Well, that's the small talk, now let's get down to business. Now, your programme – *(bad Irish accent)* What's de big oidea?

**Paul**
Well, the 'big oidea' is that we want to produce a programme that appeals to modern mainstream audiences on both sides of the Irish Sea …

*While Paul talks, Alan daydreams. He is dancing in a nightclub, wearing a leather thong and Pringle jumper. Paul and Aidan, dressed as military terrorists and drinking Guinness, are seated at the table in front of him.*

**Alan**
Ooh, scary Irish men. Would you like to recruit me? I like your berets. They're worn by Saddam Hussein, Frank Spencer, and the French.

*Alan wakes up.*

**Paul**
… with some of the culture of both countries.

**Alan**
Yeah. I think the Irish are going through a major image change. I mean, the old image of leprechauns, shamrock, Guinness, you know, horses running through council estates, you know, toothless simpletons, people with eyebrows on their cheeks, badly tarmacked drives – in this country, men in platform shoes being arrested for bombings, lots of rocks, and er, Beamish. I think, I think people are saying, 'Yes, there's more to Ireland than this.' A good slogan for the tourist board – *(in a bad Irish accent)* 'Dere's more to Oireland dan dis.'

*Susan and Michael arrive with their breakfasts.*

**Susan**
There you go.

**Alan**
Oh, thanks very much …

*Susan leaves the table*

**Alan**
(*Shouting after Susan*) … er, you blonde bastard. From the future.

*Susan looks bemused. Alan puts two fingers up at her, then turns back to his food.*

**Alan**
Phwoar, this looks disgusting. Still, might as well eat it. So, er, how many people were killed in the Irish famine?

**Aidan**
Erm, two, two million, and another two million had to leave the country.

**Alan**
Right. I mean, if it was just the potatoes that were affected, at the end of the day, you will pay the price if you're a fussy eater. If they could afford to emigrate then they could afford to eat in a modest restaurant. Could we come 'live from the Blarney-stone'? I'm trying to get an angle on this.

**Paul**
See, Alan, I think you're increasingly moving towards an area we want to move away from.

**Alan**
Yep, you're absolutely right. Live TV can blow up in your face … sorry about that, you must be, er, sick of that.

**Aidan**
What?

**Alan**
You know, being blown up. Bombs.

**Aidan**
I'm from Dublin, not in Dublin.

**Paul**
We're from Dublin.

**Alan**
Oh, right. Well that's where you make them. You've come all this way and it seems to me you're just being a little bit negative.

**Paul**
Well, no …

**Aidan**
No, I was interested in something earlier. Erm, Lynn, what you were talking about when you went to Skibbereen as a child.

**Paul**
That was interesting. Now …

**Aidan**
I think there's something in that.

**Paul**
Yeah.

**Aidan**
I would be interested to know if, at the time, did you have any friends or cousins over while you were there?

*Aidan and Paul talk to Lynn. Jed arrives, pen and paper in hand.*

**Jed**
Excuse me, Mr Partridge, can I have your autograph, please?

**Alan**
Certainly, certainly. What's your name?

**Jed**
Jed. Jed Maxwell.

*Alan signs the paper. The others are deep in conversation.*

**Alan**

Jed Maxwell … Alan Partridge.

*Jed walks off. Alan tries to attract the
attention of Paul and Aidan. Failing,
Alan exhales strongly over the table.
Paul and Aidan recoil, coughing.*

**Alan**

Erm, listen. I think if we … if you stick
around for the 'Afternoon With Alan
Partridge', then afterwards you can talk
to Lynn and me … about Lynn.

*Linton Travel Tavern conference room.
'Knowing Me, Knowing You' theme tune
is playing in the background from Alan's
keyboard. Jed sits in the middle of the audience.
Paul and Aidan stand at the back. Behind a
screen onstage, Alan waits for his cue and steps
out on to the stage just as the music ends. The
crowd applaud politely.*

**Alan**

Ah-haaa!

*Jed claps fiercely.*

**Alan**

Good afternoon, and w— (*The music starts
again, then stops abruptly.*) Sorry …

*The music starts again. Alan disappears
behind the screen and tries to switch off the
keyboard. An Irish jig then a funk rhythm
play. Alan frantically presses buttons, the music
gets faster and louder before finally stopping.
Alan re-enters the stage.*

**Alan**

Sorry about that, a couple of gremlins in
the system, there. Ghosts in the machine.
Perhaps a metaphor for, er … (*pause*)
Good evening! I might as well say this now
– Sue Cook has pulled out.

*Audience groans.*

**Alan**

Yeah. So if anyone wants to leave, then
please, now's the time.

*Alan glances round nervously. Two men get
up and leave.*

**Alan**

Amazing. Absolutely amazing.

*Later.*

**Alan**

Question from that person over there …

**Woman**

Has your career gone off the rails a bit?

**Alan**

Er, no, not you. The woman behind you.

**2nd Woman**

Are you in favour of the death penalty?

**Alan**

(*Smiling broadly*) Yes, I am. Er, for treason
and murder.

*Later.*

**Alan**

Say 'pedestrianization of Norwich city
centre' to anyone and they'll probably look
blankly at you, or – hello?

*A man peers round the door, looks around,
and leaves.*

**Alan**

Why do people do that?

*Later. Alan is sitting on a sofa, arms
outstretched.*

**Alan**

(*Sighs*) Very clever men, both very clever
men. But I don't trust 'em. Gerry Adams
looks like a deputy headmaster and Martin
McGuinness looks like a clown without
make-up.

*Paul and Aidan look appalled.*

*Later. Alan has his blazer off and his shirtsleeves rolled up. A sad-faced old lady stands next to him on the stage.*

**Alan**
OK, let's recap. *(Alan mimes actions as he speaks)* We draw the gun from the holster, knock the safety catch off, there's one in the chamber, and move and fire, and move and fire, and move and fire. The terrorist *(he rests a hand on the woman's shoulder)* is disoriented from the stun grenade, he doesn't know what's going on. Remember the double-tap, bang bang. We have to neutralize the threat by incapacitating the target, and we do that in two areas. The chestal area here, anywhere down the central line, all the major organs are kept. We get one there, he's going down. If you're near enough, you can take a head shot. Again, he's going down.

*Paul and Aidan look very aggrieved.*

*Later.*

**Alan**
One more question, lady at the back …

*An old woman next to Lynn has her hand up. Lynn quickly raises hers.*

**Lynn**
Yes, Alan. I wondered if you had any more Alan Partridge tie and blazer-badge combination packs available for sale.

**Alan**
Yes, I do, as a matter of fact, I've got one here, there we go, they're available at the back or at reception, priced 19.99. Twenty pounds, the, er, penny's just … price … rhetoric …*(Alan sees Paul and Aidan leaving)*. Um, some of the boxes are a bit faded, but I was made promises about storage that were not kept. Erm so, that's all from me, thank-youverymuch, goodbye. Sorry, gotta go.

*Alan dashes out and catches up with Paul and Aidan in the lobby.*

**Alan**
Ah, there you are. So, what did you think?

**Aidan**
Well, I wouldn't be depressed.

**Alan**
Well, I'm not.

**Aidan**
Yeah. When you were berating that old woman …

**Alan**
Yeah! Did you see the look on her face? Classic!

**Aidan**
She was really frightened.

**Alan**
*(Smiling thoughtfully)* Yeah, I know. So, perhaps we could go and chat about all my other ideas in my room.

*Jed is hovering behind Alan with a large grin on his face.*

**Paul**
In your room?

**Alan**
*(Hesitating)* In my room … in my house, where I live.

**Aidan**
Right, where's your house?

*Alan hesitates.*

**Jed**
Just down the road. Our house.

*Jed grins at Alan.*

**Alan**
Yeah … *(to Aidan)* Do you remember that man who came up and asked for my autograph earlier?

*Jed smiles broadly.*

**Aidan**
No.

**Alan**
Good. Erm, this, this is Jed. He's my … driver.

**Aidan**
Oh, hello, Jed.

*Jed shakes hands with Aidan and Paul.*

**Jed**
How do you do.
– And business partner.

**Alan**
*(Uneasily)* Yeah.

**Paul**
Hello.

**Alan**
And we live together. *(Quickly)* We're not gay. I've nothing against them, it's just, as I see it, God created Adam and Eve. He didn't create Adam and Steve. So, I'm kind of a homosceptic.

**Aidan**
Right, well, whatever. I just would like to get out of here as soon as possible.

**Paul**
It'd be nice to go.

**Alan**
Ha ha! Right, let's go.

*They leave. On the way out, Jed shakes Alan's hand, Alan pulls away sharply.*

*In Alan's car, Jed is driving, Alan sits next to him, Paul and Aidan in the back.*

**Alan**
Have you, er, have you seen the film *The Crying Game*?

**Paul**
Yes, I saw it.

**Alan**
Yeah. The, er, the woman with the old, er, tadger. I suppose the sequel will, er, have a man with a … a fanny! Ha!

*They pull up outside the house, and get out of the car.*

**Alan**
This is my house, where I live ...

**Aidan**
It's nice and out the way.

**Alan**
... with Jed. After you. *(Alan looks at a small bowl on the front path)* Bowl of bread, there ...

**Aidan**
What's that for?

**Alan**
Just, er, friends. Um ...

*Alan looks irately at the bowl, then follows everyone else inside. In the hallway, Jed is grinning inanely at Aidan, who is looking rather uncomfortable.*

**Jed**
I'll put the kettle on.

**Alan**
Right.

*Jed leaves.*

**Alan**
Erm, shall we go into the ... *(he peers uncertainly around the first door in the hallway)* yes, the lounge. Grab a pew.

*There is a solitary armchair in the room, surrounded by litter.*

**Alan**
There's only the one chair. The other one, er ... burnt down.

*Paul sits down in the chair. Aidan stands next to him.*

If Jed and I are both in the room at the same time I tend to do this. Just sort of lean on the wall, like that *(he leans on the wall)*.

*Aidan sits on the armchair arm.*

**Alan**
Yeah, perched on the arm. That's a good one. I've not tried that one.

**Aidan**
Very nice picture of yourself on the, on the TV.

**Alan**
I always leave this here *(Alan pats the photo)*, so that way I'm always on the telly!

**Paul**
Who's the other one?

**Alan**
This is, er *(he picks the photo up and looks at it)*, David Copperfield. Yes, he's, er, the American magician. You know, 'I'm an American' *(Alan waves his hands around)*. Yes, he claims to have made the Statue of Liberty disappear. But it's still there. Talking out of his arse.

*Alan puts the photo back.*

**Aidan**
Is that an original?

*Aidan points to a large painting on the wall of a near-naked woman lying next to a motorbike.*

**Alan**
I don't know why I bought this painting. It's got a very haunting quality ... man and machine. I mean, I often look at this in the morning and think, 'Ooh, I'd like to kiss her!'

**Aidan**
*(Getting up)* Actually, do you mind if I use your toilet?

**Alan**
By all means.

**Aidan**
Where is it?

**Alan**
Um, it – well, I'll show you.

*Alan leads Aidan out of the room.*

**Alan**
This is the lobby. I like to read the Sunday papers in here. And, er ...

*From inside a darkened room, we see the silhouettes of Alan, Paul and Aidan as they enter.*

**Alan**
Right, I can never find the light switch in here ...

*Paul switches the light on. The walls of the room are covered with hundreds of pictures of Alan Partridge, Alan Partridge face masks, banners, posters and signs. In the middle of the room, a life-size dummy with an Alan Partridge face mask sits in an armchair. Alan looks aghast.)*

**Alan**
Oh my God. *(He turns to Aidan and Paul and forces a smile)* I am such a bighead! Two things – one, presumably you think I'm a bit odd and you'd like to leave immediately.

**Aidan**
Yeah.

**Paul**
Yes.

**Alan**
And two *(he glances around the room, looking frightened)*, can I come with you?

**Aidan**
No.

**Alan**
Right, OK.

*Jed walks in with a tray of tea.*

**Jed**
Tea's up! I'm sorry, we've only got one mug, we don't get a lot of visitors. Well, you're the biggest, you better have the mug *(he hands it to Aidan)*, you'll have to have this milk jug *(gives it to Paul)*, it's a bit like a mug only it's got a spout on it. I'll have the coffee jar, and there you go, Alan!

*Alan takes a small plastic object, full of tea, from Jed. He looks at it, a pained expression on his face.*

**Paul**
That, that's one of those ball things you have in washing machines.

**Jed**
That's right! It's called an Arielator!

**Alan**
Cheers. *(He sips from his Arielator)* Yeah, I often think I should, er, swallow this whole, and let it slosh round my system, dispensing the coffee.

*Aidan and Paul quietly slip out when Alan isn't looking, closing the door behind them.*

**Alan**
The trouble is, it'd be quite difficult to swallow, and even harder to ... wh- wh- where have they gone?

**Jed**
You don't think my room scared them, do you?

**Alan**
I think they might have found it a bit creepy.

**Jed**
It must be odd being here in a room, surrounded by photos of yourself!

**Alan**
It is a bit, yeah!

**Jed**
I like David Copperfield as well. Not as much as you, though.

**Alan**
No, no, I can see that. He's losing the battle for wall space, isn't he? *(Alan looks closely at some of the photos)* Did you take these on a telephoto lens?

**Jed**
Yeah.

**Alan**
Are you the crank caller?

**Jed**
Yeah.

**Alan**
Yep, thought so.

**Jed**
I'm just a fan, Alan, that's all. Your biggest fan.

**Alan**
Yeah.

**Jed**
I'll show you something.

*Jed turns around and takes his jumper off. He turns back to reveal a huge tattoo of Alan's smiling head on his chest and stomach. He is grinning inanely.*

**Alan**
*(Looking very worried and frightened)* Glory be!

**Jed**
*(His voice getting frantic)* It took fourteen hours! I fainted three times!

**Alan**
Jed, I'll level with you. I'm really scared. Um, in fact, I think I'll go.

*Alan moves towards the door.*

**Jed**
No!

**Alan**
No, it's OK. I'll go.

*Jed leaps in front of Alan, blocking his path.*

**Jed**
*(Almost screaming)* No, stay! Don't go!

**Alan**
*(Backing off)* All right, all right, I'll stay, I'll stay. W-w-what do you want to do?

**Jed**
Let's do an interview.

**Alan**
I think that's a great idea.

**Jed**
Do you really?

**Alan**
I think it's the best idea in the world.

**Jed**
*(Ecstatic)* Oh! Great, right well you can be David Copperfield, and I'll ... *(Jed turns away from Alan, and puts on an Alan Partridge face mask)* ... be Alan Partridge! Ah-haaa!

**Alan**
Oh God!

*Alan makes a dash for it.*

**Jed**
NO! Come back, come back, no –

*Jed lunges and pushes Alan into the wall.*

**Alan**
Not my face! I'm doing a photo shoot for Vision Express!

*Jed gets Alan in a head-lock.*

**Alan**
I'll give you a Chinese burn!

*Alan grinds Jed's wrist with his hands.*

**Jed**
Argh! You bastard!

*Jed pulls his head-lock tighter.*

**Alan**
*(Choking)* Urrrgh ... I can't breathe ... I can't breathe ...

*Jed pulls off the face mask.*

**Jed**
Look, Alan, I just want to be your friend, that's all.

**Alan**

*(Still choking)* I'll be your friend *(he forces a smile)*.

**Jed**

Oh, great. Will you come and see my brother-in-law next weekend?

**Alan**

I'd love to.

**Jed**

Bet you can't guess where he lives.

**Alan**

Erm …

**Jed**

Go on, have a guess.

**Alan**

Er, Nott, Nottingham?

**Jed**

No.

**Alan**

Oh. Er … *(Jed tightens his grasp, Alan's voice gets higher)* Chester?

**Jed**

Where?

**Alan**

*(Speaking with great difficulty)* Ches—Chester. Near north Wales, off the M56.

**Jed**

No, Leeds!

**Alan**

Oh, Leeds.

**Jed**

*(Suddenly looking concerned)* Can you smell gas?

**Alan**

Er, I think that's my breath. I ate a scotch egg. I thought it would have bro—broken down by now but I think I'm slightly constipated. Surprising, really, considering the circumstances.

*Jed releases Alan. Alan staggers away, clutching his neck.*

**Jed**

Sorry, Alan, I didn't know. Are you all right?

**Alan**
Yeah.

**Jed**
*(Enthusiastically)* So, we're friends then?

**Alan**
Best friends.

**Jed**
Oh! In the whole world?

**Alan**
Pretty much, yeah!

*Jed opens the front door, and Alan leaves in a hurry.*

**Alan**
Thank you.

**Jed**
Well, now you know where I live I hope you'll not be a stranger.

*Alan opens his car with his remote lock and paces quickly down the drive. Jed follows closely, grinning.*

**Alan**
Who … de … ver— str—, no, won't be … one …

*Alan gets in his car.*

**Jed**
There'll always be a kettle on here.

**Alan**
Oh, great.

*Alan shuts the door and presses the door lock down firmly. Jed gestures him to wind down the window. Alan winds it down about half way.*

**Jed**
I'll see you next week, then. We'll have that pint.

**Alan**
Yep.

**Jed**
Go and see my brother.

**Alan**
No way, you big spastic! You're a mentalist!

*Alan accelerates away quickly. Jed chases him for a few yards.*

**Jed**
Come back! I'll rip your bloody head off! Come back!

*The road comes to an end. Alan stops his car.*

**Alan**
*(Panicking)* Dead end! Where's the road? Where's the road?

*Alan gets out and runs off, remote locking the car behind him. He dashes down a short path, then leaps over a stile. He sprints across a ploughed field, nearly tripping up.*

**Alan**
*(panting)* He's a mentalist!

*He stops for a few seconds, hands on knees. Then he races off again.*

Help me, someone!

*Alan keeps running.*

*A Partridge*

Dear Lynn

Thanks for your note regarding expenses. There are a few things I need to query. I checked a receipt which I will summarize:

Two cups of tea
A bottle of mineral water – sparkling (!)
Toasted sandwich

This little lot came to the grand total of £7.00. Basically, Lynn – have you been in Littlewoods cafe again? There's a perfectly good Greggs virtually next door who don't charge these kind of prices. By the way, I'm assuming this little feast was alone, and you weren't 'entertaining' your friend Gordon. If you were, it's best to come clean now. Don't double-dick me, Lynn, because I will find out.

The other receipt I need to query is for the skirt you bought for the meeting with Dante Fires. I accept that I pay an allowance to cover clothing. I remember clearly the day you asked if you could purchase three A-line skirts a year under our expenses agreement and I remember agreeing.

However, I was in your area on Sunday evening, trying to find Fernando's house again. I drove past you as you were walking up the hill to church and you were wearing what looked suspiciously like the very skirt for which you're now claiming. Now obviously I'm not saying that you can't wear clothes you bought for work outside of work, that would be miserly, but I am saying that it is unfair to make me pay for them. Basically, attending mass in a skirt clearly voids its use for meetings. I mean, how am I to know you weren't wearing the blouse you bought for the Wrexham Tobacconists Conference when you went for your 'drive' to Oxwitch with your friend Gordon last week?

Obviously, if you can prove that the skirt I saw you in wasn't the skirt you bought for work – perhaps supply some photographic evidence or eyewitness statements from three separate sources (you were surrounded by fellow Baptists on the evening in question) – then the matter is closed. Otherwise, why don't we just say you repay 50 per cent, you can pray in work clothes with a clean conscience and we can move forward.

I accept your point about the late-night phone charges. I'd completely forgotten about asking you to make those anonymous calls to Carol. Come on, Lynn, I wasn't in a good way.

Regarding your increasingly regular comments about your salary barely scraping the minimum wage – fine. I can write you a cheque for ten grand now – or pay monthly into your bank account.

Or I can carry on paying the eight grand the usual way. The way I have for years.

Up to you. All it takes is a phone call. They go right back, Lynn. I will bring you down.

Cheers

Alan

# I'M ALAN PARTRIDGE

## EPISODE 6: TOWERING ALAN

*Radio Studio*

**Alan**

That was Japan, the effeminate futurists from the eighties, with *(in a Japanese accent)* 'Life Can Be Cruel In Tokyo'. It's certainly congested! I'd love to go. In the meantime it's seven o'clock. Ooh, gov'nor, he's got me bang to rights, it's Chief Constable Dave Clifton of Scotland Yard's very own plain-clothed pop force.

**Dave**

Yes, good morning, Alan, yes –

**Alan**

Whoa, whoa, let me finish …'ello 'ello 'ello.

**Dave**

Yeah, I think you're splitting hairs a little bit there, Alan –

**Alan**

Sorry, 'splidding'?

**Dave**

Yeah, splitting, you know.

**Alan**

Sorry, it's diff-difficult to understand you when you say 'splidding', because I know in real life you say 'splitting'. It's interesting, the way you substitute a 'd' for a 't' when you're broadcasting. If you ask me, it's the behaviour of a 'dosser'.

**Dave**

A 'dosser'?

**Alan**

Yes. A 'dosser' and a 'dwad'.

**Dave**
*(Chuckling)* Alan Partridge, there –

**Alan**
There's others, aren't there? There's 'didhead', and there's 'dalendless shid', and if the rumours are to be believed, you're back on the 'boddle'.

**Dave**
Er, this is 'Einstein a Go-Go'.

**Alan**
'Gid'. That's 'git'.

*Opening music*

**Alan**
*(In opening sequence, dressed in a Popeye sailor suit, on a barge)* It's moored in Miami.

*Linton Travel Tavern. Alan meets another guest as he is opening the door to his room.*

**Mike**
Oh. Home Sweet Home! Ha ha ha!

**Alan**
*(Smiling suspiciously)* Yeah.

**Mike**
These corridors!

**Alan**
Yeah, they are, aren't they?

*Mike laughs and walks off. Alan looks at him, irritated. Alan enters his room to find Lynn leaving the bathroom.*

**Lynn**
I just let myself in. I needed the toilet.

**Alan**
Well, close the door. *(Alan shuts the bathroom door)* So, um … everything all right?

**Lynn**
Oh, just a little bit of tummy trouble.

**Alan**
No, I mean generally. Not specifically the toilet.

**Lynn**
Oh, yes. Everything's fine.

**Alan**
Good. Right, so, what have you been doing?

**Lynn**
Oh, well, I've been getting your clothes ready for the country show.

**Alan**
Right.

**Lynn**
And doing a bit of tidying.

**Alan**
*(Looking worried)* Tidying? What do you mean, tidying? *(Alan walks over to the cabinet and slyly opens the top drawer)*

**Lynn**
I just did the bed. I didn't go near … your drawer.

**Alan**
*(slamming the drawer closed)* Good.

*Alan puts on a green body-warmer.*

**Lynn**
By the way, they'd like you to judge the vegetable competition.

*Lynn neatens up the body-warmer on Alan.*

**Lynn**
Very manly. It works.

**Alan**
All I need now is a shotgun. Both barrels. Bang! *(Mimes shooting Lynn)* You'd hit the wall!

*Lynn smiles.*

**Alan**

Yeah. The good thing about this is it has the appearance of a bullet-proof vest, so any fanatics would be put off altogether, or, er, they'd simply go for a head shot. In which case, I won't even know it's happened.

**Lynn**

Alan, I've told you a thousand times, no one wants to kill you. It defies sense! Why?

**Alan**

Because I'm a soft target. They're not going to go for the Prime Minister, he's surrounded by bouncers. Yet everyone knows I will be in Swaffham at 3 p.m., outside the vegetable tent.

**Lynn**

Your mind's flying.

**Alan**

Of course my mind's flying, Lynn. I've been living in a hotel for twenty-six weeks. A hundred and eighty-two days in a Travel Tavern. See, see this, look … *(Alan picks up some paper bags)* Sanitary bags! They put these in my room every day. They know I'm a man! I keep loose Werther's Originals in them. And look at this, see this … *(Alan picks up a cardboard box from the floor and empties its contents on to the bed)* That is one hundred and eighty-two bottles of body lotion. I was going to sell them at a car boot sale. I can't remember what it's like to dial a number from a telephone without hitting '9' first. *(Alan picks up the phone and dials)* Hello? Is that reception? Sorry, I must have hit a zero. *(He hangs up)* Lynn, I was at a friend's house the other night. I was trying to make a phone call, I thought there was something wrong with the phone. I'd been hitting '9', Lynn! I felt like a … ruddy idiot! I just left, I couldn't stay there after that.

**Lynn**

Would you like a Horlicks?

**Alan**

*(Looking miserable)* Yes, please.

**Lynn**

I'll make you a Horlicks.

*Lynn goes over to the cabinet and opens the drawer. Alan kicks it shut from the bed.*

**Alan**

Not in that drawer.

*Lynn opens the other drawer. There is a knock on the door.*

**Alan**

Come in.

*Sophie walks in, carrying a large box.*

**Sophie**

Hello, Mr Partridge. Everything all right with the room?

**Alan**

Yes, marvellous.

**Sophie**

This box arrived for you *(she puts it down on the cabinet)*.

**Alan**

Oh, super. I've been trying to get my hands on this box off Carol for months.

**Sophie**

*(Picking up a photo from in the box)* Is that you?

**Alan**

No, that's my daughter, Denise. Bit of a rebel.

*Sophie starts shaking with silent laughter.*

**Alan**

What's so funny?

**Sophie**
Nothing. It's just that she really, really looks like you.

**Alan**
*(Irritated)* Yeah, well, it's not me. You know, have I got a pierced navel?

**Sophie**
I don't know.

**Alan**
Well, I haven't. *(He searches through the box)* Ooh, great. Nigel Rees' book of Humorous Graffiti. This is the Koran for the after-dinner speaker, it really is. I mean, quick tip for you Sophie, if you're ever doing an after- dinner speech, you say, 'My Lords, Ladies and Gentlemen, sorry I'm late, I just popped to the toilet. *(Alan flicks through the book)* And while I was in there, I saw some graffiti and it said "I used to be indecisive, but now I'm not so sure!"'

*Alan laughs.*

**Alan**
Straight away, you've got them by the jaffers. It's witty. It's not like a lot, a lot of the graffiti you see these days in toilets. Just crude, like, you know, 'touch my this', 'suck my such-and-such', 'something all over my whatever'.

**Sophie**
My penis is so-and-so.

**Alan**
*(Looking uncomfortable)* Yeah, yeah. Oh … *(he picks up a brown folder from the box and examines it, frowning)* There we go, Lynn. Tony Hayers. I tell you something, Sophie, you've not witnessed pure evil until you've looked into the eyes of a man who's just cancelled your second series.

**Sophie**
I think he looks quite nice.

**Lynn**
The devil can take many forms.

**Alan**
*(With an irritated glance at Lynn)* All right, Lynn. *(To Sophie)* She's a member of a Baptist church. I think they're a bit – *(Alan makes the sign of the cross).*

**Sophie**
*(To Lynn)* Sorry about saying 'penis', earlier.

**Lynn**
Oh, no.

**Alan**
No, no. Don't worry about that. Trapped her finger in a car door once, she swore like a docker.

*Lynn giggles.*

**Sophie**
I brought you some more stationery. I'll just put it in the drawer.

*Sophie opens the drawer in the cabinet. Alan leaps off the bed, and slams the drawer shut before falling on his face on the floor. He climbs back on the bed, clutching his wrist.*

**Alan**
I'd rather you didn't –

**Sophie**
Are you all right for body lotion?

**Alan**
Yeah, sure. I've got one hundred and eighty-two bottles.

*As Sophie leaves she opens the drawer and steals a glance inside.*

**Sophie**
Bloody hell! *(She laughs)*

*She runs out. Alan looks after her, anxiously.*

*Swaffham Country Fayre. Alan is giving
a commentary on the PA system.*

**Alan**

Clydesdale horses, twelve hands high.
Hands, of course, the ancient system for,
er, measuring horses that's been around
since medieval times. 'Course, tape
measures, in those days, were viewed with
suspicion. Anyone who could unfurl fifteen
feet of thin sheet metal from a pocket-sized
box would have been killed as a witch. It's
'er, tragic, really, to think that girls, some as
young as the ones holding balloons over
there, would have been burnt at the stake.
May God have mercy on their souls.

*Inside a tent. Alan is judging the entries in a
vegetable competition. A man follows him with
a notepad.*

**Alan**

Nice tray of plums, there. Just, just put 'nice
plums'. This is lovely, this *(stroking some
leeks)*, this is sort of like, like an old lady's
hair. An old lady's blonde hair. Quite
attractive. I mean, put that down as a plus
point. These are nice *(pointing to some
courgettes)*. Got a nice, kind of glossy finish.
I knew a bloke who had fingers like that
once. He's dead now – an Irish navvy – of
angina. Wasn't pleasant. Cabbages, don't
like cabbages at all. Come on, let's get
through this lot. *(Alan walks quickly past the
cabbages)* Cabbages, all one and the same.
Take your pick. I'm not sure about these
*(looking at some onions)*, because I don't
know whether this protrusion is a good or
bad thing. Actually *(Alan holds up an onion
by the stalk)* this would make a very good
murder weapon because you could beat
someone to death, then eat the evidence.
Agatha Christie's probably already thought
of that one. 'The Onion Mystery' ...
'The Onion Murders'. Good idea for a
programme. *(The man with the notepad looks*

*concerned)* Not that the BBC would
commission it – they wouldn't know a good
onion idea if I hit them over the head with
it ... and then ate the evidence.

*Alan provids a commentary on the PA system
to various scenes at the fair.*

**Alan**

Fire! Fire! The fayre's on fire! *(Everyone
ignores him)* Um, I'm joking of course, it's
not, but that's the kind of thing you can see
from er ... the ... oh, what are they called?
The local fire brigade, I don't know the
district, in tent four. My own tip is 'never
throw water on a fat fire', it'll take your face
off. Yes, the stocks are now open for custard-
pie throwing. Tell you who I'd like to put in
the stocks – Tony Hayers. He's the Chief
Commissioning Editor of BBC Television.
And it wouldn't be custard pies I'd be
throwing at him, either. I'd like to throw
cabbages, hot Bovril and gravel. I don't
know if you're familiar with BBC
commissioning policy, they, they are
obliged to contract out a certain percentage
of their programmes to independent
programme-makers, and ... I mean ...
you're not even listening, are you? You
people. Er, I'm going. It's all wrapping up
in about an hour, anyway, so I don't think
you'll miss me. Thank you, goodbye.

*Alan puts the microphone down on the table
and walks off.*
*In the hotel lobby, Lynn is busy reading.*

**Alan**

Hello, Lynn.

**Lynn**

Oh, sorry, I was just doing the catalogues.

**Alan**

Let's have a look. *(Alan takes it off her and
starts flicking through it)* You looking at the
big girdle section?

*Lynn looks embarrassed.*

**Alan**
Interesting, isn't it, that these women are technically models. Where do they get these men from? Who smiles at a Black and Decker Workmate, for goodness' sake?

*He puts down the catalogue and sits down.*

**Lynn**
How did the country show go, Alan?

**Alan**
Erm … I walked off.

**Lynn**
Who's upset you this time?

**Alan**
Pfff … Just … people. I just … hate the general public.

*The phone rings at reception.*

**Susan**
*(Calling over)* Excuse me, Alan, there's a phone call for you.

**Alan**
Who is it?

**Susan**
It's Sue Cook.

**Alan**
*(Walking over to reception)* Oh. What does she want? Hello, Sue, it's Alan. Yeah, Sue, take the fag out of your mouth, I can't tell what you're saying. *(Perking up)* What? Really? Oh my God. *(He puts his hand over the receiver)* Tony Hayers is dead!

**Lynn**
*(Getting up and punching the air)* Yes!

**Alan**
He, um, fell off the roof of his house trying to remove the aerial. Broke his neck!

*Alan grins at Lynn then speaks into the phone.*

**Alan**
So, who's replaced him as head of programmes? Chris Feathers?

*Alan makes a silent cheer and raises his fist.*

**Alan**
*(Composing himself)* That's an interesting choice. Right, I mean, he's definitely dead. Right. Presumably, there's going to be some sort of funeral. They're cremating him, good, good. Right, um, and will Chris Feathers be at the funeral? *(Gives a thumbs-up sign to Lynn)* Right, right. Can you hold on a moment, Sue? *(Alan puts his hand over the receiver and talks to Susan)* Chris Feathers likes me! He likes *me*! *(Smiling at Lynn)* Doesn't he, yeah? He likes you! He used to flirt with Lynn all the time! *(Lynn giggles)* Mind you, that was twenty years ago. *(Lynn stops smiling abruptly)* *(Back on the phone)* Right, I think I'll be going along, yes. Well, it's the least I can do. All right, thanks, Sue. You can puff away now.

*Alan puts the phone down, and turns to Lynn.*

**Alan**
Kiss my face! *(Alan strokes his cheek)*

**Lynn**
*(Holding her arms open)* Alan!

**Alan**
*(Holds his hand out)* Put it there, Lynn.

*They shake hands. Lynn walks off as Mike enters the lobby.*

**Mike**
Hello. *(Chuckles slightly)*

**Alan**
Hello. You going to the lift too?

**Mike**
Lift, yes.

*In the lift, Alan presses the button.*

**Alan**
First?

**Mike**
Yes. *(Chuckles)*

*The silence is broken every few seconds by a chuckle from Mike. Alan looks increasingly anxious.*

**Alan**
Ping.

**Mike**
*(Still smiling)* Pardon?

**Alan**
Oh, I'm just doing the noise the door makes –

*The lift pings, and the doors open.*

**Mike**
Oh! *(Chuckles)* Excellent.

*Alan steps in front of Mike.*

**Alan**
Neeow.

**Mike**
Oh, it's like cars, this!

**Alan**
That's right.

**Mike**
Excellent!

*Mike walks off, laughing. Alan looks annoyed.*

*Tony Hayers' funeral. Alan wanders into the reception area.*

**Alan**
Chris? Chris Feathers? Hi!

**Chris**
Alan! How are you?

*They shake hands.*

**Alan**
Very well, very well. I mean, considering.

**Chris**
Oh, yes. Brilliant man.

**Alan**
Oh, yes. He had a second-class honours degree in Media Studies from Loughborough University. What a waste.

**Chris**
Did you know they've asked me to take over Tony's job as er, Chief Commissioning Editor?

**Alan**
I had heard … something. Can, can I –

**Chris**
Just two minutes.

*Chris walks over to someone else.*

**Alan**
Right.

*Alan turns around, revealing 'Castrol GTX' written on the back of his black bomber jacket.*

**Alan**
*(Alan walks over to Tony's widow)* Jane.
*(They shake hands)*

**Jane**
Thank you for coming.

**Alan**
Can I offer you my deep, deep … despair, on this very bad day.

**Jane**
Thank you.

**Alan**
I mean, how are you coping?

**Jane**
Well, terrible, really. We'd booked to go on holiday next week.

**Alan**
*(With over-exaggerated sympathy)*
Oh, bugger!

**Jane**
He'd have been forty-one next month.

**Alan**
God. All those people who go around saying 'Life begins at forty'. They're notable by their absence. The nerve. Were you close?

**Jane**
He was my husband.

**Alan**
Yes, yes, of course. What was he doing on the bloody roof?

**Jane**
He was getting the aerial down because we were moving.

**Alan**
Yeah, I know. I was being rhetorical. I mean, did he actually bring the aerial down with him?

**Jane**
Yes, he did.

**Alan**
Comforting to know that the last thing he did was an act of kindness.

**Jane**
Thank you for the travel clock.

**Alan**
Oh, you got it? Littlewoods are very quick, aren't they?

**Jane**
They are, yes.

**Alan**
Anyway, um, commiseration's, hang on in there, I'm sure you'll bounce back. And if there's anything I can do, just ask. Apart from heavy lifting, I've got a bit of a bad back.

*Alan's mobile phone rings.*

**Alan**
*(Hesitating)* Er – should I leave that?

**Jane**
Yes –

**Alan**
I'd better answer it. *(Cheerfully)*
Hello, Partridge?

**Jane**
*(Annoyed)* Can you go outside?

**Alan**
Yeah, all right, all right.

*Alan moves towards the door.*

**Alan**
Oh, Curry's, great. No, I was, er, just, just talking to a, to a widow, yeah. I want two speakers for an Alba stereo syst— hello?

*Alan looks at his phone.*

**Alan**
Battery.

*He walks over to Chris Feathers, who is standing alone. Just as he gets there, someone else goes over and shakes Chris's hand. Alan recoils.*

**Chris**
Peter!

**Peter**
Chris!

**Chris**
Oh, Alan, have you met Peter? He's just revamped our news and current affairs.

*Alan looks at Peter and shrugs. He turns to Chris.*

**Alan**
Chris –

**Chris**
– just two minutes, two minutes.

*Chris leaves again. Alan looks agitated.*

**Alan**
Right.

**Peter**
Bad day.

**Alan**
Right, right, mm.

**Peter**
Ironic, really. He worked in television his whole life, and died getting an aerial off a roof. So in the end, it was television that killed him.

*Alan keeps glancing over Peter's shoulder towards Chris.*

**Alan**
Yep, very good, that, yeah. Have you got a battery for an Ericsson?

**Peter**
Er, no, sorry. I wonder if he's up there now, looking down on us?

**Alan**
What, on the roof? Oh, I see! You mean in heaven … with the apostles … *(Alan is still looking for Chris Feathers)*

**Peter**
Interesting thing about news and current affairs –

**Alan**
Would it be terribly rude to stop listening to you and go and speak to somebody else?

**Peter**
No, no.

*Alan chases after Chris, who is talking to Jane.*

**Chris**
Jane. *(He notices Alan hovering behind him)* Oh, Alan! Have you met Jane?

**Alan**
Yeah, I've done her.

**Chris**
Oh, oh good.

**Alan**
Chris, can I just –

**Chris**
– just two minutes.

*Chris walks off again.*

**Alan**
*(Annoyed)* He keeps saying that!

*Alan finds himself alone with Jane again.*

**Alan**
I'm just trying to … ahem, trying to think of something to say.

**Jane**
Well, there's nothing to say.

**Alan**
Well –

**Jane**
No, no. There's nothing you can say.

**Alan**
Well hang on, hang on. Erm … it's all … a pain in the arse, isn't it? Have you got a battery for an Ericsson?

**Jane**
No!

**Alan**
No, right. Of course not.

*Alan keeps glancing agitatedly across to Chris.*

**Jane**
Is something the matter?

**Alan**
Erm … I want to go and talk to him over there.

**Jane**
*(Annoyed)* Well, go and talk to him, then.

**Alan**
Thank you. Oh, erm –

*Alan walks over to intercept Chris. On the way, he turns back to Jane and makes a sobbing gesture.*

**Alan**
Er, Chris, Chris, can we have a chat?

**Chris**
Yes, of course, of course. Dreadful business.

**Alan**
Oh, awful, awful business.

*Alan whistles and mimes someone falling. The mime finishes with a loud crash just as Jane pushes past Alan and Chris.*

**Alan**
Oh, sorry.

**Chris**
I tell you what; can you see me tomorrow, in the office?

**Alan**
I'd love to.

**Chris**
I need to pick your brains.

**Alan**
Pick away, pick away.

**Chris**
You've got the common touch.

**Alan**
Thank you.

**Chris**
You've been away too long. Alan, I want you back on the telly.

**Alan**
*(Punching the air with both fists)* Jurassic Park! That is … that is fantastic. I mean, great.

**Chris**
The old team, eh?

*They shake hands.*

**Alan**
Absolutely, yeah.

**Chris**
Well, I'll see you tomorrow.

*Chris walks off. Alan with a big smile on his face turns to leave, stopping to shake hands with another mourner on the way out.*

**Alan**
Terrible news, terrible news.

*Alan steps out into the sunshine, singing.*

**Alan**
*(Singing)* Life isn't everything …

*Linton Travel Tavern. Alan enters the lobby singing, carrying a large cardboard box.*

**Alan**
*(Singing)* Life is the name of the game,
and I wanna play the game with you, baa
ba ba ba …

*Alan places the box on the counter at reception.*

**Susan**
How was your –

**Alan**
*(Singing)* Bam!

*Susan looks shocked, then regains her smile.*

**Susan**
How was your day, Alan?

**Alan**
I went to a funeral, which was very sad, and
then I popped into 'Hi-fi Serious' to pick
up a top-of-the-range Bang & Olufson
stereo system. Do you like it?

**Susan**
Well, it's in a box, Alan.

**Alan**
Bit like Tony Hayers! Er … Susan, Susan,
will you go out with me?

**Susan**
No.

**Alan**
Would you go out with me if I was younger
and more attractive?

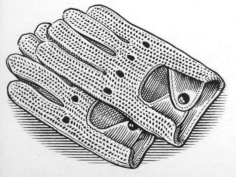

**Susan**
Erm, yes, I think I probably would.

**Alan**
I better go and build that time-travel
gymnasium, then. I'll come back aged
twenty-five, built like a brick shit-house!
Then you'll kiss me.

**Susan**
If you'll excuse me a moment, Alan, I have
to leave the desk unattended.

*Michael walks in carrying a large box.*

**Michael**
There you go, Mr Partridge *(he places the
box on the counter)*, I'm going to have to
make two trips, man, I keep dropping bits
of it. *(Alan looks worried)* Right, I'll go and
get your other bits and pieces.

**Alan**
OK.

*Ben arrives.*

**Ben**
Bang & Olufson? Wow, that's serious, man.
Whose is it?

**Alan**
It's, er, it's mine.

**Ben**
I didn't know you were into music. I know
you're a DJ, but I've heard your show.

**Alan**
Oh, yeah. I mean, I like all the bands. I like
… I've got a broad taste, you know. From
the Britpop bands like UB40, Def Leppard,
um, right back to classic rock, like Wings.

**Ben**
Who's Wings?

**Alan**
They're only the band the Beatles could
have been.

**Ben**
Well, I love the Beatles.

**Alan**
Yeah, so do I.

**Ben**
What's your favourite Beatles album, then?

**Alan**
Tough one. I think I'd have to say 'The Best of the Beatles'.

**Ben**
Gum? *(Offers some chewing gum to Alan)*

**Alan**
Yeah, cheers. So, er, who's your favourite singer, then?

**Ben**
Oh, anything, really, you know. Frank Sinatra, Kurt Cobain.

**Alan**
Who's he?

**Ben**
Nirvana. Blew his head off with a gun?

**Alan**
Why?

**Ben**
He was depressed.

**Alan**
Why, were they not very good?

**Ben**
No, they were great.

**Alan**
Oh. Someone should've told him!

*Mike walks past and sees the hi-fi on the counter.*

**Mike**
Hello again! Ooh, what's that?

**Alan**
Bang & Olufson.

*Mike laughs loudly and walks off. Alan looks at him anxiously.*

**Alan**
Uh, Ben, can you take this up to my room?

**Ben**
Yeah, sure. No problem.

*Ben raises his hand for a high-five. Alan raises his higher, and misses. He walks off towards the lift.*

**Alan**
Cheers …

**Mike**
I'll hold the door for you.

**Alan**
Thank you.

**Mike**
Hold tight!

**Alan**
Yeah.

*The lift doors close and the two men stand side by side. Every few seconds, Mike laughs out loud. Alan gets increasingly agitated with each laugh.*

**Mike**
Nearly there!

*Alan starts laughing with him, and they both start laughing louder. As the lift doors open, Mike walks off with a particularly loud chuckle.*

**Alan**
Unbelievable.

*BBC Television Centre. Alan and Lynn are in Chris Feathers' office. Chris and Alan laugh together.*

**Alan**
Join in, Lynn.

*Lynn smiles.*

**Alan**
So, Chris, what's your strategy?

**Chris**
God alone knows, Alan.

**Alan**
Can I say one word to you? Streamlining.

**Chris**
That's ... sacking people?

**Alan**
Well, basically, yeah.

**Chris**
*(Looking at some papers)* Well, where do I start?

**Alan**
Who was that man who was boring me at the funeral?

**Chris**
Oh, Peter Linehan? Well, he's just revamped News and Current Affairs.

**Alan**
Yeah, but he's finished revamping it now. So, er, give him a painting of a Spitfire and let him go.

**Chris**
OK.

**Alan**
*(Also checking names on the list)* And ... er, Susan Picardie. Know her?

**Chris**
Oh yeah, documentaries. Feminist, with the flat chest. *(Smiling at Lynn)* She doesn't have that problem, does she?

**Alan**
No.

*Lynn looks embarrassed and crosses her arms.*

**Alan**
Don't crush them, Lynn!

**Chris**
*(To Lynn)* How are you? Did you get married?

**Lynn**
Er, no.

**Chris**
No, I got divorced. Yeah, well ...

**Alan**
I'm sure Lynn would be happy to go for a drink with you, if that'd help things.

**Lynn**
*(Quietly)* Yes, yes.

**Alan**
Do you want to make a note of that, Lynn? 'Go for drink with head of programmes'. Great. Right, let's get down to business. Can we talk about *me*?

**Chris**
Yeah, all right! What can I do for you?

**Alan**
Right, bottom line, Chris. I want a six-month contract at the BBC to make television programmes.

**Chris**
No, Alan, I'm not going to give you a six-month contract.

**Alan**
*(Furious, Alan stands up)* Yeah, you're just like all the rest, aren't you? You sit there on your fat, spotty behind, in dead man's chair, leching at her like a piece of meat –

**Chris**
Alan, Alan, Alan! I'm not going to give you a six-month contract, 'cause I have prepared a five-year one. *(He produces a document from his desk)*

**Alan**
*(Grinning widely, his voice a little choked)* Yeah? That's brilliant.

**Chris**
Two hundred thousand pounds a year.

**Alan**
That's a million pounds. *(Raising a fist in the air)* Jurassic Park! I'm sorry for saying you were fat, before. I just mean you're big-boned.

**Chris**
*(Chuckling)* That's all right. How about celebrating? Let's get a bottle of Bolly!

**Alan**
Sod that! Let's have some champagne! On me. Go on, Lynn, go and get it.

*Lynn leaves.*

**Chris**
Right then.

*Chris begins to sign the contract and Alan turns to look out of the window. Chris coughs three or four times, the last time rather painfully. When Alan turns around, Chris is frozen, slightly slumped over his desk, pen still in hand.*

**Alan**
I suppose you want to check the small print … come on, Chris! You must have seen a dozen contracts like that …

*Chris slumps sideways*

*(In mock fear)* Oh no! … Oh, no … Chris? *(Really scared now)* Chris? Oh God. Um –

*Alan goes over to Chris and listens in his ear.*

Er *(shouting into Chris's ear)* Hello, Chris! A-Are you dead? Erm, oh God.

*Alan picks up the phone on his desk and dials. He notices that the contract is unsigned and Chris still has the pen in his hand. Alan looks around slyly then hangs up.*

…finish signing it, there. *(Alan pushes Chris's hand across the paper)* Chris …

Feathers … Bit tedious, all this contract business. Oh, you've, er, got the date wrong, there, so just … initial that … my copy *(Alan signs another contract underneath, still using Chris's hand)* Er … here's to the future! *(He picks up a glass and clinks it with Chris)* Sorry …

*In Alan's room, Alan and Lynn are admiring a banner hanging from the ceiling, which reads 'Thank You Staff, and Goodbye'. On the cabinet are various party foods.*

**Alan**
*(Looking at the banner)* You think that's all right? Not too sentimental?

**Lynn**
No.

**Alan**
*(Indicating his brand-new hi-fi)* Excellent. Do you want to, er, you want to put something on?

**Lynn**
Oh, yes.

**Alan**
I'll just go and, er, check the party bags.

*Alan goes into the bathroom, where there is a collection of sanitary bags. Alan is filling each with Werther's Originals and Cheesy Wotsits. Music starts playing.)*

**Alan**
What's this, Lynn?

**Lynn**
It's the theme tune from 'Black Beauty'.

**Alan**
It's brilliant!

*Lynn nods. There is a knock on the door.*

**Alan**
Hello? *(Alan opens the door and Michael enters, wearing an oriental silk shirt)* Ah, Michael!

327

**Michael**
(Loudly) Aye-aye, Mr Partridge!

**Alan**
Uh, Michael (indicating a half-finished bottle of cider that Michael is carrying), do you want me to take that?

**Michael**
Er, no, I, I, I've had a fair bit already. I'll stick with it, man.

**Alan**
That's fine, but it does preclude you from the alcohol that I've provided.

**Michael**
(Sitting down in the armchair in the corner of the room) Oh, you're all right. I'm all right with the scrumpy! Aye!

**Alan**
Right.

Michael takes a big gulp from his cider.

**Alan**
That's a nice shirt.

**Michael**
(Getting up and turning round to show Alan the back) Aye, I got married in this. Do you like it? I got it from Manila.

**Alan**
I didn't know you were married.

**Michael**
Aye. I married a Filipino lassie, like. It didn't work out. She didn't like Newcastle and she didn't fit in with the culture.

**Alan**
Right, so she's gone back home?

**Michael**
No, she moved to Sunderland. She's shacked up with my brother.

**Alan**
Oh, right.

**Lynn**
Er, Michael, would you like a miniature scotch egg?

**Michael**
Oh, not for me, pet, I've got myself a steak and kidney pie. (He produces the pie from his back pocket) Oh, look at that, I've sat on the bastard, would you believe it.

**Alan**
(Quietly, to Lynn) Er, can you keep an eye on him?

**Lynn**
Yes.

There is another knock on the door.

**Alan**
Oh, thank God for that.

**Michael**
Aye-aye.

Alan answers the door to Mike, carrying a bottle of white wine.

**Mike**
Hello! (Laughs)

**Alan**
Ah! Come in!

**Mike**
Thank you very much, thank you.

*Mike puts his bottle down on the cabinet. He opens the drawer and laughs out loud at its contents. Alan shuts it quickly, looking annoyed.*

**Alan**
You want a glass of wine?

**Mike**
Oh, thank you very much. Cheers! Thank you.

**Alan**
*(Quietly, to Lynn)* What's he doing here?

**Lynn**
You said invite a guest.

**Alan**
Lynn, that's just a phrase, I didn't mean it.

**Mike**
Nice room.

**Michael**
So, er, who are you?

**Mike**
Oh, er, Mike Sampson.

*Mike and Michael shake hands.*

**Mike**
Nice to meet you.

**Michael**
Oh, hey, I'm Michael an' all!

**Mike**
Oh! Ha ha ha ha!

*Mike and Michael laugh. Alan and Lynn join in, half heartedly.*

**Michael**
So, have you got a job?

**Mike**
Oh, yes, yes. I supply fitted kitchens.

**Michael**
Oh, aye?

**Mike**
Um, the funny thing is, that I've been in the business for fifteen years, but I can't actually cook!

*Michael laughs heartily. Lynn and Alan chuckle lightly.*

**Mike**
You see a cookery book here *(picks up a book from the table)* it wouldn't be much use to me!

*Michael laughs again.*

**Michael**
Mr Partridge, he said he sells kitchens, right, for fifteen year', but he cannot cook!

**Alan**
*(Smiling)* I know, I heard him, yeah.

**Michael**
Then, right, he sees the cook book, and he says, 'That'd be no good to me, that, would it?'

**Alan**
*(His smile fading)* I know, I heard him.

**Michael**
Ah, come on, lighten up, you stuffy get.

*Michael bites into his squashed pie.*

**Alan**
*(Quietly, to Lynn)* Lynn, this is terrible. This is terrible.

*There is a knock on the door.*

**Alan**
Oh good, great.

*He opens the door to Susan, Ben and Sophie.*

**Alan**
Oh, the cavalry! Come on in! Great, come in. Look at the sign, there, it says 'Thank You Staff, and Goodbye'.

*Lynn hands everyone drinks.*

**Alan**

Oh right, marvellous. It's all happening now. This is Michael, he sells kitchens.

**Mike**

Yes, I was just saying to the others, I sell kitchens but I can't actually cook myself!

*Mike and Michael laugh loudly again. Alan looks irritated.*

**Michael**

Right, and then he spies that cook book, right, and he says, 'That'd be no use to me, man!' He's crackers, man.

**Ben**

Er … so, Mike, where do you live?

**Mike**

I come from Acton, in west London.

**Sophie**

Is it nice?

**Mike**

Yes, it's quite nice … few too many blacks.

*Mike chuckles. The others look stunned. Mike is shown out of the door by Alan.*

**Alan**

If you don't mind, it's just some people find what you said, you know, a bit racist.

**Mike**

Mmm. *(Laughs)*

**Alan**

Party bag?

*Alan hands Mike a sanitary bag.*

**Mike**

Ooh, thank you very much. Bye bye.

*Mike walks off, chuckling to himself.*

**Alan**

Watch the fire hose!

*Mike laughs even more when he walks past the fire hose. Annoyed, Alan turns back into his room to find the other guests huddled round the drawer in the cabinet. Everyone jumps back when they see Alan. There is an awkward pause. Lynn suddenly starts to sing and dance a Scottish jig.*

**Alan**

*(Watching Lynn, arms folded, unimpressed)* Extraordinary. So, er, what do people think about the pedestrianization of Norwich city centre?

**Michael**
(*slurring drunkenly*) Eh – aye, I, I reckon it's a really good idea, like.

**Alan**
Mmm. You're wrong …

**Michael**
Oh, man, what about, you know, mothers with pushchairs and little bairns and that, you know?

**Alan**
Oh, Michael, you've got a lot to learn.

**Michael**
(*Getting angry*) No, man, look, it's *you* who's got a lot to learn, right, because folks should be giving up their cars –

**Susan**
Michael, Michael! Mr Partridge is still a guest in this hotel. Now I think perhaps you've had just a little bit too much to drink, and maybe it's time that you should leave.

**Michael**
Oh, well, if that's how you all feel.

*Michael walks off, grumbling. Alan looks smug.*

**Susan**
(*To Ben and Sophie*) Now, you two can stop giggling.

**Alan**
(*Smirking, he sidles up to Ben and Sophie*) Dunno what her problem is!

**Susan**
(*Screaming at Alan*) I'll tell you what my problem is! Having to listen to your crap for the last six months! You've been in this hotel for a hundred and eighty-two days, you little shit!

*Susan is advancing towards Alan, who is backing off. He picks up a drink, avoiding eye contact.*

**Susan**
(*Still screaming*) Ben and Sophie, I want you on reception! (*They hurry out*) And you! Check-out is twelve noon tomorrow!

**Alan**
Do you want one of these? (*Offers her a party bag*)

**Susan**
A sanitary bag!? What are you trying to say!?

*Susan slaps Alan hard around the face and storms out.*

**Alan**
(*To Lynn*) I think that went quite well. Shall we clear up? I fancy an early night.

**Lynn**
Shall I put 'Black Beauty' on again?

**Alan**
Yes, we can, er, we can clear up while we listen to 'Black Beauty'. Great.

*Lynn puts on the hi-fi and the music starts. Lynn picks up a couple of unfinished glasses of wine.*

**Lynn**
Down the sink?

**Alan**
Yep.

**Lynn**
OK, down the sink.

*Lynn goes to the bathroom. Alan picks up the paper plates and turns the music up. He starts daydreaming – he is dancing on stage to the theme tune of 'Black Beauty', wearing a leather thong and Pringle jumper. This fades into Alan running happily through a field of corn.*

# AGREEMENT

Dated     **18 July 2002**     *So far so good.*

Between     **ALAN PARTRIDGE** — *So far so good.*

(hereafter called **'the Author'**)
of the one part and

       **TURRET PRESS**

whose registered office is at

12-15 Fernlea Road
(Opposite the library)
Norwich
NR9 4EZ

(hereafter called **'the Publishers'**)
~~of the other part~~

The Agreement concerns the following work:     *Oh for Christ's sake!*

Title:        **BOUNDING BACK**    *BOUNCING BACK!*
Description:    An autobiography.    *BOUNCING BACK!!*

(hereafter called **'the Work'**)

*I only hope this is a mistake and not a creative suggestion along the lines of "Have you considered a bit of help with the writing" after I turned in the first manuscript.*

1. **Grant of rights**

    (a)   In return for the payments set out below, the Author grants to the Publishers for the legal term of copyright (including any renewals or extensions) the sole and exclusive right to reproduce, exploit and sell and to ~~licence others to~~ reproduce, ~~exploit~~ and sell all or part of the Work in any printed form in the English language, exclusively in the UK and Commonwealth ~~including Canada~~ (see appendix) and non-exclusively ~~throughout the rest of the World~~ excluding the US, ~~its dependencies~~ and the Philippines.

*Exploit? We're not having 7 year olds in Korea making trainers! It's a book people!*

    (b)   The Author shall not prepare any work for any other publisher in the exclusive territory covered by this Agreement which reproduces or adapts any material part of the Work, or any work which might prejudicially affect the sales of the Work.

    (c)   All rights other than those specifically granted to the Publishers are reserved to the Author.   *Whatever.*

1

2. **Warranties and Indemnities**

(a) The Author warrants to the Publishers and their licensees:

*✷ Very* ⟶

(i) that he has full power to make this Agreement, that the Work is an original work, has not been published in any form in the exclusive territories covered by this Agreement and is in no way whatever an infringement of any existing copyright or licence or is otherwise actionable at law; —— *fine*

(ii) ~~that the Work contains no defamatory or otherwise unlawful matter and that all statements in the Work purporting to be facts are true;~~

(iii) that the Work contains no obscene, ~~blasphemous or~~ improper material;

*Meaningless* ✓

(b) ~~The Author shall indemnify and keep the Publishers, and any party whom the Publishers indemnify in the ordinary course of their business, indemnified against any loss, injury or damage occasioned to the Publishers in consequence of any breach of these warranties or arising out of any claim alleging that the Work constitutes in any way a breach of these warranties. The indemnification shall include any legal costs or expenses and any compensation costs and disbursements paid by the Publishers on the advice of its legal advisers to compromise or settle any claim.~~ The Publishers shall notify the Author before settling any claims.

(c) The above warranties and indemnities shall survive ~~the termination of~~ this Agreement.

3. **Delivery and Approval**

(a) The Author undertakes to deliver to the Publishers not later than 31 July 2001 two complete clean typescripts of the Work. ⟵ *You have the work* *does already*

(b) The Work ~~shall~~ comply with the description and with the agreed form, content and style as a result of which this Agreement was entered into. The Work ~~shall be~~ professionally competent and suitable for publication by the Publishers. ~~The Publishers may decline to publish the Work if it does not fulfil these criteria and shall be entitled to terminate this Agreement and to recover the fee paid to the Author.~~ The Publishers shall, in that event, give their reasons in writing for rejecting the Work within one month of receipt. *it's a 'rap' print it.*

(c) ~~If~~ the Author fails to deliver*ed* the complete Work by the above date ~~or any revised date that may have been agreed in writing, the Publishers shall be entitled to terminate this Agreement and to~~

2

recover the fee paid to the Author. It is understood that time is of the essence.

(d)   The Publishers shall not amend or otherwise alter the Work without consulting the Author

4.   **Advance**

The Publishers shall pay to the Author the following advance against all sums due under this agreement of: **£10,000 (ten thousand pounds)** payable in the following stages:

*Three fifths* ~~one third~~ on signature of this Agreement by both parties hereto;

*One quarter* ~~one third~~ on delivery and approval of complete Work as described in Part I;

*One quarter* ~~one third~~ on United Kingdom hardcover publication of the Work by the Publishers.

*It to One eighth?!*

*You do the math*

5.   **Accounting**

The Publishers shall make up accounts of the monies due to the Author half yearly to the 30th day of June and 31st day of December each year and pay these amounts to the Author on or before the next succeeding 30th day of September or 31st day of March respectively.

6.   **Royalties**

The Publishers shall pay the Author the following royalties on copies of the Work which they sell:

(a)   **if published as a hardcover:**

   (i)   **home royalty:**   **2.5%**   on copies sold of the full-priced hardcover edition of the Work in the United Kingdom and the Republic of Ireland (except as otherwise provided), calculated on the United Kingdom published price.

   (ii)   **export royalty:**   **2.5%**   on copies sold of the full-priced hardcover edition of the Work for re-sale outside the United Kingdom and the Republic of Ireland, calculated on the amount received by the Publishers.

(b)   *When* ~~if~~ **published as a paperback:**

   (i)   **home royalty:**   **2.5%**   calculated on the United Kingdom published price (except as otherwise provided).

3

# APPENDIX

## EXCLUSIVE TERRITORIES

*I think we're over egging the pudding. Why not just say Africa?*

### Europe

Andorra
Austria
Belgium
Cyprus
~~Denmark~~
Faroe Islands
Finland
France
Germany
Gibraltar
~~Greece~~
~~Greenland~~
~~Iceland~~
Israel
Italy
Liechtenstein
Luxembourg
Malta (including ~~Gozo~~)
Monaco
Netherlands
~~Norway~~
Portugal (~~including~~ ~~Madeira and the~~ ~~Azores~~)
Republic of Ireland
San Marino
~~Spain~~ (including the Canary Islands)
Sweden
Switzerland
Turkey
United Kingdom (including Northern Ireland, Isle of Man and Channel Islands)
~~Vatican City~~

### Africa

Botswana
Cameroon
Gambia
Ghana
Kenya
Lesotho
Malawi
Mauritius
Namibia (South West Africa)
Nigeria
Other S. African Dependencies
Seychelles
Sierra Leone
Somali Republic
South Africa
St Helena
Swaziland
Tanzania
Uganda
Zambia
~~Zimbabwe~~ *Unless Mugabe goes*

### Middle East

Egypt
~~Iran~~ *Nice girl! only joking!!*
Iraq
Jordan
Kuwait
~~South Yemen~~
~~Sudan~~

### Asia

Bangladesh
Brunei
Burma
India
Malaysia
Pakistan
Singapore
Sri Lanka
*CHINA*

### Australasia

Australia
Australian Islands
Fiji
French Polynesia
Kiribati
Nauru
New Zealand
New Zealand Islands
Papua New Guinea
Pitcairn Islands
Solomon Islands
Tonga
Tuvalu
Western Samoa

### Canada

### South America

Belize
British Antarctic Territories
Falkland Islands

### West Indies

Antigua
Bahamas
Barbados
Bermuda
British Virgin Islands
Cayman Islands
Dominica
Grenada
Guyana
Jamaica
Montserrat
St Kitts-Nevis
St Vincent
St Lucia
Trinidad-Tobago

*(And don't claim 'they won't sell British ~~books~~. That's Bollocks I saw a documentary.)*

Initials

# I'M ALAN PARTRIDGE

SERIES 2

## EPISODE 1: THE TALENTED MR ALAN

*Radio Studio*

**Female caller**
Well, I enjoyed *The Hobbit* more than Riverdance … and I think lots of boys on an island killing a fat boy is not so enjoyable as Gandalf with a long white beard –

**Alan**
OK, if you've just joined us, we're talking about who is the best lord: lord of the rings, of the dance, or of the flies. That's tonight's hot topic.

**Jingle**
*(Alan)* Hot topic!

**Alan**
OK, the votes are closed and clearly the rings and the flies have been roundly trounced by the quick feet of blouse-wearing tycoon Michael Flatley. *(In Humphrey Bogart accent)* Flatley, my dear, I don't riverdance! *(Usual voice)* Give a damn. It's 11 p.m. – time for Alan's love asylum.

**Jingle**
*(Alan)* Alan's love asylum. *(Moan)*

*Alan mimes stabbing someone.*

**Alan**
It's basically sex music.

*Opening music*

**Alan**

*(In opening sequence, mouth full of ice cream)*
See you later.

*Radio Studio*

**Alan**

That was The Corrs. Three little birds I think we'd all like to, er, prey upon and steal their eggs. Er, anyway, I'm off now. Time to leave you in the very capable hands of Dave Clifton, who's going to be with you until 4 a.m. with his Nightclub. What've you got lined up for us, Dave?

**Dave**

Actually, it's Ladies Night tonight – special night.

**Alan**

Whoo-hoo! Maybe a wet T-shirt competition?

**Dave**

Ooh, you never know. Could be, could be. *(Laughs)*

**Alan**

*(Laughs)* How does that work on radio?

**Dave**

You could, er, use your imagination, Alan, actually, and, er, I tell you what, there's a, rather a lot of ladies in here tonight.

*Noise of ladies squealing.*

**Dave**

Whoo, whoo, steady girls, steady. *(Laughs)*

*Alan laughs.*

**Dave**

Ooh, I'm all wet.

*Alan and Dave laugh.*

**Alan**

I can hear 'em. I can't see 'em.

**Dave**

Yep, that's because you're not in my room.

**Alan**

All right. Well, I'm off for a mushroom slice at a BP garage.

**Dave**

Oop, get me one, chum. *(Laughs)*

**Alan**

*(Looks at Dave as if he were an idiot)*
Mmmm.

*Alan leaves studio.*

**Dave**

All right, OK, let's open the Nightclub tonight, folks, with The Joe Boxers …

*Alan drives along in his car. In petrol station shop.*

**Alan**

Two Flavio frothy cappuccinos coming right up.

**Michael**

Oh, you're a gentleman.

*Alan stands in petrol station shop, holding cup; talks to Michael, who's serving behind counter.*

**Alan**

Oh, look. There's that idiot in the black Hillman Imp. Is he gonna get petrol?

**Michael**

*(Shakes head)* Uh-uh.

**Alan**

No, he's just using the forecourt to turn round. He thinks he's Rod Stewart.

**Michael**

Huh. Aye. Ay, er, your road safety video's doing well.

**Alan**

What, *Crash, Bang, Wallop, What a Video!*?

**Michael**

Aye, aye. We've sold three. It's doing a bit better than your book, like.

**Alan**

Yeah, well, unfortunately, Michael, we live in a world where people would rather watch clips of idiots driving cars like maniacs into berks than a book which has been described as – and I quote – 'lovely stuff'. Not my words, Michael, the words of Shakin' Stevens.

**Michael**

Well, you could always, er, reduce the price, like.

**Alan**

What again? No, Michael, you're not pushing them hard enough. Pretend I'm a customer and try and sell me the book. *(Alan steps up to the counter)* Hello.

**Michael**

Er, what pump number?

**Alan**

Erm … three.

**Michael**

Three.

**Alan**

No, no, four. No, it doesn't matter, does it?

**Michael**

No, it doesn't matter, it doesn't matter. Four.

**Alan**

Four.

**Michael**

Four.

**Alan**

No, three. No, it's got the paper hand towels. I like three. You know.

**Michael**

Three, three. Er, would you also like this book?

**Alan**

What's it about?

**Michael**

Oh. It's about this local feller, what used to be on television, right? Er, but he wasn't very good, so now he's not. He went right down, right, and he had a – rock-bottom, man, and now he's on his way back up, right, but, I mean, he'll never get back to where he was 'cause them days is over, like. But, er, 'e, 'e, 'e, 'e, 'e's coming back a bit.

**Alan**

Well, I don't want to read that. That sounds depressing.

**Michael**

You just want the petrol then?

**Alan**

Michael, your sales technique is awful. Are you low on Bodyline brushable joint sealer?

**Michael**

Oh, aye, we are. Erm, Captain Partridge, would you look after the fort while I get on a resupply mission? *(Laughs nervously)*

**Alan**

*(Sighs)* You work in a petrol station, Michael. Not the Gulf War. Which, ironically, is like a large petrol station.

*Michael leaves by back door. Alan moves behind counter; stands with his back to shop.*

**Alan**

*(Singing)* Sail away, sail away, sail away, Sail away, sail away, sail away

*Man clears throat.*

**Alan**

*(Turns round)* Oh, I say. It's all right, I'm not Enya.

**Man**

Erm, pump number three. *(Passes Alan his credit card)*

**Alan**

Good pump! *(Looks at name on credit card)* F. Raphael. That's funny – I used to have a teacher at school called, er, Frank Raphael, yeah. 'Sweaty Raphael' we used to call him. He had, er, great big sweating stains under his armpits. I've just realized it's you. How the devil are you?

**Frank**

Alan Partridge.

**Alan**

The very same. So what are you up to now?

**Frank**

I'm still at the old school, but *(laughs)*, well, I'm the headmaster now.

**Alan**

Good call.

**Frank**

Yes, I – I remember you. Didn't you use to be on the television?

**Alan**

Yeah, I got out of that. Er, unpleasant people. Yeah. Bitter bastards.

**Frank**

Mmm. Yes, in education authorities you find quite a few of those as well.

**Alan**

Yeah, I think every profession has its, er … shits. Sorry about the bad language. Actually, I don't have to apologize any more, do I? Big balls! Fanny hair.

**Frank**

And a bag of Minstrels.

**Alan**

Ooh. Yeah, we, we all sweat, don't we? I mean, I used to sweat like a zoo, you know.

And I do mean the smell as well, because although you sweated, you didn't smell. That was another teacher – that was Cacky Raphael. That's you as well. Shoot me in the head with a massive gun! Er. And I remember you, you, you once caned me for having a chalk penis drawn on the back of my blazer.

**Frank**

*(Laughs)* Oh well, that was a long time ago, Alan.

**Alan**

Yeah. That, that's what Nazi war criminals say.

**Frank**

Funnily enough I bumped into another old boy recently, er, Tony Spillane.

**Alan**

Yeah?

**Frank**

He came and gave a talk to our sixth-formers.

**Alan**

Mmm. You realize there's no way I could have drawn a chalk penis on my back? Ask yourself two questions: how and why?

**Frank**

Well, lovely to see you again, Alan.

**Alan**

I could come and give a talk to the pupils.

**Frank**

Oh, well, if we need someone to tell the boys and girls about working in a petrol station *(laughing)* I'll be on to you.

*Frank walks away as Michael returns. Alan presses emergency buzzer and locks Frank in shop.*

**Alan**

Do you think I work in a petrol station?

**Frank**

Well, I just paid you for petrol and a packet of Minstrels.

**Alan**

No, he, this is the man that runs the place. *(Points at Michael)* Well, he doesn't run it, he's the – he's the work Geordie. No, he's … I'm not at his level. He's always been at this level.

**Michael**

Aye, 'cause when I was in the army I used to put –

**Alan**

Yeah, yeah, yeah, w-w-w-what, whatever. I'm doing much better than him. I left the BBC, formed a production company. That went into liquidation – voluntarily – er, then I was out of work for two years, I was clinically fed up – boo-hoo –

**Frank**

W-w-why do I need to know all this?

**Alan**

Because I bounced back. People bounce back. Dennis Hopper. Rolf Harris. There are others.

**Frank**

Can I get to my car?

**Alan**

It's not going to drive off by itself. It's not Herbie. Look, the point is, I now have the third best slot on Radio Norwich, I have a military-based quiz show on cable television called *Skirmish* and I've got a girlfriend … now, and I – I think your pupils are going to want to know about that.

**Frank**

Absolutely. I'll – I'll, er, be in touch.

**Alan**

If we set it up now, then Michael can press the button to, er, to, to let you go.

**Michael**

Would you like this book in a bag?

**Alan**

Not now, Michael.

**Frank**

All right, then. Well, why don't you come and give a talk on, er, Wednesday evening?

**Alan**

Michael, release the headmaster.

*Lynn walks past the building site and enters caravan, in which Alan is standing.*

**Lynn**

Yoo-hoo.

**Alan**

Hello, Lynn. Would you like a coffee?

**Lynn**

*(Shakes head)* Oh, no.
Coffee machines are the future, Lynn. Kettles are saaaad. OK, Lynn, what do you think of the polo neck? Balls out of the bath on this one.

**Lynn**

I think it's rather snazzy.

**Alan**

I think your hair's snazzy. Is that your mother's money coming through?

**Lynn**

Yes.

**Alan**

All part of the bereavement dividend.

**Lynn**

Well, I did change her sheets every day for ten years.

**Alan**

Yeah, I don't know how you managed it. I mean, she was a bit of a heffalump, God rest her soul. Yeah, she was a *big* woman. I'm tempted to say she was big-hearted but that would be bullshit. OK, Lynn, make for the banquette.

**Lynn**

OK, thank you. *(She sits next to Alan)*

**Alan**

Thanks for changing the gas bottles. I – I heard you clinking. OK then, what have you got for me? Shoot from your hip. Your new hip.

**Lynn**

Oh, er, now, you've got a one o'clock meeting with Siobhan from Meteor Productions to talk about *Crash, Bang, Wallop, What a Video! 2*. Do you – do you need me to be there?

**Alan**

I don't *need* you anywhere. I'd like you to be there. Your problem with Meteor, Lynn, is that you don't like them because they make wet T-shirt videos. It's not hardcore super sex. You know, if you – if you'd taken the trouble to watch *Boob Olympics*, as I have, then, er, you'd realize that there is a competitive element.

**Lynn**

As long as it makes you happy.

**Alan**

Lynn, the money that pays for the black granite work surfaces in the kitchen, the brass dimmer switches, your eight grand a year – all comes from Meteor, who happen to produce *Boob Olympics*, *The Eurovision Thong Contest* and *Wet Christmas*.

*House is covered in scaffolding. Alan walks into house, followed by Lynn.*

**Alan**

All right, guys?

**Builder**

Y'all right?

**Alan**

Yeah. See the match?

**Builder**

Which one?

**Alan**

Dunno.

**Builder 2**

How's it going, Mr Partridge?

**Alan**

Yeah, cool. Cool.

**Builder 2**

You see what I done in the toilet?

**Alan**

W-what do you mean?

**Builder 2**

Well, I retiled it.

**Alan**

Oh, right.

**Builder**

'Ere, I tell you what, mate, we've got summat for you.

**Alan**

Oh yeah?

**Builder**

Yeah.

**Alan**

What? What?

**Builder**

*(Passes Alan a hard hat)* Stick this on.

**Alan**

*(Puts on the hard hat which has 'boss' written across the front)* Oh! There you go! *(Laughs)*

**Builders**

Hey!

*Builders and Lynn laugh.*

**Alan**

*(Turns to Lynn)* Yes. Even though it is amusing there is a serious reason why I'm wearing this, Lynn: insurance. And, er, no offence, Lynn –

**Lynn**

Oh, none taken.

**Alan**

Well, you don't know what I'm going to say yet. You know, wait until I, I've said what I'm going to say before you decide not to take offence. You see, no offence, Lynn, but your life is technically not worth insuring.

**Builder 2**

Can we talk about the office area?

**Alan**

OK, all right, yeah. Because I was going to say that, er, I'd like the office to double as, er, a chill-out room.

**Builder**

I didn't think you were a raver.

**Alan**

I'm not a raver: I'm straight. I, I've got a girlfriend, yeah. She, she's only thirty-three. Yeah. Cashback. Yeah, I'm, er, between you and me, there are things I do with Sonia that I would never have done with my ex-wife Carol.

**Builder**

Really?

**Alan**

Yeah. I mean, occasionally I durst venture south. And, er, when I go south, I've got to say, it's like a breath of fresh air. But, er, two years ago I was a mess. Yeah. I put on weight. I had breasts.

**Builder**

Really? *(Laughing)* Bet they were the only ones you copped hold of, weren't they, as well?

**Alan**

*(Laughs)* They were actually, yeah. I was repellent to women for two years. Yeah. Running along jogging, and my breasts were there, with tassels, you know. You can make them that way *(rotates fingers clockwise)* and you make them go that way *(rotates fingers anticlockwise)* but you can't make them go that way *(rotates one finger clockwise; the other anticlockwise)*.

*Builders and Alan laugh.*

**Alan**

Imagine dreaming about that and waking up screaming. Because that's what happened.

*Sonia enters.*

**Sonia**

Hello, Alan.

**Alan**

Oh. See, told you.

**Sonia**

Hello, builders.

**Alan**
Watch.
*(Alan kisses Sonia several times on cheek)*
See, she's not stopping me.

**Sonia**
Brilliant story to tell. Last day I was in a coffee shop – where I work – and then a man came in and he said he wanted coffee. He was a smelly man. Tommy did not like him. Tommy said we didn't have any coffee. *(Laughs)*

*Alan laughs.*

**Sonia**
*(Still laughing)* And then the man just went. *(Continues laughing)*

*Alan laughs nervously.*

**Lynn**
I don't quite understand the joke. Is it –

**Alan**
Drop it, Lynn.

**Builder 2**
So, it's a coffee shop, but then one man says to another man, 'You can't have a coffee.'

**Alan**
That, that is the story. Believe me.

**Builder 2**
Yeah, but it doesn't make sense, does it? 'Cause I mean, you got, you know, man coming in for a coffee –

**Alan**
Yeah, help me out, mate.

**Builder 2**
Very funny story.

**Sonia**
Yes, it's a funny story!

**Alan**
Yeah, yeah, it is a funny story.

**Builders**
Yeah, yeah.

**Alan**
It is. It *is* a funny story. I think those stories are kind of best in the caravan.

**Sonia**
I have a present for you.

**Alan**
Why don't we go in there now?
*(Alan leaves)* Grab her, Lynn!

*Lynn grabs hold of Sonia's arm and leads her outside the house.*

**Alan**
*(Standing at caravan door)* Guess which one of you two ladies I'm going to make love with now?

*Sonia laughs.*

**Lynn**
I'll, er, just go on up to the club and – and meet that video woman.

**Alan**
See you later.
*Lynn leaves; Sonia goes into the caravan.*
Well, Sonia. Let's be appalling.

*Alan shuts caravan door. Peeks head out from caravan window as Lynn walks past.*

**Alan**
Oh, Lynn, I reckon forty, forty-five minutes. How long?

**Lynn**
Well, about, about that.

**Alan**
Yeah, actually, better make it an hour because I want to have a shower before and ideally afterwards.

**Lynn**
OK.

*Choristers Country Club; Lynn and Siobhan are sitting inside. Alan enters.*

**Alan**
Hi!

**Siobhan**
Oh, Alan.

*Siobhan jumps up and gives Alan a kiss. Lynn jumps up.*

**Alan**
*(To Lynn)* Stay down. *(Alan sits down)* Ah. Sorry I'm late. Had to have a shower. Got a bit clammy. *(Looks at Lynn, who looks embarrassed)* Yeah.

**Siobhan**
So, how've you been, Alan?

**Alan**
Ruddy bloody good, actually. Yeah.

**Lynn**
Yes, his panic attacks have all but stopped.

**Alan**
Thanks, Lynn.

**Child**
*(Sitting behind Alan, Lynn and Siobhan)*
Mum, mum, I want my Gameboy.

**Alan**
Hello. Excuse me. What's his name?

**Child's mother**
It's Todd.

**Alan**
What, Todd? Seriously? Hello, Todd. Very snazzy jeans you got on there.

**Todd**
Thank you.

**Alan**
*(Laughing)* You're welcome.

*Waiter approaches Alan.*

**Alan**
Er, correct me if I'm wrong – there is a zero tolerance policy on denim in the bar?

**Waiter**
Yes.

**Alan**
Oh. I think there's a chap over there wearing jeans. Chap of about six?

**Waiter**
Right.

**Alan**
*(To Siobhan)* They're lovely at that age, aren't they? *(Shouting, as mother and child are asked to leave)* Did they get you on the old jeans rule? *(Laughs)* Nazis! But with excellent facilities. As had the Nazis.

**Siobhan**
OK, shall we get started?

**Alan**
Yes. I have a thought. Now, because the last video was called 'Crash, Bang, Wallop, What a Video!', and this video will feature helicopters, er, pursuing these bad prats across fields, I thought perhaps a better title would be 'Scum on the Run'.

*Lynn grimaces.*

**Siobhan**
You all right, Lynn?

**Lynn**
Yeah.

**Alan**
Yeah. Lynn doesn't like the old *(taps video box on table)* water sports.

**Siobhan**
No, well, we don't do that.

**Alan**
Yeah, well, you know, the wet T-shirt thing.

**Siobhan**
Yeah, well, that's not water sports, Alan.

**Alan**
Well, w-what's water sports?

**Siobhan**
You don't know?

**Alan**
No, I don't.

**Siobhan**
You mean you don't know what water sports are?

**Alan**
*(In American accent)* I believe we've established that.

**Siobhan**
Well –

**Alan**
Tell me what you mean by water sports.

**Siobhan**
Well, it's when people relieve themselves on each other.

*Silence. Lynn looks appalled. Alan whistles.*

**Alan**
Did you know that there are no Dutch elms left in Britain? Completely wiped out. *(Pause)* Disgusting. Absolutely disgusting.

**Lynn**
Perhaps those people were caught short?

**Alan**
*(Disgustedly)* They do it on purpose, Lynn. Well, that's the small talk over with. Let, let's go on with the thorny issue of the fee.

**Siobhan**
No, no, there's no negotiation about the fee.

**Alan**
Siobhan, when you hire me, you don't just get some guy who used to be on TV, presenting a cheap video. You do get that – but you also get my voice. And let me remind you – Britain has some of the safest roads in Europe. But this isn't Britain. *(Speaks in German accent)* This is de autobahn. I bring an element of humour.

**Siobhan**
Alan, I'm sorry, I just can't move on the fee.
Now, you know we love your work.

**Alan**
I know, I know, and I love your – videos
of women in bikinis being hosed down in
car parks.

**Siobhan**
Well, it's a little bit more tasteful than that.

**Alan**
It's called *Titsnade Zoo*.

**Siobhan**
Alan, I am not negotiating. *(She stands and
collects her things)*

**Alan**
You may not be, but I am.

**Siobhan**
Well, then, you'll be negotiating on your
own.

**Alan**
So be it.

**Siobhan**
That doesn't work. Lovely to see you, Lynn.

*Siobhan leaves.*

**Alan**
*(Shouts after her)* I don't know why you
don't just go the whole hog and have me
chased down the street by a helicopter in
wet underpants. I mean me, not the
helicopter. Although I wouldn't put that
past you – some sicko'd probably buy that.
A big helicopter in giant underpants. Or
a, or a plane in a giant bra having a slash
on an airport. *(To Lynn)* Why did you say
I had panic attacks? You made it sound
like I had a breakdown.

**Lynn**
You did. You drove up to Dundee in bare feet.

**Alan**
*(Fiercely)* Lynn, I know what really
happened. You make me sound mad now.
Say I didn't have a breakdown.

**Lynn**
You didn't have a breakdown.

**Alan**
I know.

*Alan and Lynn sit in Alan's car in the car
park.*

**Alan**
I'm OK. I'm OK. Look, let's go and get a
couple of Soleros. I need to get my head
together.

**Lynn**
There goes Siobhan.

**Alan**
Right, I'm going to box her in at the squash
court and drop my price.

*Alan accelerates and hits a parking barrier.*

**Alan**
In to me! Aargh! I'm all right. Your airbag
went off – why didn't mine, Lynn?

**Lynn**
*(Frightened)* I can't move my head. It's just
not going. Can you see? I'm trapped.

**Alan**
Calm down, Lynn!

**Lynn**
It's just not moving.

**Alan**
Calm! Calm! *(Presses horn)* Eh! *(Presses
horn)* Eh! *(Presses horn)* Eh! Calm down,
Lynn! You're suffering from minor women's
whiplash. It's normal. Your – your airbag's
deployed. Mine hasn't. *(Sighs)*

**Lynn**
You haven't got whiplash, have you?

**Alan**

I know! I know I haven't got whiplash, Lynn, because my head was in contact with the headrest in the correct way. You were leaning forwards with your handbag like that, crouching like a mouse, like that.

*Siobhan comes over.*

**Siobhan**

You all right?

**Lynn**

Oh. I, I, I, I've just got minor whiplash. *(Laughs nervously)*

**Alan**

Yeah, it was me that told her that.

**Lynn**

Yeah, him.

**Siobhan**

But you need to take her to a hospital, Alan.

**Alan**

Mmm, I know, I know. In fact this has all put things in – in perspective, so that I will now do the video for the same amount as last time. Yes, to help Lynn.

**Siobhan**

Alan, I think you should be taking her to hospital and perhaps we'll chat about that later, OK?

**Alan**

Yeah, all right, OK. And, and by the way, this was probably caught on CCTV camera, and I will throw the footage in gratis. I know it's only a minor collision but … you can start off with a small one like this and then build to a big one with, you know, like a huge lorry sliding along on its back for ages, you know. I'm taking my top off. I'm babbling.

**Siobhan**

All right then. Bye-bye. Bye-bye, Alan. Talk to you later. Bye-bye.

*Siobhan leaves.*

**Alan**

She goes on a bit, doesn't she?

**Lynn**

Hmm.

**Alan**

Her. Yes. Weird, isn't it, this airbag? Sort of all that powder on your face – you look like a clown.

*Lynn laughs.*

**Alan**

Don't smile! You've broken your neck.

*Sir William Dunwoody's High School, Norwich; Alan and Lynn – in a neckbrace - are led into room.*

**Frank**

Here we are then. Well, just make yourselves comfortable … and I'll give you a shout when we're ready for you. If there's anything you need, just let me know, Alan – or you, Mrs Partridge.

*Frank leaves.*

**Alan**

*(Shouting up corridor)* She's not my wife! *(To Lynn)* I hate it when that happens. Lynn, can you pop to the shops and get me … two packets of Toffos?

*Lynn leaves. Man enters room.*

**Phil**

I heard you were in the building. Phil Wiley! We were at school together?

**Alan**

Oh, yes! You were in my class.

**Phil**

*(Laughs)* Alison Partridge!

**Alan**

No, Alan, Alan.

**Phil**

No, Alison's what we used to call you.

**Alan**

Oh right.

*Phil laughs.*

**Alan**

I didn't know that. So, erm, what are you doing hanging around at school? A bit weird, isn't it?

**Phil**

Oh, no. I'm one of the big boys now, Alan.

**Alan**

What, a prefect?

**Phil**

No, I, I teach here.

**Alan**

Oh, right. I see.

**Phil**

*(Laughs)* I've just remembered – remember the day you caught me in that darkroom snogging the lab assistant, hey? *(Laughs)* What on earth were you doing there?

**Alan**

*(Laughs)* Developing photographs.

*Phil and Alan laugh.*

**Alan**

*(Sternly)* Because that's what it was for.

**Phil**

Hey, it was the, er, the day that you got caned. Do you remember that?

**Alan**

Yeah. I remember I got a chalk penis drawn on my back by some shit. I'd love to get my hands on him.

**Phil**

Yeah, that was me.

**Alan**

I know it was. Yeah, but I really admire you teachers, you're very heroic, you know, to do what you do for such rubbish money. Tell me this, tell me this, exactly how much do you teachers earn?

**Phil**

You'd be surprised. I'm, I'm earning more than you think, Alan. You know, I'm Head of Modern Languages. *Ich weiss nicht was soll es bedeuten. (Laughs)*

**Alan**

Yeah. I've got a girlfriend.

**Phil**

I've got a wife.

**Alan**

Is she older than you or younger than you?

**Phil**

Well, if you must know, Alan, she's older than me. She's fifty-two.

**Alan**

My girlfriend's thirty-three. I'm forty-seven. She's fourteen years younger than me. *(Lifts leg as if kicking a ball)* Back of the net.

**Phil**

Right then, well, if I can just put you in this room I can get the kids. *(Guides Alan towards the door)* Just like –

**Alan**

Don't draw a cock!

*Alan is talking to a room of schoolchildren.*

**Alan**

Hi, kids. It's great to be back in my fine old school. Er, I nearly sent my son Fernando here, but I came into some money and was able to educate him privately. You, you can't muck about when it comes to your own kids. Now, let me tell you a bit about myself. I present a military-based quiz show on a daytime digital channel called UK Conquest. It's got 8,000 viewers. Let me put that in perspective: it's eleven times the population of Hemsby. Basically, terrestrial TV is a dead duck. And who watches a dead duck? Not even its mother. She just flies off, depressed. I'm going to show you an example now of, er, the kind of sell-through video that I make. By the way, there are some strobe effects in this, so, er, please, any epileptics, get out now. Because statistically one of you is. And two of you are gay. By the way, guys, if you are gay, please remember: rubber up. At your age it's still illegal. You don't want to end up in prison. Because some of those guys don't care how old you are. Or if you're gay. OK, now, this was filmed two years ago and I had let myself go a little.

*Alan presses button on video recorder and turns the lights off. Action turns to video footage of heavily overweight Alan.*

**Alan**
Crash! (*Shot of car crash*) Bang! (*Shot of car crash*) Wallop! (*Shot of car crash*) What a video!
Hi, I'm Alan Partridge and I drive a car … but not like this. (*Shot of car crash*)
Let's have a look at what this idiot did … in America. (*Shots of several car crashes*)

*Alan walks over to police car. Scantily clad policewoman is handling a truncheon.*

**Alan**
Thankfully that man was plastic. (*To policewoman*) You can stop giggling or I'll take down your particulars. But what if he hadn't been … plastic?

*Closing music to video; footage of Alan smiling at policewoman and then at camera for several seconds.*

**Frank**
(*Claps and walks to front of room*) Thank you, Alan, for a very interesting talk.

**Alan**
That's all right.

**Frank**
Are there any questions?

**Alan**
Yeah. You know this guy? He caned me for drawing a chalk penis on my back. Which I couldn't possibly do.

**Frank**
We'll be having coffee next door now, Alan.

**Alan**
Yeah, no, I'll show you. It's impossible … for me to draw … watch. (*Tries to draw chalk penis on his own back*) See?

**Phil**
But you've more or less managed it, Alan.

**Alan**
The, the, the one you did had more detail. There were, there were hairs at the base and a dotted line emanating from the crown. (*Laughing*) I'll tell you something about this guy: he got the lab assistant pregnant, he never sees the kid. Back of the net.

*Cut to Frank's office.*

**Frank**
That was an appalling thing to say. You've placed me in a rather invidious position.

**Alan**
Don't know that word. Carry on.

**Frank**
You leave the school again and we're left with a detritus.

349

**Alan**
Knock it off with the fancy words, mate. Say it like it is: it went tits up. You know, you speak like you're from the nineteenth century. And you sweat.

**Frank**
Well, I'd like to see you sweat over your work like I do over mine.

**Alan**
I don't because I use Lynx Africa. Gonna cane me?

**Frank**
No, but I might throw a chair at you.

**Alan**
It's still corporal punishment. See you in Strasbourg.

*Petrol station shop*

**Alan**
You know, on tonight's show we're talking about coffee.

**Michael**
Oh, really?

**Alan**
Yeah. Apparently they're opening a Starbucks on Beachy Head.

**Michael**
Oh, nice, you know, er, have a cup of coffee, admire the view, put a bit of spring in your step.

**Alan**
Yeah, well, a spring in your step's the last thing you need up on a cliff top. I mean it's a suicide hotspot.

**Michael**
What, Starbucks?

**Alan**
How are you going to kill yourself in Starbucks?

**Michael**
Shotgun in your mouth.

**Lynn**
Alan, there's that teacher chap.

**Alan**
Right, Michael, if he hits me will you hit him first?

**Michael**
No, aye, he's a customer. I cannae hit customers, I've been told. Er, I'll go and get some stock.

**Alan**
Yeah, chicken stock.

*Phil enters shop.*

**Phil**
Hello, Alan.

**Alan**
Lynn, hand me the apple pie.

*Microwave pings. Lynn hands Alan apple pie.*

**Alan**
And remove yourself from the theatre of conflict.

**Lynn**
What do you mean?

**Alan**
Go and stand by the Yakults.
*(To Phil)* The temperature inside this apple turnover is 1,000 degrees. If I squeeze it, a jet of molten Bramley apple is going to squirt out. Could go your way; could go mine. Either way, one of us is going down.

**Phil**
Alan, I've just come to make peace.

**Alan**
What, you're not going to kick my head in?

**Phil**
*(Laughs)* No, I'm not. I just think we should shake hands, you know? Yeah?

**Alan**
You've not got one of those –

**Phil**
Electric buzzer? No, I haven't.

*Alan and Phil shake hands. Phil makes electric buzzer noise.*

**Alan**
Aargh! You're all right, you.
*(Alan takes bite from apple pie.)*
ARGHH! How long did you put this in for, Lynn?

**Lynn**
Eight minutes.

**Alan**
It's hotter than the sun.

**Phil**
OK, Alan I'm going to go now. No hard feelings, all right?

**Alan**
Yeah, yeah, OK. Help yourself to a honeycomb Yorkie from the glovebox.

**Phil**
Yeah?

**Alan**
Yeah.

**Phil**
All right, I will. Take care, OK?
*Phil turns to go, a chalk drawing on the back of his coat.*

**Alan**
*(Quietly)* Lynn, that is not a penis.

**Lynn**
It's the best I could do.

**Alan**
It tapers at the end. It looks like a mouse's head.

*Phil leaves shop.*

**Michael**
Hey, look, Mr Partridge. That bloke's just told him.

**Man in car park**
*(To Phil)* It's there on your back, mate.

*Alan presses emergency buzzer to lock shop.*

**Phil**
*(Shouts)* Open the door! Open it!

**Alan**
*(Via Tannoy system)* According to Michael there are enough supplies in here to last three weeks. Want a Mars bar? Swivel. If you came in here for a Twix I'd stick one in your eye, one in your ear and … one up … your bum. And I'd have to break into another packet, and I'm not prepared to do that. I, I, I, I'd use a four-fingered one. Yeah. And save one for myself at the end. Having washed my hands. Having said that, I've just remembered I've got a radio show to do, so, er … can we make friends and then I can be on my way? Please? If you let me go, I will give you £200 in cash. Or, or, or a cheque for £230, which I imagine is a month's wages for someone like you. Hello?

*Blank screen for a couple of seconds.*

**Male voiceover**
Is Alan up for this?

**Male voiceover 2**
Yeah, he doesn't want a stuntman.

**Male voiceover**
All right. Scum on the Run. Scene eight, take one!

*Music; Alan crashes his car in slow motion, his head collides with the airbag.*

List of possible names for my house

Coleman house
Atlantis
Ace House
The Cottage
The New Rectory
Barn Cottage
Folly Foot
Large Cottage
Steed Manor
Rockford House
Flambards

Brideshead House
Futures
The Skirmishes
Tomahawk
Skeptre House
The Cinnamons
Classic House
The Classics
Manor House
Bentley Cottage
Lord House

# I'M ALAN PARTRIDGE

## EPISODE 2: THE COLOUR OF ALAN

*Radio Station*

**Music**
*Put out the red light*
*Put out the red light …*

**Alan**
That was 'Roxanne' by The Police or, as they're now known, Sting. A song there about a prostitute. Doesn't say what her surname is. Must give her a call sometime, although the effects of twenty-three years on the game would not render her pleasurable to mine eye. (*Clears throat*)

**Alan**
(*Jingle*) Alan's funny stories.

**Alan**
(*Laughs*) Just time for one quick funny story before the news. On line four we have Roy from Bungay. Hello, Roy.

**Roy**
Hello.

**Alan**
Funny story: what is it?

**Roy**
I sold this Makita cordless power drill in the local paper and then six months later I received the very same one back as a Christmas present from my brother-in-law – minus the power pack.

**Alan**

I see. So you, er, you, the present you gave away, you then got back?

**Roy**

Yeah, that's it. Goodbye.

*Phone goes dead.*

**Alan**

*(Laughs)* What a funny story.

**Jingle**

*(Alan)* Alan's funny stories.

**Alan**

That was a funny story. *(Laughs, looking at clock: 15 seconds to midnight)* Er, wonder who got the power pack? *(Looks at clock: 10 seconds to midnight. Laughs in forced way for 10 seconds)* News.

*Opening music.*

**Alan**

*(In opening sequence)* I mean, how can you set fire to your hands?

*Alan's house covered in scaffolding. Alan enters house, followed by Lynn.*

**Alan**

Oh. *(Laughs)* Hello –

**Lynn**

*(Quietly)* Carl.

**Alan**

Carl. There's a lot of room in here. It's nice to be able to sort of jog around *(jogs around room)* – excuse me – in this space. Yeah. Yeah. It's good, it's good, it's good. *(Stands still)* I'm in quite a good mood today because I just found out my wife's been struck off my life insurance. Spiceworld! You married?

**Carl**

Yeah.

**Alan**

Yeah. Divorced. Yeah. I've got access to the kids but *(puts on American accent)* they don't wanna see me.

*Alan and Lynn walk away.*

**Lynn**

*(To Alan)* John.

**Alan**

Hello, John.

**John**

Al. Yeah, we've, er, concreted the floor.

**Alan**

No bodies underneath there, I hope?

**John**

What?

**Alan**

I'm just joshing with you, you know. *(Puts on Yorkshire accent)* Have you put t'corpse under t'patio? I expect you get that all the time.

**John**

Not really.

**Alan**

Oh. Actually, that skirting board does seem a bit too low. Could you, could you change it again?

*John violently pulls skirting board away and throws it to the floor. Walks off.*

**Alan**

*(In Yorkshire accent)* Eeee, 'appen he thinks I'm a right indecisive tit.

**Carl**

I don't think he likes it when you do that accent.

**Alan**

Well, I'll – I'll – well, I'll stop then. *(Puts foot on workbench)*

**Carl**
Can you not put your foot on –

**Alan**
I wasn't going to. I was just going to do a Cockney walk. (*Does Cockney walk. Nearly bumps into John, coming back into the room with a new piece of skirting board*)

**John**
All right?

**Alan**
Hello. (*Claps his hands together*) Actually, I've got some good news, because I've just come into a r-r-rather substantial amount of money because I'm going to host a sales conference for Dante's of Reading, the Ferrari of the coal-effect gas fireplace industry. And if this job comes off then, as regards decision-making, I think we'll be in a can-do go situation. I won't bore you with the details –

**Carl**
Great.

**Alan**
Right.

**Michael**
(*Offstage*) Oi! Hands off your cocks –

*Michael enters house.*

**Michael**
– on with your socks! Oh, hello, hi.

**Alan**
It's all right, Lynn. It's just an army saying. Give us another one, Michael.

**Michael**
Er (*shouts*), kill! Kill! Stab! Twist! Kill!

**Alan**
Michael's going to be staying here for a bit until they, er, put his front door back on.

**Michael**
Aye.

**Alan**
Welcome aboard the … good ship … my house.

**Lynn**
Do you want to tell Michael there's no smoking in the house?

**Alan**
(*To Michael*) Er, th-th-there's actually no smoking in the house.

**Michael**
(*Lighting a cigarette*) Do you want to tell her whose house it is?

**Alan**
(*To Lynn*) It, it's my house.

**Michael**
(*to Lynn*) You've got owt to say, you can say it to me face.

**Lynn**
It's a matter of hygiene.

**Alan**
Oh, whoa, whoa, whoa, whoa, whoa. Hey. Back off. Seconds out. Round One. Ding ding! No, I'd never let that happen. (*To Lynn*) He'd batter you. Come on, tell me what you've got.

**Lynn**
Right. Well, you've got your book signing at twelve o'clock –

*Alan walks outside; Lynn follows.*

**Lynn**
– and your meeting at Chorister's with Pete Moran from Dante Fires.

**Alan**
Mary Poppins! What's that?

*Michael sticks his head out of door.*

**Michael**
Oh that? Hey, that's me bike. That's Desert Storm.

**Alan**
I'm sure the Iraqis must have been petrified when they saw that coming over the horizon. Especially if it had one of those cigarette cards in the spokes, so it went frrrrrrrrrrr. *(Alan pretends to be Iraqi, screaming)* Why don't you two bury the hatchet over a machine coffee? After you, Lynn.

**Lynn**
OK.

*Lynn enters caravan; Alan stops Michael.*

**Alan**
Pr-probably me next.

*Alan and Michael join Lynn.*

**Alan**
Lynn, I need to speak to you about something.

**Lynn**
Oh.

**Alan**
Sonia has made me this. It's a mug with my face on one side and a cat on the other.

**Lynn**
What does it mean?

**Alan**
I don't know. I've no idea. And I think she's planning something much worse. She's talking about selling this stuff down at the covered market.

**Lynn**
That's terrible.

**Alan**
It's a disaster. I don't want my face on … on this. *(Alan holds up a jug with a photo of his face on the side)* I want it on … this. *(Holds up a copy of his autobiography,* Bouncing Back*)* I might put it on a jar of pasta. Did you hear back from Dolmio about my pasta-gravy sauce?

**Lynn**
No.

**Alan**
Let it go.

**Michael**
*(Picks up a box)* Ay, do you fancy a cup of delicious microwavable soup?

**Alan**
Er, yeah. Yeah, just pop it in the microwave. Hey, Michael, can you imagine if they had, er, microwaves in medieval times?

*Michael laughs.*

**Alan**
Yeah. There's a giant microwave. You could just pop a witch in it.

**Michael**
Aye.

**Alan**
Horrific.

**Michael**
If she bursts, she's innocent.

**Alan**
Yeah. Yeah, and if she comes out looking normal but cold on the outside and hot in the middle, she's a witch.

**Michael**
Have to remember to take the foil off first.

**Alan**
Yeah, no, that's just pies.

**Lynn**
Do you mind me watching *Farrow* on UK Gold?

**Alan**
No, no, no. As long as you pop the earphones on. Oh, you have. Look at her. Dead to the world. She's sitting in the exact spot where me and Sonia have it off.

**Michael**
So are you still, er, doing it twice a day?

**Alan**
Yeah, you know. Diary permitting.

**Michael**
Careful you don't give yourself a heart attack.

**Alan**
No, it's actually quite good for you. It's good for you … it's cardiovascular exercise, 'cause if you think about it, it's like, it's like press-ups, isn't it?

**Michael**
Aye, suppose, yeah. 'Cause you are, you know, you are sort of working the major muscle groups, like, you know. *(Michael simulates having sex)*

**Alan**
That is a woman?

**Michael**
Aye, aye. That's just lo-long hair.

**Alan**
Could be Brian May. Mind you, that's not his cup of tea. No. That's the other one. God rest his soul. Actually, I've got a book signing to do later. I've got to pop up to Choristers and get the PA.

**Michael**
Oh, right.

**Alan**
If they haven't lost it. The security's terrible. They'd probably even let someone like you in.

**Michael**
That's ridiculous.

**Alan**
I know. And the person who stole your front door.

**Michael**
*(Laughs)* Aye. Oh, there's Sonia. Talking to the builders, like. Yeah.

**Alan**
Oh, God!

*Cut to house.*

**Sonia**
You just take normal photograph into Snappy Snaps and he put photo on cushion. And this cushion is called scatter cushion. It's brilliant. I call it, er, scatter love cushion. Because it, er, represent my love for Alan.

**Carl**
You could sit on his face.

*John laughs.*

**Sonia**
What do you mean?

**Carl**
You could sit on Alan's face, you know. It's – it's a joke.

*John laughs.*

**Sonia**
*(Cross)* It's a very filthy joke! *(Hits Carl and John with cushion)* And Alan is hitting you –

**Alan**
*(Entering house)* Whoa, whoa, whoa, whoa! That's English for 'stop a horse'.

**Sonia**
He's being very disgusting.

**Alan**
What did he say?

**Sonia**
He say I sit on your face.

*Builders laugh.*

**Alan**
Have you been spying on us?

**Carl**
No.

**Alan**
Sonia, I'll handle this. Go and sit in the static home.

*Sonia leaves.*

**Alan**
Sorry about that. *(Alan leaves)*

*Choristers Country Club. Alan presses button on gateway.*

**Alan**
Hello. I'm a communist with a gun. Er, I hate you lot. I've just thrown the royal family out of a plane. Can I use your toilet?

*Gate buzzes open.*

**Alan**
Utter, utter nutters.

*Train station. Alan is standing at book stall in ticket hall, promoting* Bouncing Back *and wearing a headset.*

**Alan**
Hello, commuters with your computers. This book would fit ideally into, er, an attaché case or the thigh pocket of a pair of fashionable combat trousers. Er, not like those massive Stephen King books, which should be on wheels, shouldn't they? Yeah. It's embarrassing. Idiot. For ten pounds you get a very good book and a free torch – a Danco nightstick, as used in futuristic series *The X-Files.* There's a demonstration model tied to the chair with a skipping rope by that woman. *(Points at Lynn)*
Wh-what is it you want? *(Alan leans forward to listen to woman in crowd)*
Right. Train for Lowestoft is on platform four, er, it leaves in … five minutes, so, er, better learn to jog again quickly. No, seriously, run. You will miss it.
This book is a top business aid. As I'm sure, er, as I'm sure you are, sir. Look at that: not even listening. Off to London, no doubt. Go to London! I guarantee you'll either be mugged or not appreciated. Catch the train to London, stopping at Rejection, Disappointment, Backstabbing Central and Shattered Dreams Parkway.

**Lynn**
Alan! Alan! There!

**Alan**
What?

**Lynn**
It's Pete Moran from Dante's Fires. He's just got off the train.

**Alan**
Right. He can't see me.

**Lynn**
Why not?

**Alan**
To the untrained eye, this could look like it's rubbish and I haven't bounced back.

**Lynn**
But you have.

**Alan**
I know! Just point him out to me.

**Lynn**
He's got a beard.

**Alan**
Got him. *(Runs over to Pete, still wearing headset)* Hi. I'm Alan Partridge.

**Pete**
Ah, Pete.

**Alan**
Yeah, yeah. You don't mind if I just do that *(grasps Pete's hand and turns him to face away from the book stall)* … like that?

**Pete**
Oh, no, no, not at all. Er, I wasn't expecting for you to come and meet me at the station.

*Alan and Pete walk outside, Alan still wearing headset.*

**Alan**
Yeah. Sorry about the smell of urine, but, er, you know, there really is nothing to do round here. You know, with Apache it is a one-stop shop.

*Alan's car approaches Choristers Country Club.*

**Alan**
What part of Birmingham are you from?

**Pete**
No, Alan, I'm actually from South Africa.

**Alan**
Oh yes, of course. *(In South African accent)* I should have guessed.

*Alan and Pete walk up to Choristers' gateway.*

**Alan**
This is a bit of a laugh. Security card, yeah? Hello, security? I am an arsonist with a big box of matches. Please can I come in to set fire to the staff?

*Gate buzzes open.*

**Alan**
Unbelievable.
*Alan and Pete enter country club.*
It is ridiculous, you know. I mean, they know who I am, you know, but, er, you, you could be a sex offender. I mean, all right, yes, you've come to use the excellent facilities, but you're still a sex offender.

**Pete**
But I'm not a sex offender.

**Alan**
It's all right. They won't ask you about it.

**Pete**
But I'm not a sex offender.

**Alan**

Great. That's something we've got in common. But, er, no, the security is terrible here. I mean, I actually booked the room under the name of the Real IRA. They didn't bat an eyelid. I'll just go and tell them it's me.

*Alan opens door to room and enters; several policemen are waiting inside.*

**Alan**

*(Leaving room seconds later)* I've got to get out of here.

**Pete**

What's the problem?

**Alan**

Crossed wires.

**Pete**

Well, er, shall we go to Apache?

**Alan**

What, my house? There's no electricity.

**Pete**

Well, you know, I'd just like to see the set-up.

**Alan**

Yes. We'll go straight to Apache after a pub lunch for an hour.

*In Alan's house.*

**Pete**

Hey, Alan, there's some really nice houses around here.

*Alan and Pete stand outside Alan's house.*

**Alan**

Yeah, a-a-actually, I'm sorry it's a bit of a building site. I mean technically you should have a hat hard-on. What am I saying? I mean a hat hard-on. Done it again! *(Laughs)* Come in.

**Michael**

*(In posh accent)* Hello. How do you do? How nice to meet you.

**Pete**

How do you do?

**Alan**

This is Michael.

**Pete**

It's a very unusual accent you've got there. Where are you from?

**Michael**

I'm originally from Newcastle, like, but –

**Alan**

Michael's in charge of our, er, Internet computer.

**Michael**

Aye. There's nae porn on it.

**Alan**

Did you understand that?

**Pete**

No.

**Alan**

Good. This is Lynn. *(She smiles)* Close your mouth, Lynn. Well, shall we move through to what is clearly the conference area?

**Pete**

So, this is Apache Communications?

**Alan**

Yeah, yeah. We, we, we normally have three clocks on the wall there. Telling the time in London, Paris … and Dublin. Which is the same as London, but I do think sometimes you need to be reminded of that.

**Pete**

Yeah, I'm dying to hear your ideas for the fireplace conference, Alan.

**Alan**

Er, grab a sofa.

**Pete**
Just over here?

**Alan**
Sure, yeah. Let me tell you a bit about the set-up here. You can't use the toilet because it's blocked. Yeah, you see, at Apache we waaaaaaaay – *(Alan rests hands on one end of table, which seesaws under his weight)* Sorry, er, this a new table. It's not quite finished. Do you want to pop this on? *(Picks up a hard hat from table)* Oh no, it's hiding a handle. *(Puts hat back)* Piece of fruit? *(Picks up bowl of fruit to reveal men's toilet sign)*

**Pete**
Er, no, thank you.

**Alan**
Did you see that?

**Pete**
Yes.

**Alan**
Yeah. Yeah. I, er, I think the designer has gone for that, er, toilet door balanced on a Black and Decker Workmate effect.
*Alan sits on sofa opposite Pete; table is between them.*

**Pete**
Er, Alan? I can't see you.

**Alan**
No, that's fine. No problem. I'll just, er, hop up here. *(Alan sits on back of sofa.)*

**Pete**
The caravan, Alan – whose is it?

**Alan**
The, the builders live in there. Yeah. Lynn sometimes goes in there. I don't think there's anything going on. You know. I've told her I disapprove of, er, workplace relationships but, er, shit happens. Whoa!

*Sofa tips backwards; Alan falls to the floor and laughs exaggeratedly.*

**Alan**
You've got to laugh when you fall off a sofa. Bloody sofa! I like this time of evening when the lighting gets quite bad.

*Lynn enters room, carrying tray of tea.*

**Alan**
You know –

*Lynn goes to put tray at one end of table.*

**Alan**

Meeeeeeeeeeee, Lynn! (*Alan grabs fruit bowl from middle of table*) Three, two, one (*Alan places fruit bowl at one end as Lynn places tea tray at other*), land.

**Pete**

So, er, shall we start, Alan?

**Alan**

Yes.

**Pete**

Now, the main thing, the main thing –

*Lynn picks up Pete's cup of tea from tray; Alan grabs piece of fruit from bowl.*

**Pete**

– the main thing is we need something quite quick.

*Lynn picks up Alan's cup of tea from tray; Alan grabs another piece of fruit from bowl.*

**Pete**

Now, as we always say at Dante's Fires, what is the burning issue?

*Alan laughs exaggeratedly.*

**Alan**

Yeah, it's good that. Burning issue – fireplaces – I like it, yeah.

**Pete**

So, er, what we want to do is, we want to give our sales force something inspirational.

*Alan laughs exaggeratedly.*

**Pete**

What are you laughing at?

**Alan**

No, no, I'm just still laughing at the, er, the burning issue thing. Very, very good joke. (*Rolls orange to other end of table; puts his cup down as orange hits the tray*) Splashdown.

*Pete goes to put his cup on table.*

**Alan**

Eeeeeeeeeeeee.

**Pete**

You want me to put it in the middle?

**Alan**

That would be tremendously helpful.

**Pete**

OK.

**Alan**

(*Sighs*) Shall we put the lights on, or shall we, shall we, shall we wait fifteen minutes?

**Pete**

Never mind that, Alan. All I want to know is, can you give us a pyrotechnics and light show.

**Alan**

Absolutely. We can do you (*in South African accent*) pyrotechnics. Erm, but I recommend you start with a couple of humorous comments, a couple of jokes perhaps.

**Pete**

We don't want a clown, Alan.

**Alan**

Oh God, no, no, you don't want a clown. No, no. I mean they'd never get to the podium with those long shoes on. Actually, how do clowns go down in South Africa? You know, because with all that make-up on they're neither one thing nor the other. Are they allowed on buses?

**Pete**

(*Looking annoyed*) Look, Alan. No clowns, no gags.

**Alan**

Just a couple of jokes?

**Pete**
No, Alan, no!

**Alan**
Please?

**Pete**
*(Shouts)* No, you can't!

**Alan**
Well, there's no need for that. I only wanted to do a couple of jokes.

**Pete**
*(Shouts)* You can't –

**Alan**
You've done it again. You've said it again. Just because I've got a shit table. What do you want?

**Pete**
I want you to turn the lights on.

**Alan**
Good call. *(Shouts)* Michael!

**Michael**
Aye.

**Alan**
Oh, you're there. Sorry. Erm, shall we pop the lights on?

**Michael**
All right, hang on. Mind your head. It's coming down.

**Alan**
Yeah. Yeah, i-i-i-it, er … now … it does look to me like, er, torches attached to a bicycle wheel. *(Alan and Michael switch on torches individually)* Probably designed by the same person who did the table. Yeah. I like South Africa. And I hated those people who wouldn't trade with you in the eighties. Yeah. I carried on buying your tomatoes all through that period. You say tomato, I say *(in American accent)* tomato. You say *(in*

*South African accent)* tomato. I say potato, you say *(in South African accent)* potato. Let's call the whole thing a thoroughly nice chap and, er *(in South African accent)*, doesn't matter what race he is.
*(Shouts)* Lynn!

**Lynn**
Yes.

**Alan**
Oh, you're there. Erm, I, I, I don't think this is quite bright enough. I think we're going to have go nuclear.

**Pete**
Look, Alan. *(Shouts)* It's too late to cancel!

*Pete rests hands on one end of table; Alan rests hands on the other.*

**Pete**
I'm sorry. I'm sorry.

**Alan**
It's easily done. Look, if you're gonna be angry, if you don't mind being angry down the centre of the table. I tell you what, when this meeting is over I'm taking this table back: it's bloody useless. *(Sighs)*

*Room flashes red.*

**Alan**
*(Shouts)* You've hit the hazards!
*(Sighs)* If I said 'full beam' once, I must have said it a dozen times. Level with me, Pete: have I got this job?

**Pete**
Given that it's too late to book anyone else *(sighs)* the answer has to be yes.

**Alan**
Jacka-nacka-nory.

*Room bathed in white light.*

**Alan**
Ah, that's better. *(In South African accent)* Full beam.

*Alan on the phone in the caravan.*

**Alan**
For the conference I'd like four glitter explosions, twelve puff flashes and, yeah, so the sequence would be puff-flash-puff-flash-bang. Yeah, well, basically could I have a condensed Pink Floyd concert for £500? Yes. OK. Thanks, Lynn.

*Puts phone down.*

**Sonia**
You want it?

**Alan**
What have we got?

**Sonia**
We got eggs, we got chicken.

**Alan**
Which came first?

**Sonia**
Well, I just buy the chicken on Thursday –

**Alan**
Yeah, all right. Chicken's fine.

**Sonia**
It's empty.

**Alan**
Wh-what do you mean?

**Sonia**
The chicken is empty.

**Alan**
Wh-what do you mean, it's empty? What, it's hollow?

**Sonia**
No. Where is the chicken inside the chicken?

**Alan**
You didn't, you didn't buy a display model, did you?

**Sonia**
The chicken inside.

**Alan**
You mean the giblets?

**Sonia**
Yeah, giblets. Yeah. Where's that?

**Alan**
That's awful.

**Sonia**
I like them.

**Alan**
You might eat them in your country, sweetheart, we don't here. You know, I don't want to eat an intestine or a chicken heart on a, on a, on a mini-muffin. It's like some sort of voodoo canapé.

**Sonia**
You want to make love? The bed's ready.

*Points to bed with a huge knife. The pillows have pictures of Alan and Sonia on them.*

**Alan**
No, I'm fine, thanks. Just gonna check on Michael.

**Sonia**
OK. *(Shouts after him)* Alan, I love you!

**Alan**
*(Shouts back)* Thanks a lot.

*Alan enters house; Michael in garden chair and sleeping bag.*

**Alan**
Hello, Michael.

**Michael**
Oh!

**Alan**

Do you, do you want to be on your own?

**Michael**

Oh no. No. Fine. It's nice to have a bit of company, you know? Keep the … demons at bay. *(Laughs)*

**Alan**

Yeah, I was just thinking, actually, can you imagine if we were the last two people on earth, camped out up here?

**Michael**

Cor, aye, yeah, eh. We'd, we'd have to breed.

**Alan**

Yeah, I, I think I'd prefer to adopt. Men can these days.

**Michael**

Aye. I'd, I'd adopt a greyhound. 'Cause the last one I had was right clever, you know?

**Alan**

Yeah. If they were that clever they'd know that thing that they chase after isn't a rabbit.

**Michael**

Mind, you know, if this, er, fireplace conference goes well you could get yourself a helicopter.

**Alan**

Yeah, I'd love to fly a helicopter. There's no doubt about it, Michael: the world's getting smaller.

**Michael**

Aye, it's global warming.

**Alan**

No, that's something different.

**Michael**

Oh.

**Alan**

I'd just like to fly a helicopter all round Norfolk, you know. Swoop down over a field, scare a donkey so it falls into a river … and hover over one of those annoying families that go on holidays on bikes.

**Michael**

Aye.

**Alan**

Yeah. And shout at them, 'Get out of the area!' And watch them panic.

*Michael laughs.*

**Michael**

Me, I'd, I-I-I'd have an, an Apache attack helicopter.

**Alan**

*(Enthusiastically)* Oh, great.

**Michael**

Aye. I'd gan back to school. But first I'd take out the labs *(makes machine gun noise)*, and then I'd type into the attack computer 'Mr Cragg, chemistry teacher'. *(Makes explosion noise)* Blow 'im to bits.

**Alan**

*(Laughs)* Yeah, I know the feeling.

**Michael**

And then I'd go looking for Tom Donaldson. I'd be hovering just down the road from his house, there. And he'd see us, but I'd duck down behind the trees, and he thinks he's safe, right? And he's just about to put the key in his front door, and I come up from behind the hedge *(makes machine-gun noise)*, 'Hello, you bastard.' He panics, right? And he goes in the house, so I get the 30-millimetre canon and I take out the fish pond *(makes firing noise)*, coy carp in there *(makes firing noise; Alan looks worried)* couple of rounds each, right? And then I just tilt the helicopter over to one side *(makes machine-gun noise)* and the machine-gun bullets is chewing up the drive, right? He comes out. 'Oh no! Not me Triumph Stag! I've just had it resprayed!' *(Makes machine-gun noise)* I cut it right in half, right? And then he goes, 'Ahhh!' He runs up on to the garage roof. I say, 'Right. This is for you, Tom.' He goes, 'No, no!' He's begging us, he's begging us man, 'No, please, don't!' *(Makes rocket noise)* And then I fly off to Cornwall and I just smash in the sea in a big ball of flames.

**Alan**
*(Looking dismayed, stands up and goes to leave)* Sleep well, Michael. Erm, who's Tom Donaldson?

**Michael**
Oh, he's just a mate.

*Choristers Country Club. Alan is at the gateway.*

**Alan**
Hello. I've just swallowed a load of Anthrax and I'd like to let off like mad in the club bar. Can I come in? You haven't opened the gate: well done. Now, I've just remembered, I've forgotten my card. Er, I was showing it to a Geordie last night. Er, he asked to hold it and I've gone and left it in his bloody hands. Hello?

**Intercom**
*(Male voice)* Hello.

**Alan**
Right. I think what's happened here is that I made a complaint about you, and you're pursuing a vendetta, which I can understand. Hello?

**Intercom**
*(Male voice)* Hello.

**Alan**
Right. You, you do know who I am?

**Intercom**
*(Male voice)* No.

**Alan**
Oh. Erm, I've got it! There's a complimentary copy of my book, *Bouncing Back*, behind reception. Can you see it?

**Intercom**
*(Male voice)* Er, yeah.

**Alan**
Right, great, well, I'll replicate the cover stance.

**Intercom**
*(Male voice)* OK. Go on then.

*Alan holds stance for several seconds.*

**Intercom**
*(Female voice)* Hello? Can I help you?

**Alan**
Yeah, yeah, is Sean there?

**Intercom**
*(Female voice)* No. He just knocked off for the evening. Can I help you?

**Alan**
Er, no, no, it's fine, fine. Thank you.

*Alan tries to climb over railings.*

**Lynn**
Alan, what are you doing?

**Alan**
Climbing over a fence.

**Lynn**
Oh, you should watch yourself. You're nearly fi—

**Alan**
Were you going to say I was nearly fifty, Lynn? I might be nearly fifty, Lynn, but at least I can – *(sharp intake of breath)*

**Lynn**
What?

**Alan**

*(Face contorted)* Lynn, I've pierced my foot on a spike. It ruddy frigging hurts like – *(the spike has gone right through Alan's foot)*

**Lynn**

Alan, put yourself in the recovery position.

**Alan**

You're just quoting bits of *Casualty* now.

**Lynn**

Pull it off all at once.

**Alan**

Then all the blood will run out the hole in my foot, you old mis—

**Lynn**

Pull your foot up now.

**Alan**

Can't I leave it on the spike?

**Lynn**

Well, pull it off the spike. After three –

**Alan**

*(Groaning)* No, I'm not going to do it, Lynn. You pull your foot up.

**Lynn**

Well, mine's not on the spike.

**Alan**

There's someone coming. Be normal, be normal. Hello, Dante Fires, just through there. Oooooh, you're gonna have a good time. Just being a bit camp.

*Alan and Lynn inside Choristers.*

**Alan**

I can feel the blood squelching in my shoe. Can you hear it squelching?

**Lynn**

Oh.

**Alan**

Just listen, listen, listen.

**Lynn**

Yeah.

*Alan's foot is covered in tissue paper and blood. He moves his foot around to make it squelch.*

**Alan**

Argh!

**Lynn**

Oh, look at you, Alan. You should be in hospital.

**Alan**

Lynn, some of these people have come from Stoke. I'm going on.

**Lynn**

Shall I go on for you?

**Alan**

Lynn, you couldn't present a *cat*.

*Applause and music: 'The Heat Is On'. Alan makes his way to the stage.*

**Alan**

*(Clings to podium; speaks through clenched teeth)* Ah-haaaaa! What a year it's been for Dante. Fires. Maybe you're here tonight with a wife or an old flame.

*Silence*

**Alan**

But what is the burning issue?

*Silence*

**Alan**

*(Voice thick with pain)* Hit your targets or you'll be … fired.

*Silence*

**Alan**

But today's also about fun. Have you all got your fun packs? I've got one here. *(Picks up a bag and drops it)* Dropped it. It's all right. I've got a list. Here. It should contain a torch, a Curly Wurly, a book of stamps, a free digital watch with denim strap, a vodka miniature, a Bic-style razor and *(voice wavers)* a copy of the *Daily Express*. *(Groaning)* Ooooooh, it's a good paper. Now, first award tonight is for best Christ. Not Christ. Er, sorry. Keep saying 'Christ'. Er, I know some of you may be religious and to those people I apologi— *(makes strangled noise; vomits behind podium. Hits button on podium – explosion goes off and glitter descends)* Sorry. I was supposed to hit that later. I'll just wait for it to finish. A, a glittering year ahead. *(Sighs)* You might want to read your *Daily Express*. Don't shine that torch in my face, mate. I've just lost a pint of blood. On now as we look at a fantastic year for – I'm going to be sick again *(vomits behind podium and retches several times)*. You know that feeling when there's nothing coming up. *(Retches several times more)* Urrgh. Jesus. *(Retches some more)* Urrgh. August knocked the trend for downturn in fireplace sales *(retches)*. Oh God. *(Retches)* Oh, I sound like the devil. Bits come out my shoe. That's not going back in again. You want some more glitter?

*Presses button on podium. Explosion; glitter falls on stage.*

**Alan**
Two grand, that cost. I was gonna give out some … some awards. But, er, that's not going to happen. Look at me. Go and eat some coffee. Erm, drink it. It's soup you can eat – that's not so liquid.

*Music: 'The Heat Is On'; Alan limps offstage.*

*Screen goes blank.*

**Alan**
Are we nearly there?

*Alan, in semi-darkness outside caravan. He has a tie covering his eyes.*

**Michael**
Move forward. I mean, keep, keep, keep moving. You're going in the right direction. That's it.

**Alan**
Michael, I'm not the Vietnam. Can I just take this off –

**Michael**
No! Leave it. Leave it for a minute.

**Alan**
Michael, this doesn't feel like a treat.

**Michael**
All right. That way. That way. *(Directs Alan)* Take it, take it off now.

*Alan takes tie off his eyes.*

**Michael**
There look. I've made you a helicopter landing pad.

*Shot of chalk circle with 'h' drawn in centre.*

**Alan**
It's a small H.

**Michael**
No, man. It's big. Look, you could see that from space, man.

**Alan**
Michael, I don't want aliens to see this from space. It would be embarrassing. They would look down through their giant telescope and say, 'Look at that idiot. He's got a baby H.'

**Michael**
I, I, I done it just to cheer you up, like. You know, because the fireplace job was knackered and … Apache Productions is probably gonna gan down the pan like all the other companies which you've started.

**Alan**
*(Slurring)* Michael, that may very, wery well be the case. But I am happy. Now that may very wery well be because I am on morphine.

**Michael**
You're on morphine? Oh, man. They should have put an M on your forehead.

**Alan**
Why?

**Michael**
Well, that's what you do with battlefield casualties, ay? You know, you put an M on their forehead so that the doctors know they've had morphine. It's dangerous.

**Alan**
Not so a little helicopter can land on your forehead?

**Michael**
No, a helicopter doesn't begin with M.

**Alan**
*(Laughing)* I'd like that, though. I'd like that. A little helicopter land on your head with its rotor blade would cool you, cool you down like a little hand fan. On your forehead.

**Michael**
Right, come on. You've definitely had morphine, haven't you? Come on.

**Alan**
Yeah. Do you want some Sugar Puffs?

**Michael**
Aye, that'd be nice. We'll have Sugar Puffs.

*Michael leads Alan back to caravan.*

**Alan**
Ahhhhh. Still thinking about the helicopters.

**Michael**
Aye.

**Alan**
The little helicopters.

**Michael**
Yeah – helicopters –

**Alan**
Yeah. Like the beginning of *M\*A\*S\*H*. That begins with an M.

# COMMENTS AND SUGGESTIONS
Please drop in box provided

The fruit bowls in the members' lounge — wouldn't it be an idea to put a paper doily in the bottom of the bowl, which you wouldn't see when the bowl was full of fruit but would be revealed when you got to the last piece of fruit.

It could be a very simple lace doily which would have a two-fold effect, aesthetic and practical, being

a) it would absorb any moisture or cud which might leak from a damaged or prematurely rotting plum, and

b) it's a very nice decorative thing, it makes people feel good, they don't see a bowl bereft of fruit, they see a rather attractive doily at the bottom of the bowl.

Also, I feel the staff should replenish more regularly those bowls of nuts that look like the polystyrene shapes you pack hifi equipment in.

# CHORISTERS COUNTRY CLUB

# I'M ALAN PARTRIDGE

SERIES 2

## EPISODE 3: BRAVE ALAN

*Radio Studio*

**Woman**
*(Laughing)* That was truly amazing, June.

**June**
*(Laughing)* Yes. Still pulling ourselves together after a visit from the unforgettable Lester Price, who's had us in stitches.

*Laughter; Alan looks annoyed throughout.*

**Woman**
Chaos. Maybe – say it's time for us to hand over to our old friend, Alan Partridge. He's here with Norfolk Nights. Are you ready, Alan?

**Alan**
Yes. Good night.

*Laughter*

**Woman**
Good night, Alan.

**June**
Good night.

**Woman**
Night.

**Alan**
The Nesbitt sisters there. Tonight we're talking about death.

**Male voiceover**
Wivenhoe. Flitwick. Tiptree. Hulbeach. Pinchbeck. Tarrington St Clement. Fetford Forest. It's 10 p.m. This is Norfolk Nights with Alan Partridge.

**Alan**
How would you like to be disposed of when you're dead? We're taking letters and e-mails on that tonight, er, starting with a, a letter from Mike, who's twenty-four. He'd like to be buried in a large satin-lined coffin with a couple of page-three stunners. They're

alive, he says. I'm not reading that out. No. No. Erm, another letter here from Susan from Spicksworth. Er, she says she'd like her ashes to be scattered in a nice field or meadow. That's the kind of thing we want. *(Alan reads Mike's letter for several seconds.)* Sorry. Er, we're also taking e-mails, er, on the big question: what happens after we die? Er, Frederick e-mails to say he has four children, he is the proud father of a new baby boy, Joshua, and his daughter Susan, five, has just started school, and he thinks that after death there is nothing. OK. Two questions: how are we going to eat and what floor's the restaurant on? The answer is 'The Chinese Way' and Level 42.

*Opening music*

**Alan**
*(In opening sequence)*
*Looking in his pint of beer*
Dead … dead daddy-long-legs. You can still drink it.

**Alan**
Ooh. That was Terence Trent D'Arby. Cocky man from the eighties, helping everyone relax in Alan's Deep Bath.

**Male voiceover**
*(Jingle)* Alan's Deep Bath.

**Alan**
*Gentle music playing in the background*
We're down to the final lather. Just relax. There's a foamy bit on your shoulder. Let's make it more frothy with a squirt of light lemon liquid. Don't you feel good? Relax. Don't fall asleep and slip under – some terrible statistics about that. Er, let's just finish your neck off now with some final suds … Mmmm.

**Jingle**
*(Male voiceover)* Alan's Deep Bath bath bath bath *(echoes)*

**Jingle**
*(Alan)* Brought to you by Dettol.

**Alan**
It's 1 a.m. Calling all pigeons! There's a cat amongst you, and that cat's name is Dave Clifton. Prrrrropping up the bar in his fictional nightclub.

**Dave**
*(laughs)* Yeah, well, er, better being in a fictional nightclub than in a fictional bath, Alan.

**Alan**
*(laughs)* Yeah, well, it's better than having fictional listeners, Dave. Er, it's bad enough sitting on your own in a real nightclub – which I've seen you do – but, er, sitting on your own in a fictional one has got to be the worth of boast worlds.

**Dave**
Sorry, Alan … don't you mean the worst of both worlds?

**Alan**
Er, no. No, no, no, I do mean the worth of boast worlds. I.e. in the world of boasters – not the biscuits, but people who boast, like you – they're worth is worth … you know –

**Dave**
OK. Here's, er, Matt Bianco!

*Alan and Michael in petrol station shop*

**Alan**
Chap there parked on the wrong side of the pumps. It's amazing the number of people who still think the petrol cap to a Ford Focus is on the offside rear.

**Michael**
When will they learn?

**Alan**
You know what that is, Michael? It's saaaaad.

**Michael**
Aye.

**Alan**
There's no point pulling it, mate, it's not going to reach. He's determined to make it reach. Oh, he has done.

**Michael**
So, er, was it a good show tonight? Did anybody actually phone in?

**Alan**
Had a fascinating discussion about reincarnation with a chap from Spicksworth, who, er, was convinced that in a previous life, er, he'd been Arthur Askey. I pointed out that his and Askey's life had overlapped –

**Michael**
Oh.

**Alan**
– and he backed down.

**Michael**
I believe in, er, reincarnation, like. I, I'd like to come back as an animal. Like, er, er, a dolphin.

**Alan**
Dolphins are quite intelligent, Michael.

**Michael**
I could jump through a hoop and catch a fish in me mouth.

**Alan**
Would you really?

**Michael**
Yeah, yeah.

**Alan**
Can you do this? *(Makes clicking noise with mouth)*

**Michael**
What's that?

**Alan**
It, it, it's a dolphin chatting.

**Michael**
Oh, I can do a whale. Whoooooo.

**Alan**
No, no, no, no, that … that's a homosexual.

**Michael**
Oh.

**Alan**
No, no, but it's a fascinating subject, reincarnation. Yes, er, I always wonder what Lynn would come back as.

**Michael**
*(Laughs)* Aye, aye. A badger. I've always seen her as a, as a badger.

**Alan**
Yeah, I can imagine her coming out of her hole, sniffing the air.

**Michael**
Aye, and you could smack her head with a shovel.

**Alan**
Yeah, no, I wouldn't do that. I wouldn't do that, Michael. You know, even if she was a badger.

**Michael**
You've got to control them, man. You know, they've got TB.

**Alan**
Yeah, but so had the Brontë sisters. I wouldn't hit them over the head with a shovel, no matter how bad the books were. Heathcliff – PANG! Then you really would be wuthering.

**Michael**
Aye. Aye, look, a Lexus. Hey, it's a better one than yours. *(Laughs)*

**Alan**
It's interesting, Michael, since owning a Lexus it's amazing the number of Lexi you see around. 'Cause that's the plural.

*A man enters the shop. He places a newspaper on the counter.*

**Alan**
The *Daily Mail*.

**Dan**
Yep.

**Alan**
Arguably the best newspaper in the world.

**Dan**
Oh, yeah.

**Michael**
Nice Lexus.

**Dan**
Yes, I, er, I love Lexi.

**Alan**
Yeah, I always have a thing I say about Lexus – it's like the – er –

**Dan and Alan**
Japanese Mercedes.

**Dan**
Yeah, well, I hate Mercs. People who drive them are just saaaaaad.

**Alan**
Are you wearing Lynx?

**Dan**
Well smelt *(man holds up his arm)*. Voodoo.

**Alan**
*(Alan holds up his arm in the same way)* Java. Alan Partridge.

**Dan**
Dan Moody.

*They shake hands.*

**Alan**
Pleased to meet you.

**Michael**
I wear Tommy Hilfinger.

**Alan**
It, it, it's Hilfiger.

**Michael**
No, it says Hilfinger on the bottle.

**Alan**
Did you buy it down the market?

**Michael**
Aye.

**Alan**
Oh, that's why. It's amazing, this Lexus connection, you know. Next you'll be telling me you drink Director's bitter.

**Dan**
I've got it coming out of my taps.

**Alan**
Have you?

**Dan**
I'm joking.

**Alan**
Great! It's amazing. We both like the *Daily Mail*, we both drive Lexi –

**Dan**
Plural.

**Alan**
Plural. And, er, we both drink Director's bitter. It's like *The X-Files*. Bu-bu-but a pleasant *X-Files*.

**Dan**
The Lex Files.

**Alan**
God, that's good. Can I shake your hand again?

**Dan**
Take a card.

*They shake hands.*

**Alan**
Oh, you combined the card with a handshake?

**Dan**
Yeah.

**Alan**
I used to do that, but, er, I kept getting it wrong. Gave a paper cut to a man from Nestlé. *(Looking at the card)* You *own* Kitchen Planet on the A416?

**Dan**
The very same.

**Alan**
It's massive.

**Dan**
Oh, 10,000 square feet of sheer kitchens. And I know who you are – Norfolk Nights?

**Alan**
The very same. And, er, and of course, er, *Skirmish*. Military-based general knowledge quiz show on, er, digital cable channel UK Conquest that has the largest audience share for a digital channel at that time of day in the Norfolk area.

**Michael**
Y-you should do him a cheap kitchen. He wants a kitchen –

**Alan**
Michael, Michael, I wouldn't insult this man by asking for a 25 per cent discount on a kitchen.

**Michael**
You're looking for a kitchen, I can get you a kitchen: let's talk.

**Alan**
Fancy a Flav?

**Dan**
Flavia? Good call.

**Alan**
King of coffees.

**Dan**
Oh, in off the red.

**Alan**
*(At the coffee machine)* How do you take it?

**Dan**
Unleaded.

**Alan**
Mine's diesel.

**Dan**
What does that mean?

**Alan**
*(Returning with coffee)* I don't know. You know, we've got a lot in common. We should go for a proper drink. I mean, you … you, you provide quality kitchens and I provide –

**Dan**
Quality radio.

**Michael**
And I work in a petrol station.

**Alan**

Yeah, but it's just me and Dan that's going for the drink.

**Michael**

(*Good-naturedly*) Oh, yeah, fine. I'll just get hammered on me own.

**Alan**

Well, I'll – I'll – I'll walk you to your Lexus.

**Dan**

Great.

**Michael**

Shall I put these on the tab?

**Alan**

Tab? I haven't got a tab. Wish I could! Wish I could afford a tab. (*To Dan*) I can … I can afford one. I've got a six-figure income.

*Sonia stands in caravan kitchen; Alan enters kitchen, doing up his trousers.*

**Alan**

Well, Sonia, that was classic intercourse. So, er, so thanks. OK. Let's just, er, pop the extractor fan on. Get a through draught going.

**Sonia**

Alan? Do you want an egg in a bap?

**Alan**

Yes, please.

**Sonia**

Here comes your egg in a bap (*laughs*).

**Alan**

(*Wearily*) Oh, oh, great. Mmmm. Yum-yum. (*pulls egg out of bap*) Ah, it's plastic.

*Sonia laughs loudly.*

**Alan**

Yeah … I'll look back on that as an excellent practical joke, yeah. I presume there's some sort of Whoopee Cushion in here somewhere?

**Sonia**

(*Laughing*) Yes.

**Alan**

Look forward to that taking me by surprise.

*Alan sits on banquette. Whoopee cushion makes noise. Sonia laughs loudly.*

**Alan**

Where's Lynn? She's never normally late.

**Sonia**

So, this Dan. The kitchen man. You like him: you think he will be friend?

**Alan**
Yes, I'm convinced he's my best friend.

**Sonia**
It will be difficult day for me today in coffee shop. There is new stock coming. I have to cut the carrot cake.

**Alan**
They say nurses have it tough.
*Knocking at door.*
Oh good, Lynn. Come in.

*Lynn enters caravan.*

**Lynn**
Sorry I'm late. I know I'm … I mean I know I'm not late. I'm just a little bit late.

**Alan**
Yeah, that's fine. Did you get my, er –

**Lynn**
You see, I couldn't find my keys. You see, I had a bit of a late night last night. We went for a curry and when we were about to leave, the heavens just opened, and we were stuck in the foyer, and we were just pointing at the rain, saying, 'We're stuck, we're stuck, we're stuck.' *(laughs)*

**Alan**
Lynn, has your mother's death just hit you?

**Lynn**
No. We were stuck in the foyer –

**Alan**
Hang, hang, hang on a sec. Who's we?

**Lynn**
Me and my friend from church.

**Alan**
And what's her name?

**Lynn**
It's a he.

**Alan**
Right, Lynn, sit down.

*Lynn sits down. Whoopee cushion makes noise. She looks shocked.*

**Alan**
Don't worry about that. It's just a cushion that simulates rectal gas. Now, what's his name?

**Lynn**
Gordon.

**Alan**
How long has Gordon been a member of the church?

**Lynn**
A few weeks. He's just moved into the area.

**Alan**
He's a con-man.

**Lynn**
No, he's a retired policeman.

**Alan**
Lynn, bigamists have several identities. To men like that, the building society books of women like you make fascinating reading.

**Lynn**
*(Smiling)* Sorry. Just thinking of Gordon and me stuck in the rain.

**Alan**
Stop laughing, Lynn. You're laughing at weather. You're like your mother in her last few weeks. *(Uses electric nasal hair trimmer)* We're going to have to have a serious talk in the morning.

*Phone rings. Alan picks up receiver.*

**Alan**
Hello, Partridge? You're through to the static home. Dan! Dan. Sir Dansworth of Moodyshire, as I live and breathe. Yeah, knew it was you. I keyed it in last night when I drove home. Nearly hit a badger. Yeah, well, they, they're pests, aren't they? Yeah … yeah, they carry TB. So, er, so

how's it hanging? *(Laughs)* Yes, I dress on the left, too. *(Laughs)* I'd love to. Love to, love to, yeah. *(To Sonia)* Er, Dan has asked me to present a prize at the Norfolk Bravery Awards tonight. Isn't that nice? Isn't that nice? *(Speaks into phone)* Yeah. I'd be delighted. Well, you've got to put a bit back.

*Sonia lunges at Alan with a hammer and hits him with it repeatedly.*

**Alan**
*(Shouts)* NO, PLEASE! HELP! HELP!

*Sonia laughs loudly.*

**Alan**
Oh that's … I'm sorry. I'm sorry. No, my Ukrainian girlfriend was attacking me with a rubber hammer. She's mildly cretinous. OK, bye. Bye-bye.
*(Alan puts receiver down.)*
You know, er, you know who's going to be at the Norfolk Bravery Awards?

**Sonia**
Who?

**Alan**
Who? It reads like a *Who's Who* of anyone who's anyone who's in the Norfolk area.

**Lynn**
Do you want me to come, Alan?

**Alan**
Er, no thanks, Lynn. Sonia and I'll be fine. You and Gordon can go and laugh at drizzle.

**Sonia**
Tonight I will try out some of my jokes, and make brave people laugh again.
*(Laughs and leaves caravan)*

**Lynn**
Do you need me to be –

**Alan**
Just keep her away from the dignitaries.

**Lynn**
What about brave people?

**Alan**
Oh, she can mingle with them. As long as she doesn't use her Whoopee Cushion on someone with M.E.

**Lynn**
I'll be off then.

**Alan**
OK. One more thing, Lynn.

*Alan holds up knife as if to attack Lynn. Lynn grabs Alan by the throat.*

**Alan**
*(Scared)* Argggh! Arggh! It's a joke knife! It's a joke knife! It's a joke knife! It's … it's funnier than rain.

*Alan, Lynn and Sonia in car. Sonia sits behind Alan and Lynn. Lynn is smiling broadly.*

**Alan**
Dan's a fantastic man. He really is. I was making him laugh this morning. I was on the phone to him. He was asking me what kind of phone I had, and I said, 'A Motorola Timeport,' and he said, 'That's saaaaad. You want to upgrade.' And I said, 'So do you – to a new face.' He nearly soiled himself. He said he laughed so much he had Kenco coming out of his nostrils. And that made me laugh. *(Laughs)*

*Lynn laughs politely.*

**Alan**
But, er, my nostrils were clear. You could drown in a cup of coffee. With an inch of water.

*Sonia pokes her finger in Alan's ear.*

**Alan**
Ay! Yeah! What are you doing?

*Sonia laughs loudly. She holds a fake beard up to her face.*

**Sonia**

Alan, look. You're taking a man to the party. *(Laughs)*

**Alan**

Get it off her.

**Lynn**

Oh, look! Look, Sonia!

*Lynn points out of window. While Sonia's not looking, Lynn grabs beard and passes it to Alan who throws it out of the sunroof.*

**Sonia**

*(Shouts)* Alan!

**Alan**

Well done, Lynn. That was textbook.

*Choristers Country Club.*

**Alan**

*(Getting out of the car)* I will. I will. But Lynn, please, have a word with the builder, because the other day his jeans were so far off his backside you could more or less see his anus.

**Lynn**

Mmm.

**Alan**

There's Dan! *(shouts)* Dan! ... Dan! ... Dan! ... Dan! ... Dan! ... Dan! ... Dan! ... Dan! ... Dan! ... Dan! ... Dan! ... Dan! ... Dan! ... Dan! Er, no, he's not seen me. I'll get him later ... DAN! Fine, fine. Oh well.

*The Colman's Mustard Bravery Awards. Alan stands on stage; applause.*

**Alan**

These awards are about people like Susan Cresswell. Susan is braver than ten firemen or a dozen policemen. Four years ago, Susan lost her hand in a cake-cutting machine. She managed to walk 400 yards holding her hand in ... in her other hand, where she hailed a taxi. One can only imagine what that must have looked like. The quick-thinking taxi driver drove her to a newsagent, where the hand was packed in Soleros, Magnums, Mini-milks and a Feast. After six hours of surgery, the hand was sewn back on. Sadly it didn't work, so off it came again. But she still had one good hand, and she was damned if anyone was going to take that off her – but n-no one was suggesting they were going to do that. Anyway, the point is, four years later she is credit controller at Cromwell-certificated bailiffs. Ladies and gentlemen, please give a big han—, welc—, applaud. Applaud like mad for Susan Cresswell.

*Applause. Alan passes Sue her award and stands staring at her prosthetic hand.*

*At the award ceremony reception party.*

**Alan**

*(To Lynn)* Single-hand Sue there, tackling the buffet. Like a human JCB.

**Dan**

See man over there with the big head and small face.

**Man**

Yeah.

*Alan wanders over to join Dan.*

**Dan**

That's Mike Yapley.

**Man**

What, who owns the car supermarket on the A47?

**Dan**

The very same.

**Woman**

He is such a character. But he's got a heart of gold.

**Dan**

Yeah. Teeth of gold as well.

*They laugh.*

**Alan**
I heard he hit a prostitute.

**Dan**
Alan. How was your visit to the lavatory?

**Alan**
Er, mission accomplished. Splashdown.

**Man**
Did you see Mr Brown and his friends off to the coast?

**Alan**
Yeah. Actually, I tell you what? I should get a bravery award for that, I tell you. No, seriously, it was textbook.

**Dan**
*(Motions to man)* Alan, this is Bob Fraser.

**Bob**
I own Sexton's Garden Centre.

**Alan**
Wow. Hey, I tell you, if a bomb went off in here tonight, the whole of society would collapse … in, in Norwich. For a bit.

**Bob**
Yeah, look, lovely to meet you, Alan. I'm just going to have a chinwag with Mike Yapley.

*Bob walks away.*

**Alan**
OK. Don't dress as a whore, he'll thump you.

**Dan**
Alan, you must meet my lady wife, Kerry.

**Kerry**
I love listening to your Deep Bath, Alan.

**Alan**
Well, Dan has told me all about you.

**Kerry**
Oh, what did he say?

**Alan**
Well, he just said he was married.

**Dan**
Well, give the man a twirl. Let the dog see the rabbit.

*Kerry turns around slowly.*

**Alan**
Oh yeah. But which is which? *(Laughs)* Sorry! I … obviously, I, I, I'm the dog. I'm the dog, yeah. You're a terrific rabbit. Oh, er, lovely olden days map of Norfolk there.

**Dan**
Yeah. They call Norfolk the rump of Britain.

**Alan**
Yeah.

**Kerry**
I think it looks more like a boob.

**Alan and Dan**
Oooh.

**Dan**
I stand corrected, said the man in the orthopoedic shoes.

**Alan**
Cracking.

**Dan**
Ooh, there, there goes Karen Colman.

**Alan**
Is that Karen Colman, Colman mustard's Colman?

**Kerry**
Yeah.

**Alan**
She is the Grace Kelly with black hair of Norfolk.

**Dan**
Yeah. Her house is massive.

**Alan**
I know. They use it in Hammer Horror films. It's Draclea's house. Can I just go and talk to her?

**Dan**
It's a free country.

*Alan walks away; Lynn comes up to him.*

**Alan**
Oh, this.

**Lynn**
I'm just keeping a close eye on Sonia.

**Alan**
Just make sure she hasn't got any

stinkbombs strapped to her body. She detonates those, it'll be the mother of all pongs. Then we'll see who's brave.

*Alan walks up to circle of people surrounding Karen.*

**Karen**
… about 300? I just started my speech when the heavens opened *(Alan laughs)*. I mean, everybody got absolutely drenched. So we quickly moved ourselves into the marquee, which was leaking like a fish, and there was …

*Alan runs over to woman in wheelchair.*

**Alan**
Erm, would you like to meet Karen Colman?

**Patricia**
Well, yes, I don't really know her –

*Alan pushes woman over to Karen's circle.*

**Alan**
Room for a brave one? Beep beep! Come on, mate. We're on wheels here. Erm, excuse me, mustard? I mean, er, Karen? Hello. Er, this, this lady would, would love, love to meet you.

**Patricia**
Hi, I'm Patricia Lessing.

**Karen**
Oh, Karen Colman. Nice of you to come.

**Patricia**
Nice to meet you. Hello there.

**Karen**
Well, I hope you're being looked after.

**Alan**
Oh, do you want to meet Bob? He owns a garden centre.

*Alan pushes woman in direction of Bob.*

**Alan**
Yes. She's an amazing woman. An amazing, amazing woman.

**Karen**
My grandfather was in a wheelchair.

**Alan**
Really? Oh. Was he born in a wheelchair? Not sure what I meant by that.

*Woman in wheelchair comes up to Karen again.*

**Patricia**
Karen, I wonder if I could bend your ear for a moment.

**Karen**
Yes, of course.

**Patricia**
Erm, I run a project in Ipswich where we help disabled people set up their own businesses, and –

**Karen**
Oh, really?

**Patricia**
Yes –

**Karen**
Well, we must talk. Let me get you a drink.

**Patricia**
Oh, thank you.

*Karen turns away.*

**Alan**
Would you be brave enough to let me finish my conversation?

**Patricia**
I, I just wanted to talk about my project.

**Alan**
Yeah, listen, love. It's just a meet and greet. Come on. Come on, you can push your way to the front of the buffet queue. It's not all doom and gloom.

*Alan pushes woman away.*

**Karen**
Where's she gone?

**Alan**
I think she drove off. Erm, now, as a mustardess, if you, if you like *(clears throat)*, what's your view on the new kids on the block. I mean things like, er, Tobasco sauce and, er, soy. I mean, I mean, do those keep you awake at night?

**Karen**
Well, as we say in our family, 'Too much mustard gets up your nose.'

**Alan**
*(Laughs)* That's marvellous!

**Karen**
So many brave people here today.

**Alan**
They're so ruddy bloody brave. I love brave people. Sir Donald Campbell, Evel Knievel, Braveheart and, er, and of course yourself.

**Karen**
Oh, I'm not brave. I just do my bit at events like this and fundraising for mental health charities –

**Alan**
Yeah, that's one charity I avoid, actually – mental health. Don't want to get tarred with the mad brush.

**Karen**
– but I really should go and mingle now.

*Karen walks off, Alan follows.*

**Alan**
I had mental health problems.

**Karen**
Oh, I'm so sorry.

**Alan**
Yeah.

**Karen**
I should have realized. Although I did wonder when I first met you.

**Alan**
I won't bore you with the details, but, erm, I drove to Dundee in my bare feet. Yeah. After buying the rights to K-9 – the robot dog on casters from *Dr Who*.

**Karen**
Oh, well, listen, we must talk. I, I've done an awful lot of work in that field.

*Dan walks up behind Alan.*

**Dan**
Did you find out how much she's got? *(Laughs)*

**Alan**
*(Under his breath to Dan)* It's all right. It's fine.

**Dan**
Hey, you know that thing you were saying about Norfolk being like a breast? Well, Kerry just said, 'The A47 ring road is the areola.' *(Laughs)*

**Alan**
Yeah, yeah, that's not really my kind of humour, er, actually …

*Karen turns away.*

**Dan**
Anyway, Alan Partridge, I arrest you on suspicion of sucking up to a mustard magnate.

**Alan**
You're not a copper.

**Dan**
Well, it's a citizen's arrest.

**Alan**
Well, I'll shoot you then – bang!

**Dan**
Well, I'm wearing a bulletproof blazer.

**Alan**
Well, I'll go for a head shot – bang!

**Dan**
I'm the Terminator: you can't kill me.

**Alan**
*(Desperately)* I've got your kids. I, I've got your kids, Dan.

*Alan turns and notices Sonia talking to Karen.*

**Alan**
Oh, cook a cat.

**Sonia**
Well, I met a guy called Geoff on the Internet. Got married, and then he went back to his first wife, and my boyfriend call him Jack Shit. *(Laughs)*

**Alan**
Is this lady annoying you?

**Karen**
No, not at all. She's been telling me the problems in getting into this country. I think people like Sonia should be helped to settle here. Permanently.

**Alan**
I think you have to judge each case on its merits.

**Karen**
Listen, things are beginning to wind down here. Um, I've got some friends coming for a drink at the house.

**Alan**
Splendid and tremendous.

**Karen**
It's a girls-only night tonight.

**Alan**
Oh, all right, what, loads of women talking blabbering crap?

*Sonia turns around wearing glasses with eyes on springs.*

**Sonia**
Look, I am brave – my eye is falling out. *(Laughs loudly)*

**Alan**
That's the tip of the iceberg. *(Karen laughs)* Oh, you think it's funny.

**Karen**
*(Laughing)* I love it. I'm sorry.

**Alan**
Yeah, well, this'll make you laugh. This *(stammers)* 'too much mustard gets up your nose?' nonsense.

*Alan picks up a pot of mustard and eats a large spoonful, then grimaces.*

**Karen**
*(Speaking slowly)* I'm going to give Sonia a telephone number. There's someone you should talk to.

**Alan**
I'm fine. I just need … just need some water.

**Sonia**
Bye, Alan!

*Karen and Sonia leave.*

**Alan**
*(To Sonia)* I won't kiss you goodbye. I'll kiss you later, and the rest – whoorr.

*(Takes a large gulp of water.)*
Oh, Lynn, Lynn. Er, have you seen Dan?

**Lynn**
Er, no, I haven't. *(Alan blows his nose)* I think everyone's gone now.

**Alan**
Right. And, er, what, what are you doing?

**Lynn**
Well, I'm going out with Gordon. You're more than welcome to join us.

**Alan**
No, no, no, no! I've got lots of plans.

*Alan in amusement arcade, playing video games.*

**Alan**
Shitty zombies!

*Alan in petrol station shop.*

**Alan**
Michael! Michael.

*Female assistant walks behind counter.*

**Alan**
Oh. No. No. No.

*Alan leaves shop.*
*Alan walks up to a front door and knocks.*

**Male voice inside house**
Someone lock the dog in!

*Door opens.*

**Michael**
Oh, it's Partridge.

**Alan**
Hello, Michael.

**Michael**
Oh, I cannae sell you any petrol.

**Alan**
No, no. Just … just passing, you know. Just thought I'd er –

**Michael**
Oh, right.

**Alan**
– say hello.

**Michael**
Would you like some soup?

**Alan**
I'm not a tramp, Michael.

**Michael**
No, no, no. I'm just offering you something to eat, like.

**Alan**
Oh, yeah, well, what, what have you got?

**Michael**
I could do you a cup of beans.

**Alan**
A cup of beans?

**Michael**
Have you never had a cup of beans, man?

**Alan**
No. No.

**Michael**
Oh, aye, you're in for a treat here.

**Alan**
Oh great.

*Alan starts to follow Michael inside house.*

**Michael**
No, stay there.

**Alan**
Yep, right.

*Michael comes back, several seconds later.*

**Michael**
There you go. As ordered: one cup of beans. And I've, I've put a sausage in an' all. It's a Michael special.

**Alan**
Marvellous. That's lovely. It's like, sort of like a savoury 99.

**Michael**
Aye. Aye. You can use the sausage for to scoop the beans out.

**Alan**
Oh, I see, yeah. Have you got a spoon?

**Michael**
No.

**Alan**
You haven't got a spoon?

**Michael**
There's one in the bathroom, but I've no cause to use it.

**Alan**
*(Eating his beans)* You all right, Michael? You seem a bit, er, at a bit of a loose end.

**Michael**
I'm watching a documentary about triads, like.

**Alan**
Oh. I always wondered, you know, how did they get those swords through Customs.

**Michael**
Aye. Probably just put them inside a cardboard tube, like what you'd put a poster in there.

**Alan**
Yeah, that's a good idea.

**Michael**
Yeah, bye.

*Michael shuts front door in Alan's face.*

**Alan**
Goodbye. What do you want me to do with this cu—

**Michael**
Put it on the step.

**Alan**
Yeah. Right.

*Alan walks away. He talks into his mobile phone.*

**Alan**
Hello, Lynn. I'm at Dan's big house. Can you come with the kitchen brochures? So that's, er, Smeg, Neff, Poggenpohl and, er, Bosch.

*Dan and Alan enter living room.*

**Dan**
Come on in. Come on in.

**Alan**
Hi. Thanks. Yeah, Dan, I, I, I, can we still talk about kitchens?

**Dan**
I speak no other language. Get you a drink?

**Alan**
Yeah. Nice big fat shot of Director's bitter.

*Dan leaves. Kerry enters living room, dressed in a silk dressing gown.*

**Kerry**
Oh, hello, Alan.

**Alan**
Oh, hello.

**Kerry**
Budge up.

**Alan**
Er, yeah. All right. Sorry. Sorry I'm, er, a bit late.

*Kerry sits close to Alan on the sofa.*

**Kerry**
What have you been up to?

**Alan**
Er, tried to outdance a computer: impossible. *(Kerry begins to stroke Alan's knee)* And then I fought some zombies with a boy in care. Wiped the floor with him. Yeah. Your hand is about 30 mil. from my gland … and, er, if I was dressed on the other side it, it would be in *(voice rises)* contact. Your little finger just touched it. I'll just, just, just pop that there.

*Alan moves Kerry's hand on to her knee.*

**Dan**
*(Returning with drinks and a video)*
The kitchen?

**Alan**
*(Moves further along the sofa)* Oh, good.

**Dan**
This is the one for you.

*Dan puts video in machine.*

**Dan**
Budge up.

**Alan**
What, *(points to Kerry)* that way?

**Dan**
Yup.

*Alan sits between Dan and Kerry on sofa. They watch video.*

**Alan**
Oh, that's a, that's a good, er, stainless steel hob. Very futuristic. *(To Kerry)* That's you! You're naked. And there's you. Hello, Dan. Is that a granite work surface that, that's supporting you both? Not corian, a man-made marble substitute?

**Dan**
Well, corian is to marble and granite what, er, MDF is to wood. I've got wood there.

**Alan**
No, that's MDF. Oh, I see. You're making a joke. *(Turning to Kerry)* MDF's banned in America.

**Kerry**
*(Nods at screen)* So's that.

*Alan turns back to screen.*
*Groans from film.*

**Alan**
Oh, all done. I think I'll go

**Dan and Kerry**
Alan.

**Alan**
No, I've, I've got, I've just remembered my dad is still dead. Er ... my dad's dead.

**Lynn**
Alan! Alan!

**Alan**
Er, that was quick!

*Lynn enters living room.*

**Lynn**
You rang earlier to tell me to bring over the kitchen brochures.

**Dan**
Can I get you a drink, Lynn?

**Lynn**
Oh, a Baileys please.

**Dan**
Take a seat.

*Kerry pats hand on sofa.*

**Alan**
*(Points towards armchair)* Sit there! Sit there, sit there, sit there.

**Lynn**
Oh, this is a comfy sofa.

**Alan**
Oh, Jesus.

**Dan**
I'll, er, I'll get the drinks. *(Puts his hand on Alan's shoulder)*

**Alan**
*(Moving away)* Aargh.

**Kerry**
I'll see where your drink is.

**Alan**
Lynn, these are sex people.

**Lynn**
What do you mean?

**Alan**
They're sex swappers! Lynn, this is Death Con 1. Look!

*Alan presses play on video.*

**Lynn**
Urgh.

**Alan**
Don't make the same noise as them! They'll think you want to join in! I'll pause it. Oh, I've hit fast forward. Oh, it's like a sort of hardcore Benny Hill. That, that's the kitchen work surface I was telling you about.

**Dan**
Lynn! Lynn, your Baileys.

**Lynn**
Er, no thanks. I don't want to be part of your sex festival.

**Alan**
(Looking confused) Sex festival?
(Lynn leaves.) Er, can I be very rude? Not like that.

**Dan**
Try me.

**Alan**
No, no. Come on, pack it in, mate. I don't want to have sex with your wife. I mean, you know, even though from the promotional video I can see that I … I, I, I would have a … a ruddy good time.

**Kerry**
A little hug?

**Alan**
A quick one.

*Kerry and Alan hug.*

**Alan**
Don't rub your fanny on me!

**Kerry**
Look forward to listening to your Deep Bath later, Alan.

**Alan**
Yeah. Yeah.

*Radio Station*

**Male voiceover**
(Jingle) From Felixstowe to Spalding, all the issues.

**Alan**
It's 11.30. Time for my Deep Bath.

**Male voiceover**
(Jingle) Alan's Deep Bath.

**Alan**
That's the last one. We're stopping this after

tonight, so … there's the bath, hop in, wash yourself, there's a loofah. It can, er, do, do, do, do be clean. Er, there's a big coarse towel on the radiator.

*Dan and Kerry sit at home smiling at each other and listening to the radio.*

**Alan**
And don't forget to rinse the bath once you've drained the water. Use the shower nozzle to blast off the scum. Here's Brian and Michael.

**Music**
He painted Salford's smoky tops
On cardboard boxes from the shops,

*Dan and Kerry look downcast.*

**Music**
And parts of Ancoats, where I used to play.

*Music continues; we see Alan in the studio, interspersed with him playing video games in an arcade.*

**Music**
I'm sure he once walked down our street,
'Cause he painted kids who had nowt on their feet;
The clothes they wore had all seen better days.
And he painted matchstalk men and matchstalk cats and dogs.
He painted kids on the corner of the street that were sparking clogs.
Now he takes his brush and he waits,
Outside them factory gates,
To paint his matchstalk men and matchstalk cats and dogs.

**Alan**
(Playing shoot 'em up video game)
King of Anglia!

**Music**
Now canvas and brushes were wearing thin …

Lord House
10 Pentney Lane
Norwich

Dear Jack

Thanks for your message. I'm replying this way to avoid a repeat of our last phone conversation. I apologize if I was abusive, but you must agree it was all a bit of a shock to me.

When I met Sonia in October, I was obviously unaware that she was still married to you. It's a mystery quite why she failed to tell me about you flying her over from the Ukraine, marrying her, moving to Lowestoft, then panicking after two weeks and running back to your wife. If you hadn't called last week to ask for Maureen's watch back, I'd still be in blissful ignorance. I'm not saying I wouldn't have got involved with Sonia if I'd known I'd be sitting here now filling in an Immigration declaration to take over her support from a sixty-one-year old man who's clearly emerging from some kind of extremely belated midlife crisis. But I may at least have run a few background checks.

What were you thinking, Jack? She's 52 per cent your age. You must have known it wouldn't work. And to just dump the girl in Carphone Warehouse like a spent Nokia or that little phone with arms and legs in the advert that walks along tragically in the rain – breathtaking. God alone knows what would have happened to her if I hadn't gone in there to get a holster for my Ericsson.

Anyway, enough of the small talk. Without fail, I need all the relevant paperwork (most importantly the Decree Absolute). Bottom line, Jack: I love the car – where's the log book? Don't send the papers here, as my PA Lynne is unaware of this cock-up and I want it to stay that way. She'd tear my head off. Instead meet me at the car park of Harry Ramsden's on the A6 outside Flitwick on Thursday. I will text you the exact time. I also need you to bring the letter I forwarded for you to sign, confirming that it was you who got Sonia from ukrainewife.com and not me. As I said in the phone call, I've been the subject of some not entirely pleasant ribbing about Sonia's origins at my country club, and having the letter on my person should shut a few people up.

As regards the rest of your message, congratulations on your remarriage. Maureen's either a remarkably forgiving woman or stupid. A little bit of both I imagine. Quite how you persuaded her that secretly closing your joint account, leaving her and acquiring an international e-bride for a fortnight consituted a 'moment of madness' is, to say the least, impressive.

Thanks for your suggestion that when all this is sorted out, the four of us go for a meal. I think not in the circumstances.

Yours faithfully

Alan Partridge

# I'M ALAN PARTRIDGE

## SERIES 2

## EPISODE 4: NEVER SAY ALAN

*Radio Station*

**Music**
I loved you
But you left me.

**Alan**
That was Norwich-based singer-songwriter
Christian Laveau, with a self-penned song
entitled 'I Loved You, But You Left Me'.
Apparently he can't get a record deal.
There's no justice, Christian … Laveau.
Well, it's the Bank Holiday weekend. A
terrible time for the lonely, which, I think,
Christian testifies to on his second track –
yes, 'Lonely … 'Cause You Left Me'.
Tonight we're think about which celebrity
you would like to spend a Bank Holiday
with, and what would you do. Er, Sue from

Paston says she'd like to sit down with some
hotpot and red cabbage and watch *Chitty
Chitty Bang Bang* with Sting. And, er, T.
Blatham, er, e-mails to say he'd like to clear
out the attic with the lovely Kate Winslet.
OK. On the line we have, if I'm not
mistaken, Roy from Caster St Edmunds.
Roy, hello.

**Roy**
Hello.

**Alan**
It's Bank Holiday! Whatcha doing? 'Oo's
with ya?

**Roy**
I'd like to go round Legoland with Sean
Connery and then afterwards we'd go for a
lovely lamb lunch in the centre of Windsor.

**Alan**
Got to say, Roy, I don't think that's Connery's cup of tea. I think Sean would rather do something like wander round the wildfowl park in Pepperstock *(in Scottish accent)* wi' a bottle of Scotch.

**Roy**
I don't agree. He'd go to Legoland. Bye.

**Alan**
Well –

*Phone goes dead.*

**Alan**
Sorry. Music! Hide the steak: it's Chrissie Hynde.

*Opening music*

**Alan**
*(In opening sequence)*
When they found him he, er, still had the remote control in his hand.

*Radio Station*

**Alan**
That was moving rabbit classic 'Bright Eyes'. Another cheeky chappy who's staring into the abyss of having to spend three days with himself, the insomniac's boyfriend David Clifton. *(Alan laughs)*

**Dave**
Yeah, good evening to you, Alan. Actually, do you know what? Er, I'm not so sure about that, Alan, because I'm going to be seeing a friend at the weekend.

**Alan**
Oh-oh. Johnny Walker or Jack Daniels?

**Dave**
No.

**Alan**
Glen Morangie?

**Dave**
No, I'm going to be, I'm going to be seeing Tony Hadley from, er, Spandau Ballet.

**Alan**
Rubbish.

**Dave**
Oh, yeah. I'm actually doing an archery weekend with him.

**Alan**
Really?

**Dave**
Yeah, yeah. I mean, we both do archery. I'm, er, grade three at the moment. I'm hoping – fingers crossed – to get, er, my grade four there this weekend.

**Alan**
How do you, how do you, who … can I –

**Dave**
So, er, what are you doing this weekend then, Alan?

**Alan**
I'm, er, watching all the Bond films back to back with my friend Michael.

**Dave**
Oh, what, the guy who works at the BP garage?

**Alan**
I know where he works.

**Dave**
OK. There goes, er, Alan Partridge, er, licence to kill … time in his caravan by watching videos. *(Laughs)*

**Alan**
Oh, that's good. Tha-that's … good one. Good one.

**Dave**
Yeah. Yeah.

**Alan**
Arrows, arrows are deceitful. When a cowboy fires a gun, there's a bang. It's a warning. Gives you a chance to duck. When a cowboy has an arrow fired at him, he hears nothing. If he's lucky, it sticks in his hat and he just looks daft. But more often than not, it sticks in his back and he dies, slumping forward on the horse that rides off with him just on top of it, going like that.

**Dave**
Yeah, OK. Bye, Alan. See you later, pal.

**Alan**
Yeah, and also, archers – I hate archers, *The Archers* and Jeffrey Archer. You're all deceitful cowards. I've just realized that only applies to archers and Jeffrey Archer, but not *The Archers* who, to be fair, are a mixed bag. Goodbye.

**Dave**
OK, and, er, what are we doing to the planet? Well, er, it's 'Purple Rain'.

*Alan enters petrol station shop with a jump, pretending to fire a gun.*

**Alan**
*(Shouts)* Bang!

**Michael**
*(Miming blood gushing out of his neck)* Pshhhhhhh.

**Alan**
I'm James Bond.

**Michael**
Got us right in the neck.

**Alan**
You can survive that if it doesn't sever the spinal column.

**Michael**
Aye. Mind you, I wouldn't be able to talk. I'd just go *(makes strangled noise)* like that. Hey, I love the gadgets.

**Alan**
Yeah.

**Michael**
Like, 'Pay attention, Bond. Simply remove the top of this pen, jab it in somebody's eye and smash it in with yer hand like that.'

**Alan**
That's not a gadget, Michael. That's just monstrous use of a biro.

*Man walks up to Michael, dropping newspaper on counter.*

**Tex**
Check it out. There's an advert for it.

**Michael**
Way-hay, Truckfest! Hey look, it's coming to Ipswich. Oh, David Soul's gonna be there.

**Tex**
Yeah.

*Man and Michael pretend to pull on truck horns and make honking noises.*

**Tex**
Hey, imagine that, ay, Mike?

**Michael**
Phoooooo.

**Tex**
Driving across the States –

*Michael laughs.*

**Tex**
– on one of them roads, Route 66, sleeping in motels –

**Michael**
Aye. Just going into a shop and buy a gun.

**Tex**
Yeah.

*Man and Michael pretend to pull on truck horns and make honking noises.*

**Alan**

They're, they're, they're actually left-hand drive, those lorries. So if you were doing that, you'd just be grabbing photographs of your family. Or perhaps rosary beads if you were driving up from Mexico.

**Tex**

Hey, Mike, do you wanna serve this guy?

**Michael**

Oh no, it's all right. He's a friend an' all.

**Tex**

Oh! All right. The name's Tex.

**Alan**

Text?

**Tex**

No, Tex. Like, er, short for Terry and, er, you know, like Texas an' that.

**Michael**

He likes American stuff.

**Alan**

Oh.

**Tex**

Yeah.

**Michael**

Alan likes James Bond.

**Tex**

Ah, you're a Bond guy, are you? My man's gotta be Wayne.

**Alan**

What, Wayne Sleep? Just the jacket and the boots, you know. *(Points to Tex's cowboy jacket and boots)*

**Tex**

No, you know Wayne, er *(in American accent)*, get off your horse and drink your milk.

**Alan**

Yeah, yeah – Wayne Sleep.

**Tex**

Hey, er, Mike, I'm just gonna grab a Dr Pepper from the cooler. Stick it on me tab.

**Alan**

Yeah, yeah, Michael, I'm just going to get a Ginsters from the fridge. Put it on the slate.

**Tex**

Ah yeah, Mike. Can't wait to get back to the States.

**Michael**

Aye.

**Alan**

Yeah, I used to hang around the States.

**Tex**

Where'd you get to?

**Alan**

Florida, mainly. Yeah. You know, a fortnight in Florida. Yeah, yeah. Good days.

**Tex**

Florida, ay? Walt Disney.

**Michael**

Aye.

**Tex**

Now there's a guy who lived the American dream. Built a huge empire.

**Alan**
Yeah. I thought he just drew pictures of mice. I prefer David Attenborough. Yeah. At least he's more honest, you know. He interviews real mice.

**Tex**
Anyway, erm, I'm gonna hit the road. Check you later, Mike.

**Michael**
Check you later.

*Tex and Michael make honking noises. Michael laughs.*

**Tex**
Nice to meet you, Colin.

**Alan**
Colin?

*Tex leaves.*

**Alan**
Walt Disney, you know … animals never wore clothes.

**Michael**
Hang on, hang on.

*Truck horn honks several times.*

**Michael**
*(Laughing)* Oh! There he goes.

**Alan**
Is that his pick-up truck?

**Michael**
Aye. He calls it 'Convoy'.

**Alan**
Convoy?

**Michael**
Aye.

**Alan**
Michael, you're hanging around with a man who uses a collective term for a single vehicle.

**Michael**
Oh, he, he, he just likes American things.

**Alan**
What, like Dr Pepper?

**Michael**
Aye.

**Alan**
Tastes like fizzy Benilyn. So, er, how long's Like a Rhinestone Cowboy been coming in here?

**Michael**
Well, about eighteen month. No, two year. Aye, two year.

**Alan**
Do you chat to any other men?

**Michael**
Aye, including you – er, four regulars, like.

**Alan**
Michael, what the hell's going on?

**Michael**
Well, it's just, you know, men who want someone to talk to, you know. They're just, they're just lonely. Look, I cannae not talk to the customers, man. Look, what does it say on me badge? 'Michael. I'm here to help.'

**Alan**
No, it doesn't. It just says Michael.

**Michael**
Oh, aye, it does.

**Alan**
Why did you think it said the rest?

**Michael**
I don't know. I must have dreamt it. So anyway, hey, Bond weekend. Me and you.

**Alan**

I don't remember inviting you to the Bond weekend, Michael. I think what you've done is you've put two and two together and you've made five, or as the Americans say, fahve.

**Michael**

Do you want that Kit-Kat?

**Alan**

No.

*Alan sticks two fingers of Kit-Kat up at Michael. He leaves them on counter and walks away.*

**Michael**

You'll have to pay for that.

**Alan**

Put it on the slate. Oh, actually, I'll eat it.

*Alan walks back to collect the Kit-Kat.*

*Alan's house. Alan dives through front door and pretends to stalk someone with an imaginary gun.*

**John**

*(Approaching while Alan's back is turned)*
All right, Al.

**Alan**

Aaarggh! Hi, hi, what're you doing here? It's a Bank Holiday.

**John**

I had to come in, do those dodgy floor joists, didn't I? What was that you were doing just then?

**Alan**

Oh. I was, I was just walking through my house … in, in the style of James Bond.

**John**

Oh, it was quite good. I think you'd make a good James Bond.

**Alan**

Do you really think so?

**John**

I like that *Goldfinger*. That bit where the laser beam's going up his jaffers.

**Alan**

Yeah. We should talk more, you know. I've got lots of subjects I love to chat about. I used to chat to another bloke about them, but, er, he likes American things now. What do you think of American things?

**John**

They're a bit full of themselves.

**Alan**

Abso-bloody-exactly.

**John**

Not my cup of tea.

**Alan**

Actually, we could do a Bond film. I could be Bond and you could be my stuntman. You know, because you've got a good physique.

**John**

Yeah, well, I don't like to get too big, you know. No, it's your pec muscles you've got to start off with, you know. Got to sort out your pecs, do your bench presses. Yeah. Have a prod o' that.

*He sticks out his chest and Alan prods it quickly.*

**Alan**

Mmm. Yeah, very firm. Very firm. Yeah, mine are more or less the same, they're just fractionally more flaccid. Apart from that, erm, I've just got a smooth chest with a ring of hairs round each nipple … and a thin line that sort of builds towards the usual place.

*Silence*

**Alan**
Bye.

*In the caravan*

**Alan**
Right, Sonia, let's sort this timetable out. Nine a.m: *Dr No*. Break for a pee. I need at least three minutes to urinate. Seems to take for ever these days. I never thought when I was in my twenties I'd have to push.

**Sonia**
*(Writing)* Next?

**Alan**
11.05: *From Russia With Love*. 1.15: *Goldfinger*. Strawberry Nesquik, fish cakes. 3.35: *Thunderball*. Dump – question mark. See how I feel after the fish cakes.

**Sonia**
How long?

**Alan**
Twenty minutes. Better allow for complications. 6.15: *You Only Live Twice*. Tin of Director's. 8.20: *Diamonds Are Forever*. Put the roast on as soon as you see the moon buggy.

**Sonia**
You're very brilliant. This is a clear schedule.

**Alan**
Thank you. *(Pats her on the head)* I love you in a way. You could be a Bond femme fatale with your broken English. You're sexy, but I don't trust you.

**Sonia**
James Bond doesn't live in a caravan.

**Alan**

No, but this could very easily be a compact Swiss chalet … about to be stormed by fifteen bad bastards in boilersuits.

**Lynn**

Hello.

*Alan turns round, startled.*

**Lynn**

*(Firing imaginary gun at Alan)* Bang. Bang. Bang, bang!

**Alan**

You look like you quite enjoyed that.

*Lynn makes machine-gun noise. Alan pretends to be riddled by bullets.*

**Alan**

Was that a snub-nosed Uzi?

**Lynn**

Yes, I think it was.

**Alan**

You're in a remarkably cheerful mood, considering it's the first anniversary of your mother's death.

**Lynn**

Well, life goes on.

**Sonia**

Can we finish writing the Bond schedule?

**Lynn**

Oh, you've made allowances for the visit to my mother's grave?

**Alan**

Yes, that's in the schedule. Visit to your mother's grave. Then *Dr No*. The underground base of an evil genius … and then *Dr No*.

*Alan and Lynn smile. Sonia looks confused. Alan passes his hand over the top of his head and makes whistling noise.*

**Sonia**

You make him take you to grave. Then we will be late for film and all work we did will be destroyed.

**Lynn**

Can't you cut one of the less important films?

**Alan**

Whoa! Whoa, whoa, whoa, whoa, whoa, whoa. Whoa. Whoooaaa, whoa, whoa, whoa. *Which* are the less important Bond films, Lynn? I've got to hear this.

**Lynn**

One of those Welsh ones.

**Alan**

What, you mean the Timothy Dalton ones?

**Lynn**

Mmm.

**Alan**

He didn't play it as a Welshman. He didn't say, 'The name's Bond. *(In Welsh accent)* Jones, the Bond. Double O sev-en. Licence to Kilch.' *(Sniffs)* Lynn, are you wearing perfume?

**Lynn**

Yes.

**Alan**

For a corpse?

**Lynn**

No. I'm going to have lunch at TGI Friday's with Gordon.

**Alan**

What, the retired policeman who's not a conman?

**Lynn**

Yes.

**Alan**
Well, you can have Death by Chocolate while he rifles through your building society book. Right! Spectacles, driving gloves, phone, wallet, keys … Sonia – did you get the piccalilly?

**Sonia**
Yes.

**Alan**
Chunky?

**Sonia**
Yes.

**Alan**
Excellent. Let's go to the graveyard.

*Alan pushes in front of Lynn as they leave.*

*Alan and Lynn sit in Alan's car at the cemetery.*

**Alan**
*(whistles)* Graveyards are so depressing. They remind me of … death. There's a grave over there that I saw. It's of a man who died in 1872. And he was only three.

**Lynn**
Snazzy headstone there.

**Alan**
Yeah. That's one of those eighties one, isn't it? Yeah. Black granite. It's a waste really, because if you sliced that three-ways and laid it end to end, you'd have the lion's share of the work surface for a Poggenpohl kitchen. In fact I bet a lot of these gravestones go missing. I wouldn't be surprised if they ended up as the work surfaces in luxury kitchens. They'd have to turn them upside down, of course, so that, you know, it didn't, er, reveal the details of the dead … in their recessed lettering, which would also collect crumbs. Lynn, the anniversary of a dead mum is always a tough one.

**Lynn**
Mmm.

**Alan**
But I am up against it with this James Bondathon, so if you could limit your mourning to *(in German accent)* no more than ten minutes – I'm trying to lighten the mood with a Nazi voice.

**Lynn**
But you don't need to lighten the mood, Alan. I am not down.

**Alan**
You've got ten minutes. Go give it to her.

*Lynn leaves car. Alan puts on loud music and drums along to it.*

*Alan winds down window and presses car horn.*

**Alan**
Ten minutes, Lynn!

*In Alan's house*

**Lynn**
That's the first year over.

**Alan**
Yeah, she's probably up there in heaven right now, complaining about, er – what did she used to call them? – brown people? I'll give her this, Lynn, she stuck to her guns with all that. Right to the end. Even on the last day. The way she looked at that nurse. God rest her racist soul. She'd be horrified. I mean, Jesus was from the Middle East.

**Lynn**
Was he? Jesus wasn't brown.

**Alan**
Lynn, let's not have that discussion now.

**Gordon**
Can I come in?

**Alan**
Sorry, we don't need our drive tarmacking, thank you very much.

**Lynn**
This is Gordon.

**Alan**
Oh, sorry! Sorry, sorry. I thought you were a tinker with tarmac. Sorry.

**Gordon**
Nice to meet you.

*They shake hands.*

**Alan**
And you. Well, erm, there's Lynn. Look after her and make sure she's back here by ten o'clock and don't get her pregnant. I believe you're quite keen on the Bible?

**Gordon**
I live by it.

**Alan**
I was reading the book of Genesis the other day. I got to say, that bloody snake.

**Gordon**
Do you suppose, erm, you'd be prone to temptation like Adam?

**Alan**
I think I'd be more preoccupied by the fact that I was encountering a talking snake. I think whether I wanted an apple or not would be a side issue for me. I mean, even if it wasn't a talking snake, even if just rolled an apple towards me and sort of went – *(nods his head)* – I think I'd still be troubled. After that I think I'd just, erm, put some trunks on and sit down on the grass.

**Lynn**
Well, we'll be off then.

*Lynn leaves.*

**Alan**
Great.

**Gordon**
Well, I'm glad we're on our own, Alan. I've been, er, wanting a word with you about Lynn. I don't like the way you treat her.

**Alan**
*(Surprised)* Oh.

**Gordon**
I think you're a bully, and if you don't start treating her better, I'm going to knock your block off. Do I make myself clear?

**Alan**
*(Scared)* Yeah, yeah.

**Gordon**
*(Speaking slower)* Do I make myself clear?

**Alan**
Yeah. *(Gulps)* Yes.

**Gordon**
*(Brings finger to his head)* Well, keep the thought –

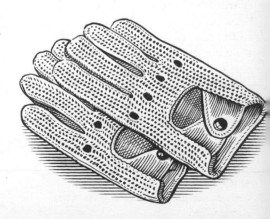

**Alan**

Ayyyy! Sorry. I thought you were going to attack me with your finger.

**Gordon**

I know when I'm being lied to, you know. I've spent a lot of my life being lied to.

**Alan**

*(Laughs)* Well, with respect, you know, as an ex-police officer, if you hang around with criminals, you're gonna get lied to.

**Gordon**

*(Leaving)* Think on.

**Alan**

I'm thinking on. I'm thinking on.

*In the caravan, Alan is dropping videos into a box. Sonia is ticking a list.*

**Alan**

Let Die. Golden. Raker. Eyes Only. Pussy. Daylights. Nutty Professor II: The Clumps. What's this doing here?

**Sonia**

I got it for 90p in a brilliant charity shop called Scope.

**Alan**

Scope! Why do they change their name and ruin it? Consignia and Scope. It's the Post Office and The Spastics Society. Oh, butter my arse! I've, I've just realized, we haven't got *The Spy Who Loved Me*. I've just remembered: I lent it to that bloke I used to chat to at the petrol station.

**Sonia**

Michael?

**Alan**

Is that his name? Mmm. Yeah, I'm going to have to go and get it off him.

**John**

Hello!

**Alan**

*(Turns and karate kicks the air)* Hoo!

**John**

You know, I reckon I could do a bit of that Bond stuff.

**Alan**

Yeah. Unfortunately though, I don't think society's ready for, er, *(in Yorkshire accent)* View T'Kill. Eeeeee! Octipussy.

**John**
Dr Nowt.

**Alan**
Lovely stuff. Listen, I've just cracked open a bottle of Sunny Delight. They're quite big and, er, I can't manage a whole one … fancy a shot?

**John**
No thanks. Er, I've got to go off to the, er, timberyard.

**Alan**
I'll take you. Erm, just, er – here you are – get a couple of straws. *(Puts two straws in a large bottle of Sunny Delight)* No problem. So, yeah we'll stop off at the, er, petrol station on the way.

**John**
How is yer Geordie mate?

**Alan**
Well, you got to ask yourself some serious questions about a man who sits in a petrol station all day talking to other men.

*Alan hands John the bottle of Sunny Delight, who takes it looking confused.*

*Petrol Station Shop*

**Alan**
Have a look round, John. See if there's anything you fancy. I'll treat you.

**John**
Cheers.

**Alan**
*(To Michael)* Has the Duke of Hazzard been in?

**Michael**
Er, no he's not.

**Alan**
Erm, I'd like you to return my *Spy Who Loved Me* video and any other property that you have of mine.

**Michael**
Look, I haven't got it here. It, it's at home.

**Alan**
Where, in America?

**Michael**
No, Lismouth Street.

**Alan**
This is my friend John. John, don't be shy. Come out. Show him, show him, show him your toolbelt.

*John comes over, lifts his shirt and turns round slowly.*

**Michael**
Ooh, smart.

**Alan**
Yes, it's interesting, Michael, this, this, this obsession you have with American things, and yet you work for British Petroleum. Yeah. I mean, hello?

**Michael**
Hello.

**Alan**
No, it's a thing people say.

**Michael**

So do you want any petrol?

**Alan**

No, I'm going to be getting it from across the road from now on. Your petrol's a bit, erm, it's a bit obvious. It's a bit petrolly. Come on, John. *(In American accent)* Let's saddle our horses and, er, get ourselves a curly Cumberland sausage from the little bitty chef – *(in ordinary voice)* Li-Little Chef.

**Michael**

Oh, er, hey! I taped that, er, documentary for you: *The World's Worst Storms*. Hey, there's footage of a tsunami, and it comes in, and it crashes down on this village and wipes them all out.

**Alan**

What, programmes about storms? Get a life! Come on, John. Let's go to Sprouston.

**John**

*(Quietly)* I haven't got time for that, Al …

**Alan**

*(Quietly)* Well, we'll just go … we'll go, we'll go straight to the timberyard –

**John**

*(Quietly)* … ten minutes.

*Alan enters caravan. Sonia, Lynn and Gordon are inside.*

**Alan**

Oh. Oh, hello, Lynn. What are you doing here? A wonderful woman like you should be at home relaxing.

**Lynn**

Y-you asked me to get you a black marker pen.

**Alan**

Oh. Thanks. In fact, erm, I'll give you a raise. Eight, eight, eight and a half thousand? N-nine. Nine? Nine and half? Te-tehhhhhhll *(sings)* you what. Tell you what, it's nine and a half thousand pounds. Let's all sing it:

**Alan and Lynn**

*(Sing)* Tell you what, tell you what, it's nine and a half thousand pounds.

**Lynn**

*(Smiling)* Thank you, Alan.

*Lynn jumps up and kisses Alan.*

**Alan**
Oh, Mrs Robinson, are you trying to seduce me?

**Lynn**
*(Laughing)* Sonia, why don't we get some juice while the men set the world to rights?

**Gordon**
Still watching you, Alan.

**Alan**
Yeah, I know. And, and I'm thinking about it in my block … that you may knock off.

**John**
*(At caravan door)* All right. Cement's dry now, Al, so I'll be off.

**Alan**
Er, no, wait, wait. *(Alan jumps up and runs to door)* Will you stay and watch a Bond film, please?

**John**
I can't, Al. I've got too much to do.

**Alan**
Listen, I have been physically threatened by an ex-fuzz. If – if you hang around, I will pay you. I mean, h-h-how much is a monkey?

**John**
Five hundred.

**Alan**
How much is a mouse?

**John**
There's no such amount. Pony's one fifty.

**Alan**
Right, I, I, I'll give you two hundred. That's a pony and a bag of hooves.

**John**
Go on.

**Alan**
Great.

**Lynn**
I got Sunny Delight for you –

**Alan**
*(Shouts)* Don't kiss me again!

*Lynn trips and and falls, dropping two large jugs of Sunny Delight into Alan's box of videos.*

**Alan**
Aarghh!

**Lynn**
Alan, I, I've spilt Sunny Delight all over your James Bond videos.

**Alan**
*(Angry)* Lynn, you … *(looks at Gordon, who has stood up; speaks calmly)* shouldn't worry about it.

**Lynn**
Are they repairable?

**Alan**
*(Quietly)* I'll, I'll just check them. Yeah. They're ruined. Excuse me.

*Alan walks to kitchen and picks up several boxes of cereal.*

**Alan**
I'll, er, I'll just be a minute.

*Alan takes cereal outside and smashes boxes with a hammer, shouting incomprehensibly.*

**Alan**
Hello, Michael.

**Michael**
What are you doing?

**Alan**
Just, er, just destroying my cereals.

**Michael**
Careful. F-folk might say you're a, you're a cereal killer. Ha!

**Alan**
Yeah.

**Michael**
Here's your tape: *The Spy Who Loved Me*.
And all, all, all your other stuff.

**Alan**
Can we make friends? I mean, I know,
I know, I know I said all that stuff –

**Michael**
No, no, please – phhhhh!

**Alan**
Phhhh!

**Michael**
Phhhh!

**Alan**
Phhhh!

*Alan and Michael start spitting, smiling.*

**Alan**
Come on! Let's go and watch *The Spy Who
Loved Me*.

**Michael**
Aye. Oh, er, it's a bit difficult 'cause, erm,
I've –

*Truck honking noise*

**Michael**
We're just going to drive round and blow
the horn.

**Alan**
Michael, you could have blown the horn
in my Lexus. All you had to do was ask. You
could have sat in the passenger seat and
reached across. It's not on the end of a
stalk, it's on the central steering wheel
boss, behind the airbag.

**Michael**
Aye, well you see, it's precision engineering,
isn't it? It's like what you always say: it's the
Japanese Mercedes, eh?

**Alan**
God, I've missed you.

**Michael**
I missed you an' all, man, you know. I really
have. I just … I feel –

*Michael goes to give Alan a hug. Alan backs
away and falls on floor. Gets up and finds
himself staring at Gordon's crotch. Backs
away on hands and knees towards Michael.
Tex enters.*

**Alan**
Hi, Tex. We're having a hoedown. I'm, I'm,
I'm down. B-b-b-but I'm not a ho.

*Alan gets up.*

**Tex**
Do you know there's a load of Frosties on
your step?

**Alan**
Yes, I know. I've been destroying my
cereals. *(In American accent)* Gotta problem
with that? You're welcome to come and
watch *The Spy Who Loved Me* with us.

**Tex**
Well, thanks very much but, er, me and
Mike are getting off to the, er, Truckfest.
You know, we'd better, er –

**Alan**
*(Stepping in front of Michael)* He's staying
with me.

**Michael**
We could see it at Skegness. T-T-Timmy
Mallett's gonna be there. I mean, it won't
be as good, but –

**Tex**
All right.

**Alan**
Oh, great. Right. Fantastic. OK.

**Tex**
*(Sitting down)* Thanks very much.

**Alan**
Let's watch *The Spy Who Loved Me*!

**Tex**
The, er, Chevvy 68, right?

**Michael**
It's got flames down the side.

**Tex**
I did that meself.

**Sonia**
You paint yourself?

**Tex**
Yeah, yeah, yeah, yeah.

**Alan**
Stop talking about American things and let's watch the best film ever made.

**Video**
Welcome to *America's Strongest Men*, where the toughest, mightiest Titan –

**Alan**
*(Stopping the video)* Have you taped over *The Spy Who Loved Me* with *America's Strongest Men*?

**Michael**
No, I haven't. It was Terry. I gave him the tape. He's done it. It's his fault.

**Tex**
I'm really sorry. I, I, I, I really wanted to see *America's Strongest Men*.

**Alan**
Well, now you've got Norfolk's maddest man. I wanted to watch Roger Moore necking with Fiona Fullerton. And instead I have to watch a giant Michael Bolton lookalike in a tight vest throwing an oven over bales of hay.

**Sonia**
*The Spy Who Loved Me* is a brilliant film. It begin in forest in Germany –

**Alan**
It's Austria! *(Shouts)* Austria!

**John**
What's the one where the laser beam goes up his jack—

**Alan**
*(Shouts) Goldfinger*!

**Michael**
What's the one with the, with the volcano, and it splits up and a big rocket comes out with all Chinkies jumping up and down?

**Tex**
Isn't that, er, *Thunderball*?

**Alan**
No. *(Shouts)* No! No! No! Stop getting Bond wrong! I'll tell you about *The Spy Who Loved Me*. All do that with your fingers round your eye. I am Roger Moore. Bang! Blood dribbles down. We're on a submarine. Two sailors sit down and have a game of chess. Then the cups start wobbling and then a man who used to be in *The Oneidon Line* comes in and goes, 'Why are the cups wobbling? What's going on?' And then … yeah, you can stop doing that now. And then he peers down the periscope thing and looks through it and goes, 'Oh my God. The submarine's being eaten by a giant tanker.' And then we cut to Moscow. And there's a man there and he's Russian – he's got eyebrows, you know – and he's on the phone going, 'What, a whole submarine? You're joking! I'm gonna have to tell some other Russians. See ya!' Right, and then, and then, it cuts to James – Roger Moore – and er, yes, *(laughs)* he's with a lady. Yeah. Yeah. He's, he's necking with her. And he goes, 'I've got to go, love. Something's come up.'

**Michael**
Aye. He means his cock.

**Alan**

Anyway, then he, he, he puts on his underpants and his ski suit and he gets on his skis and he starts skiing. And he's being chased by these Russian shits in black jumpsuits with lemon piping. And, er, he's just skiing along like that, and they start shooting at him, and he goes, 'Right! I've had enough of that! Just stop it!' And he turns round with his gun and then he does a backward somersault off this ramp, and he, he lands on his feet – I'm not sure why, but he's not showing off. And then, then he goes over a cliff and he's falling and you think, oh God, James Bond's going to die! *(Shouts)* He's going to die! But then at the last minute –

**Michael**

He pulls a ripcord, right? And a, a, a parachute comes out and it's got a Union Jack –

**Alan**

*(Wails)* Michael! Michael!

**Michael**

But that's how it ends.

**Alan**

That's not the end of the beginning. The end of the beginning goes like this: *(sings)* glang! Glanalangalangalangalangalang! Glanalang, langalangalanga, nobody does it better – *(speaks)* and I'm a naked woman in silhouette with a gun, spinning round – *(sings)* Makes me feel sad for the rest. Nobody does it – *(speaks)* ooh, bit of nipple – *(sings)* quite as good as you. Baby, you're the best. Da, da, da – *(speaks)* and now a really big bounce right over and I land on my feet. *(sings)* Da, da, da, da, da, der. I wasn't looking, so now you found me … *(speaks)* ooh, bit of bush, er –

*(sings)* I tried to hide from your love life – *(speaks)* and a woman swinging on a Luger, a giant Luger; ooh, look at that … *(sings)* Like heaven above me – *(speaks)* and now another naked woman walking along the top of a gun, completely Billy Bollocks … *(sings)* The spy who loved me is keeping all my secrets safe tonight – *(speaks)* and then one more big swing from the woman; legs go right up – ooh, what was that? Too late … *(sings)* Nobody does it half as good as you, baby you're the best!

**Sonia**

Yes! Brilliant! Brilliant!

*Applause*

**Alan**

Yes, so er, do you wanna hear some more?

*Everyone (except Alan) is watching television.*

**Video**

Welcome to *America's Strongest Men*.

*Alan is running about outside caravan, with imaginary guns and explosives.*

**Michael**

*(Watching video)* He's strong, eh? Look. Go on, lift it.

*Alan splashes Sunny Delight over caravan.*

**John**

*(Watching video)* His fingers are like Schwarzenegger's arms.

*Alan pretends to light match, jumps inside house with hands over his ears. Sits on step and drinks the rest of the Sunny Delight.*

## Henry VIIIIth (9th)

Synopsis for novel. Copyright A. Partridge, April 2002

The year is 3000AD

The whole of Norfolk is waterlogged. Home insurance is a
thing of the past. You would think in the future things
would get better but, no, they're worse. A lot of people
are mad and eat pets. The anti-hunting lobby have finally
won the day and foxes have, as feared, grown to five times
their normal size and now carry off babies and small electrical goods. People have 3D TVs on their wrists and go
around on monorails like the one at Gatwick.

There are two main plots, between which the story alternates
but somehow comes together at the end (I haven't worked
this out yet).

## Plot A

People are fed up voting for governments which just take
taxes, and teachers taking liberties. A big fat king is in
charge again, and he's got six wives, but not separately —
at the same time, that's the twist. Three turn out to be
evil robots. Anne of Cleves, Catherine Howard and Jane
Seymour are robots. They only find out when they chop their
heads off and there are a load of wires. But they keep
talking for about an hour until the batteries run out.

## Plot B

It's the aftermath of a nuclear ratings war between two TV
stations, one of which is based on Pluto. TV presenter Jack
Jupiter has twenty-four hours to do something but each day
is ten hours because they've gone metric on time. The diary
industry is in turmoil. That's a subplot (plot C). But one
rebel, called Alec Parsons, wants to return to a seven-day
week because it makes sense, and he goes back in time to
the present to see what a week's like.

# I'M ALAN PARTRIDGE

SERIES **2**

## EPISODE 5:
## I KNOW WHAT ALAN DID LAST SUMMER

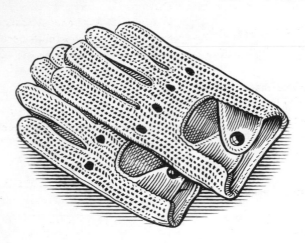

*Radio Station*

**Alan**
That was sweating lunatic Iggy Pop, part of our Tuesday-night punk pack, which is climaxing at midnight with Madness. This is Norfolk Nights with Alan Partridge, and we're in the middle of Supertalk.

**Jingle**
*(Alan)* Supertalllk!

**Male voiceover**
Brought to you by Ginsters pasties.

**Alan**
Tonight we're supertalking about evil dogs. We've all seen them in those, er, undesirable areas. Er, Donald from Hemsby has e-mailed us to say, 'Dangerous dogs should simply have their teeth replaced with strips of rubber.' I think that's an excellent idea, and I'm going to make him our E-mail of the Evening.

**Dalek voice**
E-mail of the Evening.

**Alan**
And Donald wins our top prize, which is a kind of Action Man military figure. It's got all kinds of features and, er, on the box it says, er, 'Not suitable for children'. I wouldn't take any notice of that. Er, although my cousin did once buy a pirated Tweenie from a covered market in Brondell and it was full of soiled bandages. Anyway, time for music now. Who's this beautiful blond man with a lovely voice? It's Annie Lennox.

*Opening music*

**Alan**
*(In opening sequence)* Fat arms, big beards, and that's just the men – women.

**Alan**
That was Bill Withers, who, thank the Lord, is still with us. Erm, I'll be back again tomorrow with another fun prize – er, it's a piggy bank. It's 1 a.m. As the whole of Norfolk sleeps, something truly evil stirs.

**Dave**
*(Laughs)* All right, Alan. Actually –

**Alan**
Shhh! His – no – his coffin lid opens with a shuddering creak *(creaking sound effect)*. An owl hoots –

**Male voiceover**
Danny Francetti's jazz box this Sunday at –

**Alan**
Sorry. It's a new digital system. *(Owl hoot sound effect)* Out pops the vampire: Count Daveula of Cliftonvania. He's very fed up. Not because he can't see his reflection, but because he can.

**Dave**
Yeah. That's right, Alan. Actually, do you know, I've been, I've been up all night drinking human blood.

**Alan**
Is that all?

**Dave**
And, er, I tell you – there is one person that I would *love* to drive a stake through.

**Alan**
Well, that's the only thing you'll be driving.

**Dave**
What do you mean by that?

**Alan**
Since your ban.

**Dave**
Well, well, er, maybe *you* should be banned from broadcasting, Alan, after some of those truly shocking prizes you've been giving away. *(Laughs)*

**Alan**
This – this coming from the man who, er, once gave away a CD removed from the cover of a music magazine.

**Dave**
Ah, yes, yes, yes. All right, folks. We're gonna Go West.

*Alan and Sonia in caravan.*

**Alan**
Ah. That – that was the best full English breakfast I've had since Gary Wilmot's wedding.

**Sonia**
It was bloody superb.

**Alan**
Oh yeah. I would, erm, I'd have that three times a day if I could. But, er, I'd be dead.

**Sonia**
It kill you?

**Alan**

Yeah. It's, er, it's cholesterol. Scottish people eat it. Few, few of them make sixty. Why are there holes in my *Daily Mail*?

**Sonia**

I do collage. Look. I cut out the heads of U2 and then I put on top of space clothes.

**Alan**

Ah, I see. And the idea is that U2 are going into space?

**Sonia**

Mmm.

**Alan**

Yes, an interesting thought. You should send it to the fan club.

**Sonia**

I already have.

**Alan**

Oh! You're not just sexy, you're also … a very good, er, fan-club member.

**Sonia**

I also write to tell them that my boyfriend is very good friend with Bono.

**Alan**

Yes, yes, I am. Yes.

**Sonia**

When are you going to introduce me?

**Alan**

Yeah.

**Sonia**

Can I put in journal that I am very good cook of full English breakfast?

**Alan**

Yes, you can. In fact I've made a few notes. Erm, yes, er, bacon: ten on ten. Button mushrooms: bingo. Black pudding: snap. Erm, minor criticism: more distance between the eggs and the beans. Erm, I, I, I may want to mix them but I want that to be my decision. Use a sausage as a breakwater. But I'm nitpicking. Er, on the whole a very good effort: seven on ten. Let's make love.

**Sonia**
OK.

**Alan**
Yeah, I always find, er, a fried breakfast makes an excellent aphrodisiac. Excuse me. *(Belches and waves hand in front of face)*

**Sonia**
You don't want to wash the dishes?

**Alan**
Uh-uh. Let's make love right here, right now. OK, just, er, fold this table away. You should feel it clip in the housing. Yeah, I'm gonna hump ya. Right, er … no, that's it, that's it, yeah. Like Deputy Dawg … would hump ya. There we go. Right.

**Sonia**
You want fitted sheet?

**Alan**
No, we'll just use a large beach towel.

**Sonia**
Alan, I buy you another present.

**Alan**
What?

**Sonia**
It's a London love taxi.

**Alan**
Ahhh.

**Sonia**
I have put my heart in back of taxi and tell driver to go to you.

**Alan**
Ahhh. Don't know *what* you're talking about. Just, er, pop that up there with the others. Getting a bit crowded now. Like London, yeah. Which I spell S.H.I.T.H.O.L.E. Shithole. Let's start with, er, some petting.

*They both sit down and start to take their shoes off.*

**Lynn**
*(Knocking)* Alan! Alan! It's me!

**Alan**
Get in, Lynn. Lynn, what do you think is Sonia's best feature?

**Lynn**
Er, her hair?

**Alan**
Nope.

**Lynn**
Her neck?

**Alan**
Try again.

**Lynn**
Her eyes? Her eyelashes?

**Alan**
No, it's going to take for ever, no. It's her feet – lovely dainty feet. I don't like big feet. Reminds me of gammon.

**Lynn**
Have you decided what you're going to call the house?

**Alan**
I've, er, narrowed it down to Lord House, Ace House, and The Cinnamons.

**Sonia**
I want to call it Our House.

**Alan**
Yeah. W-w-w-we could call it that. Erm, do you want to make a note of that?

*Lynn writes on her clipboard. Alan takes her pen and puts line through it.*

**Lynn**

Now. Now, Alan. I need to know you're completely ready for the Inland Revenue. Have you got all your receipts?

**Alan**

Yes. Some are on a spike over there. You've got some in a fat envelope and the rest are in a shoebox which I threw off a ferry. That was a low point.

**Lynn**

Now. Be prepared. These tax people can stay indefinitely.

**Alan**

Lynn, if I have to put back my roger with Sonia one more time, I'll be fit to burst, you know. I'll have to resort to, er, Plan B.

**Lynn**

Have you got everything ready for the meeting?

**Alan**

Well, you're, you're going to be there with me.

**Lynn**

Well, they're not investigating me.

**Alan**

Lynn, we're in this together.

**Lynn**

Well, w-w-what are you trying to hide?

**Alan**

Nothing ... All right. Bill Oddie gave me a dressing gown as a Christmas present. He enclosed a receipt so I could take it back if I wanted to. I submitted Oddie's receipt for tax purposes. I'm guilty as hell, Lynn. And if I'm going down, you're going down with me. I want you to lie for me.

**Lynn**

Oh, I can't do that, Alan. In the eyes of God, I mean –

**Alan**

Lynn, Lynn! I'm on God's side. I can't *stand* the Devil. I think he's bang out of order. I think he's an evil, evil idiot. And I know in the Ten Commandments it says, 'Thou shalt not lie', but if, if the Elephant Man came in here now, with some lipstick on and a nice dress, and said, 'How do I look?' would you say, Lynn – bearing in mind that he's depressed and got respiratory problems – would you say, 'Take that blusher off, you ugly, misshapen-headed, elephant tranny'?

**Lynn**

No, I'd say, 'You look very nice.'

**Alan**

Exactly. You'd say, 'You look nice ... John.'

**Lynn**

Now, Alan. The tax people are coming in an hour. You've got one hour to get ready.

**Sonia**

Alan! Look what I draw.

**Alan**

What's that?

**Sonia**

It's an alien judge.

**Alan**

Golly. An alien judge.

**Sonia**

And the alien judge ... the alien judge is shooting the tax man, and the tax man's head has come off and all the blood has spurt out. *(Laughs)*

**Lynn**

Alan, you promised me Sonia wasn't going to be here when the tax people came.

**Alan**
I know, and I've ruddy gone and forgotten, haven't I? Speak-very-quickly: she-can't-understand-it.

**Lynn**
What-can-we-do-about-her?

**Alan**
That's very good. I-could-send-her-into-Norwich-on-an-errand. Er, Sonia? What are your plans?

**Sonia**
I go to coffee shop, of course.

**Alan**
Problem-solved.

**Lynn**
Pardon?

**Alan**
Problem solved. Er, Sonia? Lynn's going to give you a lift to work.

**Sonia**
OK.

**Lynn**
And, er, the house names?

**Alan**
Oh, yes. I've decided I'm going to call it Excalibur Cottage. Can't mess about on this one, Lynn.

**Lynn**
You will get ready for the tax people?

*Sonia and Lynn leave.*

**Alan**
Yeah. Chill out, babe – love – Lynn. The last one.

*Alan sticks head out of caravan door.*

**Alan**
See ya! Wouldn't wanna be – oh, she's gone.

**John**
Hello, Alan.

**Alan**
Oh! Hello … er … *(in child's voice)* tell me your name.

**John**
John.

**Alan**
All right, John, me ole mucker?

**John**
I'm from Manchester.

**Alan**
M62. How's it going in the lounge?
Uncovered any old fireplaces?

**John**
No. It's a brand-new house, innit?

**Alan**
Yeah. Good call. Well, if you need me I'll be
*(in Cockney accent)* in the caravan. *(In usual voice)* Sorry. You're from Manchester. Yeah.
Cotton and guns.

*Alan goes back inside caravan, puts on music and clears away breakfast plates, wiping them clean with one of Sonia's London teddy bears. Starts playing air guitar.*

*Knock at door. Alan kicks it open, still playing air guitar.*

**Monica**
Mr Partridge? We're from the Inland
Revenue.

**Alan**
No, you're not.

**Catherine**
Yes, we are.

**Alan**
Oh! Er, come in then. Come in. Hello.
Sit over there.

**Monica**
There?

**Catherine**
Hi.

**Alan**
Ah! Wolves at the door! You'll huff and
you'll puff and er … where's the other one?
Where's the other pig? Sorry, er … sorry.
I only just met you. Got off to a bad start.

**Monica**
I'm sorry. We are a bit early.

**Alan**
Yes, that old one: the being early trick.
Mind games. *(Makes whizzing noise)* I'm
shit-chatting – sorry, chit-shatting.

**Monica**
I'm Monica. This is Catherine.

**Catherine**
Hi.

**Monica**
And, er, what today's all about – it's purely
a straightforward random investigation.

**Alan**
OK. Do you want something to eat?

**Catherine**
No.

**Monica**
No, thanks.

**Catherine**
No, thank you.

**Alan**
I'll check the fridge. OK. We've got a
net bag of Babybels – you can't have
those: they're for the car; I'm driving to
Harrogate. Er, do you want a beer?

**Catherine**
No.

**Monica**
No thanks, no.

**Alan**

Yeah, that's another old trick, isn't it? Er, spike the drink, er, pop you in the boot of the Lexus and then dump you in the North Sea. Yeah. Could tie a jack to your leg: you'd sink like a stone.

**Catherine**

It's all right. We, we've eaten, thanks.

*Alan ducks down to pick up teddy bear from floor.*

**Alan**

Do you want a little teddy bear? It's got bean juice on it. I could pop it in the washing machine.

**Monica**

Do you think we could see you?

*Alan remains behind kitchen counter and jiggles teddy bear on top of counter.*

**Alan**

*(In high-pitched voice)* Hello. My name's Graham. Erm, don't be horrible to Alan. He doesn't avoid tax, he only evades tax – no it's the other way round – *(in usual voice)* oh, shut up.

**Catherine**

Please, why don't you just sit down?

**Alan**

Yeah. *(Alan sits down next to tax inspectors and sighs)*

**Monica**

So, let's have a look at a couple of your company records. Now there's an entry here – Tomahawk Leisure. What was that?

**Alan**

*(Screws up his face)*

That was a company which we set up ... er, we looked at its operation and then we closed it down again: it was inoperable. I wonder if I can walk like this. *(Walks along with hands holding his ankles)* I could have been R2-D2.

**Catherine**

OK. What about Apache Communications?

**Alan**

Yeah, I've got a leaflet on that. Mine's a pint. *(Jumps up and skips over to a drawer)* It's not here! *(In high-pitched voice)* It's not here! *(In usual voice)* That's the bear again. This is going quite well. Do you want a chicken drumstick?

**Monica**

No. No, thanks.

**Alan**

I've got a chocolate Marble Arch. It's very well rendered. Should have got them to do the house. Better than these bastards. Still, at least they're cash in hand.

**Monica**

Alan. Er, cash in hand? It, it's not a phrase we like.

**Alan**

Yeah.

**Catherine**

Look, Alan. Just relax, OK? As long as everything's above board you've got absolutely nothing to worry about.

**Alan**

I've got nothing to hide. *(Holds legs up by his ears)* Search me! Search me! Oh no, that's Customs and Excise, isn't it?

**Monica**

Right. Erm, could we have a look at the receipts on your spike?

**Alan**

Yes. I have a confession to make: when I raised me legs then, something happened which was unplanned. I released an unexpected but potent gust. And I'd like to apologize in advance if it registers, because it is out there.

**Catherine**

Look, Alan. We understand if you're nervous, yeah?

**Monica**

There's a receipt here for a cinema ticket for one to *Shrek*.

**Alan**

Research. Next question.

**Monica**

Seems to be on the same day there's a receipt here for a pair of shoes from Dolcis in Dundee.

**Alan**

Yeah, I had no shoes. Can't go and see *Shrek* in your bare feet.

**Monica**

We've got a receipt here for a dressing gown. Do you want to tell us about that?

**Alan**

Yes. Can you hold these please?

*Alan passes Catherine his glasses and goes outside.*

**John**

All right, Alan?

**Alan**

All right … All right …

**John**

John.

**Alan**

John, yeah. Sorry. I, I always think of you as, erm, as bleachy head, because of your hair. Bleachy head – I could throw myself off the top of you. If I get depressed again. Just er … just let off in a tax inspectress's face.

**John**

*(Laughing)* Let off.

**Alan**

And it was mostly deliberate. Yeah.

**John**

Do you want one, Al? *(Offers Alan his rolling tobacco)*

**Alan**

No, I don't smoke. I'm one of the anti-cancer set. Yeah. We're a dying breed. Well, we're not – you are. Not that you've got cancer, you know … if, if, if, well, maybe you have. If you haven't, I apologize. If you have … please take the rest of the day off.

**John**

No, I've not got cancer, Al.

**Alan**

You can't be too careful. Testicular – that's the one, isn't it? Always got to check for extra lumps.

**John**

Aye.

**Alan**
Yeah. Some … some guys feel a bit uncomfortable about it, but I always say, why not combine it with a scratch?

**John**
You could get your girlfriend to do it.

**Alan**
Yeah. *(Laughs)* Yeah-heah. Yeah, I've got a girlfriend. Yeah. We were bonking like mad last night in the caravan.

**John**
Getting down to it, ay?

**Alan**
We were. Yeah *(laughs)*, I tell you what, i-i-if it weren't for the telescopic dampers on all four corners of the caravan, that place would have been wobbling like a very rude house. I say telescopic dampers; I mean rigid stays. How's the grouting coming along?

**John**
Well, it's not. 'Cause we haven't decided on the tiles yet, have we?

**Alan**
Yeah, all right. Well, just er … just, just carry on building the house.

*Alan puts some loose change into John's hand.*

**John**
What's that?

**Alan**
It's a tip. I, I, I panicked. But do declare it.

*Alan enters cavaran.*

**Alan**
Sorry about that. Just having a chinwag about cancer. Yes, it's a serious subject, yeah. I once found a lump under my arm. Awful, awful, awful. Yeah, turned out in the end it was just a knot in my vest.

**Sonia**
Hello, Alan.

*Sonia stands at caravan door.*

**Alan**
Oh, she's here. Sonia, what are you doing back?

**Sonia**
I had a row with Tommy. I tell him to put his coffee shop up inside his ass.

**Alan**
I just realized: I'm in a static home with three women. Hmmm. Just don't all go off to the toilet and talk about me behind my back. Because it really is too small. But it is a solid bog, you know. The chemicals in that loo will dissolve a corpse.

**Sonia**
You tell tax people they won't find your money?

**Alan**
Sonia, these are very important people.

**Sonia**
She wears no make-up!

**Alan**
That's irrelevant. *(To tax inspectors)* Excuse me.

*Alan draws curtain across living-room area so that tax inspectors can't see him and Sonia talking.*

**Alan**
Do you want to go to prison? Do you? Do you want to go to prison?

**Sonia**
You tell me prison is very cushy. It's like holiday camps.

**Alan**
I was making a point about something else.

**Sonia**

Just go out, and you say, 'No, I don't pay. Tax is rubbish.'

**Alan**

*(Shouting)* Sonia, you are not the Chancellor of the Exchequer. You're my girlfriend. If you took over, the country'd go to pot.

**Sonia**

You want me to be good little shut-up Sonia? Zip.

*Sonia leaves caravan, slamming door.*

**Alan**

Thank you.

*Alan steps forward into kitchen area, which the curtain does not reach.*

**Alan**

*(To himself)* Oh. Oh, God. It's all right, it's OK, it's OK, it's OK, it's OK. Wawawawawawawawawawawawawawawa. *(Turns round and notices tax inspectors)* Oh, did you see all that?

*Tax inspectors nod. Lynn enters caravan, carrying envelope. Alan pushes back curtain.*

**Alan**

Oh! Great! Lynn! The fat envelope! Not you, Lynn. I'm just gonna, er, pop to Choristers. Lynn'll answer all your questions. Bye!

*Alan leaves caravan and enters house.*

**John**

Where do you want these sockets, Al?

**Alan**

*(Speaks quickly)* Er, two there. Two there. One in the middle of the floor for the computer.

*Choristers Country Club. Alan enters bar area. Two men are sitting in armchairs, reading newspapers. Alan looks at the men and picks up a charity money box from bar.*

**Alan**

*(Barks)* Guide dogs for the blind. It's cruel really, isn't it? You know, forcing a dog to pull a man round all day. Not fair on either of them. *(Puts money box back on bar)* Cheers. Yeah.

*Alan sits down in armchair facing one of the men and sips a half pint of beer.*

**Alan**

*(To man)* Yeah. Girlfriend's left me. Yeah. I got to be honest, I'm chuffed like mad. She weren't expecting that. Yeah, when I get home tonight I'm just gonna have a sandwich and watch Trevor McDonald.

*Man reads newspaper, ignoring Alan.*

**Alan**

Thank you very much. Probably won't even brush my teeth … Sleep in my trousers … Yeah, some of the things me and my girlfriend do is pretty top shelf. I mean, top shelf in this country, not abroad. I don't want to see an erection. Unless it's in the mirror, right, guys? Finished with the *Daily Mail?* Yeah, cheers.

*Alan picks up newspaper from table, unfolds it and folds it back up again.*

**Alan**

Yeeah. *(In American accent)* Yeah, I think I'll go and read Simon Heffer … on the veranda. Ain't no one gonna stop me …

*Alan walks away.*

**Alan**

Urgh.

*In petrol station shop*

**Alan**
I don't know what I'm gonna do, you know? We have it off *all* the time.

**Michael**
Well, at least it'll be an end to all that London crap, ay? You know, all them Big Ben teddy bears and all that sort of – you hate London, hey?

**Alan**
Oh yeah. But there is an upside because all those small taxis and little Tower Bridges sometimes make me feel like a giant.

**Michael**
Aye.

**Alan**
Yeah, in fact, one day when Sonia went out I arranged them all on the floor and I just marched round, saying, 'Fee! Fi! Fo! Fum! I smell the blood of an ungrateful bunch of bastards.'

**Michael**
Hey, mind, she's a good cook.

**Alan**
Oh, yeah. Yeah. She can do a *fantastic* full English breakfast.

**Michael**
Aye.

**Alan**
That's daft. That's daft. A *good* English breakfast.

**Michael**
Right. She's still making it a bit too bunched up?

**Alan**
Yes, yes, yes, yes.

**Michael**
Aye. With the egg too –

**Alan**
Too close to the beans, yes.

**Michael**
Too close to the beans. *(Laughs)* When will they learn, ay? Mind, she was sexy. You know. She wore … she wore a G-strap.

**Alan**
Yes, well, that's for hygiene reasons too. Lets the buttocks breathe.

**Michael**
Oh, right.

**Alan**
Yes.

**Michael**
'Cause you don't know whether to wear it or floss your teeth with it, ay? *(Laughs)*

**Alan**
*(Laughs)* Or slice cheese with it.

**Michael**
*(Laughs)* Aye … or, or all three!

**Alan**
Yeah, no, that's unhygienic. Problem is, I did have a girlfriend and now I haven't got one any more. What am I going to do?

**Michael**
Well, get yourself another!

**Alan**
No chance. British?

*Lynn enters shop.*

**Lynn**
Alan. I've called the police.

**Alan**
What for?

**Lynn**
Oh, I thought it was best.

**Michael**
She'll turn up – one way or the other.

**Alan**
This isn't *Silent Witness*.

*Sonia enters shop.*

**Sonia**
Hello.

**Alan**
Sonia.

**Lynn**
Where have you been?

**Sonia**
I buy another present for Alan. Guess what I buy?

**Alan**
I don't know. A bear dressed as a Beefeater.

**Sonia**
Yes! And then I went by the caravan and chucked out the tax woman. *(Laughs)*

**Alan**
Lovely stuff.

**Sonia**
So ... did you buy me a present to say sorry for being cross to me?

**Alan**
Yes, I did. And I'll just go and get it.

*Alan walks to back of shop and returns holding video.*

**Alan**
There ... there we go. It's a video by the West Country comedian Jethro, and it's signed by Bono.

**Michael**
Do you know Bono?

**Alan**
Yes, I do.

**Sonia**
He is great friends with Bono. He tell me.

**Alan**
Yeah.

**Michael**
When did you get him to sign that then?

**Alan**
When I was round at his house with Jethro.

**Sonia**
You've been to Bono's house?

**Alan**
Yes, I have.

**Michael**
Bollocks! You don't know Bono.

**Alan**
I do know Bono!

**Sonia**
You take me to Bono's house.

**Alan**
You want to go to Bono's house? OK. We'll go ... we'll go to Bono's, we'll go to Bono's house. But you'll look stupid.

*Sonia leaves.*

**Alan**
*(Angrily)* Thanks, you two, for dropping me right in it.

*Alan picks up two large bottles of Lucozade.*

**Alan**
Put these on the tab.

*Alan and Sonia in Alan's car.*

**Sonia**
Alan, you don't remember where is Bono's house?

**Alan**
Yeah, I will remember. I will remember. Because the last time I was there, I took some pot and I was briefly mindless. And as I say, he has a huge dog and he may well be drunk and unleash it, because normally I ring ahead.

**Sonia**
I'm not scared to dogs.

**Alan**
Well, you should be, because these are more like fat horses. You will either look thick or it'll have your hands and feet off before Bono can whistle it to stop.

**Sonia**
What sort dog is that?

**Alan**
The sort of dog that the Nazis used to chase Steve McQueen. They're trained and they are very right-wing.

*Alan's car turns in to gravel driveway.*

**Alan**
This is it. This, this, this is Bono's house. Eureka! Those spiky trees …

**Sonia**
Yes.

**Alan**
I think are Joshua trees.

**Sonia**
This is Joshua tree?

*Sign reads: The National Trust, Blickling Hall, Open to the Public.*

*Alan and Sonia get out of the car.*

**Sonia**
Who are all these cars?

**Alan**
Th-these are all, er, Bono's.

**Sonia**
All these cars?

**Alan**
Yes. Yes, he's got the biggest collection of, er, hatchbacks in the country. *(Shouts)* Bono! BONO!

*Alan and Sonia enter the house; people are wandering around.*

**Alan**
Well, this is it. This is where the idiot lives. Lo-lovely pictures up there of, er, lads with big hair. Henry VIII – he was a shit.

*Alan and Sonia enter a room full of paintings.*

**Alan**
Bono? Nah, nah. He's not here. Do you fancy a curry?

**Sonia**
No. I want to see.

**Alan**
All right. OK.

*Alan and Sonia enter a lavishly decorated bedroom.*

**Alan**
Yes, this is Bono's bedroom. Not sure if he's in. Bono? No, he's not. He sometimes likes to lie there though, with the *Sunday Express* and, er, the biggest bowl of Alpen you've ever seen. Massive, it is.

*They return to the room full of paintings.*

**Alan**
What's the name of a U2 album?

**Sonia**
Joshua Tree?

**Alan**
Yeah, I knew that because he composed half of that over there. And the other half … over there.

*Alan and Sonia sit in the coffee shop area.*

**Sonia**
These people are friends of Bono?

**Alan**
Oh, still on that, are we?

**Sonia**
Why the red rope everywhere? Why the plastic fruit?

**Alan**
The man is mentally ill. I've seen him eat a plastic pie.

**Sonia**
But in normal house you don't have forty tables all the same.

**Alan**
The very fact that you're questioning my, my, my, my, my, my …

*Lynn enters, standing next to man wearing U2 T-shirt and huge sunglasses.*

**Alan**
… my God.

**Lynn**
Hello, Alan. Good news.

**Alan**
You got my text then?

**Bono**
Hello, Alan.

**Alan**
Hello, Bono. Give him a seat.

*Bono sits with Alan and Sonia.*

**Alan**
How's er … how's the Edge?

**Bono**
The Edge is fine.

**Lynn**
How's Adam Clayton?

**Bono**
Adam Clayton is fine.

**Alan**
How's um … the drummer?

**Bono**
The drummer is fine.

**Alan**
When did you last see the gang?

**Bono**
I saw dem last Thursday at a pop concert.

**Alan**
Who were playing?

**Bono**
We were.

**Alan**
Right. Didn't see that advertised. You should sack your PR people.

**Bono**
We have.

**Alan**
Good.

**Sonia**
How long you live in house?

**Bono**
Since the eighties *(looks down at lap and reads from leaflet)*, Linkington Hall was built by Sir Henry Morgan. The Jacobean house is built on the site of a late-medieval predecessor.

**Sonia**
He is not Bono. He's rubbish.

**Alan**
He is, isn't he? Lynn, are those your mother's cataract glasses? *(Points to Bono's sunglasses)*

**Lynn**
Yes, they are.

**Alan**
What's your name?

**Bono**
Andrew.

**Alan**
Andrew, who is, I'm guessing, a friend of Lynn's from the Baptist church.

**Bono/Andrew**
Yes, that's right.

**Alan**
What do I owe you for your trouble, Andrew?

**Bono/Andrew**
Oh, just a contribution for the church.

**Alan**
OK. A fiver?

**Lynn**
Thirty?

**Alan**
(Surprised) Thirty?

**Bono/Andrew**
That's very generous.

**Alan**
I've been ambushed. There we go. Help yourself to a scone. You're probably sick of canteen food from being on tour. I forgot: you're not Bono.

*Evening; Alan and Sonia emerge from house carrying pizza boxes and head towards caravan.*

**Alan**
Yeah, I've, er, I've changed my mind about Excalibur Cottage. Think I'll just call it … Ye House.
*Alan turns caravan lights on and notices giant teddy bear in living-room area.*
AARGHH! Aarghh! Aaarghh!
*(Alan grabs receipt spike and stabs teddy bear)*
AARGHH!

**Sonia**
What you doing?

**Alan**
(Agitated) I've killed a bear! Who is he?

**Sonia**
He's a second-hand bargain Beefeater bear.

**Alan**
(Angrily) Sonia, Beefeaters do not live in caravans. They live in the Tower of London and they are restaurants.

**Sonia**
He is brilliant present.

**Alan**
(Angrily) It's not an appropriate gift for a man approaching fifty. It's too big! How did you get it here?

**Sonia**
On the bus.

**Alan**
(Angrily) You took *that* on the bus? Sonia, anyone who knows us might have thought it was *me* inside there. Me wearing a bear costume. They'd think I'd lost it again.

**Sonia**
It's very nice.

**Alan**
Look, I'm sorry. I'm sorry. When I, when I've calmed down I'll, I'll, I'll kiss him better where I stabbed him … just next to his thorax. He'll be fine. I'll make it up to you, OK? Tomorrow is your day. You can do whatever you want. Anything you like.

**Sonia**
I want to go to London.

**Alan**
(Pretends to look happy) That's fine.

*Closing music; Sonia and Lynn sit on top of an open-top bus looking at London sights. Alan plays air guitar inside the caravan. He throws the giant teddy bear out of the caravan and drags him off by the legs.*

look at somebody like Eamon Holmes and I think, you poor man, you just don't get it, do you? Just another of these sad celebrities sitting in their metal kitchens for money. It's a cry for help, surely. What is it with these people and their need to show off their possessions in magazines? Noel Edmunds – the thick man's Richard Branson – buys a helicopter, thinks he's Christ.

Of course there are famous people out there who are more down to earth. Paul McCartney does a nine to five. Writes his songs at a desk, dashes off a few letters to the terminally ill, has a tuna bap, sees his accountant and goes for a walk. Arnold Schwarzenegger spends five minutes a night going over his desk diary. Warren Beatty has an English Pub in his house. He had it built about nine years ago. Hasn't actually used it since 1996. Ex-Deep Purple guitarist Ritchie Blackmore likes nothing better than to sit down with his collection of episodes of Hettie Wainthrop Investigates. Says it takes his head to another place, away from rock.

It's amazing how careers can just take a downturn. A friend of mine who works in a BP garage says he served Gary Davies the ex-Radio 1 DJ. And, get this – the man looked awful. Had a sleeping bag in his car. What's going on there? Matthew Pinsent is doing poster adverts for insurance companies, dressed in his old rowing gear. But there's no boat. He's not rowing. Not rowing but drowning. And making a few quid. Good luck to you, Matt. Better than selling your medals, I suppose.

And it was with dark thoughts like this that I found myself considering suicide. Was my career as sunk as Pinsent's? I sat there in the car, with the garden hose attached to the exhaust pipe with two 3X2 bulldog grips, Vangelis on the CD. It had been a dark day. My Toblerone addiction was out of control. I'd got up in the middle of the night and stuffed a whole Toblerone, not a small one, into my mouth. Spewed up in a thermos. No prizes for guessing what I did with that. I threw it away.

Dark, dark days. My divorce had just come through. Awful business. I'd been forced to cite her drink problem as part of the grounds. You meet a lady in a lovely red dress and you marry her. And out come the jogging bottoms and the whisky miniatures. She secreted sherry. I'm not saying she sweated sherry. Well, she did in the end.

I'd tried everything to raise my spirits. I went to Legoland to get my head together. You need a day. It was more than I could do to stop myself from kicking over a large lego robot who in my twisted mind had become the chief commissioning editor of the BBC.

I even took a Ryanair flight to Stuttgart, £10 return, just to try and clear my thoughts and make some sense of it all. I was depressed. I stared into the abyss. And then I saw a chaffinch in the summer sun, pecking at a discarded beefburger, and I thought, he's not trying to throw himself off a cliff. And I just drove home, with the garden hose trailing from the exhaust pipe like a giant mouse's tail. Stopped off at a place called Buffalo Bills. They've got old shell pumps and photos of a young Malcolm Brando from *It's the Waterfront*. Don't look for it. It's not there. It's a Carpetland. And I never looked back, even when I found the lump. It turned out to be a knot in my vest. Now I've bounced back I don't wear

# I'M ALAN PARTRIDGE

## EPISODE 6: ALAN WIDE SHUT

*Radio Station*

**Mary**
I think we'll be giant super-beings … really.

**Alan**
Yeah. We're, we're talking about how people will look like in a billion years' time. Carry on, Mary.

**Mary**
Well, I don't think we'll have hair, you see. I think we'll be completely hairless.

**Alan**
Are you hairy, Mary?

**Mary**
*(Quietly)* No.

**Alan**
What?

**Mary**
No!

**Alan**
Ri-right.

**Mary**
And I think at the end of the day what will happen is we'll all be more or less the same but with bigger hands and eyes and sex organs.

**Alan**
I wonder what that will look like?

**Mary**
Look in the back of a spoon … in the bathroom.

**Alan**
Goodbye, Mary. Traffic!

**Jingle**

*(Car beeps)* **Alan:** Get away, you f—ing idiot!
*(Car beeps)* **Alan:** You could get a bus through there, you f—ing c—t.
*(Car beeps)* **Alan:** You stupid f—ing c—t. Let me through! Help! *(Car beeps)* **Alan:** No! Not in there! No!

**Alan**

*(Trying to talk over jingle)* We've got a traffic report – *(Car beeps)*

**Alan**

We've got a … I'm just gonna get rid of that: it's annoying. *(Jingle stops)* On the A146 just past Luddon, a lorry filled with livestock has jackknifed, shedding its load over both lanes. I wonder what that looks like. Probably looks like something from *Saving Private Ryan*, but, er, but with animals.

*Opening music*

**Alan**

*(In opening sequence)* Tom Spotley? When?

*Radio Station*

**Alan**

Now, listeners, I have someone on the line who fears he may be a gay. He's married, so he wishes to remain anonymous. I shall only be using his Christian name. I'm talking to Domingo in Little Oakley. Oh, he's gone. Oh, that's a pity. Marvellous little tapas bar there. Erm, well, we're just coming up to two minutes to one, so we might as well go straight to Dave Clifton.

**Dave**

Yeah, hello, Alan. How're you doing? All right?

**Alan**

Yeah. What's that you're reading?

**Dave**

Actually it's incredible: this is the, er, the biography of an East End gangster and it's, er, it's called *Bad Slags*. It's amazing stuff. It's incredible.

**Alan**

Yeah, yeah, I think, I think there's another word for it really. I think it's saaaaad that people find it entertaining to read about men who call themselves things like Stan the Stabber, who chop people's heads off in half, set fire to their eyebrows and knock people's teeth out with a toffee hammer just because they couldn't repay a loan at a very uncompetitive rate of interest.

**Dave**

Is, is your book in trouble with Stan the Stabber then, Alan?

**Alan**

What do you mean?

**Dave**

Well no, it's just that, er, from what I hear, all the unsold copies are being bundled into the back of a truck and driven to a big warehouse where they're going to be, er, quite literally pulped.

**Alan**

There's only one word for people like you, Dave –

**Dave**

*(Smiling)* Yeah?

**Alan**

*(Pause)* I'll tell you tomorrow.

**Dave**

OK. Here's, er, S—

**Alan**

Fri-Friggis! Friggis! That's it: Friggis!

**Dave**

– Salt 'N' Pepa.

*Alan in caravan, sitting on banquette.*

**Alan**

Hit me! Hit me! Hit me with your rhythm stick. It's nice to be a lunatic. Hit me! Hit me! Hit me. Only a few more nights in the caravan, Sonia. I thought we'd celebrate tonight by watching *Spartacus* with corned beef hash. Then afterwards we'll make sweet love. Then I'll drive you home.

**Sonia**

OK.

**Alan**

Actually, let's bring the love-making forward. Come 'ere.

*Alan pulls bottle of mouthwash out of cupboard, takes a gulp, gargles and swallows.*

**Alan**

Ah! Come here, you lucky, lucky lady.

*Alan and Sonia are about to kiss, when Lynn enters caravan.*

**Alan**

Oh, Lynn! Lynn!

**Lynn**

Hello.

**Alan**

Hi. Just having some hygienic snogging.

**Lynn**

*(Out of breath)* Oh.

**Sonia**

*(Leaving caravan)* Bye.

**Lynn**

Right. I've nearly moved everything into the house. Oh! That's for you.

**Alan**

What's this?

**Lynn**

Oh, it's just an invitation to my baptism.

**Alan**

Baptism?

**Lynn**

Mmm.

**Alan**
Lynn, how will they get you up to the font?
They'll need four men to lift you.

**Lynn**
No, no. It's not a font. It's a special pool
that they lower you into.

**Alan**
Right, and if you sink you're a Baptist, and
if you float ... you're evil. It's touch and go.

**Lynn**
*(Laughs)* Alan, I just want you to stand by
me with a towel to help me dry myself off.

**Alan**
Lynn, five minutes ago you were my PA and
now you're inviting me to some sort of
religious wet T-shirt competition.

**Lynn**
Right. I've got you that *Bad Slags* book you
asked for. And also, do you still want to do
the radio show, since all your books have
been incinerated?

**Alan**
Yes, I do want to do the radio show, Lynn,
and the books aren't being incinerated,
they're being pulped. My book could very
well end up being reconstituted as a trestle
table in a home for battered women. I'm
putting something back.

**Lynn**
Still annoyed about that *Bad Slags* book?

**Alan**
I am. I don't know why people buy this
rubbish ... about these East End thugs who
lend you £100 and a week later you owe
them a million. I'm not exaggerating. Or
you buy a car off them and find out its two
front ends welded together ... and you send
off for an MOT and you get a note back
saying they've found some chap's ribs in
the oil sump. Or you take a lid off the gear-
knob and find a teste.

**Lynn**
Alan, er, the builders are waiting to sign off.

**Alan**
OK. I'm gonna miss this caravan. I used
to enjoy sitting here like this. Sometimes
like this. *(Puts arms on back of banquette)*
Sometimes I'd lean forward and watch
the TV.

**Lynn**
Well –

**Alan**
No, hang on, there's a fourth position.
Sometimes I used to like sitting here like
this *(lies on his side on the banquette, with his
legs open)* ... waiting for Sonia. Yeah, we
had some good times on the banquette.

**Lynn**
Alan.

**Alan**
Oh! *(Alan grabs his crotch and sits up)*

**Lynn**
The builders.

**Alan**
Yes.
*Alan enters office in his new house. Builders
are sitting on sofa.*
Ah! You've already made yourself
comfortable on the banquette. Great.

**Carl**
You don't think it's a bit tight in here?

**Alan**
Mmm, not really. No. You know, people
always go on about space, don't they – ooh,
ooh, it's nice to have a bit of space, you
know. People forget you can get lost in
space. Yeah. Could have done with a
skylight really. Oh well. I presume, er, we're
all going to keep in touch, you know, now
the work's finished.

*Silence*

**Alan**
I, er, got you all a present for your hard work.

*He hands them each a wrapped gift – the same shape and size as his book.*

**John**
Ta, Al.

**Unnamed builder**
Cheers, mate.

**Alan**
I won't tell you what it is.

**Carl**
Oh, cheers.

**Alan**
It's a surprise. Lynn! What the frig have you got on your feet?

**Lynn**
Shoe covers.

**Alan**
You look like you live on a ward.

**Lynn**
I just got fed up getting my feet dirty.

**Unnamed builder**
They look like a pair of Action Man bodybags.

**Alan**
Yeah, yeah, and it's fine to join in.

**John**
They're like bibby bags for your feet, you know. If they want to sleep or summat, you know.

**Alan**
Yeah, sort of a development of what he said, isn't it? But again, fine to join in. Erm, Carl, do you want to add anything about Lynn's shoe covers? Perhaps say that they're like, er, a marquee for toes? Or, or, or a foot tent? Something like that?

**Carl**
No.

**Lynn**
Right. I've got some stuff for your bedroom. Have you decided which room it's going to be?

**Alan**
Yes. Now, the bedroom. Down the corridor, last door on the left.

**John**
That's the box room, Al. I mean that's the same size as your bedroom in the caravan.

**Alan**
Is it?

**Lynn**
Yeah, yeah.

**Alan**
Fine. Just, you know, squeeze a double bed in there and I can open the door and just step up on to the bed.

**Lynn**
Where are your clothes going to go?

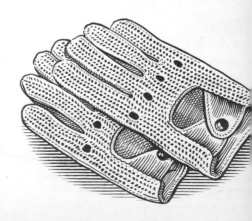

**Alan**
In a storage room. Just a short naked jog across the landing.

**Lynn**
What happens when you've got guests?

**Alan**
Lynn, I'll cup myself. I don't mean with an actual cup.

**Carl**
More like an eggcup.

*Builders laugh.*

**Alan**
It wouldn't be an eggcup. It'd be two eggcups and a kidney dish.

*Alan and Michael in petrol station shop. Alan is sitting by counter, reading newspaper.*

**Michael**
Do you want a pickled onion?

**Alan**
Er, no. I hate them.

**Michael**
Oh.

**Alan**
It's a very laidback petrol station, this.

**Michael**
Aye.

**Alan**
You could have a couple of sofas in here, couldn't you. People'd come in, relax, you know. You've got your petrol, it's fine.

**Michael**
Aye. This week's guest petrol is Texaco. And er, next week's guest petrol will be …
Texaco again.

**Alan**
Yeah, and you've got a great forecourt. You could have a lovely barbecue out there.

**Michael**
Oh no. You're not allowed naked flames on the forecourt.

**Alan**
It's political correctness gone mad.

**Michael**
Aye.

**Alan**
I'll tell you what amuses me, Michael. Really amuses me when people criticize my book just because I happen to use the phrase 'Needless to say, I had the last laugh' fourteen times. Because you and I know, in my life to date I've actually had the last laugh –

**Michael**
Twenty-five times.

**Alan**
Twenty-five times. Exactly.

*Microwave pings.*

**Alan**
Oh! There's my toad in the hole.

**Michael**
There she blows. Oh, lovely, man. Now, look at that: I bet you never thought that you could make toast in a microwave.

**Alan**
That's not toast, Michael. That's hot floppy bread.

**Michael**
So what'd you do last night?

**Alan**
Oh, I just stayed in and watched a documentary on quicksand. Then Sonia and I took our tops off and had a cuddle. Followed by mince and onions. Doesn't get much better than that.

**Michael**
Ay, it did for me. I done a bit better than a cuddle last night. I had full sex with a woman.

**Alan**
Go on. Go on.

**Michael**
She was all over us, man. I mean, uh, she's a bit older than me, like. She's sixty.

**Alan**
Sixty?

**Michael**
Aye. What's wrong with that? Same age difference as you and Sonia.

**Alan**
Yeah, that's just wrong. Shouldn't do it the other way round.

**Michael**
We did. *(Laughs)*

**Alan**
I suppose sixty's not really old, is it? I mean, look at Bob Dylan.

**Michael**
Aye. She looked a bit like him. Aye.

**Alan**
What, the big nose and lots of mad hair?

**Michael**
Aye. Do you know her?

**Alan**
No. How'd you meet her?

**Michael**
Outside Thresher's. She was loading all this booze into her car, and she says, 'Oh, I've had a bit to drink, like. Would you drive us home … to Cardiff.'

**Alan**
Cardiff?

**Michael**
Aye. I come back this morning on a National Express coach. It was sort of like a SAS operation, you know. Uh, your mission: gan till Cardiff, have full sex with a woman, come back on the coach. Sort of like, er, Operation Bravo Two Zero.

**Alan**
I think in your case, Michael, it was Bravo *Six* Zero.

*Michael laughs.*

**Alan**
By, er, Randy McNab.

*Michael laughs.*

**Michael**
*(Laughing)* Randy McKnob.

**Alan**
All right. Stop. Stop now.

**Michael**
So, er, how's you and Sonia getting on?

**Alan**
Er … never really thought about it. She'll be along soon with, er, with a hot dessert.

**Michael**
I tell you, the way she looks after you, man, you're looking a gift horse in the mouth.

**Alan**
Yeah, no, I think that's what you were doing last night, Michael.

**Michael**
So when's, er, Lynn getting baptized then?

**Alan**
Splashdown for Lynn is 1500 hours on Sunday.

**Michael**
Oh right. And is, er, lover-boy gonna be there? The ex-policeman?

**Alan**

Gordon? I hope he's not doing the dunking. I wouldn't like to be dunked by a retired policeman. 'Cause when you came up, he'd probably go, 'Where's the money?'

**Michael**

Aye.

**Alan**

You say, 'I don't know: I've just been baptized.' 'Down you go again.'

**Michael**

Aye aye. 'Ere comes Sonia.

**Alan**

Ah. The dinner lady.

*Michael laughs.*

**Sonia**

This is rhubarb crumble and custard.

**Alan**

Smashing.

**Sonia**

Alan, I am a homeless person. I live in my flat; the landlady is telling me that all the girls we have to go because she must sell this house because it will be office block. I have to find somewhere.

**Alan**

Look, if the worst comes to the worst, you can always move in ... to Lynn's mum's bedroom.

**Sonia**

I don't want to sleep in Lynn's dead mum's bed.

**Alan**

Well, Michael did something similar last night, and he's very happy. *(Sonia looks miserable)* Erm, let's see one of these. *(Pulls Sonia's mouth up at the sides)* Actually, that's just weird.

*Radio Studio*

**Tessa**

Hello, and welcome back to PrayerWave with me, Tessa McPherson. I'm talking to Kate Fitzgerald –

**Kate**

Hi.

**Tessa**

Whose book *Someone Else* charts a journey of self-discovery.

**Alan**

Good title.

**Tessa**

Er, it takes you through childhood to your drug addiction and prostitution –

**Alan**

Oh God.

**Tessa**

– and then to your recovery, er, in a very upbeat sort of a way.

**Kate**

Mmm.

**Alan**

Mi-mine's upbeat, too.

**Tessa**

Erm, I should say at this point that the other voice that you can hear is my other guest, er, Alan Partridge. Erm, now, Alan, for a while, had a TV chat show and was quite a big name up there, and then, erm, then it all went very wrong. And that's the subject of your book, *Bouncing Back*.

**Alan**

Yes, yes, I noticed, erm, although Kate in effect felt she bounced back, I ... I feel I have, had and are bounced, bouncing ... er, I felt that – do you want to carry on talking to Kate while I just, erm ... sort something out?

**Tessa**

Erm –

**Alan**

Can I borrow a pen?

**Tessa**

Yes, of course. How's the book doing?

*Tessa passes Alan a pen. He looks thoughtful and writes something down.*

**Kate**

It's doing wonderfully well. The best feedback for me is actually people just coming up to me in the street –

**Alan**

Yeah, well, I'm all right now, you know.

**Kate**

Erm, people who felt very alone, um, but through me they found a friend, they found hope, they found light in the darkness –

**Alan**

*(Stops writing)* There. There. All done!

**Tessa**

It's been very well received, hasn't it ...

**Alan**

*(Talking over Kate)* Sorry, sorry, sorry, sorry, I'm sorry.

**Kate**

Oh, it's had a positive effect, I mean it's wonderful. Can I just say it's actually quite distracting when you interrupt?

**Alan**

*(Indignantly)* But you just interrupted her!

**Tessa**

Erm, Alan, erm, *Bouncing Back* – I suspect you meant it as an ironic title, didn't you? Because you haven't bounced back, have you? I mean, certainly not ... not emotionally and I, I think in a sense not in a career way either. How do you feel about that?

**Alan**

*(Pause)* What?

**Kate**

I, I think what Tessa's saying is that, is that you haven't bounced back. I mean, I haven't read your book, I've just skimmed it –

**Alan**

Well, I have. I'm doing, I'm doing, er, Norfolk Nights and I've got a, er, a show called, a show – why are you shaking your head? Are you trying to put me off? Two can play at that game. *(Sticks two fingers up at Kate)* I know you ... I know you've had problems in the past. *(Pretends to inject himself in his arm)* The time's just coming up to 11.30, we – oh, sorry, it's your show.

**Tessa**

So, er, yes. *Bouncing Back* – you fell quite spectacularly, didn't you?

**Alan**

Yeah, all right. Do you slow down for car crashes?

**Tessa**

I suppose the point I'm trying to make really is that, you know, I've been looking for the positives in your book, and, and it is a book that's full of joy. But it's chiefly joy at other people's misfortunes.

**Kate**

Mmmm. Mmmm. I noticed a lot of bitterness. Actually, I notice you end almost every anecdote with the phrase 'Needless to say, I had the last laugh.'

**Alan**

Yeah, well, you, you could end some of your chapters with 'Nee – needles to say ... I ... I took drugs.'

**Tessa**

If I could turn to you, Kate.

433

**Alan**
Yeah, sure.

**Tessa**
You … you come from quite a privileged background.

**Kate**
Er, materially privileged, yes. But, I mean, emotionally undernourished. My father was very distant –

**Alan**
Is that because he lives in a different wing of your house?

**Kate**
Have you read my book?

**Alan**
No, but I've seen the photographs in the central spine. And I read the bit where you say you put drugs up your bottom. Why? You've got a perfectly good mouth.

**Kate**
Very easy to confuse the two. Sometimes people can actually end up talking out of their arse, Alan.

**Tessa**
Let's talk a little bit more about your drug addiction. Now, you were hooked on a variety of drugs, weren't you?

**Kate**
Yeah. Yeah. Erm, I started on crack.

**Alan**
Now, that's not the same as crackling, is it?

**Kate**
No.

**Alan**
It's a joke. I love crackling. I had some last Sunday. Had hairs on it, but I didn't mind.

**Tessa**
And then the chemical dependency grew worse.

**Kate**
Yeah. Erm, my drug of choice became ketamine, which is in fact a horse tranquillizer.

**Alan**

*(Surprised)* Shit! Sorry. Did you get that by hanging round stables? Because you do seem, you do seem quite posh. I can imagine you in wellies and one of those sleeveless anoraks.

**Kate**

Mmm. The technical name for that is actually a gilet.

**Alan**

No, that's a razor. Could have done with that for the crackling. Have you ever shaved your crackling?

**Tessa**

Erm, yes, ketamine.

**Alan**

Yeah, why give drugs to a horse? Why drag them into it?

**Kate**

They use ketamine to tranquillize the horse and then to extract the horse's semen.

**Alan**

How do they do that?

**Kate**

I don't know. In the same way that you would a human being.

**Alan**

*(Baffled)* What, send him into a cubicle with magazines? They've got hooves, for goodness sake. Four of them. It would take some doing, but I can't see it.

**Tessa**

I think we've strayed somewhat from, from the topic. I think it's interesting that you both obviously have addictive personalities.

**Kate**

Mmm.

**Tessa**

Clearly in your case it was drugs; in your case, Alan, it was chocolate.

**Alan**

Yes, specifically Toblerone. I, erm, I would wake up in the middle of the night and, er, eat an entire Toblerone. And I don't mean, I don't mean a small one. I mean a medium sized one. In fact in the best chapter in my book I talk about when I gorged on Toblerone and drove to Dundee in my bare feet.

**Kate**

*(Laughing and shaking her head)* I have to say, chocolate addiction is never going to be as destructive as drug addiction.

**Alan**

What's her book like?

**Kate**

Excuse me, I really don't like being referred to as 'her'.

**Alan**

All right. What's *his* book like? I don't know your name – Tara Peter Frampton Double-Barrelled Shotgun Kensington on the Horse.

**Kate**

*(Angrily)* You really have got a *lot* of issues.

*Kate stands up and leaves studio.*

**Alan**

Yeah, of *What Car?* magazine.

**Tessa**

Erm, that's something of a first on Prayer Wave. Never had anybody walk out before.

**Alan**

Yes, I think the atmosphere has turned rrrrather sour.

**Tessa**
Er, yes, let's see if we can smooth things over with a little bit more from Monteverdi's *Vespers*.

**Alan**
Good band.

*Music starts. Lynn appears at studio door.*

**Tessa**
Well, thank you very much for coming on the show, Alan. Slightly more exciting than I'd anticipated. *(Laughs)*

**Alan**
Yes – oh, sorry, can I introduce you? This is my PA, Lynn.

**Tessa**
Hello. *(Tessa and Lynn shake hands)*

**Alan**
You must be a guest on my show sometime. Yes, we discuss issues – erm, Europe, conspiracy theories, what happens if you just eat crisps, things like that.

**Tessa**
Mmm, that sounds interesting actually. We're, we're currently revamping this show. Erm, I'm actually looking for a co-presenter at the moment, so it would be quite interesting to talk to you about some of those ideas. You know, I'm, I'm the producer of the show as well as the presenter.

**Alan**
Oh! No! Oh! That's interesting, isn't it? I didn't know who you are and yet I still got in with you.

*Tessa laughs.*

**Alan**
Um, Ooh! I forgot to say I am *sooo* a Christian.

**Tessa**
Well, it's not a prerequisite for being on the programme. *(Laughs)*

**Alan**
Come on.

**Tessa**
*(Laughing)* But er, no, really it's more to do with our family remit.

**Alan**
Mmm. Well, I love families, you know. I used to have one. But it left me. Boo-hoo. Er … this one's a Baptist, yes. Er, Lynn's being submerged this week, for her sins. Literally. You're welcome to come along.

**Tessa**
Oh! How wonderful. Have you been preparing for it for a long time?

**Lynn**
Oh yes. Yes.

*Alan stares into space.*
*A heavily overweight Alan is in his car gorging on Toblerone and shouting 'Lynn! Lynn! Lynn!'*

*In studio*

**Lynn**
… infused with the Holy Spirit. It's quite extraordinary.

**Alan**
Shall we make tracks?

*Alan and Sonia in caravan.*

**Sonia**
So, Alan, when is your book being destroyed?

**Alan**
Sonia, it's not being destroyed. The correct term is 'pulped'. They're pulping the remaining unsold 14,000 copies of my book next Thursday.

**Sonia**
Oh.

**Alan**
So they can make room for books on Cockney killers.

**Sonia**
What is Cockney?

**Alan**
Cockney, Sonia, is an area in London where criminals live. The police don't arrest them, because – and they're very strict about this – they only slaughter their own. And they have funerals with horses and floral tributes that say things like 'Mum' and 'Stab'.

**Sonia**
They don't sound so evil. These men like flowers?

**Alan**
Sonia, these guys – some of the stunts they pull. They'll chain you to a car that's been clamped. So the only way you can get yourself free is by phoning the council, but you can't do that because they've shoved your mobile phone up your backside.

**Sonia**
Mobile phone not hurt too much. Is only small.

**Alan**
No, Sonia, this is in the late eighties when mobile phones were like big black plastic bricks with a, a rubber breadstick sticking out of the top. It was agony.

**Sonia**
*(Laughs)* Maybe it was, mmm. Vibrating phone – it quite pleasant. *(Laughs)*

**Alan**
Sonia, this is no laughing matter. You know, if you're at a funfair, these guys might put your head in a candy-floss machine. And they might be standing around having a great laugh at you with your big pink hair. But you may be very, very dizzy.
Now, Sonia, I've been thinking about your impending homelessness, and I've come to a decision. I want you to move in.

**Sonia**
*(Surprised)* Really?

**Alan**
I want you to make the place your own.

**Sonia**
*(Delighted)* I can't believe!

**Alan**
I've bought you the caravan.

**Sonia**
I don't live in the house with you?

**Alan**
Well, have you seen the size of the box room? I, I, I want you here in the caravan. You'll be my, my very own John West tinned woman. Skipjack Sonia in brine.

**Sonia**
OK. And I can come visit whenever I want?

**Alan**
Probably best if I come and see you, actually. Yeah. Or we'll set up a signalling system. If you see a bottle of ketchup in the kitchen window, it means 'let's make love' – 'I'm feeling saucy.'

**Sonia**
You want me to pay rent?

**Alan**
Oh, I'm sure we can come to some sort of an arrangement.

**Sonia**
You're sure you don't want me to pay rent?

**Alan**
No, it's fine. As I said, you know, I'm sure we can, you know, come to some sort of arrangement.

*Sprowston Baptist Church*

**Gordon**
And, er, so I came to know a warm woman with a smile for everyone. So let's hear it for Lynn.

*Applause; Lynn, looking disshevelled, laughs nervously.*

**Michael**
Go on, Lynn, lass!

**Alan**
She didn't like being in that water, did she?

*Michael laughs.*

**Alan**
You see her thrashing around?

**Michael**
*(Laughing)* Aye. I've got it all in here. *(Points to video camera)* It's hilarious, man.

**Tessa**
*(Walking up to Alan)* That was lovely.

**Alan**
Yes, it was, it was like a, it was like a very moving sheep-dip. Erm, anyway, I'm down to do a spot now, and, er, I'm going to be saying lots of interesting things about God, so if you hang around …

**Tessa**
Oh! Unfortunately I've really got to go, Alan –

**Alan**
*(Quickly)* Right, I'll, I'll, I'll do it now. I'll do it now. I'll do it now.

*Alan rings bell.*

**Alan**

Erm, hello. Erm, y-y-you probably, er, don't know me. Erm, erm, I'm Alan Partridge. I host, er, Norfolk Nights on Radio Norwich and *Skirmish*, a military-based general knowledge quiz on a cable television channel called UK Conquest. But, er, today is Lynn's day. And what a tragedy that, er, the one person who can't be here is Lynn's mum, Peggy, who is dead. Erm, we didn't see eye to eye. Erm, there was a lot of bad blood, which, coincidentally, was one of the complications she had at the end. But erm, I'm digressing. Erm, today is Lynn's day, and she has bounced back, er, in the same way that I have. Erm, because God is, is, is a very positive god. Um, even when he tried to create the world in six days, there were people who said, 'You can't do it; it can't be done.' Erm, although he hadn't created people then. Erm, but the criticism bounced off him like water o—, not off a duck's back, 'cause he hadn't invented ducks either. But erm, anyway, er, where, where was I? Or is I? Is was. Is was. *Tiswas*. Who remembers *Tiswas*? The seventies. Space hoppers and er, sweets they don't make any more and er ... er ... er ... oh ... er ... er ... *(shouts) Kojak!* Er ... er ... er ... Who loves you, baby? Errrrrrrr, a lollipop, you know. Erm, sorry, it's not going very well. Erm, *(jovially)* ohhhhh, I'm gonna kill meself. Ooh, where's me shotgun? Oh, click, click, click. *(Mimes loading shotgun and puts it in mouth)* Oh. Can't get me toe on the trigger. Oh, got it! *(Makes exploding noise)* That, that, that's it. That's it. Erm ... and ... and ... and to, to Lynn. Yeah.
*(Takes a big gulp of wine)*

*Faint applause. Tessa goes to leave.*

**Alan**

Sorry about that. Erm, I won't do the er, er, shotgun thing on the radio. That's just for the Baptists. Yes.

**Tessa**

Erm, anyway, I've really got to go.

**Alan**

Yeah, go! Go! Go! Go! Go! Go! Go! Go.

**Male member of congregation**

Hello, Alan.

**Alan**

Oh!

**Male member of congregation**

Can I just say, I love your radio show.

**Alan**

Oh, thank you very much.

**Male member of congregation**

And I read your book.

**Alan**

Oh.

**Male member of congregation**

I have to say, didn't really work for me.

**Alan**

*(Cross)* Fuck off.

*Alan walks up to Sonia, who is talking to Gordon and Lynn. Michael is filming them.*

**Sonia**

Alan was very shy before we make love. He was very shy of his body, but I just tell to me, please, it doesn't mind. It's what's inside what matter. And also Alan is pretty well hung, so –

*Michael laughs. Alan walks away.*

**Sonia**

– and then, now when we make love he's like a big good bear.

*Michael laughs.*

*Alan walks up to male member of congregation.*

**Alan**
Oh, erm, listen. I, I, I, I'm sorry about that before. I think you just caught me at a, caught me at a bad moment.

**Male member of congregation**
Perfectly understandable. So, I hear your book's being pulped.

**Alan**
*(Indignantly)* Fuck off!

*Alan's mobile phone rings.*

**Alan**
Hello? Er, y-yes he is. Did he give you my number? Er, M-Michael, it's, it's, it's a, it's a Nerys for you.

**Michael**
Hello? Oh, hiya. Oh, Nerys, aye. So I know your name now, ay? No, no, I can still smell you, 'cause I 'aven't 'ad a shower or owt.

*Alan looks dejected. He looks at Lynn, who is laughing with Gordon.*

*A heavily overweight Alan is gorging on Toblerone in the back of his car, with bare feet.*

**Alan**
*(With mouth full of Toblerone)* Lynn! Lynn!

*He gets out mobile phone and dials.*

**Alan**
Hello, Lynn? I've been eating a lot of Toblerone. I've eaten four and I've got two white ones left. 'Cause I don't like them as much as the dark ones. Mmm.

*Sprowston Baptist Church*

**Alan**
*(To male member of congregation)* Oh, hello again.

*Alan in car, mouth covered in Toblerone.*

**Alan**
Not very happy.

*Sprowston Baptist Church*

**Alan**
I'm sorry. It's just, er, you know when you have a book out and you get lots of criticism, it's, er, very difficult to …

**Male member of congregation**
Not a problem. Don't worry.

**Alan**
Unfortunately, er, people would rather read books about people called Dan the Daggerman from Dagenham, you know.

**Male member of congregation**
The world.

**Alan**
Tortures you by putting your hair in a fax machine and pressing 'Send'. What do you think was actually wrong with my book? Don't pull any punches.

**Male member of congregation**
Well, to be honest, I … I don't think anecdotes are your forte.

**Alan**
Oh, that's fair enough. Yeah. So you don't think I can tell anecdotes? Do you want to just pop that down for a second?

*Male member of congregation puts his plate on table. Alan grabs him by the lapels.*

**Alan**
*(Speaking through clenched teeth)* Right, I'll tell you an anecdote. In 1975 I was catching the London train from Crewe station. It was very crowded. I found myself in a last-minute rush for the one remaining seat, with a tall, good-looking man with collar-length hair. It was the seventies – Buckaroo. When I sat down on the chair, I looked up and realized it was none other than *(shouts)*

Peter Purvis. He was at the height of his *Blue Peter* fame. He said, 'You jammy bastard,' and quick as a flash, I replied, 'Don't be blue, Peter.' Needless to say, I had the last laugh. Now fuck off!

*Man looks completely stunned. Alan walks away.*

*In warehouse, full of bales of paper.*

**Alan**
*(To warehouse man)* Hello, Alan Partridge. Come to see my book being pulped.

*Enormous boxes of* Bouncing Back *travel up a conveyer belt.*

**Alan**
It's great to know that actually they're like putting something back … there's a lot of dignity involved.

*Alan looks into an enormous vat of pulped paper.*

**Alan**
*(Speaking loudly over the machinery)* It looks like porridge! Weird porridge! *(Alan spots copy of his book in the pulp)* *(Excited)* There's my book! There's my book! I'll pop back in sometime. *(Holds up plastic bag full of liquid)* Thanks for the souvenir. Did *Blue Peter* once do a documentary here?

**Warehouse man**
No, not here.

**Alan**
Oh, right. Must be somewhere else then.

*Alan walks off with plastic bag, then starts jogging.*

## Acknowledgements

Permission is gratefully acknowledged for the following
musical excerpts to be published.

Abba lyrics on pages 62, 140, 201 by permission
  Bocu Music Ltd, 1 Wyndham Yard, London WIH 2QF.
'We'll Gather Lilacs' on page 148. Words and music by
  Ivor Novello © 1941 Chappell Music Ltd, London W6 8BS.
  Reproduced by permission of International Music
  Publications Ltd. All rights reserved.
'Wuthering Heights' on page 279. Words and music by
  Kate Bush 1977. Reproduced by permission of Kate Bush
  trading as Noble & Brite, London WC2H 0QY.
'Goldfinger' on page 283. Lyrics by Leslie Bricusse, John
  Barry and Anthony Newly. Reproduced by permission
  of Sony/ATV music publishing.

Every effort has been made by the publishers to trace
the copyright holders, but if any have inadvertently
been overlooked please contact the publishers and any
amendations will be made at the earliest opportunity.